The Ultir Beginner's Guide to Social Media for Small Businesses

Written by Scarlett Darbyshire
www.scarlettdarbyshireuk.com

About

Social media is well and truly here to stay in the marketing world, and by all accounts, it will only further penetrate all aspects of life and work. Social media presents a huge opportunity for small businesses. More than 1 billion people are sharing, liking, commenting, and checking in on social networks, making it a necessity for your brand to get on board and let the world know that you're open for business.

According a recent Social Media Examiner Report, the most effective networks for business are; Facebook, LinkedIn, Twitter, YouTube, Pinterest and Instagram. With the top 3 benefits of using these networks being; increased exposure, driving traffic to your blog/website and building a loyal fan base.

Despite the benefits of being active on social media, many resource-strapped businesses struggle with social media marketing. They're unfamiliar with the different social networks, don't feel they have the time to effectively manage it, or in a lot of cases, they simply don't get 'it.'

This guide tackles all these issues head on. Whether you are new to social media in general or your efforts need a bit of a pick-me-up, this beginners guide is jam-packed full of tips for the major social media networks, exploring how to build a social marketing strategy from scratch, how to build a loyal following, how to measure your success, time-saving tips and tricks and much more.

Whilst this guide explores most of the major social media platforms, my best advice for getting started on social media is simple: Pick one network, build up a solid strategy and fan base there, then move on to another. Whilst it may be tempting to jump on every new and popular social media platform, it is better to do an excellent job of managing a few social media platforms the right way...than poorly managing several.

Let's get started ...

Contents

Introduction
- What is Social Media?
- How is Social Media Being Used by Businesses?
- Why Should You Join In?
- The Ultimate Checklist for Your Social Media Marketing Plan
- 24 Best Practices for Social Media Marketing Success
- Important UK Internet Usage and Social Media Statistics

Guide to;

Blogging (Page 27)
- What's good about Blogging?
- What's not so good about Blogging?
- Need to Know Facts, Stats and Tips about Blogging
- Why You Need a Blog For Your Business
- Blogging: What, and How Often?
- How to Write an Effective Blog Post
- 8 Quick Content Ideas for Blog Posts
- 8 Point Checklist Before You Publish Your Blog Post
- How to Build a Following and Amplify Your Impact
- Tips for Success
- Common Mistakes to Avoid
- Measuring Success
- Weekly Blogging Maintenance Checklist

Facebook (Page 54)
- What's good about Facebook?
- What's not so good about Facebook?
- Which Businesses Should be on Facebook?
- Need to Know Facts, Stats and Tips about Facebook
- Why You Need Facebook for Your Business
- Creating your Facebook Page and Getting to Grips with the Basic Lingo
- Checklist for Developing a Clear and Effective Facebook Strategy
- Posting on Your Wall: What, and How Often?

- How to Create an Effective Facebook Post Checklist
- A Quick Guide to Facebook Live
- Advertising Basics on Facebook
- How to Build More Members of Your Facebook Group
- How to Build a Following and Amplify Your Impact
- Tips for Success
- Common Mistakes to Avoid
- Measuring Success
- Daily/Weekly Facebook Maintenance Checklist

Twitter (Page 100)

- What's good about Twitter?
- What's not so good about Twitter?
- Which Businesses should be on Twitter?
- Need to Know Facts, Stats and Tips about Twitter
- Why You Need Twitter For Your Business
- Creating a Twitter Account and Getting to Grips With the Basic Lingo
- Questions to Help Form a Successful Twitter Marketing Strategy
- Tweeting: What, and How Often?
- How to Write An Effective Tweet
- How to Build a Following and Amplify Your Impact
- Tips for Success
- Common Mistakes to Avoid
- Measuring Success
- Daily/Weekly Twitter Maintenance Checklist

LinkedIn for Personal Use (Page 139)

- What's good about LinkedIn?
- What's not so good about LinkedIn?
- Who should be on LinkedIn?
- Need to Know Facts, Stats and Tips about LinkedIn
- Why You Need a LinkedIn Profile
- How to Create an Effective LinkedIn Professional Profile
- LinkedIn Professional Profile Checklist
- Tips for Success
- Common Mistakes to Avoid
- Measuring Success
- Daily/Weekly LinkedIn Maintenance Checklist

LinkedIn for Business Use (Page 160)
- Why LinkedIn Company Pages
- Need to Know Facts, Stats and Tips about LinkedIn Company Pages
- Who Should Have a LinkedIn Company Page?
- Setting up Your LinkedIn Company Page and Getting to Grips With the Basic Lingo
- An Introduction to Paid Advertising on LinkedIn
- Questions to Ask Before You Get Started Using LinkedIn for Business
- How to Build a Branded LinkedIn Company Page That Gets You Noticed
- Tips For Success
- Measuring Success

YouTube (Page 177)
- What's good about YouTube?
- What's not so good about YouTube?
- Should your Business have a YouTube Channel?
- Need to Know Facts, Stats and Tips about YouTube
- Why You Need YouTube for Your Business
- Creating Your YouTube Account and Getting to Grips With the Basic Lingo
- 7 Key Questions to Help Form a Successful YouTube Strategy
- Uploading: What, and How Often?
- How to Create a Branded YouTube Channel that gets you Noticed
- How to Build a Following and Amplify Your Impact
- Tips for Success
- Common Mistakes to Avoid
- Measuring Success

Pinterest (Page 198)
- What's good about Pinterest?
- What's not so good about Pinterest?
- Which Businesses should be on Pinterest?
- Need to Know Facts, Stats and Tips about Pinterest
- Why You Need Pinterest for Your Business
- Creating a Pinterest Account and Getting to Grips with the Basic Lingo
- Creating a Pinterest Strategy for Your Business
- What Should You be Pinning?
- How to Build a Following and Amplify Your Impact
- Tips for Success and Common Mistakes to Avoid
- Measuring Success
- Daily/Weekly Pinterest Maintenance Checklist

Instagram (Page 227)

- What's good about Instagram?
- What's not so good about Instagram?
- Need to Know Facts, Stats and Tips about Instagram
- Why You Need Instagram For Your Business
- How to Create an Instagram Business Account and the Basic Lingo
- How to Create an Instagram Marketing Strategy
- Creating a Content Strategy for Instagram
- How to Craft Instagram Posts That Drive Sales
- How to Find Your Best Frequency and Timing on Instagram
- How to Use Hashtags on Instagram
- How to Get More Followers on Instagram
- How to Optimize Your Instagram Profile to Increase Your Growth and Engagement
- 8 Ways to Increase Sales using Instagram
- Getting Started With Instagram Advertising
- A Quick Guide to Instagram Analytics
- Tips For Success

Other Useful Resources (Page 257)

- Useful Social Media Links and Resources
- Social Media Platform Monthly Clean Up and Refresh Checklist
- 83 Engaging Ideas for Your Social Media Content
- How To Best Incorporate Social Media Channels On Your Website
- Useful Tools and Apps to Help You Market Smart
- Powerful Call to Action Phrases you NEED to Use in Your Social Media Content!

Introduction

This beginner's guide is designed to show you how to effectively use social media for your business. It will help you to develop and maintain a social media presence that engages your audience, builds your brand awareness and drives new business. Whether you're just starting out or need to refocus your existing efforts, this is your go-to resource for tips and advice on how to approach and tackle social media for your business covering everything from summaries of the major platforms, how to build a following, to how to measure your success and much more.

What is Social Media?

Social media is the means by which people interact with others in virtual communities and networks allowing them to create, share and exchange information and ideas. With the rapid popularity growth of these new technologies, social media has had a profound impact on the way people discover, read and share news, information and content. Social media encompasses all forms of 'user generated' content, from communication platforms such as Facebook and Twitter to multimedia services such as YouTube and virtual gaming platforms like World of Warcraft. It has become extremely popular as it allows people to connect and form relationships in the online world for personal and business use.

How is Social Media Being Used by Businesses?

Social media puts you out there and brings your solutions to your prospects' doors. As such, the benefits of creating a social presence on the web have been felt by every type of business and industry. Whether you have a restaurant, retail outlet or provide professional services, social media enables you to build your online reputation, increase credibility and help generate business and drive sales. By taking advantage of social media, you can make your business gain more exposure, be more personable and generate and maintain long term connections as well as benefit from rich insights into your customers and industry. All of which can greatly benefit your business in the future.

Why Should You Join In?

With the surge in popularity in having a presence on social media, the chances are that your customers and competitors are already involved. On the web your customers will be talking, forming their opinions and its's where they're making their own recommendations to their friends and connections. Likewise your competitors may be already channelling in on those customers and reaping the rewards from engaging with, joining and listening to those conversations. People all around the world may be already talking about your business, so it's important that you get involved in the conversation and present yourself how you want to be presented on the web. Still not convinced? Here are 5 more reasons why you need social media for your business;

Social Media is Everywhere and Very Popular

Social media has become a central part of most people's lives, whether they are at home or on the go, people are actively engaging online. These users aren't just sharing updates from their own lives; they are searching for businesses, products, services and connecting with brands through their social channels. People of all ages and genders are actively using social media so no matter how old or young, or what gender your target audience may be, chances are most of them are already logging on and waiting for you to get started.

Social Media Sites are Free

Getting started on most social media platforms is completely free. Facebook, Twitter, Pinterest, YouTube, WordPress and LinkedIn all offer free accounts to users and businesses and in most cases signing up won't require anything more than an email address. There are features within some platforms that you need to pay for such as a Facebook Ad or a profile upgrade in LinkedIn, but for the purposes of getting started there's no upfront cost for most of the social networks.

Join an Existing Conversation

Social media provides you with an opportunity to listen to the conversations about your business and industry being openly discussed online. Not only does joining this conversation mean you can hear what is being said about you, it also means you can easily develop a richer understanding of your customers and benefit from insights into your target audiences. Moreover, it can also be used to create dedicated communities where you can host discussions about the products and services you offer or use your followers as an outlet for helping build new ones.

Social Media is Great for Customer Service

Customer service through social media is quickly becoming an expectation of consumers. Businesses have quickly come to realise that it offers a unique opportunity to showcase your customer service skills, promote more intimate business relationships with your customers and enables you to cater to your

customer's needs instantly. In a world where everything is fast-paced, a quick response that showcases how much you care about providing a memorable experience can create a lifelong customer. Social media allows you to continually strengthen relationships with these customers through social engagement and because this engagement is publicly visible to others, it can introduce your business to a whole new audience and enable you to reach your next customer.

It Helps People Learn More About Your Business

Social media sites are becoming the go-to place for consumers who want to learn more about a business. People are online actively searching for information about anything from product reviews to informative articles and general entertainment, so it is up to you to utilise this and use your social media presence to provide valuable, informative and entertaining news and updates to existing and potential audiences. If customers are already searching for you on Facebook or Twitter and not finding your business, you are missing opportunities to win new customers and inform and engage your existing ones so it is vital that you join in with social media and have your brand heard and seen online.

The Ultimate Checklist for Your Social Media Marketing Plan

'If you fail to prepare, prepare to fail.'

Whilst Benjamin Franklin wasn't speaking to the owner of a local cupcake company looking to start a Facebook page when he said those words, they still ring true when it comes to a business starting out on social media. Just as you wouldn't set up a business without a business plan, you can't just jump straight into social media, start aimlessly posting and expect the customers to come rolling in. Rather, you must sit down, grab a cup of coffee and develop a clear social media strategy. While there's no one-size fits all solution, you can find social media success if you're armed with the right questions to get you started. After all, a plan equals focus and focus is what is going to drive your business forward online.

What Objectives do I Want my Business to Achieve by Using Social Media?

Whether you want to use your social media presence to gain exposure for your brand, directly educate and interact with your customers, promote specific products and services or all of the above, clearly identifying your objectives is the critical first step towards a successful social media presence. Identifying your objectives in the beginning ensures a multitude of critical elements of your social media marketing, it allows you to effectively tailor your content and posting schedule, provide value to your customers, right through to helping you accurately measure your success as you will be aware of the most appropriate metrics to track efficiently.

Common Social Media Objectives

- Build Brand Awareness
- Drive Traffic to Website
- Provide Customer Service
- Engage with Fans
- Establish Thought Leadership
- Launch New Products or Services
- Generate Leads and Increase Sales
- Research and Insights
- Build Your Community
- Improve SEO
- Competitive Analysis

What is the State of My Current Social Media Use?

If you are already present on social media, you need to take a good hard look at your content from the eyes of a new (or potential) fan or follower. There is a whole host of important questions you need to ask

yourself when you look through your online presence. Here's a few taken from the checklist I use when I conduct a Social Media Audit;

- **Assess their presence:** has it been thought through? Profile/cover photo/about section completed, effective and branded?
- **Can potential followers immediately get a sense of company culture,** products and services on offer?
- **Content:** How does their content support their strategy? What content receives the most clicks, likes and shares? Are they sharing engaging content? Do they encourage engagement? Offer something valuable/useful? How often is it updated? Are they engaging back with fans? Do they use hashtags effectively? How do they use images to tell the company story?
- **How are the individual platforms being used to drive traffic to the main web presence?** Is it clear what the next step is that they want fans/followers to take? Call to actions in tweets/pins/posts?
- Record **numbers of followers and following** – are they both relevant and targeted audience?
- When the last time was their Twitter / Facebook/Pinterest etc. presence was **updated**?
- What **feedback** do they get from followers?

Who are My Target Audience?

Determining the audience that you want to reach and engage with on social media is fundamental to your strategy. Whether your target audience is your current or potential clients or customers, affiliate businesses, thought leaders or all four, your aim is to create a successful social media strategy that matches and is tailored towards understanding and acting on your target audience's behaviours online. Creating Buyer personas helps you define and target the right people, in the right places, at the right times with the right messages. When you learn important factors about your target audience from their age, job status, income, interests, problems, to their likes, dislikes, motivations, where they spend their time online and in what format they like to digest their content online then it becomes easier to target them on social media. The key is to remember that the more specific you are the more successful and targeted you are going to be with your social media strategy that will bring real results and conversions for your business.

What Platforms am I Going to use for my Business?

What platforms you choose to use will ultimately depend on where your customers are and which ones are best suited for your business. Spend the time researching where your current customers are online and what platforms can be best utilised with your resources and business. The key is to not spread yourself too thinly across lots of social media platforms just because you think this will gain your business more exposure, rather it is much more effective to run a handful of platforms consistently and efficiently and to spend the time reviewing the platforms you are on to make sure they are as effective as they can be. You should also keep up to date with research into new technologies and platforms that your business could potentially utilise in the future.

Selecting the Right Social Media Platforms for Your Business

Each social media platforms is unique, with its own best practices, style, and audience. The key to choosing the right social media platforms relies on you having a clear understanding of your objectives for social media, your target audience and what resources/ information you have available to share. Simply put, choose the ones that best fit your strategy and the goals you want to achieve on social media. You don't have to be on them all—just the ones that matter to you and your audience.

To help you decide the best platform, ultimately ask yourself these questions;

- **Purpose** – What information do you want to share with and communicate to your audience?
- **Format** – In what format is the best way to present this information? Videos, Podcasts, extended pieces of writing etc.
- **Platform** – Which social media platform will allow me to share this message best and which platform has the correct audience that I want to reach?
- **Time** – How much time can I devote to a social network? Aim for at least an hour per day per social network. Once you get going, tools like Buffer can help you effectively manage your time.
- **Resources** – What personnel and skills do you have to work with? Visual social platforms like Pinterest and Instagram require good quality images. Social platforms like blogging emphasize quality content. Do you have the resources to create what's needed?
- **Audience** – Where do your potential customers hang out? Which social network has the right demographics for you?

Have I Done my Research?

A successful social media presence is always aided by a good, solid foundation of prior research. You should look to do initial research into key areas such as your competitor's social media, your target audience demographics, the latest trends and news in social media, marketing and business as well as many others. Conducting research and paying attention to changes in your industry and audience for example should also be a regular and active occurrence as things, especially social media, evolve and change so you need to keep up to date to ensure your strategy is as relevant and effective as possible.

- **Market Research** – Who is your target audience? How do they behave on social media? Where are they online?
- **Competitors** – Which platforms are your competitors using? Are they directly engaging with prospects online? What are they good at online? In which areas could they improve? Can you get case studies? (Both successful and unsuccessful examples?)
- **Latest Business and Social Media News, Trends and Techniques** – Do you know the latest techniques on your social media platforms that are effective? What is changing in social media and/or business that could affect your marketing?

Am I Clear on My Marketing Voice and Tone?

The temptation at this point might be to jump right in and start sharing. Before you do however, it is crucial to cultivate a voice and tone of your marketing that effectively encompasses your brand.

To help you with this, start with questions like these:

- If your brand was a person, what kind of personality would it have?
- If your brand was a person, what's their relationship to the consumer? (A trainer, friend, family member etc.)
- What do you want your customers to think about your company?
- Describe what your company's personality is not
- Are there any companies that have a similar personality to yours? Why are they similar?

Who is Going to set up and Maintain my Businesses Social Media Platforms?

In the beginning you will need to decide who will implement and maintain your social media accounts. Whether you want to run them in-house or hire a social-media marketing manager or firm, you need to ensure that the person who oversees your platforms can effectively represent your brand and has the know-how to create and maintain a successful social media presence. That person is going to ultimately control how your business is presented to others in the online world so you need to be absolutely confident that they are the right person for you and your business.

Have I Chosen My Core Topics?

The key to a successful content strategy is finding the core topics you want your business to be known for and the topics that attract and keep the attention of fans and followers. What topics or categories best represent your company? For most this is a combination of 3 areas,

- **Your Passion** - the topic you are passionate and love to talk about
- **Your Assets** - the topic you're known for and skilled and trained in
- **Market Reality** - is there a demand on social media for the type of content you are offering?

What Resources/ Content do I Have at my Disposal?

Each social media platform has a certain type of content that is best suited towards it, for example Pinterest is inherently visual and as such requires good-quality and memorable images to be effective. From this, you need to understand what type of content that the platforms you are using is most effective and importantly what content resonates best with your audience. Once you are clear on both these aspects, you will be able to form an effective content strategy with maximised effectiveness. It is important that you share with your audience a diverse and interesting mix of content types that encourages engagement so you need to think about the types of questions you will ask, updates you will share and ultimately what resources you have that you can utilise and repurpose for your social media platforms.

What Should I be Posting?

A quick glance through any social media article, research and blog post will show an emphasis and push towards sharing visual content. This trend towards the visual has plenty of anecdotal evidence too, with it being a widely known fact that image posts get more views, clicks, re-shares, and likes than any other type of post. On Facebook, photos get 53% more likes, 104% more comments and 84% more click-throughs on links than text-based posts. Similarly, for Twitter, in a study of over two million tweets from verified users across a number of different industries, Twitter found that photos have the greatest effect on retweets. Photos average a 35% boost in Retweets with Videos getting a 28% boost. What does this mean for your business? Simple. You must prioritise producing good quality visuals in your social media content strategy.

So now we have established that you need to incorporate the visual into your content strategy. It's time to take a look at what elements should make up your other content. There are hundreds of rules, strategies and theories on the best way and most effective ways to structure your content, the most used and most simple but effective strategy I use is the 70:20:10 rule.

The 70:20:10 rule

As a general rule of thumb, the rule states;

- 70% of posts should add value and be brand and business building, stuff that your followers will find interesting, valuable and insightful and that supports who you are as a company.
- 20% should share ideas or content from other sources e.g. blogs, digital PR, websites, other social media channels etc.
- 10% should be self- promotional - your offers, discounts, marketing and promotional, sales etc.

21 Quick-Fire Example Content Ideas

- **Business Tips**: People love to hear valuable business tips.
- **Humour/Relatable**: Whether it's a funny meme or something funny that's happened in your life or your business, share it.
- **Inspiration/Motivation:** Inspiration is the number one most shared type of content across every social media platform.
- **Open-Ended Questions:** People love to talk and they love to answer questions.
- **Offers and Deals:** Did you know that getting deals is still the number one reason that people like brands on Facebook? We all love a good deal.
- **Behind the Scenes/Sneak Peeks:** People love to feel like they're a part of what's happening in your business.
- **Opinions:** You can give yours and/or simply ask for theirs. People love to give their feedback and feel like their voice is being heard.
- **Industry News:** There's a huge value proposition in this. Firstly, you are educating your community on things that are happening in your space or in your niche. Secondly, doing this routinely will help you become an industry news or thought leader.

- **Fill in the Blanks:** It's an alternative way to phrase a question and the best ones only require a one or two-word answer, which makes it easier for your fans and followers to answer and engage with.
- **Strike Up a Conversation:** Take the time to strike up a conversation. It's a great way to build relationships.
- **Testimonials:** Let people know that other people value your services or your products.
- **Open Q&A's:** Are a great way to provide value and get some real-time engagement with your followers.
- **Polls:** You can use a poll for a number of different things like collecting opinions and/or ideas. Polls are a great engagement tool, but it's also a great way to get great information.
- **Caption a Photo:** Asking your fans and followers to caption a photo normally elicits good engagement.
- **Make Predictions:** People love predictions. They want to know what you think.
- **Crowd Source Ideas:** Ask other people for ideas. Whether you're getting ready to do a new product or anything of that nature...ask!
- **Highlight Your Customers:** Let your social media followers know that you value them. It's important.
- **Tech Tips or Tools:** People love tools and they love tech tips.
- **Advice:** if you have some great advice and you feel like its valuable then share it.
- **Share Video or Audio Clips:** In some cases video and audio posts are more impactful than a simple text based or image post.
- **ASK:** Ask your followers what content they want to see.

What is my Publishing Schedule?

Whilst it is wonderfully easy for you to be told from a social media expert that you should post 2 Facebook posts a day, 10 Tweets and 2 Blog posts a week for example, the ironclad and definitive answer to the questions 'What, When and How often should I post?' is simple: It depends. Everything about the social media experience is about your individual audience and niche. What works for you might not work for me... the important thing is that you experiment and learn what does work for you.

Your publishing schedule is going to be ultimately dictated by three things, your business capabilities, the platform you're using and your audience needs. In the beginning you will need to experiment to find a publishing schedule that works best for your business, goals and readers and is the perfect balance of what you want and what your audience wants. Part of this consideration is also understanding the nature of the platform you're using to publish and whether it is one such as Twitter that favours several short updates per day or Facebook where posting 7+ times a week is effective. Ultimately, when you are creating a publishing schedule you need to ask yourself, Can you keep this schedule consistently? Can you always publish high-quality content at this rate? And will you have enough content for this schedule? Once you've discovered the most effective schedule for you, being consistent with your publishing schedule has the benefit of increasing SEO value, maximising value and engagement from readers and encourages readers to come back regularly for more.

How Often Should you be Posting?

As you have come to realise, everything about a business social media experience is unique to you. There is no one size fits all approach to what content to post, just like there is not one for about how often to post to social media either. Some of the factors that will impact your specific sharing frequency may include your industry, your reach, your resources, the quality of your updates and the social network you're using. The best way to discover the ideal posting frequency is by looking at your own analytics and several tools available in the market, these are a great way to show you the best time of day to post on your social media platforms, how often and even when your audience is online. So what are you to do if you are just starting out on these social networks, with no audience and no history? This is where best practices come in. As a good example, SumAll, which compiled timing research from sites like Visual.ly, Search Engine Watch, and Social Media Today has created a great visual resource of what their extensive research found in terms of timing.

- **Twitter** – 1-3pm weekdays
- **Facebook** – 1-4pm and 2-5pm weekdays
- **LinkedIn** – 7-8:30am and 5-6pm Tuesday, Wednesday, and Thursday
- **Instagram** – 5-6pm weekdays and 8pm on Mondays with a sweet spot at 6pm
- **Pinterest:** 2-4pm and 8-11pm weekdays with weekends being the best

How am I Going to Ensure my Business Branding is Representative and Consistent?

Having a social media presence is a great way to show a wider audience who you are, what you stand for and ultimately why they should love you. From this, it is important that you know clearly what your brand stands for and how this is going to be conveyed consistently and accurately across your platforms. This consideration needs to be applied to everything from the voice you want for your brand that can be consistently applied across all your posts to the creative aspects of your platforms- that is the overall presentation including the colour scheme and typography. By setting consistent guidelines over the presentation and integration of your branding into your social media platforms it ensures that all these factors support and are in line with your overall branding and help reinforce your message and brand.

Am I Going to Have to Create a Written Social Media Policy for my Employees?

If there are going to be several different administrators of your platforms or you run a business with staff members who have personal and/or business social media accounts, it is well worth creating a social media policy for your staff to sign so everyone is clear on their responsibilities and what is deemed appropriate and inappropriate behaviour when they are representing or discussing your business online.

Have I Considered My Mobile Strategy?

With ever increasing numbers of people accessing the internet and social media platforms from their mobile devices, it is vital that you optimise your profiles for mobile users and give them a mobile friendly experience. Therefore, you should test and experiment with your platforms to see how they look on both

your desktop and a variety of other mobile devices to ensure you provide a seamless experience for those visiting your social media platforms no matter what device they are viewing them from. When assessing your site from different devices, you should check for several key areas such as; do your images remain high quality? Are the social media sharing buttons clearly positioned and working properly? If text is used, it is readable on a small screen? The time you spend to perfect your platforms from your desktop should also be spent on making your site work for mobile too, if you fail to do so then you could lose traffic and sales as you will not be providing all users with a good experience.

How am I Going to Measure the Success of my Social Media Marketing Efforts?

Tracking your social-media marketing metrics is a fundamental part of the social media marketing process as it helps gauge which tactics are successful and which areas are in need of improvement. Put a plan in place that allows you to track, measure and assess your results consistently to see what content/strategies resonates best and to ensure you are successfully meeting your social media objectives and if they are still relevant to you. Adjust your strategy and your content when appropriate to keep your social media content fresh and your information topical. The more you post, the more you'll discover which content, timing, and frequency is right for you.

Ultimately, Have I got a Clear Strategy?

Having a clear idea on every aspect of your social media marketing strategy is key to its success. Ultimately, you should easily be able to answer confidently and with clarity the below questions that form a basic social media marketing strategy. Part of maintaining a strong, successful presence is also to regularly assess whether certain aspects of your original strategy have changed (For example are your objectives still the same? Is there a new social media platform that your audience is using?) and then adjust your efforts accordingly. As you become a regular participant on social media you will find ways in which you need to improve certain areas and areas in which you excel in, so never stop learning and listening to what your audience and your analytics tell you.

Keep referring back to this handy checklist;

Setting Goals

- ✓ Why have I joined social media?
- ✓ What is my brand's overall purpose?
- ✓ What does my business aim to achieve with social media?

Audience

- ✓ Who is our target audience?
- ✓ Which social networks do they use?
- ✓ What topics and sources of information are most important to them?

- ✓ What problems can I help them solve?
- ✓ What jobs can I help them complete?

My Brand

- ✓ What is my brand voice?
- ✓ What is the overall tone of my social media updates?
- ✓ What emotions do I hope to convey through my brand's messaging?

Content

- ✓ What types of content should I post on which social platforms?
- ✓ What type of content best supports my content marketing aims?
- ✓ What are the main topics, categories or messages that support my brand?
- ✓ Should I use social media to provide customer service?

Content Creation

- ✓ What realistic resources do we have?
- ✓ Who should set up and maintain my company's social media accounts?
- ✓ What is the workflow from content creation to publication?
- ✓ How often should I post new content on my social networks?
- ✓ How does social media fit with our other campaigns?

Measuring Success

- ✓ How will I measure ROI and define success with my social media strategy?
- ✓ What is working with my social media marketing efforts?
- ✓ What is the customer journey from search to purchase?
- ✓ Where does social media fit within my funnel?

24 Best Practices for Social Media Marketing Success

Want to ensure your social media presence is ultimately going to be a successful addition to your marketing strategy? Take note of these 24 best practices!

Have Goals and Objectives

Like every other marketing and business initiative, you need to have a goal or objective that you what your social media presence to achieve. Whether you want to use it to improve brand awareness or as a new outlet to interact with customers, having clear objectives for your platforms helps to optimise their reach and impact. In addition, having well-defined objectives also makes it clearer for you in what to measure for your return on investment. It is also worth noting that return on investment with social media marketing cannot always be measured in money. Whilst it can drive sales, the real power of social media marketing is in building relationships with customers. Whatever your objectives, make them achievable and relevant for your business and remember as you progress these objectives may change.

Portray Yourself Consistently

It is important that before you engage in social media that you are clear on what kind of image you want to portray of yourself and make sure to keep it consistent across all platforms. This consistency equally applies not just to the 'voice' you portray but also to the creative aspects, that is the overall presentation including the colour scheme and typography. If your brand or company uses certain colours then be sure to apply these consistently across the presentation of all your social media platforms. This also extends to a company logo or picture, make sure they are up to date and reflective of the image you want to portray. Having a social media platform is a great way to show a 'human' side to your business that customers appreciate and prefer. From this, it is important to have an idea of what voice you want for your page that can be consistently applied across all your posts, especially if your company page is going to be managed by several different contributors. In general, avoid generic corporate speak and replace it with your own unique voice and customers will be more drawn to and engage with you. By setting consistent guidelines over the presentation and integration of your branding into your page it ensures that all these factors support and are in line with your overall branding and help reinforce your message and brand across all social media platforms.

Be Where Your Customers Are

It's important to have a presence where your customers are looking to interact with you. To find out where you should be there are two easy ways; research the demographics of your intended social media platforms and ask your customers yourself. When you start researching what platforms you think are best for your business, be sure that their main audience are the ones you want to target. The other option is for you to ask your existing customers where they are active online; this will then help guide your platform choices.

Get In The Habit Of Checking The News

If you're not already doing this at least once a day, you need to start. Get in the habit of checking both industry news and the news in the world. You don't need to read an entire newspaper and several journals, just look to bookmark a few key sites and blogs and at the very least, skim the headlines. Social media covers all aspects of people's lives and the more you understand about them in a wider context, the more you can understand where your brand will fit into your followers' newsfeed. The added benefit of scanning the news daily means it will also help you to find real time opportunities that you can utilise for your social media content.

Learn To Manage Your Time Effectively

On average, 64% of marketers spend at least 6 hours a week on social media. As more social media platforms, tools and features are added into your marketing mix regularly, it can become overwhelming to keep on top of your timing and not to have your social media management impact your other duties. Timekeeping is one of the most vital skills for an efficient social media marketer, so make sure you're getting everything done by creating checklists for regular tasks and using social media tools that help you work smarter.

Focus on Building a Community Rather Than a Number of Followers

The number of people following you can only take you so far. Having 10,000+ followers is noteworthy, but at the end of the day it doesn't matter how many followers you have if they're not interacting and paying attention to your content. So what can be done to build a community and increase engagement with your current and potential followers? Simple, always insert some personality, humor, and life into your brand and always converse directly with your followers: which is as simple as having a conversation with them, retweet them, like and comment on their posts, and directly ask them to interact with your content.

Create a Powerful Presence Across all Social Channels

If you want your audience to stay engaged, you need to be engaging. One of the great ways to do this by creating powerful social campaigns that run consistent across all your social platforms. How do you do this? Start by...

- **Telling a powerful story**: Think of ways you can use your social channels to tell powerful, motivational and therefore compelling stories to your viewers. For example, you can share a story rooted in charity work that you do or support. Alternatively, you could share stories from your happiest clients on your blog and then create a social campaign with a unique slogan and hashtag to promote and create a movement around their stories. Team this strategy with...

- **Brand your movement with a unique name and hashtags:** Branding your movement will make it memorable and stick out in the mind of your followers. Take time to brainstorm actionable ideas that will get followers involved, whether that is done by posting photos and using your hashtag to group them, running a contest, or throwing events run by your business. For example, you could use the inspirational aspect of getting fit, or New Year's resolutions, or whichever angle you believe your customers would gravitate towards. Test out a few hashtags, find the one that resonates best, and brand your movement by announcing it on your blog and social platforms.

Suck Up to Influencers

The goal is to get these influential people to like you and like your brand. Once you get in with the people that matter, your business will exponentially grow because you are exposed to their audience and authority. Make a thorough list of key industry influencers and actively take the following steps to socially connect with them:

- **Favorite, like, comment, and re-share their content:** Don't favorite/like everything they post however, that is too obvious. Try to like and favourite a few times per week and comment when you genuinely have something educational and valuable to say.
- **Tweet at them:** Whether it's asking their feedback on your content or asking industry related questions, this strategy works very well as they will be flattered that you thought of them and consider them to be a valuable resource/influencer.
- **Use the same hashtags:** This way when they're reviewing their hashtag feeds, they'll see your content, and perhaps spark their interest.

Share Trending Content

Your platforms don't exist to be solely self-promotional, this strategy will only make you be seen as boring and obnoxious. Rather, you need to strike a balance between sharing promotional content that markets your brand, interacting with your followers and influencers, and sharing other useful and entertaining content and news from other valuable resources. To help you become an industry influencer and produce content that is share-worthy, follow these four tips:

- Look for viral videos on YouTube of hilarious children, adorable animals, and inspirational moments and re-share with your own unique spin.
- Scan the news for the highest covered media stories and add a unique perspective keeping relevant to your brand.
- Follow and use relevant trending hashtags to add your voice to the larger conversations happening on social media. For example, on Twitter you can see "Trends."
- Use a popular tool like Buzzsumo to find content that resonates. It's the easiest way to search related industry news sites and blogs, keywords, influencers, etc. to find the content with the highest number of social shares. Study the headlines that were shared and re-share those

articles/headlines with your followers. This will continue the train of sharing, but also show your followers that your social posts are intriguing and follow-worthy.

Focus On Creating Content That People Care About and Inspires Conversation

On social media, you can't depend on passive followers to convert themselves. You need to create as many opportunities to engage people as possible, and it all begins with your content. As people spend longer on social networks, their community expands and with every person followed, page liked, or friend added, they have a whole new set of posts and stories vying for their attention. Brands who have little respect for what people want in their newsfeed will find themselves further fenced off than before, therefore it is vital that the content you share is what your prospects and former customers generally respond well too. This may be a video about how your products work, interesting insights about the culture of your company or shocking stats about inefficiency in your industry for example. Whatever the case may be, build social content that gets your prospects talking to you.

Utilise Every Opportunity to Make Social Media Content

Every piece of content that you post is part of your story that you share with your audience. Everything from your ups and downs, your proudest achievements, to your charity work and the people behind your business are all prime areas in which you can create content that you can share with your viewers. So whenever you launch a new product, attend a conference or find a new way to use one of your products for example, look at the ways in which you can squeeze content out of it for use on your social media platforms.

Promote your Platforms

Anywhere your customers interact with your brand is an opportunity to encourage them to engage with you online. Once you begin, remember to promote all your social media platforms and that includes mentioning them on your e-newsletter, your email signature, business card, product packaging and anywhere else your customers will see it. Your customers and fans need to be told where they can connect with you through social media, so make it clear where you are.

Make Providing Value a Top Priority

Social media is centred on having conversations and engaging with people. That being said, unless the aim of your platforms is to be akin to a personal journal, the content you post should not be simply an update of what you are thinking or doing no with no real substance or value in what you are writing. To avoid making this mistake every post and tweet should have a clearly defined topic as well as delivering something valuable to the reader, whether that be entertainment or information. You must also write your content with your target audience in mind so rather than trying to appeal to a generic wider audience, write content that contains specialised information and analysis that those interested in your

services or in your sector would read. By openly giving out valued advice and information you will become an online repository of specialist knowledge and this will attract the attention of your target audience. Central to being effective is also realising that conversation is a two-way process so you also need to listen to what people are saying to you and about you and respond to them accordingly.

Be Active and Consistent

In order to get the most out of using social media as a marketing tool, you need to post content often. It is therefore vital that in the very beginning you figure out a comfortable writing routine that works with your editorial calendar, be it posting daily or several times a week, and stick to it in order to maintain consistency and maximise your impact. Although it takes some experimentation to find the best publishing schedule for you, there are two things that should always be considered and will dictate your posting schedule; your business goals and what your audience wants.

Respond Quickly

The fact that customer service through social media is quickly becoming an expectation of consumers means you're publicly open to both criticism and praise online. From this, it is vital that you watch for any negative things that are being said about you and respond quickly and accordingly. Rather than simply deleting any negative comments you receive, as even the most universally loved businesses receive negative comments, view them as an opportunity to win over a customer offering help, guidance or even acknowledging where something went wrong. By dealing with negativity in an open and authentic way you can help build rapport and trust with your customers. Also remember that often you will get praise online in the form of a great review or comment, do not forget to say thank you.

Coordinate Your Social Channels

Your success will be limited If you treat each social media platform as a stand-alone effort. Your networks should work together to help you achieve your goals, with your website acting as your brand's home base. Coordinate and cross-promote your social media efforts to reach new audiences, boost your following and to push people to your website where they can buy your product or service.

Boost Results With Social Advertising

If you want to accelerate your social media performance, it's worth your time to explore paid advertising options. Facebook offers several advertising options to help boost sales, brand exposure, audience engagement and website traffic. Twitter has two advertising solutions: promoted content that helps you cut through the noise and serve your content to tailored audiences and promoted accounts which help increase the size of your Twitter following. Likewise, LinkedIn also offers opportunities to reach specific audiences by advertising or using the sponsored updates feature to increase your brand's visibility. Even

if your budget is limited, don't dismiss social advertising. Used strategically it can produce great results to boost your visibility and success on social media.

Find Leads Using Social Media Monitoring Tools

Tracking and monitoring conversations happening around your brand and products is a time consuming but vital task that can be made manageable using social media monitoring tools. Ensure you actively make the effort to monitor mentions of your name, your business name, your products and any other keywords related to your business to find conversations already happening in your industry. Jump into those conversations and provide answers, guidance or helpful information where needed. Being useful is one way to start to build relationships with your target market.

Participate in Other People's Communities (OPC's)

Actively join and engage the discussions in the communities populated by people likely to use your services and share some of your expertise when it's relevant. Make it your aim to become and trusted member of these communities. You never want to be promotional in social groups, but if you're consistently helpful and engaged, prospects will likely be interested and click through to your profile where they'll find your posts and marketing collateral.

Send Regular Emails with Valuable Content, Deals and Promotions

As your social media connections move into your email list, you can and should continue to provide valuable information, notify them of upcoming deals and promotions and provide general interesting business news and updates. At this point in the funnel you have likely already become a trusted source of information, meaning your subscribers are warmed up to buying from you. Social media is all about building connections with your target market and making yourself the first name that comes to mind when they're ready to buy. Take this opportunity to craft perfect email campaigns, using segmentation whenever possible to be sure your content and offers are targeted to specific groups of subscribers and by the strategic use of strong calls to action in your emails to make sure your subscribers know what you want them to do, and what to expect when they click on your offer/content. By continuing to cultivate them with engaging, valuable and entertaining information in your emails, you will help to build connections that will result in long-term, profitable relationships.

Create Customer Advocacy Opportunities

Customer advocacy is where your marketing ROI can take off. You'll be putting in less effort to reach your marketing goals because your customers will effectively sell for you.

- **Continue to engage qualified leads and customers**

There's no reason why people should stop learning from you after they become customers. If they're on an email list or subscribed to your blog, actively send out informational reminders for them to connect with your company on social networks.

- **Offer occasional incentives for customers to review your services or share certain posts**
Depending on your business and market, offering vouchers or bargains such as free consultations can work well. The benefits for you are twofold: You'll increase brand exposure and subtly help customers become your advocates.

- **Engage customers specifically about your products and services**
If your company offers a complex product, it might be a good idea to create a forum on your website or an entirely hub that's purely for continued customer support, just for you and your customers to interact around your products. Externally, LinkedIn showcase pages and Facebook groups might be possible hubs for product-based conversations that build increased trust for your brand and position your company as worth advocating for.

- **Provide substantial advocacy opportunities for repeat customers**
Over time, you might form mutually beneficial partnerships with repeat customers. Consider rewarding these relationships with more substantial opportunities such as inviting them to networking events.

Monitor Social for Un-Tagged Brand Mentions

Not every person who mentions your brand or products on social media will tag you in the post. In fact, many social posters may assume that you'll never even see the posts they create mentioning you. Actively scan your social media networks for these types of mentions and join the conversation by provide pleasantly surprising customer engagement. You should look to actively monitor;

Your Own Brand Terms: make sure to monitor for all variations of your company's name, including nicknames and common misspellings.

Your Own Product Terms: A less frequently used strategy involves monitoring social for some of your popular products, as well as the common nicknames and misspellings.

Create an Internal FAQ Document

Consult with everyone who manages your social pages and build a document that houses all these questions and some solid answers. Whilst you should never simply copy-paste those responses over to your customers, you can use this document to quickly guide your response.

Do What Is Right for You

As you become a regular participant on social media platforms, you will find unique ways in which they can be used to the best advantage for your business. Nobody knows your customers and what they expect from you better than you yourself so delivering the content they want and engaging with them is the most important thing and will dictate your decisions surrounding your social media marketing

efforts. As with any other marketing efforts, you will learn in time what works and what don't, the important thing is to learn by doing.

Important Internet Usage and Social Media Statistics

Internet

- In 2017, 90% of households in Great Britain had internet access, an increase from 89% in 2016 and 57% in 2006 *(ONS,2017)*.
- In terms of access, 73% of adults accessed the internet "on the go" using a mobile phone or smartphone, more than double the 2011 rate of 36% (ONS,2017).
- In terms of purchases, 77% of adults bought goods or services online, up from 53% in 2008 (ONS,2017).
- Clothes or sports goods were purchased by 56% of adults, making these the most popular online purchase in 2017 (ONS,2017).
- In 2017, 93% of adults who had bought online in the last 12 months, had done so from online sellers in the UK, while 31% had bought from sellers in other EU countries and 31% had bought from the rest of the world (ONS,2017).
- On average, Google gets over 100 billion searches a month. Additionally, more than half of those searches are coming from mobile devices.

Social Media

- The power of social networking is such that, the number of worldwide users is expected to reach some 2.95 billion by 2020, around a third of Earth's entire population.
- Facebook is the first social network having surpassed the 1 billion monthly active user mark and as of the first quarter of 2017, has more than 1.94 billion MAU worldwide.
- For context, as of January 2019, total worldwide population is 7.7 billion
- The number of internet users worldwide in 2018 is 4.021 billion, up 7 percent year-on-year
- The number of social media users worldwide in 2018 is 3.196 billion, up 13 percent year-on-year
- The number of mobile phone users in 2018 is 5.135 billion, up 4 percent year-on-year
- On average, people have 5.54 social media accounts
- The average daily time spent on social is 116 minutes a day
- 91% of retail brands use 2 or more social media channels
- 81% of all small and medium businesses use some kind of social platform
- Internet users have an average of 7.6 social media accounts
- Social media users grew by 320 million between Sep 2017 and Oct 2018. That works out at a new social media user every 10 seconds.
- Facebook Messenger and WhatsApp handle 60 billion messages a day
- Social networks are the biggest source of inspiration for consumer purchases with 37% of consumers finding purchase inspiration through the channel.

- 21% of consumers would rather message a brand on social media instead of calling up customer service.
- The most common reason why consumers reach out to brands on social media is because they have a question.
- The second most common reason is to have an issue with a product or service resolved.
- 34% of people reach out to brands on social media so they can commend them on their products or services. Brands should use all of these instances as an opportunity to build relationships.
- 21% of consumers are more likely to buy from brands that they can reach on social media.
- Close to half the world's population (3.03 billion people) are on some type of social media.
- 64% of online shoppers say that a video on social media helped them decide on a product to buy.
- Only 43% of online stores receive significant traffic from their social media pages.
- 77% of Twitter users appreciate a brand more when their tweet is responded to. It takes about 10 hours on average for businesses to respond to a tweet, even though customers want a response within four hours.
- 59% of adults between 18 and 29 are using Instagram.
- The average person spends about 20 minutes on Facebook or one in every six minutes a person will spend online.
- 1.57 billion YouTube users watch about 5 billion videos on average every single day.
- 86% of women will look at social media before deciding to make a purchase.
- People are accessing 69% of their media on their smartphones.
- 89% of people on smartphones are using apps, while only 11% are using standard websites.
- Pinterest is number one for mobile social media, with 64% of referral traffic being driven by smartphones and tablets.
- 57% of all mobile users will not recommend a business if their mobile website is poorly designed or unresponsive.
- 40% of all mobile users are searching for a local business or interest.
- Mobile websites that load in 5 seconds or less will end in a viewing session that's 70% longer than their slower counterparts.
- Share of web traffic by device highly favours mobile at 52% (+4% year-on-year change), whilst Desktop remains in second place with only 43% of device share to all web pages, down by 3% year-on-year.

Google

- Google processes 100 billion searches a month
- That's an average of 40,000 search queries every second
- 91.47% of all internet searches are carried out by Google
- Those searches are carried out by 1.17 billion unique users
- Every day, 15% of that day's queries have never been asked before
- Google has answered 450 billion unique queries since 2003
- 60% of Google's searches come from mobile devices
- By 2014, Google had indexed over 130,000,000,000,000 (130 trillion) web pages
- To carry out all these searches, Google's data centre uses 0.01% of worldwide electricity, although it hopes to cut its energy use by 15% using AI.

BLOGGING

Blogging offers an easy way for businesses to share informative content with subscribers, fans and followers. Blogs are often considered at the heart of social media as they present the opportunity for you share better, more engaging content than a typical update on social media. This allows you to provide more value in every piece of content you create, helping you to connect with your audience more and become a valued source of information.

What's Good About Blogging?
- A great tool for improving search engine rankings
- Adds personality to your website, showing a 'human' side to your business
- Helps boost industry perception and can place you as an authority in your sector
- It's inexpensive, there are many blog platforms such as WordPress that allow you to set up a Blog for free

What's Not so Good About Blogging?
- Not useful for companies that cannot be open with information
- A successful blog takes a lot of thought and time so is not suitable for businesses without the time, talent or expertise

Need to Know Facts, Stats and Tips About Blogging
- On WordPress alone, 74.7 million blog posts are published every month
- Blogs have been rated as the 5th most trusted source for accurate online information.
- From 2014 to 2017, there was almost a 400% increase in paid content promotion from bloggers. Bloggers today are spending more money on paid ads to drive traffic.
- The average word count of top-ranked content in Google is between 1,140 and 1,285 words.
- Companies who blog receive 97% more links to their website.
- Blog posts that incorporate video attract 3 times as many inbound links as those without video.
- Featuring a blog as a key part of your website will give you a 434% better chance of being ranked highly on search engines.
- 10% of blog posts are compounding, which means organic search increases their traffic over time.
- Compounding blog posts generate 38% of overall traffic.
- Companies that published over 16 blog posts per month received almost 250% more traffic than companies that published up to four monthly posts.
- Bloggers that post daily get 5 times more traffic compared to those that don't.
- Titles with 6 to 13 words tend to attract the highest and most consistent amount of traffic.
- On average, companies with blogs produce 67% more leads per month.

- Once you write 21 to 54 blog posts, blog traffic can increase by up to 30%.
- Companies that blog get twice as much traffic from their email marketing than those that don't.
- 94% of people who share posts do so because they think it might be helpful to others.
- Using images in your blog posts gets them 94% more views.
- 47% of buyers consume three to five pieces of content before making a purchase decision.
- 43% of people tend to skim blog posts.

Why You Need a Blog for Your Business

It's Great for SEO

Blogs are a fantastic resource for improving search engine rankings as filled with relevant content they provide an ideal platform for your targeted keywords to be used in a natural setting. A blog also encourages people to link to your website that adds to your credibility in the search engine's eyes and also allows you to build internal links within your site, making it more easily navigated by search engine spiders. By providing regular and fresh content search engines will visit your page more frequently helping you gain maximum search exposure as quickly as possible.

Allows you to Easily Keep People Informed and Shows Your Personality

The internet can often be an impersonal place, however, having a blog offers an informal and chatty platform for your opinions, stories, humour and advice that gives your business a human face. This great ability to humanise your business through blogging ultimately makes your business appear more engaging, relatable and trustworthy to others. The space that blogging gives you to go over and above the basic, everyday postings on social media presents the opportunity for your customers to get to know you better, so whether you are sharing industry expertise, reviewing a product or sharing an aspect of your brand story, each post acts as a small piece of your business puzzle that each makes up the elements of your story. As those pieces all fit together, they give your customers the wider picture and put your business into context, helping them to better understand who you are, what you do, and ultimately tells them why they should care about you.

It Increases Your Authority

By regularly updating your corporate blog with valuable, interesting and relevant industry analysis and comment, it shows that you have a deep interest in your sector and are more informed than the average participant; giving potential customers a compelling reason to choose you over competitors. Moreover, those customers will continue to visit and spread the word to others of your valuable and interesting blog.

Blogging: What, and How Often?

Before you jump in and start blogging there are seven key strategic questions you must answer in order to ensure your blog is going to be in line with your business objectives and ultimately be a successful addition to your social media marketing strategy.

Have You Determined Your Blog's Business Objectives?

One of the first things you must do is determine what you want your blog to achieve for your business. Whether you want to use it to support sales by giving potential customers useful information in the form of how-to videos, or use it as an outlet to build your brand by providing content that supports your offering, having clear objectives for your blog helps optimise its reach and impact and when you later come to measure your success, you will have a clearer idea of what metrics to track.

Common Blogging Goals

- Build Brand Awareness
- Attract new Customers or Generate Leads
- Provide Post-Sales Support
- Inform, Educate and Entertain your Audience
- Demonstrate your Expertise and Become and Authority in Your Sector
- Drive Direct Income
- Build Long-Term Relationships with your Community

Where Will You Host Your Blog?

One of the initial hurdles when forming a blog is picking a service that will be right for your business. Many businesses choose free providers in the beginning such as WordPress and switch to self-hosted sites once they are more comfortable with blogging. Much like when you choose what other social media platforms to be on, you need to choose a platform that is relevant for your business and that offers you the services you are looking for.

Have You Defined Your Target Readers?

In addition to determining your objectives, having a clear idea of your target readers is paramount as your posts can then be tailored around content that maximises interest and engagement from your readers. It is also important to consider how your demographic behaves on social media for example how they like to receive their information and whether they are people who actively comment or not, as blog posts can then be tailored accordingly in order to maximise your potential for impact and engagement.

Have You Developed Your Blog's Voice?

Blogs are a great way for business to show a 'human' side to your business that customers appreciate and prefer to interact with. From this, it is important to have an idea of what voice you want for your blog that can be consistently applied across all your posts, especially if your business blog is going to be managed by several different contributors. Put simply, avoid generic corporate speak and replace it with your own unique voice and customers will be more drawn to and engage with your blog.

Have I Chosen the Best Blog Layout?

One of the first things you need to do when you start a blog is to choose a blog template layout. Do you want your blog to look like a traditional website? Or an online portfolio or magazine? Most blogging applications offer a variety of themes to choose from. Here are the most commonly used blog layout options to help you decide which one is right for your blog:

- **One-column** typically looking similar to online journals, this layout includes a single column of content with no sidebars on either side of the content. The benefit of this template is that readers give 100% of their attention to your content, however this template layout doesn't leave you with room for promotion of additional information, except throughout or at the end of posts. Choose this layout if you have a personal blog and have no need to display any additional information other than the content of each post.

- **Two-column** This is the most common layout as it allows bloggers to offer more information and features on the same page as their blog posts. This blog layout template includes a wide main column, which typically takes up at least three-quarters of the screen width, as well as a single sidebar that can appear to the left or right of the main column. Usually, the main column includes blog posts and the sidebar includes additional elements such as ads, links to archives, RSS subscription links for example. The key to making this layout work for your business is to ensure that the sidebar focuses on your business goals, with the most important elements at the top.

- **Three-column** A three-column blog template layout includes a main column that usually spans approximately two-thirds of the screen width as well as two sidebars. Blog posts are usually displayed in the main column and additional elements are shown in the two sidebars. If you produce a large amount of content that you want to promote alongside your articles, the three-column layout gives you plenty of space for promotion. This layout can distract readers from the main article but can also keep them on your website longer, as they'll have plenty of related content to click through to.

- **Magazine** A magazine blog template layout uses a variety of boxes of content, or featured spaces, to highlight specific content such video, images, and blog posts. This makes the home page look more like a page on a newspaper than a blog, however, interior pages can look like traditional blog pages. This type of layout is best for a blog that publishes a significant amount of content each day and as such needs a way to display a lot of content on the home page at the same time.

- **Photo, Multimedia, and Portfolio** If the majority of your blog content is made up of images or video, this type of template layout would be perfect for your blog design. These layouts are used to show a variety of images or videos in an appealing way, with images or videos displayed attractively across the home page.

- **Website or Business** This type of template layout makes your blog look like a traditional website. If you want your blog to look like a website, use a website or business blog template layout.

- **E-Commerce** An e-commerce blog template layout is designed to make it easy for you to display products using images and text and usually incorporate a shopping basket function as well. If you plan to sell products through your website, this template layout would be a good option for you.

- **Landing Page** A landing page blog template layout turns your blog into a sales page that is designed to drive conversions using some type of form or other mechanism to capture desired results. This layout is perfect if you're using your blog as a place to capture leads, sell an eBook or drive app downloads, for example.

- **Mobile** A mobile blog template layout enables you to create a site that is completely mobile-friendly. If you know your audience will be viewing your site through mobile devices this template layout is vital as it ensures content loads quickly and accurately on smartphones and tablets

- **Resume** A popular layout among job seekers and individuals who are trying to build their brand online. If you're looking for a job or need a site to communicate your skills and experience, a resume blog template is a very good option for you.

Whichever blog template layout you choose, remember these top tips!

- Unless you're an affiliate marketer or a publisher that generates income from advertisers, **don't give visitors any external links to leave your website,** unless they point back to your main website.
- **Strive for simplicity**: Simplicity is the best rule in design. Whilst Many WordPress themes come with lots of colours, complex layouts, flashy animations, etc. in most cases you don't really need all that. Simply put, find a theme that looks good, is not overly complicated but without compromising on usability and simplicity.
- **Responsive is Not Optional**: Responsive themes adjust their layout across different screen sizes and devices. Google shows mobile friendly websites on top in their mobile search results and a significant number of web traffic today is generated from mobile devices. This means that regardless of your site's topics and demographics your blog needs to be responsive and fully mobile ready. Most WordPress themes are already responsive by default, but ensure you check that the theme you are choosing for your website is mobile friendly.

Have you Listed Features to be Regularly Included in Your Posts?

Deciding on what major content categories you want to include regularly helps you to stay focused and maintains a clear direction for your posts to go in order to ensure your content is in line with your business goals and is targeting reader's needs. Part of this process is to also determine how often you will post new content on your blog as having a clear schedule of when you will be posting is paramount in order to ensure it supports and is in line with your wider social media strategy.

Have You Outlined Your Creative Elements?

Consistency should also be applied to the creative aspects of your blog that is the overall presentation including the colour scheme and typography. By setting consistent guidelines over the presentation and integration of your branding into your blog it ensures that all these factors support and are in line with your overall branding and help reinforce your message and brand across all social media platforms.

Have You Included Multiple Opt-in Forms?

If you want to convert blog readers into email subscribers to promote your business products and services, you need to have multiple opt-in forms on your blog. There are several different ways to implement them on your blog with SumoMe, for example being a popular tool that allows you to add a variety of opt-in forms to any website. You can add opt-in forms anywhere on your site, including the sidebar, footer, after a post, in floating bars, in slide-ins and in pop-ups. Whilst you don't want to go overboard, it is important to make sure that there is an opt-in form available on your blog so readers can subscribe at any time.

Have You Included Social Sharing Buttons?

Social sharing buttons are vital for your blog post content as they make it easier for your readers to share your content on the social networks. If you're comfortable editing your blog design, you can choose to add the official sharing buttons from Twitter, Facebook, LinkedIn, Pinterest and your other chosen networks. If you'd rather use a plugin, there are a vast number of tools available with Shareaholic being a popular example as it works with most major website platforms including Bigcommerce, Blogger, Drupal, Joomla, Magento, Shopify, Squarespace, Tumblr, Typepad, Weebly, Wix and WordPress. The advantage of using a social sharing platform rather than installing the buttons manually is the analytics that become available to you, allowing you to learn more about how your content is shared and who shares it.

Have You Installed Content Analytics?

Besides the above social sharing analytics, there are several additional analytics tools you need to set up on your blog to help you assess how well your content performs. Two popular tools are Google Analytics with functions such as The Behaviour report that show you details about the traffic your content receives. In addition, Google Webmaster Tools has a great feature called the Search Analytics report which shows you how your content performs in search based on the number of times seen, the number of clicks and the average position in search. By utilising these tools and regularly analysing your blog content analytics you will optimize your content marketing strategy to ensure that you're driving the best results from your blog posts.

Have You Created Unique User Accounts?

If you have multiple people blogging for your business, whether they're employees, guests or freelance writers, you should create a unique user account for each new person. Platforms like WordPress already allow each author to have a custom author bio with their posts and an author page that archives all of their articles. Not only is this beneficial from an organised point of view it can aid your SEO efforts as when people search for the author in Google, they might stumble upon your blog. If you have dozens of popular authors, this will allow you to get additional visibility in search and increased traffic to your blog.

How Will Your Blog Align With Other Marketing Efforts?

Maintaining a blog should fuel and enhance your overall content marketing efforts. So similarly, when you create a clear posting schedule for your blog be sure to consider how each post is going to fit in with and enhance your other marketing efforts. Consider questions such as how am I going to use my other platforms to promote my blog posts when they are published? And how can each blog post supplement this week's promotional strategy?

Now it's time to write your Blog, there are several fundamental basics to follow to ensure you create a powerful and engaging Blog post.

Say Something Interesting and Useful

Write your blog with your target audience in mind so rather than trying to appeal to a generic wider audience, your content contains specialised information and analysis that those interested in your services or in your sector would read. By openly giving out advice and information you will become an online repository of specialist knowledge and this will attract the attention of your target audience.

Be Creative

People always respond better to something that is new, fresh and clever so always brainstorm ideas in the mind-set of producing something that is creative and breaks the mould of other generic blog posts. You are competing in the fast-paced and growing world of social media marketing, so you need to make yourself stand out and give potential customers a compelling reason to choose you over your competitors.

Keep it Short and Sweet

An ideal blog post is between 400- 1,600 words in order to be easy enough to digest quickly. It is widely accepted that online readers are becoming lazy and it becomes difficult and unappealing to read something crowded with text and heavy paragraphs so keep paragraphs succinct and sentences short and snappy. Keep in mind that readers will often read less and less the further down an article or post they read so may sure the important point or link you want to make is made early on.

Never go for the Direct Sell

When you first start blogging it may be tempting to go with the direct sale approach posting information about how wonderful your business is and all of the things you sell or offer. This however is not a successful approach and, in most cases, will see you viewed as a spammer and will quickly lead to people losing interest in your blog. To avoid making this mistake you must strike a balance between subtle business blog posts and ones centred on customer engagement, with a favourable emphasis on the latter.

Have a Compelling Title and Leading Paragraph

It is paramount to draw the attention to your post by making your headline and introduction exciting. Choose the major point of your post and outline it clearly in the beginning, this is essential if you are going to encourage your readers to click through to the full post.

Balance SEO with Good Content

Whilst it is important to include keywords in your blog, especially within titles, you need to strike a balance between catchiness and SEO. Don't flood readers with keywords but do pay attention to the basics such as clean URLs and Meta descriptions.

Include a Call to Action (CTA)

Blog posts should end with something that moves the reader onto a next step be it a call to comment or to connect on another social media platform, this should not be an opportunity to directly hard sell a product however, as this often loses your readers trust.

How to Write an Effective Blog Post

Headline

The headline represents one of the most important parts of your blog post. It is the deciding factor on whether a reader is compelled enough to click on and read your blog post or not and for this reason it needs to grab attention and be concise in stating to the reader the benefit of clicking the link and reading the content. Don't stress out over your blog titles before you start writing. Often, the best titles come after you have already written a post. That being said, it can be helpful to come up with a basic title before you start writing. Whilst 9 times out of 10, you'll change this title later, it will in the beginning give you some direction and focus as you write. Whilst there is no definitive perfect headline template, there are several key characteristics of a powerful headline that compels the reader to click on. Powerful headlines are very concise and specific, they focus on the reader and what interests them and are keyword-optimised ensuring the right type of reader is going to find them.

- *Focus on Blog Title Accuracy*
  Whilst it may be tempting (and is relatively easy) to come up with a headline that gets clicked, for example "10 Tips to Increase Your Productivity By 10,000%". These types of crazy, outlandish headlines will ultimately destroy your credibility. You need to ensure that whichever headline format you decide on, the basic premise of your title is accurate and when people click

on your headline, they are genuinely pleased with the content they discover as it meets their expectations and delivers on whatever promise the headline made.

- **Keep your Blog Title Length Short**
  According to Kissmetrics, the ideal length for a headline is just 6 words as it is easily digestible, short and snappy. When it's not possible to stick to a 6-word limit however, Buffer suggests using your most important words at the beginning and end of your titles where readers are most likely to notice them.
- **Optimise your Blog Title for SEO and Click-throughs**
  If you want your blog posts to rank for specific keywords or phrases, placing these in your title is vital. Using keywords in your titles is also very important for getting people to click on your posts in the SERP's (search engine results pages). When people search for a particular phrase, they're highly likely to click on search results that closely match their search term.
- **Google Search**
  While it is important to include your keywords in your title, you also want to make sure your title is catchy and clickable and makes readers actually want to click through.
- **A/B Testing can Make all the Difference**
  Testing out various headlines on your audience is a time consuming but vital task as having the right headline can make all the difference

Example Headline Templates That Grab Attention

- How to Get The _____ you Want Using _____
- 5 Secrets your _____ Won't Tell you About _____
- 10 Things _____ Can Teach You About _____
- 5 Little Known Ways to _____
- The Ultimate Step by Step Guide to _____
- Best Practises for _____
- 100 Shocking Statistics About _____
- Now You Too Can Have _____ with These 5 Easy Steps
- How to be a World-Class _____ Like _____
- How to _____ a _____ You Can Be Proud Of
- 10 Things you Must Know About _____ But Don't
- 15 Things you Never Knew about _____
- 5 Unexpected ways to be Successful at _____
- Why Your Business Needs to Know About _____
- 3 Things You Must Do After _____
- How to _____ in _____ Days
- 20 _____ Every _____ Should Include
- 10 _____ Mistakes that I Should Have Done Differently
- Why I Don't Do _____
- 11 _____ Tips I Wish I Had Known

Opening Paragraph

The opening paragraph or introduction is meant to provide the setup for the main content and put the subject matter into context. This section of the blog post needs to clearly explain to the reader what your blog post is going to address and compel them to feel as though they will achieve a significant benefit from reading on and taking in what you have to say. As a general guide there are several key characteristics of a successful opening paragraph that you need to include.

- **Be Direct**: Online readers prefer to be clearly told what they are about to read and why they should do so. So avoid over complicated, artsy style writing and make it clear to the reader what you are talking about and why they should listen and take note.
- **Be Concise and Compelling**: The success of getting readers to read your whole post lies in how well you convince them at the start of your blog post that they simply have to read on. So whether you are offering exclusive content, a competition or some highly valuable advice, make it clear to the reader and in doing so give them a compelling reason to want to read on.
- **Be Bold and Creative**: Ensure you set yourself apart from other generic blog posts by being creative. Don't stick to generic writing styles, layouts and subject matter as being bold but still informative and valuable can attract a lot of attention and encourage a reader to carry on and read the whole post.

The Main Body

The main section of your blog will provide the substance to what you have outlined in your title and opening paragraph. It is important within this section you adhere to several characteristics that constitute a well written blog post;

- **Logical Structure** - You need to ensure that your blog follows a clear and logical structure that flows coherently, making the topic easy for your reader to understand.
- **Short and Succinct Sentences** – Short and succinct sentences ensure readers keep interest as it makes your content easily scannable and digestible, an important aspect for skim readers.
- **Examples and Evidence** – Providing evidence and examples that back up your points helps you appear more of an authority with your writing as well as helping your readers to grasp concepts by offering clear and obvious examples that clearly support what you are discussing.
- **Images** – Having a variety of images helps the visual appeal of your post as they break up the blocks of text and help to visually illustrate specific points.

Conclusion

The conclusion should be a short statement that clearly summarises and wraps up your post. This is the area when you should also include a clear call to action in which you direct the reader onto a next step after they have finished reading your post. Whether it is a link to an external site or encourages them to subscribe, you need to ensure the connection with you doesn't end when your blog post does.

Proof Reading and Optimisation

Once you have finished writing your blog you need to consider the important factors of proof reading and optimisation before you publish your post. This process includes a thorough read through of your blog looking into areas such as formatting, grammar, spelling, keyword placement and other optimisation opportunities. Look to analyse these several key areas;

- *Strategically Placed Keywords* – By including relevant keywords and phrases that your target readers are using and strategically placing them throughout your blog post you tailor your content in a way that is going to ensure you are targeting reader's needs and the chance for maximum search engine visibility. Look to strategically place these keywords across your post from your URL, to your blog title and subheadings.
- *General Formatting* – Ensure your blog post is readable and visually appealing by thoroughly checking your formatting and paying attention to key areas such as including sub-headings to help break up text, breaking large blocks of text with images, being consistent with font choice and text size and generally ensuring ease of read with succinct sentence structure and clearly made points.
- *Correct Links and Visuals* – If you have included links ensure that they point to the correct location. If you have included visuals such as pictures and videos also ensure you reference and credit where you got them from.

8 Quick Content Ideas for Blog Posts

- **Tips and How-To's**
  Providing informative tips, advice and how-to posts can be very useful to your customers and has the added benefit of promoting your product and its uses.
- **Behind the Scenes/ A Day in the Life of**
  People love to see behind the scenes as it shows them an aspect of your business that they wouldn't normally see. 'Day in the life' posts are a popular example.
- **Contests and Other Exclusive Content**
  Running a contest and sharing exclusive content always generate engagement and interest. Just make sure the content and/or prize you offer is relevant and valuable to your audience.
- **Relevant Industry News and Updates**
  If you know any relevant news/ events that are going to interest or affect your customers then share it with them and you will become a trusted industry news source.
- **Compile a Useful Resource List**
  If you come across any valuable and informative resources such as links, websites, books and products related to your business and industry, then share it with your customers. This can go some way towards establishing your blog as a trusted source of information.
- **Customer Testimonials / Success Stories**

A customer testimonial goes a long way in terms of establishing credibility and interest in your product or service. So if you have received a good recommendation or someone has found another useful use for your product then share it on your blog.

- **Interviews with Industry Leaders/ Key Figures**
  If you have an industry expert that is of interest to your customers or have celebrity contacts then conducting an interview and sharing it on your blog is a sure fire way to attract attention, even more so if they share exclusive content.
- **Content that Helps Humanise Your Brand**
  Sharing stories from your business founders, staff members, charity work to your business morals and values and your business highs and lows helps your audience get to know and care about you as it shows there exists a real human behind your real business.

Top Tip: There are plenty of ideas for content out there. Every book you read, event you attend, blog you visit and interview on the news you hear, is rich with ideas for content. So keep your eye out and keep a notepad handy so you always write down any ideas. But what happens for those times when you run dry? Here are four tools to help generate content for your blog:

- **Google Trends:** Google Trends keeps you up to date on the day-to-day pulse of your audiences' interests. With Google Trends you can see the frequency and popularity of Google searches related to your topic and test the subject with Google Trends.
- **MyBlogU:** This free online platform allows you to crowdsource and brainstorm with other content creators.
- **Quora:** This is a crowd-sourced, question-and-answer website where questions are asked, answered, edited and organised by its community of users. This can help lead you to the types of questions that real people are asking. As well as having the benefit of building your authority, engagement, and traffic from being a regular contributor on Quora.
- **Buzzsumo:** A fantastic source for research, with Buzzsumo you enter a topic or a URL in its search box and then displays a wealth of information. Buzzsumo provides backlinks and shows the content that performs best on social media.

8 Point Checklist Before You Publish Your Blog Post

Have I Met my Goal for This Blog Post?

Whatever you set out to achieve with your blog post, whether it's getting people to take part in research, purchase a product or sign up to your newsletter make sure that the material and links fully support your

aim and you have clear and relevant call to actions. Having clear goals also makes it easier to measure your success later down the line and assess whether the blog post achieved what it set out to do.

Is my Post Easy to Read, Well- Developed and Presented?

Having a well- formatted blog post is crucial for both ease of read and keeping the attention of readers. Blog posts even when the tone is causal are ultimately still professional papers and when writing them you are representing your business as much as you do when at meetings and in general. From this, it is vital that you generate a structured blog template and form a routine before you publish around proofreading your post, paying particular attention to several key areas;

- Is your information bulleted and has numbered lists for easy consumption?
- Are the links you use relevant and pointed to the correct webpage?
- Have you used short and succinct sentences to get your point across successfully?
- Are your section headings clear and specific to their individual points?
- Is your post well concluded with good evidence?
- Does the tone of voice/language fit the overall tone of your blog, and your brand's editorial guidelines?
- Did you use custom-made images and screenshots instead of stock photos whenever possible?
- Have you given proper credit to the images/content you used in your blog post?
- Have you taken to time to proofread and made sure your format is consistent with spacing between paragraphs as well as font styles and sizes?

Have I Directly Targeted my Audience in This Post?

You need to ensure that your blog post has been directly written with your target audience in mind. This involves you knowing and learning aspects about them from what content resonates best with them to what needs, interest, problems and questions they have as customers. So ensure your content contains specialised information that your customers will want to read. In doing so will not only will you be maximising interest and engagement from your readers, you will be proving your expertise in your industry.

Does my Post Contain Relevant Keywords?

In order to increase the potential for your blogs reach, every blog post you write should focus on and reiterate certain relevant keywords for your business. Ideally, when you are writing keep in mind 5-10 keywords and weave them into your content from the title through to the main sections of you post, taking care to not over flood your content making it unreadable and incoherent. As you become more comfortable with writing your posts you will soon find that you develop this skill to fully optimise your posts confidently.

Does the Title Grab my Attention and Make me Want to Click on it?

The main section of your blog post may be full of brilliant and valuable content, but if you don't invest the time into creating an optimised your title that makes readers want to click on it, you are making a mistake. When forming a title consider whether you yourself would click on it, is it going to solve a common problem? Improve and aspect of your life or is it exciting exclusive content? Whatever you decide, make sure it is compelling enough to click on and is optimised with keywords. You should also pay attention to the length of your title, bearing in mind that the optimal length is between 40 – 69 characters long. A shorter title may not be as descriptive and specific enough to capture attention, and a longer title will be cut off at 69 characters in search results, making your click-through rates likely to decrease.

Have I Backed up my Points with Good Evidence?

One of the key ways to become a trusted source of information is to provide content that is reliable and backed up with solid evidence to support what you are claiming. So before you publish your post make sure all the points you make are coherent and evidence is there that supports and justifies what you are claiming. Remember people may be making business decisions based on what you write so you must appear informed and reliable and give them clear reasons why what your saying is true and accurate.

Have I Included a Clear CTA?

By ensuring you include a clear call to action in every post you are making sure that each post is purposeful for your business. Whether you direct the reader to an external site or ask them to leave a comment for example you need to consistently encourage the reader to continue the interaction with you.

How am I Going to Promote this Post?

To ensure maximum reach and impact you need to consider how you are going to promote your post once it's published. There are many tips later on in this section, but also consider the means of promotion you personally have at your disposal that can help get your blog post seen more.

> Although it takes some experimentation to find the best publishing schedule for you, there are two things that should always be considered and will dictate your blogging schedule; your business goals and what your audience wants.

In general, publishing one new blog post a week is optimal because it helps maintain good relationships with customers, attract natural search traffic, and avoids burnout from writing too often. This however may vary depending on what works best for your company, goals and readers so it is important to experiment to find a blogging schedule that works for you. For example, if your goal is to become a cutting-edge information resource, you might want to post shorter articles more often or if your main audience is mostly interested in technical or behind-the-scenes details, you'll probably publish longer articles less often. So the first step to determining your ideal blogging frequency is to find the perfect balance of what you want and what your audience wants.

To maximise the benefits of having a blog you need to ultimately ask yourself, Can you keep this schedule consistently? Can you always publish high-quality content at this rate? And will you have enough content for this schedule? Once you've discovered the best times to blog, being consistent with your publishing schedule has the benefit of increasing SEO value and encourages readers to come back regularly for more.

How to Build a Following and Amplify Your Impact

Writing your blog post is only the beginning. The next challenge is to promote your blog in order to get maximum exposure and attract attention. Having a loyal band of readers who regularly engage with your blog and come back for more is fundamental to achieving success as a blogger. You may have the best blog in your niche filled with valuable and informative content, but what good is that if you don't have a regular stream of readers to appreciate and act on your work? Not matter what else, you need faithful readers who keep coming back for more.

Relying solely on search engines mixed with a bit of promotion might get you a few eyeballs, but fundamental to your success is recognising that building a loyal readership isn't something that happens overnight. Rather, it is an ongoing conscious effort to create, maintain and learn what works best for you, through the use of employing smart marketing techniques and tactics.

Syndication

One of the most powerful mechanisms of a Blog is its RSS feed that allows you to automatically feed your Blog's content to many different places, including many social networking sites. This can significantly expand your reach and saves you hours of time where you would otherwise have to post your content manually. There are also many other social sites that allow you to plug in your blog's RSS feed, make sure to link it to all of your available platforms and the potential reach of your blog becomes significantly increased.

Seek Out and Comment on Other Blogs with Similar Topics

Providing helpful, valuable comments on other blogs can be a great way to generate traffic, develop relationships and build a following. Once you have finished a blog post on a topic it is worthwhile to do a quick search to find other blogs covering the same topic, you can then add your viewpoint in a genuine, non-self-promotional way. Showing yourself to be insightful and willing to provide advice is always welcomed and appreciated and is often rewarded in the form of new relationships with other bloggers who are more likely to mention and promote your blog.

Promote your Blog

Anywhere your customers interact with your brand is an opportunity to encourage them to look at and interact with your blog. There are several key areas in which you can promote your blog, from mentioning it on your e-newsletter, your email signature, to your business card and product packaging, promoting it across all your other social media platforms and reaching out to influencers in your niche when you publish great content.

- **Email Marketing** - highlight your blog post by including a clear link to and/or a section of your blog post to help drive traffic to your blog and your website.
- **Twitter** - Tweet a summary of your post, a quote pulled from the post, or share a link to and encourage others to comment on the post itself. You can also include your blog's URL within your Twitter bio to help drive traffic.
- **LinkedIn** - Share your post with your groups and others that you know may be interested in it, this can start discussions, encourage engagement and debate that can fuel new content for future blog posts.
- **Pinterest** – Create a board that is purely for your blog posts remembering to use an interesting and relevant image to be pinned along with it and keep the boards location high, so it is clear and one of the first boards that is seen when on your profile.
- **Guest Post Opportunities** – Be proactive in looking for other bigger websites and blogs that have opportunities for guest posters. This is a great opportunity for more attention from a potentially new audience and linking back to your own blog can help with traffic. Similarly, you yourself can encourage others to guest post that can bring with it a new audience and following.
- **Meetings, Events and Giving Presentations** - Remember that whenever and wherever you meet people this presents an opportunity for you to promote and refer the audience to your blog. Similarly, for the very savvy marketer, you can also utilise digital technologies such as QR codes on your packaging that can allow people to quickly and easily subscribe to your blog.
- **Social Media Advertising** – For particularly important and popular posts, consider using social media advertising to promote shares of your blog posts on Pinterest, Facebook, LinkedIn and Twitter.

Utilise Website Banners

A website banner provides the perfect opportunity and space to create a clear call to action for driving traffic to your blog. Consider placing calls-to-action banners on different pages of your website and use

language that encourages people to want to go forward and view your blog. One of the most popular website banner CTA's for blogs is to emphasise the number of people who are already subscribed to your blog and encourage the person that is reading to join them.

Encourage and Ask for Participation

Blogging is a great way to build an engaged community. By writing your posts in a way that fosters interaction and discussions from your readers you benefit from an active and interested community that will respond to what you write. By listening to what your readers have to say you will gather important information about them from their opinions, interests and ideas to suggestions about your business, all of which are greatly beneficial as they will help guide future content creation and inform business decisions.

Host a Contest

Hosting contests are a popular and successful way of attracting attention from an audience. From asking people to pick their favourite blog posts of yours and why to having other bloggers publish a post on their blog about you, any relevant and engaging contest will help to expand your blog's reach and attract new visitors.

Publish on a Consistent Schedule

You need to publish quality content on your blog, but it's also important to publish quality content on a consistent schedule. Aim to publish a new blog post at least once a week as readers will come to expect a new blog post at a certain time and that will keep them on the lookout for it. They'll know that if they go to your blog once a week, they'll be greeted with new content. Similarly, if they go back to your blog and never see new content, they probably won't return. Making it vital to create and maintain a consistent posting schedule.

Offer Multiple Ways to Subscribe

Whilst growing your email list is one of the most important things you can do for your business, email shouldn't be the only subscription option that you offer. Not everyone wants to receive more email in their inbox, and if visitors can only subscribe via email, they likely won't. Everyone should be able to find at least one option (email, RSS, Facebook, and Twitter for example) that suits their preferences.

Show Off More of Your Content

Visitors who enter your blog through your homepage should see lots of content options, however, take the care to not make it overwhelming. Showcasing lots of content means readers will more likely find something of interest and stay on your blog for longer. However, if you prefer to maintain a minimalist

design on your blog page, you can showcase extra content on your individual posts. You can do this by ensuring readers get to see related content and are encouraged to read more posts by referring to related blog posts using text links throughout your content. These links should compel visitors to click through to more of your content since it relates to the current blog post.

Get Content Ideas From Visitors

One of the best ways to get visitors to keep coming back to your blog is by letting them know that you want to create content just for them. You can do this by adding a quick and simple survey feature to your blog that asks visitors what they want to read about next. A survey not only helps you learn more about what content your visitors want, but also ensures that you won't run out of relevant topic ideas. An added benefit is that once visitors submit a topic idea, they might subscribe to your blog so they can see if you use their suggestion for new content.

Allow Comments

There is a recent trend to turn off comments on blogs in favour of social media engagement or, in some cases, to reduce the amount of moderation required because of spam. By allowing visitors to leave comments on your blog you turn a site with informational articles into a community. Visitors just want their voice to be heard and if they know they can ask the author questions and interact with other readers, it makes them more likely to return. To encourage visitors to become loyal readers and members of your community, be sure to actively reply to comments on your blog after a post has been published.

Tips for Success

Write for People

With all the technical aspects of blogging to consider when you are writing it is easy to forget that you are ultimately writing for people. Whilst it is important to consider aspects such as keywords, the most successful bloggers are those that never stop listening to their audience and strive to better understand their needs and interests and as such this passion and genuine intention of getting to know their customers is reflected their content that is always valuable and engaging.

Show Your Personality

To stand out from the crowd you need to humanise your blog by sharing your personality, interests and stories that helps people to get to know you and really connect and care about your brand. Consumers

want to know the real people behind a business and by showcasing your personality and what makes you unique you will ultimately grow a collection of loyal followers.

Keep Going

Maintaining a successful blog is a process involving a lot of effort, time and thought and as time progresses often gets neglected or becomes lower down in a business list of priorities. The key is to keep going and keep it one of your top priorities as search engines and readers want regular, fresh content that will keep them coming to your blog otherwise they will both soon lose interest.

Deal with Negativity in a Positive Way

Rather than simply deleting any negative comments you receive, as even the most universally loved businesses receive negative comments, view them as an opportunity to win over a customer offering help, guidance or even acknowledging where something went wrong. By dealing with negativity in an open and authentic way you can help build rapport and trust with your customers.

Include Your Key Contact Information

You need to remember to include your key contact information clearly within your blog as you want to make it as easy as possible for a potential engagement or business opportunity to get in touch with you.

Make Sure you Include Social Media Sharing Buttons

To help give your blog content extended reach ensure that you include social media sharing buttons on every post. This encourages readers who have enjoyed your post to share it within their own personal networks and this will expand your posts reach beyond your own connections, opening your content out to a whole new audience.

Include Visuals

Typically, blogs that include visuals such as a photograph, infographic or video tend to perform better than posts that are purely text based. So be sure to include some type of visual content within your post that is relevant and position it to make the format more visually appealing to readers and breaks up blocks of text.

Make Your Post Easily Digestible for Skim Readers

In order to keep readers attention, it is important to format your post in such a way that it is easily digestible for skim readers. This involves using sub headings, bullet points and short, succinct paragraphs that ensure there are no heavy paragraphs and your post is clear and easily readable.

Don't Forget Your Sidebar CTA'S

The homepage for your blog is a great area in which to utilise and help generate leads and interest. Make sure you place prominent and interesting CTA banners and buttons at the top of and on the sidebar of your blog. These are great areas to encourage others to connect with you on your other social media platforms to promoting your latest offers and more.

Don't Forget to Ask For Feedback

Remember as you grow your blog and develop and gain new audiences it is vital that every so often you conduct a survey on your audience to gain feedback and ensure that the information you are posting is still resonating with them and they are finding it useful and interesting. Questions should address topics such as what formats they prefer to receive their content (text, video or audio etc.) and remember to give readers the opportunity to make their own suggestions that will ultimately benefit your efforts and provide future content ideas for you.

Invite Guest Bloggers

Inviting guest bloggers has several benefits, from giving your audience a fresh perspective to driving new audiences and helps relieve a bit of pressure off you if you do not have the time to post a blog yourself that week/month.

Read and Learn

Reading and learning from other blogs in your industry is a great way to better your own posts. Not only will you boost your own knowledge in your field and become a better writer, you can learn other important aspects of other business blogs, from what they write and how their audience responds and what they say as well as giving yourself the opportunity to voice your opinion and add your thoughts to the conversations of others. Reading lots of other blogs will also help guide future content creation for you as you can share any valuable blogs or articles you come across and of course you can be inspired to create your own posts based on ideas/debates/topics you have seen or read.

Common Mistakes to Avoid

Not Enabling Conversation

Your blog is an on-going social conversation, and not allowing conversation to occur on your blog is a mistake. Whilst allowing blog comments can open you up to criticism and negativity, it also provides an invaluable opportunity to connect with your audience. Your audience is vital to the success of your blog and likes to know that they are being heard so you need to open yourself to the conversation and enable

and encourage your audience to respond to what you write. Beyond enabling commenting on your blog, you also need to remember the conversation is two-way, so respond to the comments readers leave and you are likely to develop a community around your writing that can help turn your customers into fans who will promote your products and services and provide you with quality feedback.

Posting Inconsistently

Over time blogs often become neglected and not updated regularly as businesses let it slip down their list of priorities. An inactive and forgotten blog can have negative impact on your online image so is not going to benefit your business or be a successful addition to your marketing strategy. It is therefore vital that you continually assess your time and resources and if you find yourself unable to maintain your writing routine comfortably then edit and change it in order to maintain consistency and maximise your impact.

No Diversity Among Post Types

When businesses struggle to generate fresh and interesting ideas for their blogs this often leads to posts sounding generic and similar. When this is teamed with another common mistake in not including media content such as relevant videos and pictures, blog posts can look uninviting and will not capture a reader's attention. To avoid making this mistake make sure to post insightful and valuable content that your readers will want to read and looks visually appealing also.

Only Talking About Your Business, Products and Services

It is very common to see businesses using their blog purely as a place to hard sell their products and services. This is one of the worst mistakes a business can make as to truly benefit from using a blog and social media in general you need to be social and develop relationships and connect with your audience. This involves getting to know them and build a rapport in order that you can directly address their needs and share informative and valuable content that is going to build trust and create a community of loyal brand advocates.

Publishing Without Promoting

Your blog could be full of ground-breaking ideas and brilliantly valuable information but that is no good if no one can find or see it. Once you have published your post, remember to promote it across all your platforms and that includes tweeting it, mentioning it on Facebook, emailing it to someone you know would find it useful and putting it into your e-newsletter etc.

Neglecting to Optimise for SEO

Whilst you are ultimately writing for people, you still need to consciously act on the various ways you can optimise your blog for search. This means utilising your blog post titles with key words and strategically placing them throughout your content. Part of this process also involves a consideration of your blogs tags and using SEO friendly Text.

Ignoring the Design Aspects of Your Blog

Remember to consider the design aspects of your blog and ensure that they are optimised to boost and generate leads and traffic for your business. From ensuring you have social media sharing buttons, a search box, a subscription CTA, clear website links and contact information to a clear, organised content filing system. All of these need to be taken into account and optimised in order to make it easier for visitors to find and view content and ultimately connect with you and take actions.

Not Really Thinking About Your Post Title

Your blog post title represents one of the most important aspects in the success of your blog as it is from seeing it that a viewer will ultimately decide whether to click on it and view your post. This means you need to take the time to understand the importance of optimising it and making sure it grabs attention, is clear and concise and directly targets and will be of interest to your audience.

Ignoring Blog Analytics

If you fail to analyse your blogs analytics you are missing out on the opportunity to gain valuable insight as to whether your blog is successful and is reaching your business goals. It also helps you to determine which types of posts are most successful and which aren't, which will help guide future content creation and ensure you make informed decisions that will ensure your blogs future impact and effectiveness.

Trying to Write for the Generic Masses

Remember when writing your posts, you need to do so with your target audience in mind as this will ensure that your content is focused, interesting and informative to those who are interested in you and your industry. Writing to please a generic mass of people will not help your goal of becoming a source of valued information and expertise in your industry, so always consciously aim to directly target and address the needs and wants of your audience within your posts.

Neglecting to Check Your Post for Typos

Neglecting to read through your work to check for typos and other errors not only makes a post difficult to read and a point harder to get across, it also negatively impacts on your corporate persona leaving the reader with a less-than-professional opinion of you and your blog. So take the time to go through and

address easily fixed errors such as spelling mistakes, typos and bad links as they can cost your business greatly in terms of readership and general opinion.

You Don't Read and do Enough Research

Doing your research on your blog topic before you write it is an important aspect of blogging. Reading allows you to be exposed to and learn from different types of literatures, writing styles, opinions and thoughts all of which will inform your own posts and help you develop a solid writing style. By gathering information and educating yourself on the debates surrounding your blog topic you also ensure that you can write a balanced article filled with accurate and relevant debates which will go a long way towards establishing your blog as a trusted and valued source of information for your audience.

You See Other Bloggers as Nothing More Than Competition

A common mistake bloggers make is to see others like themselves as competition and not utilise the great opportunities for your business that comes with collaboration. Rather than ignoring other bloggers, take the opportunity to build relationships with them and encourage interaction by joining their conversations and contributing to their sites by adding your voice with valuable and positive commentary. This goes a long way towards establishing yourself as a thought leader in your industry. By collaborating with other bloggers and sharing their articles you will also benefit from increased reach and will be opened to a whole new audience as they will likely reciprocate by sharing your content also.

You Expect Overnight Success

Having a successful and popular blog takes a lot of time, patience and consistency as it takes a while to grow an audience, find a comfortable writing style as well as posting schedule. Don't make the mistake of expecting to become an overnight success as in most cases it doesn't happen. Rather it is the result of a lot of hard work, patience and continually listening to feedback, checking your analytics to see what works and what doesn't for your blog and its audience.

Measuring Success

Like any other marketing strategy, the success of your blog must be measured against your business objectives. Analysing your blog's metrics will show you a wealth of information and insights and help determine whether your blog is having a measurable impact and whether the data is reflective of the overall goals and what you wanted to achieve by having a business blog.

Measuring Visitors

One of the most basic metrics you can track is the count of people who actually read your blog content. You can look to them to assess whether your blog is successfully growing over a period of time and importantly you can to look at this data to view visits by individual blog articles. This important metric can then help you better understand what content resonates best with your audience and help you determine what the similar factors of your most successful blog posts are and use this to create content in the future that will maximise effectiveness.

Measuring Leads

Measuring what blog posts generate leads for your business is as true measure of a successful business blog as leads are what ultimately fuel the growth and success of your business. Look to examine what leads you generate from your blog posts and the rate at which those leads then convert into customers.

Subscriber Count

Your subscribers are the base readership of your content and you want to ultimately see that readership grow. Looking at how many people subscribe to your blog provides a solid indicator of the quality and consistency of your content.

Engagement

Engagement is about gauging how much people interact with you and the comments on your blog are a good way to measure engagement qualitatively. Your aim should be to create conversation and if your readers are interacting with and responding to your blog posts then it is a good indication that you are engaging your readers making them more likely to respond to and keep coming back to your blog.

Authority

A key validating factor for a blog is when others are discussing and referencing what you say. So look to measure the rates at which your blog posts are getting cited or referenced as this will give you a good measure of your authority. If you are consistently providing valuable information to your readers that they cite and share with others, not only do you generate a conversation you also become an authority within your sector.

Blogging Maintenance Checklist

DAILY

- ✓ Look through blog posts others have posted (ones you follow, blogs of industry insiders and others that you come across) and if relevant respond by adding your thoughts and/ or sharing it.
- ✓ Look to see if any new connections from other social media platforms have a blog and subscribe to it
- ✓ During the week gather information and sources for the following weeks blog post(s)
- ✓ Respond to any interaction and comments from others on your blog post(s) daily

WEEKLY

- ✓ **Check Your Analytics** - Your analytics will help you figure out what your audience likes and doesn't like, so you can plan your future content better. It'll also help alert you to any red flags early on. Regularly go through your analytics and ask; How is the traffic? Are there specific pages on your site that people seem to be bouncing out of? What kinds of topics resonate best with your audience? What headlines grab attention? What kind of keywords are bringing people to your website?

MONTHLY

- ✓ **Update Your WordPress Installation, Theme and Plugins** - Make a habit of performing updates on a regular basis and remove unnecessary themes and plugins you're not using anymore.
- ✓ **Backup Your Site** - Backing up your blog regularly helps prevent disasters as if your site ever gets wiped out, you can simply do a restore. Backing up your data is made easy by a variety of different backup plugins. Popular examples include VaultPress or BackupBuddy.
- ✓ **Check for Broken Links** - The majority links in within your posts will still work even months and years from today. But some of them won't. When that happens, it reflects very badly on you. To avoid broken link issues, scan your site for broken and whenever possible, replace your old links with new resources.
- ✓ **Check Your Ads** - If you are running ads on your site, get into habit of checking what ads are showing up on your site and that they are relevant and more importantly aren't offensive in nature.
- ✓ **Check Your RSS Feeds** - Make sure your RSS feeds are working properly. It's best to check on several different RSS clients as sometimes feeds can work in one reader but not another.

- ✓ **Review Your About Page** - Is your About page up-to-date? If anything about you, your blog, or any other content on your About page has changed since you published it, then you should update it.
- ✓ **Test Your Forms** - If you have any forms on your blog, be sure to test them to ensure that they are functioning correctly. This is particularly important for your blog's contact form. If you use third-party plugins or tools to create and manage forms on your blog, make sure you always keep them updated with the latest upgrades and fixes.
- ✓ **Delete Spam and Trash Comments** - Clean out your comments by deleting spam and trash comments. These can add up quickly so make sure deleting them is part of your ongoing blog maintenance.
- ✓ **Clean up Your Sidebars** – Regularly assess that all of the elements in your blog's sidebar are still timely, useful, and relevant. Keep it clean and useful by deleting extraneous elements and placing the best content in a prominent position.

FACEBOOK

Facebook is the largest and most active social network, with over two billion active users sharing more than more than 2.5 billion pieces of content per day. Businesses have utilised the benefits of Facebook, recognising that it's easy-to-use interface and extensive potential for user engagement makes it a fundamental tool in their marketing efforts. Perhaps the greatest feature of Facebook is the ability for your followers to share your content with their friends at the click of a button and is what cements Facebook as a successful word-of-mouth platform that can help your message reach an entirely new audience of prospective customers.

What's Good About Facebook?
- The user base is extensive and that means many of your customers and competitors may already be there
- It is compatible with any type of multimedia content meaning you can post videos, photos, and links to external content
- You can separate your personal and professional use

What's not so Good About Facebook?
- You have limited ability to customise your Page
- It can be difficult to get your content seen by fans
- It's a closed environment, although anyone can find your page, only Facebook users can 'Like' your business to receive your updates
- Facebook and its updates are moving closer to being a pay-only marketing platform to gain results

Which Businesses Should be on Facebook?
The sheer scale of Facebook's audience and its position as one of the most powerful social networks make is a must consider for any business.

Need to Know Facts, Stats and Tips about Facebook

- Users access Facebook an average of eight times per day.
- Each day, 35 million people update their statuses on Facebook.
- The average Facebook user is separated from another given user by just 3.57 degrees of separation.

- 42% of Facebook customer service responses happen during the first 60 minutes.
- More than 100 million Facebook users belong to meaningful communities—groups aimed at helping users such as new parents.
- Thursdays and Fridays between 1 p.m. and 3 p.m. are considered by many to be the best times to post on Facebook.
- The most effective length for an ad title on Facebook is four words—15 words for a link description.
- Images account for 75-90% of Facebook Ad performance.
- 26% of Facebook users who clicked on ads reported making a purchase.
- 83% of women and 75% of men use Facebook.
- 83% of Facebook users worldwide are under the age of 45.
- As of January 2017, men aged 18-24 make up the highest percentage of Facebook users by both age and gender, at 18%.
- Facebook is the preferred social platform of supermarket shoppers—89% use it.
- Facebook gets over 8 billion average daily video views.
- People are 1.5 times more likely to watch video daily on a smartphone than on desktop.
- One in five Facebook videos is now a live broadcast.
- Videos earn the highest engagement rate, despite making up only 3% of content.
- In Facebook News Feed, people consume a given piece of content faster on mobile than on desktop.
- 19% of time spent on mobile devices occurs on Facebook.
- Over 2.5 trillion posts have been created on Facebook.
- 42% of Facebook fans "like" a page with the aim of getting a coupon or discount.
- Facebook is the second favourite platform for consuming videos after YouTube. 40% of consumers said that they watch the most videos on Facebook.
- 83% pay for ads on Facebook.
- The number of local business pages on Facebook has reached 65 million.
- Total Number of Monthly Active Users: 2.072 billion
- Total Number of Mobile Monthly Active Users: 1.66 billion
- Total Number of Desktop Daily Active Users: 1.368 billion
- Total number of Mobile Daily Active Users: 1.57 billion
- Facebook users are 53% female and 47% male.
- Average Facebook user has 155 "friends".
- 56% of online Seniors aged 65+ are on Facebook and 63% are between age 50-64.
- 87% of online users of age 18-29 are on Facebook.
- More than 40 million small businesses have active pages
- A post's average organic reach is only around 6.4% of the Page's total likes
- 47% of Facebook users only access the site through the mobile app
- Videos with auto-playing sound annoy 80% of users
- Your video ad has about three seconds to capture viewer attention
- Shorter posts get about 23% more interaction than longer Facebook posts
- Video posts get more shares than any other post type.

Why You Need Facebook for Your Business

Facebook has an extensive global reach, making it an invaluable platform for businesses to grow brand awareness. Almost two thirds of Facebook users decide to follow a brand page after making a purchase, making Facebook a great tool in your marketing arsenal as it encourages users to recommend and invite their own friends to 'like' business pages that they themselves have had rewarding experiences with. Opening your business up to a potential audience of active users that has now surpassed 1 billion.

Connect With Customers and Strengthen Relationships

You will be able to connect with your customers because it is likely that they themselves are using Facebook. When a user likes your page or comments on a post, they are showing that they want a relationship with your business. This gives you an invaluable opportunity to listen to and find out about your customers, demonstrate your customer service skills, share your valuable and informative news and information, offer incentives and exclusive rewards for loyal Facebook customers. You can also use it as a channel for gaining feedback from your customers on how you can improve your product, services and your customer service, all of which can greatly help your business in the future.

Raise Awareness Through "Likes"

The Facebook 'Like' button can be seen everywhere from packaging to TV advertisements and has become a fundamental tool in the marketing efforts of businesses. Whenever a user interacts with your page by liking or sharing your content this action could get published to their friends and so forth resulting in excellent exposure for your brand and goes a long way in increasing your brand awareness. Through sharing and promoting great and valuable content that encourages interaction, you are deepening existing customer relationships at the same time as potential creating and attracting new ones, therefore making every post an invaluable opportunity to generate awareness and attention for your business.

It Shows Your Personality

The internet can often be an impersonal place; however having a business Facebook page offers an informal and chatty platform for your opinions, stories, humour and advice that gives you an opportunity to attach a face, name and personality to your brand. Having a Facebook page allows you to foster genuine social connections with your audience and as you share your brand story with others and enjoy interaction and conversation it allows others to see the human side of your business helping you create richer, more human relationships.

You Can Build a Community on Your Page

Facebook pages can work as excellent hubs for creating a community of customers, prospects and other businesses. As you continually post consistent, valuable and informative content you will be rewarded with a rich and very beneficial experience with your community in that they will share reviews, opinions, raise queries and offer feedback all of which can greatly help your business in the future. By encouraging engagement in this way you help your business build a reputation based on loyal followers making your page and brand more attractive to others who will be likely drawn to your page.

Still not convinced? Here's 8 more reasons why you need a Facebook Page

- ✓ Provides increased exposure for both your website and your brand.
- ✓ Provides website traffic by way of content sharing.
- ✓ Facilitates lead generation.
- ✓ Improves your search engine rankings.
- ✓ Free to use, though paid advertising opportunities are also available.
- ✓ Offers valuable insights into your marketplace and your competitors.
- ✓ Allows you to communicate directly with your audience.
- ✓ Allows you to create and promote company events.

Creating Your Facebook Page and Getting to Grips with The Basic Lingo

Creating a Facebook page is very straightforward. You can either go to the top navigation bar and click the arrow button to find the Create a Page option or select Create Page from the menu on the left-hand side of your news feed. Both options lead you to a page directing you to select what type of page you want to create. Your options include the following:

- Local business or place
- Company, organization or institution
- Brand or product
- Artist, band or public figure
- Entertainment
- Cause or community

From there after you select the category that best fits your business, you will then be prompted to enter basic business information like your business type, name, address and your phone number. Once the required information has been filled out, click Get Started to continue to page creation. This will lead to a page where you will be prompted to follow four steps:

- **About:** Here you will be asked to fill out a description and your website URL, as well as to confirm whether your business is a real establishment. You'll also be asked to type in categories that fit your business industry, separated by commas. This will help people find your page when they search for businesses in those categories.
- **Profile Picture:** Add a profile picture to your page, which you can do by uploading one from your computer or importing one from your website.
- **Add to Favourites:** This optional feature allows you to add your page to the top of the menu on the left side of your news feed for easier access.
- **Preferred Page Audience:** This lets you specify the kind of audience you want your page to have so that Facebook can make sure the right people find it. It will prompt you to enter targeted information such as age range, gender preferences and interests. In addition, the locations where you would like your audience to be, similarly exclude locations you don't want to reach.

You can skip these steps at any time, if you'd prefer to fill them out later.

When you first create your page, Facebook will give you a pop-up tutorial of how to navigate it. It is worth reading each information box, so you can get a better idea of how to get around your page.

At the top of your page, you'll see a white navigation bar. On the left side of the bar, you'll see four options: Page, Messages, Notifications, and Publishing Tools. You'll also see an Insights option once Page Insights has been made available to you. On the right side, there are two options: Settings and Help.

- **Page** is the default destination; it shows you your business's page. This is where you can create posts, interact with fans, update your profile information and more. Messages will take you to your page's inbox, where you can see messages you've sent and received with fans.
- The **Notifications** option takes you to a page where you see your activity such as if people have liked, commented on or shared your posts, or tagged you in a post, for example. On the left-hand side, you'll also see options to check Activity where you can monitor reviews, check-ins, mentions and more and Requests, where other Facebook users can ask you for more information about your page.
- **Publishing Tools** is where you can see your previously published posts, scheduled posts and any post drafts you may have created. You can also see your expiring posts (posts that you have set to have specific expiration dates).

Clicking the **Settings** option will take you to a page where you can fill out key information about your page and change your page's settings. Note that these settings are completely separate from your personal settings.

On the left side, you'll see a menu with several options:

General: This is where you can change many of the basic settings of your Facebook page.

- You can publish or unpublish your page with the Page Visibility setting
- Choose whether you'd like other Facebook users to be able to post to your page's wall with the Visitor Posts setting
- Turn on or off News Feed Audience and Visibility For Posts, which allows you to control which specific demographics see your posts and which don't.
- Turn on or off the ability for other Facebook users to message your page privately, and if you want other users to be able to tag your photos and videos.
- Other settings include the ability to restrict your page by country and age, block specific words from appearing on your page (like inappropriate remarks in the comments)
- Turn on a profanity filter and turn comment ranking on, making top liked comments show first, instead of new ones
- You can also turn on Similar Page Suggestions, which will recommend your page to users who view pages similar to yours.
- Facebook also gives you the option to download your page's information, merge duplicate pages and to delete your page if you choose to do so.

Messaging: This option allows you to turn on Instant Replies, which allows you to send an automatic response to anyone who messages you. Here you can also tell users who message your page what your typical response time is (which you select yourself), so they know how long to expect to wait before they hear back.

Page Info: While this option still appears in the menu, it actually no longer exists — instead, Facebook will direct you to the About tab on your business's page.

Post Attribution: This is where you can decide if you would like posts made to your page to be credited to your page or to yourself. This is just a default setting and can be changed on a post-by-post basis. If you choose to post as your page, those posts will show up as posts on the page's timeline for everyone to see. If you choose to post as yourself, these posts will show up in the Posts to Page section as if you were posting on someone else's timeline.

Notifications: This section allows you to set up what kinds of notifications you'd like to receive about your page. By default, Facebook turns all notifications on, and sends you an email each time you get a notification. You can choose to turn off email notifications if you'd rather view them on your page and

not have your notifications fill up your inbox. Or you can turn off notifications for specific events — like user check-ins, likes and more — if you prefer not to get a notification for everything.

Page Roles: If you have multiple employees running your Facebook page, this section is where you can add them to your page and adjust how much control you want them to have over it. There are five different roles you can assign to each person: Admin, Editor, Moderator, Advertiser and Analyst.

- **Admin** allows that person to manage and change any and all aspects of the page.
- **Editor** role gives them the power to edit the page, send messages, make posts and view insights, but not assign other users page roles.
- **Moderators** can respond to and delete comments on your page, as well as send messages as your page, view insights and create ads, but they can't create posts.
- **Advertisers** can only create ads and view insights, and Analysts can view insights.

The roles you assign to employees depend on what their jobs entail and what level of access they need in order to achieve their goals.

People and Other Pages: Here, you can see the full list of every person who has liked your page, as well as other pages that have liked your page and users you have banned from your page.

Preferred Page Audience: This option allows you to edit and update the Preferred Page Audience information you filled out when you created your page.

Apps: There are many apps available from Facebook and other developers that can help you add an extra dimension to your page. In this section Facebook will suggest apps that may be useful for your page, such as Facebook Events. You can also manage individual settings for each app that you have added by clicking Edit Settings under the app you want to change. You can also click Go to App to view it on your page or click Link to this Tab to copy the link specifically to that section of your page for sharing purposes.

Instagram Ads: This is where you can connect your business's Instagram account if you have one so that you can run paid ads on Instagram if you choose to.

Featured: Here, you can add other pages you've liked to your page's Featured Likes section. This is a great way to show off your business partners or suggest pages that are similar to yours. You can also

add/display a featured page owner, which is useful if you want your followers to know that you (or one of your employees) is the person running your page.

Page Support: If you have reported technical issues to Facebook from your page, this is where you can check the status of those reports.

Activity Log: This is where you can view all your page activity such as the things you have posted, searched for and more.

The **Help** button also pulls up a drop-down menu where you can access the Facebook Help Centre, go to the Facebook Help Community to ask a question, and send feedback to Facebook.

Personalising Your Page

Personalising your Facebook page is simple. Head to your page and click the About tab where you can fill out all of your basic business information, so customers and followers know what your business is and where to find you.

Example – Local Business

If you created your page as a local business, you'll see two options under About: Overview and Page Info. In the Overview section, you'll see basic information about your business, like your hours, price range, address, phone number and website. The Overview section will also show your business's location on a map, as long as your address is filled out. To fill out or change any of this information, go to the Page Info tab.

Under the Page Info tab, you'll be able to fill out and/or edit the following information:

- **Category:** This is the category you chose when you created your page (in this case, "local business or place"), so this will already be filled out. However, you can edit it if you made a mistake or think another category better suits your business.
- **Name:** This is your business's name. You can edit it if you made a mistake.
- **Subcategories:** As with your business category, this is the subcategory or subcategories that you filled out when you created your page.
- **Facebook Web Address:** Here, you can create a username or vanity URL for your Facebook page. When you do this, the URL to your page will be in the www.facebook.com/YourUsernameHere format, rather than a long collection of words, letters and numbers. That makes your page a lot easier to share, and even something that can easily fit on a business card. This is an important step in setting up your Facebook page, but make sure

you're careful — once you've set your username, you can only change it one more time before it becomes permanent.
- **Address:** Here, you can add or change your business's address.
- **Start Info:** This section allows you to highlight when you started your business. Choose Born, Founded, Started, Opened, Created or Launched from the drop-down menu, and then add the date by clicking Add Year.
- **Hours:** Here, you can set your company's hours by choosing from a list of four options: "No hours available," "Always open," "Permanently closed" and "Open for selected hours."
- **Short Description:** This is where you'll enter a short description of your business (fewer than 155 characters) that will appear below your profile picture on your page.
- **Impressum:** This is where you can enter a statement of ownership on your Web presence (up to 2,000 characters), which may be required of your business by law, depending on where your business is located.
- **Long Description:** Here, you can expand on your short description by adding more details about your business, how it started, what you do and any other details you'd like your audience to know.
- **General Information:** In this section, you can also enter any other basic details you think visitors to your page should know.
- **Price Range:** Enter the price range for your products or services here, by selecting either Unspecified or one of the following options from lowest to highest: £, ££, £££ or ££££.
- **Parking:** In this section, you can check off the types of parking available to your customers from any of these three options: Street, Parking Lot or Valet.
- **Public Transit:** If there are public transit options nearby, here is where you can let visitors know how to get to your business.
- **Phone:** Here, you can add or edit your phone number.
- **Email:** Here, you can add your email address where customers can reach you.
- **Website:** You can enter or edit your company's website in this section.
- **Official Page:** This option is only necessary to fill out if your page is not run as an official representation of your brand. This is more common when creating fan pages. In most cases, you can leave this blank.
- **Facebook Page ID:** Here, you'll see your Facebook Page ID number. This information can't be changed but may be necessary to fill in when you're using other apps on Facebook.

Changing your Profile and Cover Photo

Along with updating your business's information, you'll need to upload a profile picture and a cover photo. To upload a profile picture, simply click Add Photo in the profile picture box, and then click Upload Photo. To add a cover photo, click the small camera button right above the profile picture box. You can either upload an image or choose from a photo you've already uploaded to your page.

Your profile picture will display at 160 pixels wide by 160 pixels tall on a computer and 140 pixels by 140 pixels on a smartphone, but the image you upload needs to be at least 180 pixels by 180 pixels. If you upload an image that is not square, it will be cropped to fit.

Your cover photo must be at least 399 pixels wide by 150 pixels tall, but it will display as 640 pixels wide by 360 pixels tall on a smartphone and at 851 pixels wide by 315 pixels tall on a computer. Make sure your cover image is high-quality and eye-catching and test it out on various devices to make sure it looks good on a variety of devices.

Posting to Your Facebook Page

Posting to your Facebook page is almost exactly the same as posting on your personal profile. But instead of seeing the Status option, you'll see Post, and the Create Album and Life Event options are not there. Instead, you'll see an Event, Milestone + option, which allows you to quickly create an event to invite your followers to, or to add a company milestone. Each option will open up a pop-up box that allows you to fill out the necessary settings in order to create your event or post your milestone. You'll also see a little icon with your profile picture in the top-right corner of the post box — clicking this allows you to change from posting as your page to posting from your personal account. Otherwise, posting works the same way — you can share links, photos and videos.

Using Facebook as your Page

If you click on the arrow on the right side of the blue navigation bar at the top of the page, you'll see an option that says "Use Facebook as _____." This option allows you to switch back and forth from using Facebook as your personal account or as your page. If you are using Facebook from your personal account, there is no change to what you can do in managing your page. However, when you click on the Facebook home page, you'll see your personal news feed full of posts from your friends and the pages you have personally liked.

If you use Facebook as your page, you will instead see your page's name and profile image on the top navigation bar where your name and image usually are, and your news feed will be filled with posts from the other pages you've connected with from your business's page. You can also post to your Facebook page from the news feed in this mode.

Trending Topics on Facebook

On your news feed, you'll be able to see the top trending topics on the right-hand side of your screen. This is very useful as you can take advantage of trending topics if they're relevant to your business. For instance, if you run a bookstore, and a certain book is suddenly trending on Facebook, mentioning it in a post will allow your page to show up when users click on that particular trending topic.

Checklist for Developing a Clear and Effective Facebook Strategy

Determine Your Facebook Business Objectives

One of the first things you must do is determine what you want your Facebook Page to achieve for your business. Whether you want to use it to drive more traffic to your website, promote your events or use it as an outlet to build your brand by engaging your community, having clear objectives for your page helps optimise its reach and impact and is crucial as you later come to measure your success. So ensure you have clearly defined objectives that are realistic and achievable for your business.

Common Facebook Marketing Objectives;

- Increase Brand Exposure and Awareness
- Create a Loyal and Engaged Community
- Generate Leads
- Generate Sales

Define Your Target Audience, Are They Using Facebook?

In addition to determining your objectives, having a clear idea of your target readers and if they are themselves using Facebook is key. If you do find your target audience is active on Facebook, then you can tailor your posts effectively around content that maximises interest and engagement from your readers. It is also important to consider how your demographic behaves on social media whether they are people who actively comment or can be described as lurkers, as posts can then be tailored accordingly in order to maximise your potential for impact and engagement.

Do Your Research

Conducting research before you start using Facebook for business is fundamental to a successful presence. Your Facebook research should include these several key areas;

- ***Identify your Target Audience*** - You will need to know important factors such as where they spend their time online, how they like to digest content and other general demographics.
- ***Research your Competition*** - Find out what is and isn't working for your competition on Facebook, find out what they do well and what they don't and then apply it to your own strategy.
- ***Understand the Latest Techniques*** - Make sure you are aware of the latest updates, tends and techniques on Facebook so that you can keep your page up to date, competitive and effective.
- ***Case Studies*** - Compile examples of businesses that are similar to you and have thriving Facebook pages, look at what they do well, what their audience responds well to and other important factors that you can apply to your own efforts.

- ***Facebook's Future News, Updates and Projections*** - Ensure you track Facebook's trends and updates as they regularly change so you need to keep your business up to date and effective.

Who is Going to Manage Your Page?

Whether you yourself are going to maintain your page or you are considering hiring an external consultant or agency, you need to clearly establish the person who will be running your page and ensure that they are equipped with the right knowledge and experience to know how to effectively maintain and run a page that is representative of your business and will become a valuable asset to your marketing efforts.

How are you Going to Promote Your Page?

You need to consider how you are going to promote your page and build awareness of it which involves you having to utilise all your relevant assets that you have available. Everything from your website, e-newsletter, corporate literature, blog, word of mouth to signage and business cards present an opportunity for you to advertise and promote your page. So be clear on what tools and assets you are going to use to help successfully drive traffic to your page.

Have you Got a Clear Content Strategy? How Often Will you Post?

Deciding on what major content categories you want to include regularly helps you to stay focused and maintains a clear direction for your posts to go in order to ensure your content is in line with your business goals and is targeting reader's needs. Part of this process is to also determine how often you will post on your page as having a clear schedule of when you will be posting is paramount in order to ensure it is in line with your wider social media strategy. Creating content that people will interact with takes some thought and scheduling. Your first priority should always be to create content that your audience is interested in so look to experiment to find out the most effective content strategy and share a variety of different types of posts, at different times during the day and in different quantities. Through this initial experimentation you will find out valuable information that will guide your future strategy from what content resonates best with your audience, to the times they are most active on Facebook.

What is the Corporate Character of Your Page?

Defining the corporate character of your page has a crucial part to play in how successful your Facebook strategy will be as it is here that you will outline and determine how you are going to present yourself to your audience. This consideration involves establishing a clear vision of every aspect of your page from what your brand values are and how you will get them across, what tone of voice you will present, how you will apply your branding to the creative aspects of your page right through to the type of messages that you will be sharing.

- **Develop Your Facebook Voice** - it is important to have an idea of what voice you want for your page that can be consistently applied across all your posts, especially if your business page is going to be managed by several different contributors. Put simply, avoid generic corporate speak and replace it with your own unique voice and customers will be more drawn to and engage with your page.
- **Outline Creative Elements** - Consistency should also be applied to the creative aspects of your Facebook page that is the overall presentation including the colour scheme and typography. By setting consistent guidelines over the presentation and integration of your branding into your page it ensures that all these factors support and are in line with your overall branding and help reinforce your message and brand across all social media platforms.

Posting on Your Wall: What, and How Often?

Now it's time to start posting, there are several fundamental basics to follow to ensure you create a powerful and engaging post.

With over 15 million Facebook business pages and with users sharing 2.5 billion pieces of content each day, it can be hard to make your page and posts stand out from the crowd. For small businesses without an already established brand this is an even more difficult task to manage. There are however several guidelines available to aid you in what to post, but always remember these four key things;

Never Go For the Direct Sell

When you first start posting it may be tempting to go with the direct sale approach posting information about how wonderful your business is and all of the things you sell or offer. This however is not a successful approach and, in most cases, will see you viewed as a spammer and will quickly lead to people avoiding your page and not becoming fans. To avoid making this mistake you must strike a balance between subtle business posts and ones centred on customer engagement, with a favourable emphasis on the latter.

Try to Include Some Form of Media Within Your Posts

Not including some form of media content such as a relevant video or picture is a common Facebook mistake and makes posts look uninviting and will not capture a reader's attention. To avoid making this mistake make sure to post insightful and valuable content that your readers will want to read and looks visually appealing also. Posts with some form of media such as a photo or link always get more clicks, so it is vital that you try to include some form of relevant media.

Say Something Interesting and Useful

Write your posts with your target audience in mind so rather than trying to appeal to a generic wider audience, provide content that contains specialised information and analysis that those interested in your services or in your sector would read. By openly giving out advice and information you will become an online repository of specialist knowledge and this will attract the attention of your target audience.

Be Creative

People always respond better to something that is new, fresh and clever so always brainstorm ideas in the mind-set of producing something that is creative and breaks the mould of other generic posts. You are competing in the fast-paced and growing industry of social media marketing, so you need to make yourself stand out and give potential customers a compelling reason to choose you over your competitors.

> *Engagement on Facebook is reflected in five forms: likes, shares, clicks, comments and reactions. Here are several ways to create the right type of customer engagement with your posts;*

The Photo Post

A picture is one of the simplest ways to catch someone's attention, as it is more visually appealing than the average post. For ideas you can provide links to photographs of your employees, offices, celebrations, etc. Similarly, posting a photo and asking fans to come up with a caption is a common and successful way of encouraging fan interaction and engagement. When it comes to brands, a familiar image is also key and can be as simple as including your business logo or a face that is tied to your brand on your images.

The Fill in the Blank Post

Fill-in-the-blank posts are great at encouraging engagement. The blanks are essentially platforms for people to share their creativity and often gather fun and short comments, which then encourage your audience to interact.

The Question Post

You will get a lot more out of Facebook if you enable and encourage your customers to respond to what you write. Beyond asking questions with your posts, you also need to remember the conversation is two-way, so respond to the comments readers leave and you are likely to develop a community on your page

that can help turn your customers into fans who will promote your products and services and provide you with quality feedback.

The Tips Post

Successful posts often deliver something valuable to the reader, whether that is entertainment or information. A tip is engaging because it gives value to your audience and therefore makes them more likely to interact.

The Promotion/Discount/Incentive Post

By giving discounts or other benefits to your Facebook fans, you give them a reason to follow you and you get a captive audience for other business messaging. Common promotions offer a free gift or service upon receiving a certain number of likes. Facebook however has stringent rules when running a contest, so always consult these rules before you choose to run yours.

The Fun Post

Ensure you show your personality and inject a bit of humour into your page and posts and you will attract attention and show your brand has a personality. Strike a balance between business related posts and fun, humoured ones as you need to remember people come to businesses on Facebook to not only be informed and educated but also to be entertained.

The On Trend Post

Utilising relevant events/ observances and occurrences that are on trend is a great way to attract attention to your page. Seek out relevant trending topics and find a way for your business to join in with and share content relating to them.

The Quote Post

Quotes are one of the easiest and most popular ways to get likes and shares on Facebook. They tend to get more interaction compared to comments because quotes are often inspirational, making it personal in nature and thus showing a more human side to your brand that people are drawn to and appreciate.

The "Behind the Scenes" Post

Sharing behind-the-scenes content helps your audience to know more about you and also works towards humanising your brand.

The "Personalised Encouragement" Post

Your fans will be thrilled if you show respect and appreciation by devoting time to interact with them. Craft a short message and give your fans words of encouragement when they announce major milestones (such as a new baby, running a marathon, getting married or purchasing a first home). You can make the message more personal if you don't use any hashtags.

The "Problem-Solving" Post

Grab your audience's attention by providing valuable content that will help improve their lives. To identify what content might be valuable to your audience, read through their profiles to discover their likes, dislikes and current influences and select a common issue that they're dealing with then create content that presents a solution to their problem and promote it. Be careful to avoid creating content that is merely disguised selling tactics however as customers will quickly notice your deception. Rather than sell to them, aim to educate your followers by posting information that they'll find valuable. This is a great way to integrate your brand into their lifestyles and build more genuine customer relationships.

The "Customer Service" Post

If you offer customer service through your company's Facebook account, it's important to respond to customer concerns in a timely manner. Helping to quickly solve their queries/complaints is a great way to provide good customer service and at the same time strengthen customer relationships. Be sure to state your customer service hours of operation in your profile as if you don't people may assume a service representative is available 24/7.

The 'Video' Post

Embedded media helps keep visitors on pages longer. Videos are a great visual tool to show your personality so be creative. For example, you can post videos of employees working on a project, videos that relate to your services or products, a behind the scenes clip or something fun such as a video with you at work with your office dog.

The 'Educational' Post

Content that gets shared the most is content that has valuable information about solutions to problems. If you want to build a loyal following, provide solutions to their problems in a genuine and non-promotional way.

The 'Asking Advice' Post

Pose and problem and ask for advice. This type of Facebook post idea is great as people love to answer questions, provide their opinions and help solve problems. You can also approach it from a different

angle and ask a question that may also help them with a problem, they will be grateful for the help. Some ideas include:

- What would you do if....
- I need to make a decision and am looking for your feedback....
- What advice would you offer to a person who is struggling with...?
- One of our readers has a question. Can you help?

The 'Follow Friday' Post

On a Friday, share a Follow Friday post that allows your fans to add a link to their website/business page in the comments. This is a popular post as it give your fans the chance to showcase their business or products, but they can meet new people and make new connections.

The 'Seasonal' Post

Help humanise your brand by taking advantage of upcoming seasonal trends. This can be as simple as sharing a holiday picture, quote or greeting, changing your cover photo, and providing seasonal tips relating to your product/service.

The 'Blog Excerpts' Post

Whether you have found an external blog article that your fans will find valuable or it is your own latest blog post, when your share it be sure to include a backstory or short excerpt from the post so your fans know what to expect when they click on the link.

The 'Fan-Only' Discount Post

Offer your Facebook fans an exclusive discount, just for being a fan. This goes a long way towards rewarding loyal customers and attracting new ones. Be sure to use an image to promote the discount as this will help grab the attention of your fans and help in getting more shares.

The Cross-Promotion' Post

Team up with a business that offers a complimentary product or service and help cross-promote each other. Tag each other in Facebook status posts, recommend that your fans 'like' each other's Pages, or simply share each other's content. The benefit is that you get your content opened up to a wider and potential new audience as well as creating valuable business relationships.

Although it takes some experimentation to find the best publishing schedule for you, there are two things that should always be considered and will dictate your posting schedule; your business goals and what your audience wants.

In general, posting 7+ times a week is optimal because it helps maintain good relationships with customers, attract natural search traffic, and avoids customer attrition from posting too often. This however may vary depending on what works best for your company, goals and readers so it is important to experiment to find a posting schedule that works for you. For example, if your goal is to become a cutting-edge information resource, you might want to post shorter articles more often or if your main audience is mostly interested in technical or behind-the-scenes details, you'll probably publish longer articles less often. So the first step to determining your ideal posting frequency is to find the perfect balance of what you want and what your audience wants.

To maximise the benefits of having a Facebook business page you need to ultimately ask yourself, Can you keep this schedule consistently? Can you always publish high-quality content at this rate? And will you have enough content for this schedule? Once you've discovered the best times to post, being consistent with your publishing schedule has the benefit of expanding your reach and encourages readers to come back regularly for more.

How to Create an Effective Facebook Post - Checklist

Every post that you create must be done so with purpose and a clear goal in mind. How successful your post depends on two important factors before you even start writing;

- **Have I Built a Relevant Audience?**
  One of the fundamental aspects of whether your Facebook posts and indeed presence is successful depends upon having built an audience that is already interested in what you have to say. A relevant and invested audience is key for your success as those fans are the ones you are trying to target with interesting and valuable content as in doing so you help turn those highly targeted users into brand advocates who genuinely care about you, will interact with you and share your content, helping you to grow your fan base. No matter what any person or article says, having 100 genuine and interested fans is far better than 5,000 fans who never interact with you, share your content or show interest in building a relationship.

- **Have I Utilised Facebook Insights So I Know What My Audience Wants and When the Best Time to Post is?**
Understanding your audience and important aspects about them from their demographics, which types of content they engage with most to the times and days they are mostly online is fundamental to an effective and well performing Facebook post. You can easily find out this information through regularly analysing your analytics, so ensure you are actively looking at this data and then apply it to the content you post. In doing so you ensure your posts are going to be as effective as possible as you have directly targeted and addressed the wants and needs of your audience and will know exactly when to post the content for maximum potential for viewers.

✓ *Have I Included Visuals?*
Posts that contain visuals such as photos and videos get the highest amount of engagement on Facebook, so you need to actively and consistently incorporate visual elements into your posts. Photos and videos are more visible and take up more space on a user's newsfeed than a simple text-based post so look to include high-quality, eye-catching and relevant visuals and you will find you encourage your audience to become interactive with your page.

✓ *Is the Post Shareable?*
Your main goal when posting something onto your Facebook page is to get your fans to act on it through engagement, sharing and participation. It is widely accepted that posts containing photos, videos and links get shared more often than simply texted based posts, but ultimately none of your posts will get shared by your audience unless they are interesting, valuable and engaging which is what makes them sharable. Before you publish your post ask yourself if you would be willing to share it yourself and if you wouldn't then you need to change it. The key characteristics of sharable posts often have one or more of the following; They are informative, humorous, buck the latest trends/ events, provide a solution to a problem, have an effective and clear call to action or contain an inspirational quote or bit of advice that fans can't help but like and share.

✓ *Is the Post The Right Length?*
Facebook offers you a larger area for content that other social media networks such as Twitter, but this does not mean you should post lengthy content. The key to getting attention with your posts is to keep the length concise and easily digestible for online readers. There is no perfect length size for a post but in general the idea is to make your posts stand out in a user's news feed so you need to grab their attention with images, good links, solid CTA'S and short, snappy sentences.

✓ *Have I Removed Links from Link Copy?*
This tip is more driven by personal annoyance than necessity, but I recommend removing URLs from a Link Update. If you're already sharing the URL through Facebook's Link Share option, including the URL again in the copy is not only redundant, but also occupying precious update space.

✓ **Have I Kept my Link Titles <100 Characters?**
When you're uploading a link directly to your News Feed, if the original post has a lengthy title, be sure to click into the title to edit it. Any title above 100 characters gets cut off when posted on your Facebook Business Page, and you don't want the core message to disappear as a result.

✓ **Have I Experimented with emoticons? :)**
According to AMEX Open Forum, emoticons can impact our posts positively in a few ways:
Posts with emoticons receive a 33% higher share rate.
Posts with emoticons receive a 33% higher comment rate.
Posts with emoticons receive a 57% higher like rate.
With stats like these, it is worth testing the use of emoticons within your posts. If it works then great, if it has no impact then there is no harm done and then at least you will know for future content creation.

✓ **Does the Post have a Clear Call to Action?**
By including a clear CTA within your posts ensures that every post is working as hard as it for you to get something out of it. Importantly, a CTA doesn't have to be about getting people to buy from you, it can include a wide range of other actions from encouraging people to like or share your post, commenting on it, clicking a link to directing them to a landing page or to one of your other social media platforms. What you want your readers to do is up to you just make sure you tell what to do with a clear, simple and concise CTA.

✓ **Is the Post Relevant to My Business and Audience?**
With Facebook's continuous updates making it even harder for pages to reach their audience organically, making sure that the content they do see is highly valuable, entertaining and relevant is more important than ever. When it comes to what you post on your page you need to ensure that you stay on topic and only post relevant, high quality and varied content that your audience is interested in.

✓ **Am I Available to Quickly Respond to Posts?**
Actively watching your posts for audience comments and interaction is just as important as the post itself. You need to be regularly available to respond to the comments you receive and then consciously act on the feedback. By responding to what others write you not only provide good customer service you publicly show your audience that you are genuinely interested in interacting with them and listening to what they have to say about you and your business. There is so much you can learn from becoming sociable with your audience and listening to them and as you become familiar with them more you can then better understand their needs, wants and opinions which you can apply to future content creation and better target their needs and interests.

www.scarlettdarbyshireuk.com

A Quick Guide to Facebook Live

What is Facebook Live?

Facebook Live is a live video streaming feature on Facebook that allows you to broadcast real time video out to your audience through your company page or personal profile. Using the camera on a computer or mobile device, live broadcasters can decide who on Facebook can see their video and use this content to engage their audience during the moments that are important to them.

How to Use Facebook Live

If you're on a mobile device or going live from your Facebook profile rather than a Facebook company page, a small button will appear when drafting a post that says "Live Video." Select it to get started! If you're going live from a Facebook page on your desktop, you'll see a box that says "Live Video" below the post box.

- ✓ Give Facebook access to your camera and microphone when prompted.
- ✓ Choose your privacy and posting settings.
- ✓ Write a compelling description that's direct, actionable and informative. Your description and video thumbnail are the most important pieces of your video. Without compelling copy to entice your viewers, your live video isn't going to get much attention.
- ✓ Tag friends, choose your location, or add an activity.
- ✓ Set your camera's orientation.
- ✓ Add lenses, filters, or writing and drawing to your video.
- ✓ Click the blue "Start Live Video" button to start broadcasting.
- ✓ Interact with viewers and commenters.
- ✓ Click "Finish" to end the broadcast.
- ✓ Post your reply and save the video to your camera roll.

What happens to the Live video after the broadcast ends?

The video will be published to the Page or profile so that fans and friends who missed it can watch at a later time. The broadcaster can remove the video post at any time, just like any other post.

Where do Live videos show up on Facebook?

Videos will appear in News Feed and on the broadcaster's Page or profile while they are live. Once a broadcast has ended, live videos show up everywhere that other videos appear.

Facebook Live Best Practices

- **Tell fans when you're broadcasting ahead of time**: Build anticipation by letting your audience know when you'll be going live with a written post.
- **Make sure you have a strong connection**: Check the app to make sure that you have a strong signal before going live.. If you have weak signal, the 'Go Live' button will be grayed out.
- **Write a catchy description before going live**: A great description will capture people's attention and let them know what your broadcast is about.
- **Ask viewers to subscribe to Live notifications**: Remind your audience that they can tap on the Follow button on live videos and videos that were live so that they can get notifications the next time you go live.
- **Say hello to commenters by name and respond to their comments live:** Your audience will appreciate you mentioning their name and answer their questions when you are live!
- **Broadcast for longer**: The longer you broadcast, the more likely people are to discover and share your video with their friends on Facebook. Aim for at least 10 minutes!
- **Use a closing line to end of the broadcast**: Finish with a closing line, such as "Thanks for watching!" or "I'll be going live again soon." After you've finished, wait a few seconds until you hear the "ping" that indicates your broadcast is complete.
- **Be Creative:** Try different types of broadcasts - and go live frequently - to keep your audience engaged. Here are some examples of discussion points; Q&A's, Breaking News, 'Live With...', Performance (song, scene, sport, display your craft etc.), Behind the Scenes and sharing a Demo!

Advertising Basics on Facebook

While having and maintaining an engaging page is a great marketing tool in and of itself, Facebook has a wealth of options that you can utilise if you want to boost your presence a and pay to advertise on Facebook. According to Facebook for Business, there are several different options with each option designed for a specific outcome:

- **Page Post Engagement Ads:** These ads are intended to get more people to see and interact with (like, comment, share, etc.) your content.
- **Page Like Ads:** These ads help more people find your page so you can get more page likes.
- **Clicks to Website Ads:** These ads send visitors to your website, and you can choose a specific page of your site to advertise.
- **Website Conversions:** This option helps you track what people do on your website once they've clicked through to it from your Facebook ad.
- **App Install and Engagement Ads:** If you have an app you want to show off, this ad will help you get more people installing and engaging with your app.
- **Event Response Ads:** These ads help you create an event and get more people in attendance.

- **Offer Claim Ads:** If you want to offer a special deal or discount, you can use these ads to spread the word to new customers.
- **Video Views:** This option allows you to create and track video ads on Facebook.
- **Local Awareness Ads:** These ads allow small businesses looking to reach new customers in their area to target people by location and boost business.
- **Carousel Ads:** Carousel Ads show multiple photos or products in one ad that users scroll through and interact with.
- **Dynamic Product Ads:** These ads help you promote specific products to people who have browsed your website or mobile app.
- **Slideshow Ads:** Slideshow Ads run similarly to Facebook's video ads, but instead they're slideshows made up of photos and are designed to be more lightweight (and load more easily) on mobile devices for slower Internet connections.

Creating a Facebook Ad Campaign

1. *Choose a Campaign Objective Based on Your Goal*

The structure of a Facebook advertising campaign consists of three levels: a campaign, an ad set, and an ad. The first level, the campaign, is the basis of your ad. At the campaign level, you choose your objective, which is the action you want people to take when they see your ads. To choose the right objective simply answer the question "what's the most important outcome I want from this ad?"

The objective you select depends on your strategy. For example, If you want to run a retargeting campaign to send people from Facebook to your website, choose either the Traffic or Conversions objective, depending on what specific action you want people to take.

2. *Build Your Ideal Custom Audience*

The second stage in the campaign structure is the ad set, which specifies how your ad will run. The middle level of the Facebook campaign structure is where you choose your targeting, placement, budget, and schedule. Targeting is one of the most important elements of your campaign and it can make or break performance, even before your campaign goes live. The easiest way to target your audience is to use the demographic and interest options. Here you'll choose demographic constraints such as location, age, gender, and language. You can set basic demographic- and interest-based targeting at the ad set level. In the Detailed Targeting section, you can narrow your audience by choosing from thousands of interests, behaviours, demographics, and more. There's no rule for how large your target audience should be. Typically, you'll get the best results with basic targeting by using a layered approach, choosing a mixture of interests and behaviours to zero in on your ideal customer.

- **Location:** This allows you to show your ads to people based on their city, country or community, and is an especially useful tool for local businesses.

- **Demographics:** Facebook gives you options to target users based on gender, age group, education level, relationship status and more.
- **Interests:** Target users with interests or hobbies that align with your brand. For example, if your business sells clothing, you can use this option to reach users who have liked similar brands' pages on Facebook.
- **Behaviours:** With this option, you can target users based on the devices they use, the things they purchase and other activities they do while connected to Facebook. This is a great tool for mobile app developers — if your app is designed for iOS devices, for example, you can narrow your audience so that only those who use iPhones see your ads.
- **Connections:** Wit this option, you can reach people who have connected to your business in some way on the social network, as well as their friends. For example, if these users have RSVP'd to one of your events or have friends who have liked your page. This is a great way to engage people who are already somewhat familiar with your business.

3. Build and Test Your Ad Creative

The last stage of the campaign structure is the ad level, otherwise known as your creative. Your ad is what your audience will see. This is where you choose your ad format and creative including images, videos, news feed text, URLs and a call-to-action button. What your Facebook ad will look like depends on your advertising strategy, campaign objective, and ad format. Some objectives constrain which ad formats you can use. For example, the Video Views objective allows you to choose only video ad formats.

Top Tip: Create multiple Facebook ads and split test their performance.

The number-one best practice of Facebook ad creative is to create multiple ads as you run your campaigns. Don't just stop after you've created a single ad, by creating multiple ads to test variations in copy, image used, and even overall ad format, you can improve performance over the life of your campaign and find out what formats resonate best with your audience.

How to Build More Members of Your Facebook Group

Groups for Pages, enables the 70 million+ Pages on Facebook to create their own unique communities and feeds. More than 1 billion people around the world use Groups and more than 100 million people see Groups as the most important part of their experience on Facebook. Facebook Groups are the place to connect with other like-minded people and are becoming increasingly important for brands and businesses aiming to cultivate a community.

Whether you choose to have just a Facebook Page, Group or Both in your Facebook marketing mix, Here's a quick overview of the positive features for each:

Facebook Page

- Built-in analytics (Page Insights).
- Call-to-action button (e.g. Sign Up, Book Now, Learn More) on your Facebook Page.
- Boost your Facebook Page and Page posts with Facebook ads.
- Like and comment as your Facebook Page.
- Add apps and services to your Facebook Page, so that your fans can easily order a product, make a booking, get a quote and more.

Facebook Group

- Built-in analytics (Group Insights) now.
- Set your Facebook group as private (Closed or Secret).
- Post documents, create polls, and even buy and sell in your Facebook group.
- Group chat with your group members.
- Members receive notifications about new posts to the Group.

10 Things you Can Use Your Facebook Group For:

- Building Relationships
- Growing a Community
- Establishing Yourself as an Expert
- Share your Blog Posts
- Drive Traffic to your Website
- Grow Your Subscriber / Email List
- Launch New Products and Sell Existing Ones
- Host Trainings
- Find Partners

Tips For Growing your Group

- **Engage With Your Members Regularly**
  When your community is in its initial small stage, there might not be many posts from your community members. Help cultivate conversation by regularly (perhaps 2/3 times a week)

adding relevant, helpful conversations to encourage engagement. For example, you could welcome your new members every Monday, initiate a discussion on every Wednesday, and invite members to share their weeks' achievements on Friday.

- **Use Analytics to Inform Your Strategy**
Group Insights can be accessed by clicking on "Group Insights" on the left sidebar. Here, you can find out insights such as how your Facebook Group is growing, when your members are most engaged, and who your most engaged members are. Use these metrics and insights to inform your community-building strategy.

- **Host Regular Events**
Hosting events is a great way to get community members involved and attract inactive members back to the community. In-personal meetups help to reinforce the connections made online, making the relationships more meaningful. Here are some online and offline events you could host:
  - AMAs (Ask-Me-Anything) with a community member or industry expert
  - Q&As with someone from your company
  - Talks and panel discussions
  - Mastermind sessions or community discussions
  - Casual get-to-know-each-other gatherings such as brunch, picnic, dinner, etc.

Once you have planned your event, create an event in your Facebook Group and invite members to attend.

- **Email Your List and Invite them to Join**
If people subscribe to your email list, send them a welcome email with a link to join your group!

- **Write a Blog Post Promoting Your Facebook Group**
This is a great way to get in front of a new audience and attract more people to your group. You can use this piece of content and promote it on Pinterest, Instagram, and Facebook to expand your reach.

- **Leverage Your Friends and Group Members**
Encourage your members to invite their friends in your post, group description and per private message directly when inviting them to your group. You may also encourage your group members to help you and reward those who put in the most effort.

- **Advertise Your Group**
Remember to promote the link to your group on other social media sites like Twitter or in YouTube videos etc, wherever you can. You should also look to post the link to your group in similar groups and invite members directly to join your group via private message. Don't be spammy with this technique though, simply 'like' other members posts and write them a private

message, asking them to join your group so you can create new relationships at the same time and they will more likely have a look at your post in your own group.

Top Tip: Get rid of Spammers. *Admonish or delete spammers to keep your group clean and on topic. Decide who you are going to accept in your group and check out their profiles if necessary.*

- **Make Sure you Respond to Every Post in Your Group**
  You want to reward people for posting high quality content into your group, so reward them by commenting and letting them know how much you like what they're posting. Think positive reinforcement.

- **Give Your Group What They Want**
  You'll be surprised at how being of service will build your client base, no matter what your business is. Ask people what their needs, wants and desires are, and structure your posts around that. The more you can fill a need, the better.

How to Build a Following and Amplify Your Impact

Make Yourself Likeable

If you want to be liked on Facebook, you need to make yourself likeable first. This means you need to incentivise and attract people to your page by having an active page full of quality and consistent posts with good, valuable information and consistent engagement and interaction between your page and others.

Promote your Facebook Page on Other Social Media

Anywhere your customers interact with your brand is an opportunity to encourage them to follow you on Facebook. Once you develop your presence, remember to promote it across all your other social media platforms sharing your URL in your profile descriptions as well as sharing your most recent posts as well as mentioning it on your e-newsletter, your email signature, business card, product packaging and anywhere else your customers will see it. This also applies if you're an active participant in a forum or membership site, placing a signature with your fan page link will direct more attention to your page.

Use Tagging and Acknowledgments

Tagging an author, influencer or a popular Facebook page in your post is a great networking tool that can drive new connections. You should however have a good reason to do this, for example if the page or

author has posted something that will be useful and valuable to your fans. Be authentic and selfless in how you do it and you may be rewarded with increased attention to your page.

Reward Your Loyal Supporters

Encourage your loyal customers to join your Facebook page as supporters and reward them with special deals for consistent support. This equally applies to those already fans of your page that continually show their support. A recommendation or shout-out from a happy customer is a lot more attractive than a marketing slogan, so reward your fans and they will likely share with their friends how great you are.

Host Contests

Contests are a popular method of building an audience on Facebook and, if executed correctly, can drive huge fan growth over a short period of time which will have a big impact on your Facebook page. You should test a wide variety of different types of contests and see which resonates with your audience but always remember that you need your contest to captivate attention in a way that gets people thinking about your products or services, but make it simple enough that the majority on people can easily take part in.

Popular Contest Ideas

- Tell Us How You Would Use [Product] to Win it!
- Help Name our New [Product]
- Caption This to Win [Prize]!
- Friday Giveaway! Simply post _____ in the comments to be in with a chance to win!

Connect With Other Page Managers

Connecting and interacting with other page managers, especially local business to you can be a powerful tactic for making new connections and gathering attention. If there is a local business to you on Facebook then look to connect and work with each other to cross-promote. Not only will you develop a meaningful connection with another business that can lead to future opportunities, you will become visible to their audience which can help drive new likes and connections.

Join Conversations and Comment on Other Pages

One of the easiest ways to gain more exposure to your Facebook page is to utilise the social side of the network and interact with and join conversations of others to make yourself more visible. By actively searching for relevant businesses and conversations to interact with and join you can demonstrate your authority and authenticity by adding your relevant and valuable thoughts to conversations which will ultimately get yourself noticed by others who will likely be drawn to your page.

Utilise Print Media

Every piece of print media you use in your business from brochures to signage, business cards, magazine ads and vehicle stickers presents an opportunity for you to clearly display that you are on Facebook. Make yourself visible and you make it easier for the people you have connected with in person and who have seen other forms of your corporate literature to know you have a presence and connect with your Page.

Use Facebook Advertising

Facebook offers several paid options for you to advertise your business. From Facebook ads to sponsored stories and promoted posts, there are many customisable options for you to utilise allowing you to have the freedom to create an ad campaign that works for your business.

Give Your Fans a Reason to Connect

To make people want to connect with you, you have to give them a reason to do so. This means in addition to consistently providing quality content you need to utilise other means of incentivising people to connect with you from hosting regular competitions or giveaways to holding a fan of the week showcase, there are many options available for you to encourage people to like you. Simply learn what your target audience wants, why they like you and what content they respond well to and you will easily be able to use this information to attract more people to connect with you.

Turn Your Facebook Page Into a Community

Turning your page in to a community hub where fans are free to interact and share their opinions is a great way to learn more about your community and help build your brand. By actively getting your fans involved in your page by asking things about them and encouraging them to interact with each other, you utilise the fundamental aspect of why they are on social media, they just want to be heard. Therefore build your strategy around encouraging others to use your Facebook presence as a platform for sharing, and you will reap rewards for your business.

Be Social With Your Fans

Make it a habit to check your page daily for any new interactions or conversations you can join in with and respond to. It is by taking the time to respond to those who are talking to you that you show that you are genuinely interested in what they are talking about online and you have real conversations that build relationships. From this follows the development of a community of loyal followers that are likely to recommend you to others and share and interact with your content, allowing it to be shared and seen across whole new audiences.

Add a Facebook Like Button or Box to Your Website

Adding a Like Box to your website and blog is a great tool to utilise and it can be a big generator for likes and traffic to your page. You can place the button wherever you like on your website—perhaps in the sidebar, header or footer. You can also add the Facebook Like button to thank-you pages that appear after someone signs up for your mailing list, submits a lead form or makes a purchase. Since those visitors have already connected with your business, they will likely connect with you on Facebook as well.

Include Your Facebook Page in Guest Author Bios

When filling out your author bio or profile on a website where you contribute content, look for a place to add your Facebook page link. If there's more than one field to enter a link to your Facebook page, enter it multiple times. Some sites use plugins that will only pull from one field or another.

Connect Profiles With Pages

One very simple and effective tactic you and every employee can do to promote your Facebook page is to add your business as your current employer in your personal profile's Work section. There are many benefits to this tactic, at a basic useful level it ensures that there's a link to your Facebook page everywhere your profile appears on Facebook. An additional benefit is that when you leave a comment on a website and/or participate in industry-related Facebook groups and comment on industry blogs that use the Facebook comment platform, your page is linked within that comment as well. When you connect your page and profile you'll build a lot of exposure for your Facebook page that could lead to more fans.

Adding the link is simple. Go to your personal About page and edit your Work and Education information. Click Add a Workplace and select your Facebook page as the company. After you enter details about your position, check the "I currently work here" box and choose the dates as applicable. Make sure the visibility is set to Public and click Save Changes.

Interact as Your Page

Most users interact on Facebook as themselves (using their personal profile), but if you're looking to grow your page's audience, consider using Facebook as your page to garner more attention. Once you've chosen to use Facebook as your page, you can go to other related pages in your industry and comment on those pages' posts as your page. This way, you're bringing attention to your page, not your personal profile.

Create Facebook Groups

Facebook Groups make it easy to connect with specific sets of people, like family, teammates or co-workers. Groups are dedicated spaces where you can share updates, photos or documents and message

other group members. With the idea behind Facebook groups being that even with a small group, you can start to build a community of like-minded people.

- ✓ **An easy way to get into people's inboxes**: By default, people get emails any time there is a new wall post. That means that when you have a new product or something that important to say everyone that's in the group will get it via email.
- ✓ **A free way to create a paid member-only group**: Now, you can't do all the payment through Facebook, but you can very easily make a PayPal buy button to take payment and then you manually give the person who bought access within 24 hours.
- ✓ **Sell Products**: A great alternative/addition to selling products or digital goods on your website, you're now able to sell in Facebook groups. Once you create a For Sale group, you'll see an option to "sell something" in your Facebook update.
- ✓ **Establish Expertise**: One of the easiest ways to use Facebook groups for business is to become a resource in your field. Create a group or contribute your knowledge to one that already exists.

> ***Pro Tip:*** *If you set up a group for your business, create guidelines for the group and put them in the description area and/or pin them to the top of the group feed. You'll need to moderate the group to ensure that members are adhering to the guidelines and not spamming everyone else with their own agenda.*

Curate Content for Similar pages to Get Noticed by Their Fans

Simply send each of your targeted Facebook pages a message offering to curate content for them once a week or even just once or twice a month. It is worth noting however that the more exposure, the quicker the results. The pages you approach should appreciate the opportunity to mix up their content not to mention that it takes some of the pressure off from posting. Be sure to remember that the pages you reach out to need to be complementary, not competition. Chances are anyway that any direct competitors likely won't allow you to use their Facebook page to promote yourself.

Seek Out Promotional Swaps

Search for and list Facebook pages for products, services or communities that are complementary to yours. Once you have a robust list, craft each page a message, explaining a bit about yourself and your Facebook status and stats such as page likes and engagement. Offer to mention their Facebook page to your fans on a Facebook update if they mention yours in return. Once you reach an agreement, share your cross-promotional posts. Remember to track your results so you know which partners are good to work with in the future.

Note: This tactic works best when you have a good start with 3,000 to 4,000 likes on your Facebook page. If your page is light on fans, you may want to reach out to your email list or consider doing an inexpensive Facebook advertising campaign to increase your fan base.

Tips for Success

- *Optimise Your Profile*
  Facebook is continually working and updating its features for businesses to help them create the best experience for your audience when they are on your page. It is up to as the business page owner therefore to utilise the many features Facebook has to offer to make your page as competitive and effective as it can be.

- *Featured Video*
  The use and popularity of video has grown exponentially throughout the past few years and as such Facebook has revamped its video sharing tools to accommodate this growing trend. One of the great features you can now utilise is the ability to upload and select a featured video for your Facebook Page. The video will occupy a prominent position on your page, highlighted under the video section of your Page in addition to being visible on the left side of your Facebook Timeline. Videos are a popular and powerful way to share your story in an engaging way so ensure that the video you choose to represent your page is high quality, engaging and informative.

- *Use Photos*
  Using visual content such as photos within your posts is continually shown in studies to get the highest amount of engagement on Facebook. As such, they present a huge opportunity for brands to connect with fans and generate more likes, comments and shares. Photos and videos are more visible and take up more space on a user's newsfeed than a simple text-based post giving you the opportunity to showcase your business in a way that text alone cannot. So it is vital you regularly and consistency include high-quality, eye catching and relevant visuals.

- *Create a Unique Facebook Web Address*
  Facebook offers you the invaluable opportunity to change your Facebook URL and personalise it for your business. The URL is what people will enter to find your Facebook page and it follows the format of http://facebook.com/username. It is vital therefore that you choose a clear username that is reflective of your business as URLs are heavily weighted by search engines.

- *Keyword-Rich "About" Section* – Ensure that when you fill in your About section on your page that you not only consider making it clear, fully filled, accurate and concise but also look to utilise the SEO benefits by filling it with keyword rich information. Your About section, Mission and Company Description are all searchable on Facebook and other search engines, so it is vital that they are as optimised as they can be.

- *Build Out Your About*
  - Make sure all of your important details are placed front and centre. You have a short amount of time to gain the attention of potential fans so put the most relevant details at the top of your "About."
  - Make your about stand out with rich content. Include links to webinars, videos, upcoming events you're hosting, and in-depth information about you, your product and/or service.

- Add your mission, vision and values along with any founding details that would matter to potential clients.
- Add keywords and phrases that are relevant to your business and would be searched by any consumer looking for your small business.
- Provide success stories and examples of how you've helped others. Was there a difficult situation you were able to work through? Highlight that story.
- Remove jargon from your content and talk to fans in a conversational way.

- **Relevant, Up-To-Date Contact Information** – When someone is looking on your page it is vital that you make yourself easily contactable. Ensure that all the contact information you have on your page, from your email address to your phone number and location is all up-to-date.

- **Call-to-Action Button** - The Call-to-Action button is a great feature that you can add to further utilise your Facebook page. With this new feature, admins can choose from a selection of call-to-action buttons such as Book Now, Contact Us, Use App, Play Game, Shop Now, Sign Up and Watch Video that will be added next to the "Like" button at the top of your Facebook Page. An added benefit is that admins can edit the call-to-action button to link to a page on or external to Facebook.

Never Stop Listening to Your Audience

Listening to your customers is a fundamental aspect of having a successful social media presence. The essence of social media is based upon creating conversations, engaging your audience and listening to them showing you have a genuine interest in what they have to say about you and your business. You can then take what you learn from listening and use that information to help better many aspects of your business in the future from your products and services, to your content and future marketing campaigns. Ultimately by listening to what others say about you are armed with the valuable knowledge to know what your customers really want and need which will help your business to successfully grow.

Humanise Your Brand

The most successful companies on Facebook are those that show the real people behind the brand. Facebook offers an informal and chatty platform for your opinions, stories, humour and advice that gives your business a human face and it is through this great ability to humanise your business through the content you post that ultimately makes your business appear more engaging, relatable and trustworthy to others. Ensure you utilise this opportunity for your customers to get to know the real you better, so whether you are sharing industry expertise, reviewing a product or sharing an aspect of your brand story, each post gives your customers helping them to better understand who you are, what you do, and ultimately tells them why they should care about you.

Be Consistent With Calls to Action

By ensuring you include a clear call to action in every post, you make each post purposeful for your business. Whether you direct the reader to an external blog post or ask them to leave a comment for example you need to consistently encourage the reader to continue the interaction with you either on Facebook or externally on one of your other sites.

Be Prepared to Adjust if Things Aren't Working

A key aspect of maintaining a successful social media marketing strategy is to continually look to see what is and isn't working and how you can improve your Facebook marketing. This involves initially setting realistic objectives for your presence in the beginning and continually analysing your analytics to ensure you are meeting them. If you find you are not getting what you want from your Facebook presence, then you know you need to adjust some aspects of your strategy. It is through this adjustment that you can learn and grow as a business online which will ensure you are presenting yourself as effectively as you can online and creating better experiences for your audience.

Stay up to Date with Facebook's News and Developments

As Facebook evolves it is likely to make important changes that you as a business need to be aware of. Remember to follow the official Facebook business page and subscribe to their blog to make sure you are aware and up to date with Facebook's business updates.

Optimise the Cover Photo

Your page's cover photo represents one of the most important parts of your page. When someone visits your page, the cover image is most likely going to be the first thing a visitor will see and as such presents an opportunity to showcase your products and services, show your personality, and attract attention with eye catching and relevant photos that utilise holidays, seasons and other special events etc. all of which help towards lead generation for your business. Ensure you utilise the cover photo by creating an eye catching, good quality image with a strong CTA. Ultimately, design your cover photo with a clear primary purpose of gathering attention and prospects.

Utilise Major Events, Trends and Holidays

Major events, trends and national holidays present great opportunities for you to utilise to generate more attention for your page. From running a special competition, updating your cover photo to reflect the holiday season, to running a special promotion to coincide with a big event, there are many ways in which you can utilise these major occurrences to encourage fan engagement. Ensure you are organised, and plan ahead so make a list of major events and holidays and start thinking of ways in which you be inspired to get your business involved.

Always Make Giving Good Customer Service a Priority

Giving good customer service is essential for any brand on Facebook. You need to accept the social aspect of social media and take the time to respond and interact with those who are talking to you. Answering questions and queries and responding to complaints and issues are a natural part of any business so you need to show your fans that you are listening and care about what they have to say by responding quickly and genuinely to them. In doing so you not only boost engagement, you show your audience that you are human and that you care about what they have to say.

Let People Post Content on Your Facebook Page

There is the option on Facebook pages to not allow others to comment on your page. However whilst it is available, it doesn't mean you should use it. In fact, not allowing people to post content on your page is a mistake as you stop the ability for people to interact with you. Whilst it opens you up to the potential of public complaints and negativity, it also opens up genuinely interested audience who wants to interact with you, hear your story and share your content.

Learn From your Audience Insights

By regularly exploring your analytics, you have the ability to understand your audience from what they engage with best, what content they like most, when they are online and many other important factors that help you optimise your content strategy, target your advertising better and generate more return on investment.

Enable the Follow Button

The Follow button allows anyone to follow your public updates. If fans want to follow you, they just have to visit your profile and click the Follow button. When someone sends you a friend request, they'll automatically follow your public updates even if you haven't accepted their request. Facebook has a limit of 5,000 friends, but you can have unlimited followers,

Turn on the Follow button to allow more people to connect with you.

- Click the down arrow in the upper-right corner and select Settings.
- Click Followers on the left sidebar.
- Select Everybody from the Who Can Follow Me section (the default is Friends).

> **Pro Tip**: Since anyone who follows you can see your public updates, be sure to change your audience settings as needed to control privacy. You can choose which updates are public and which ones are only for your friends or a custom list of friends.

Share Page Posts Via Your Profile

Personal profiles are getting much more visibility in the news feed than pages. If you have some key page posts that you would like to garner more reach, share them via your personal profile. The benefit of this is that the page name travels with the post and gives your page a boost in reach, introducing your friends and followers to your page, resulting in more fans.

Craft Multi-Product Ads

Facebook now offers the ability to create multi-product (also known as carousel) ads, which allow you to rotate several products in one ad. Each product has its own title, image and landing page but all share the same text and social (like, comment and share) buttons. It's an excellent way to test which product gets the best response. While you're able to add two or more images to the multi-product ads, the best practice is to test to find out what number of displayed products maximizes your conversion rate.

There are a few things to bear in mind when creating a multi-product ad.

- ✓ Keep the headline and description text short so they'll fit the screen. For best results, limit your headline to 25 characters and your link description to 30.
- ✓ As per other ads on Facebook, you can't have more than 20% text in the image. You can measure the ratio using the Facebook Grid Tool.
- ✓ Remember, multi-product ads (both for desktop and mobile ads), work on a square dimension of 600 x 600 pixels so don't use large, wide images.
- ✓ Multi-product ads only run on the news feed and are not allowed in the right column of Facebook.

Add Featured Videos

Facebook is pushing for more video content and has hit 1 billion video views per day in September 2015. Whilst Facebook is already encouraging pages to post videos directly to the platform, one of Facebook's latest updates is encouraging pages to upload a featured video and show it prominently to people when they visit your Video tab. Setting up a featured video is easy, simply click Videos in the tab below your page's cover photo. Upload your chosen video if you haven't already done so then click Add Featured Video. Featured videos effectively bring attention to your page.

Create Video Playlists

Relating to above, Facebook has also created video playlists, which should engage users to watch and share more content. To set up your video playlist simply click Videos in the tab below your page's cover photo (which you may find in the More section). Then select Create Playlist. Create a video playlist for your content then add a title and description and click Next. Select the videos you want to add to your playlist and click Next. Now, click and drag videos to order them and select Create Playlist. Your video

tab will now display one section with your playlists and one section for all videos. This is an excellent way to group and share themed or topical video content.

Explore Dynamic Product Ads

Facebook dynamic product ads allow you to reach customers with relevant products and offers by automatically showing them ads for the products they're interested in. According to Facebook themselves this new feature is beneficial to businesses as it means you can;

- ✓ **Scale:** Promote all of your products with unique creative without having to configure each individual advert
- ✓ **Always on:** Set up your campaigns once and continually reach people with the right product at the right time
- ✓ **Cross-device:** Reach people with adverts on any device they use, regardless of their original touchpoint for your business
- ✓ **Highly relevant:** Show people adverts for products that they are interested in, in order to increase their likelihood to purchase

Collect Testimonials and Reviews

If you set up your Facebook page as a local business, you have the option to collect testimonials and reviews from your customers. Whilst you can't encourage customers to review your business for incentives, you can help yourself by letting your customers know (by putting up signs at your shop or on your corporate literature for example) that they can review your business on your Facebook page. In addition to having a Facebook page full of reviews, you can then as an added bonus put the best reviews on your website. To add a review, click on the timestamp of the review, click the drop-down arrow at the top right and select the Embed Post option.

Ask for Audience Feedback

A survey not only encourages your audience to engage with your page, it also helps you discover important information about what your customers want from you and your page. You can, for free, poll your audience with a standard post to your page or use Facebook polling apps. Your choice depends on if you want to compile the answers yourself or have the app compile the answers for you, and if you want to collect additional information (such as email addresses) that you can't collect publicly on your page.

Encourage Your Fans to Use the See First Option

Facebook now allows people to customise their news feed to prioritize updates from particular friends, groups and pages. This is great news for business pages with good content, as you can have your fans prioritise your posts. Educate your audience on how to select to see your posts first in their news feed.

The easiest way is to go directly to your Facebook page, click the Liked button and then select the See First option.

Create Saved Replies for Your Page

Saved Replies can save precious time if you have a standard message you frequently send. You are able to create generic replies for all of your frequently asked questions, then customise them before sending them out. To access your saved replies, first navigate to the Messages area of your page. To see Saved Replies, click on a particular message. The message will appear in a pop-up box and the Saved Replies will be on the left sidebar. From there, select Manage Replies to see all of the replies you've created or create a new reply.

Use the Call to Action Button

The call to action button is designed to bring a business's most important objective to the forefront of its Facebook presence. These buttons link to any destination on or off Facebook that aligns with a business's goals. You have multiple options with an unlimited amount of ways you can use them. The seven calls to action available are:

- Book Now
- Contact Us
- Use App
- Play Game
- Shop Now
- Sign Up
- Watch Video

Use Testimonials

Testimonials sharing real-life experience with your business go a long way in building credibility and can add a boost to your product sales. To encourage people to do this you need to get them excited about sharing their thoughts on your page.

Create a Posting Road Map

Many businesses start posting on Facebook without a content posting plan. As a result, their posts are often inconsistent and don't address the needs of their audience. A great tip is to create a road map for your posts covering various core topics. The more topics you add to your content bucket, the more variety you can offer to your audience. After you choose the topics you'll cover, go on to create a calendar that maps out what to post each day. If Start by creating a content calendar for one week in advance as a good rule of thumb.

Write Your Text for Skim Readers

A study by the National Centre for Biotechnology Information showed that people have an attention span of 8 seconds, which is 1 second less than that of a goldfish. If you apply that to Facebook, the first three to four words of your update are crucial to grabbing your audience's attention. Make it your priority to create compelling content in your Facebook updates.

Consider Using Brand Hashtags

Whilst the benefits of using Hashtags on Facebook are widely contested, I wouldn't dismiss the idea of hashtags altogether, before you have tested them for yourself. Using hashtags on Facebook can make sense if they are used correctly and contribute to your brand positioning. Is there a particular hashtag you use for your branding? Use hashtags when they make sense for your business. It is also effective and worthwhile to use Hashtags if you're posting about a trending topic.

Customize Your Facebook Post Descriptions

When you post a link on Facebook, it fetches the metadata automatically. Did you know, this can and should be edited to fit the post description and suit the current context? If you're republishing a post, tweak the metadata and add your own keywords. A great tip is to remember that Facebook posts are now searchable, so this is an excellent opportunity to add your keywords to the description too.

Common Mistakes to Avoid

Posting Only About Yourself

The essence of social media marketing is about creating social engagement. Therefore you need to encourage interaction from your fans by sharing valuable and informative information and comments and listening to and joining in with conversations. It is vital that you do not simply use Facebook as an outlet to push your hard sales and promotional content. Whilst you have a presence as you will ultimately want to drive sales, your posts should not blatantly reflect this, rather you need to make people love your brand by sharing stories, responding to interactions and sharing information they are going to find useful and interesting.

Posting Unrelated Content

It is important that you do not treat your Facebook business page like your own personal page. Those that have chosen to like your page expect to get relevant, valuable and informative information regarding your business or industry therefore you need to create a content strategy that clearly shows

the themes and topics you will be sharing and will ensure that every post has a relevant purpose and ensuring it is branded and directly written with your target audience in mind.

Not Responding to Negativity

Rather than simply deleting any negative comments you receive, as even the most universally loved businesses receive negative comments, view them as an opportunity to win over a customer offering help, guidance or even acknowledging where something went wrong. By dealing with negativity in an open and authentic way you can help build rapport and trust with your customers.

Begging for or Buying Likes

The more people that like you results in the more potential reach you have for your content as people interact with, like and share it. This leads many businesses to beg for likes or buy them from external sources rather than earning them through posting engaging content, interacting with others and giving incentives to encourage people to like you. Buying likes will bring no benefit to your business as whilst you may appear popular initially, those bought 'likes' are not going to be from real people that want to interact with you, so therefore you will lose out on important engagement and potential business opportunities. Begging for likes also reflects badly on your businesses reputation online as it makes you appear untrustworthy and desperate.

Connecting Your Facebook and Twitter Account

Connecting your Facebook and Twitter feeds is not recommended as each platform requires a tailored use of content from the general layout of content to the best time to post, therefore you need to treat your Facebook and Twitter account as separate entities and share your content individually tailoring them to each as opposed to having Twitter automatically tweet the same message you posted on Facebook.

Not Using Facebook Insights

If you fail to analyse your Facebook analytics you are missing out on the opportunity to gain valuable insight as to whether your page is successful and is reaching your business objectives. It also helps you to determining which types of posts are most successful and which aren't, which will help guide future content creation and ensure you make informed decisions that will ensure your pages future impact and effectiveness.

Not Checking for Bad Links and Grammar & Spelling Errors

You must remember that you represent your business with every post therefore it is vital that you review your content carefully before you share it. If you have included a link to an external site check that it is

working and points to the correct page in addition to double checking your grammar, spelling and ensuring your post is clear and concise before you post it as a post that is grammatically incorrect, incoherent or riddled with spelling mistakes will affect your credibility and reputation negatively.

Trying to Write Every Post for Everyone

Remember when writing your posts, you need to do so with your target audience in mind as this will ensure that your content is focused, interesting and informative to those who are interested in you and your industry. Writing to please a generic mass of people will not help your cause to become a source of valued information and expertise in your industry, so always consciously aim to directly target and address the needs and wants of your audience within your posts.

Measuring Success

Like any other marketing strategy, the success of your business Facebook page must be measured against your business objectives. Analysing your Facebook Insights will show you a wealth of information and help determine whether your page is having a measurable impact and whether the data is reflective of the overall goals of your business page.

Likes

In the Likes section of your Insights, you'll find 3 core metrics:

- **Page Likes**: The total Page likes for each day, over a 28-day period
- **Net Likes:** The number of new likes minus the number of unlikes
- **Where Your Page Likes Happened:** The number of times your Page was liked, broken down by where it happened.

If you're looking to build brand awareness, monitor your Page likes and ensure that you're connecting with more of the people who matter to you by targeting your posts.

Top Tips:

- You can select longer periods of time to see your metrics by using the chart at the top of the Page
- Click on a metric in the benchmark box on the right to compare data over time.

Reach

In the Reach section of your Insights, you'll find 4 core metrics:

- **Post Reach:** The number of people your post was served to, broken down by paid and organic reach
- **Likes, comments and shares:** The positive engagement that helps you reach more people
- **Hide, Report as Spam and Unlikes:** Negative engagement will decrease the number of people you reach
- **Total Reach:** The number of people who were served any activity from your Page

Top Tip: Click or drag the Post Reach, Positive Engagement and Negative Engagement charts, and the pop-up will tell you which posts people were seeing during the selected time period. This helps you tie content to performance trends in your graph.

Visits

In the Visits section of your Insights, you'll find 2 core metrics:

- **Page and Tab Visits:** The number of times each of your Page tabs was viewed
- **External Referrers:** The number of times people came to your Page from a website outside of Facebook

Top Tips: Ensure that your Page is filled in with basic information so that you can be found by the people who matter most to you.

Update your Page with:

- Category and description: Add accurate details to help people find your Page when they search
- Website and phone number: Enter relevant business info so that people can find you online
- Page web address: You can request a web address like facebook.com/marketing, which makes it easy to find you. Update your Page web address here.

Posts

In The Posts tab section of your Insights, you'll find 3 core metrics:

- **When Your Fans Are Online:** Shows you when the people who like your Page are on Facebook content
- **Post Type:** Displays the success of different post types based on average reach and engagement
- **Top Posts From Pages You Watch:** Gives you the engagement of posts from the Pages you're watching

Top Tip: Review your analytics regularly and schedule your posts to appear when your audience is most often online. You can also review your post types to see what resonates most with your audience, such as link posts or photo posts.

Video

In the Visits section of your Insights, you'll find 3 core metrics:

- **Video Views:** Number of times your Page's videos were viewed for 3 seconds or more
- **30-second Views:** Number of times your Page's videos were viewed for 30 seconds or more. If a video is less than 30 seconds long, this counts when people view 97 per cent of it.
- **Top Videos:** Most-viewed videos on your Page watched for 3 seconds or more.

People

The People tab is divided into Your Fans, People Reached and People Engaged.

- **Your Fans:** View the gender, age, location and language of the people who like your Page
- **People Reached:** See the people your post was served to in the past 28 days
- **People Engaged:** Find out who has liked, commented on or shared your posts, or engaged with your Page, in the past 28 days. Once you know who your most engaged audience is, you can better tailor your Boosted Posts to them.

Top Tip: Target your Boosted Posts to your most engaged audience to keep them interested.

Audience Engagement

Is your audience interacting with your content? This could be by: liking, commenting, reacting or sharing it. Engagement is about gauging how much people interact with you and the comments, shares and likes on your Page are a good way to measure engagement. Your aim should be to create conversation and if your readers are interacting with and responding to your posts then it is a good indication that you are engaging your readers making them more likely to respond and continue interacting with your page.

In terms of importance, you need to consider: A comment is more valuable than a like and a share is more valuable than a comment. When someone likes or comments on your content, it is not automatically shared with their followers. Facebook does take into account the popularity of your content, so it's more likely to be shared to other people if there are likes or comments. But shares are really what you want. With a share, it is a real endorsement of your content and your fan is specifically asking Facebook to share your content with their friends.

Negative Feedback

Tracking negative feedback is also an important part of the process as it can show you areas for concern. If fans are hiding your posts, un-liking your page or reporting your posts as spam, then you need to

know. For the breakdown you have to download the excel report in your Facebook insights. If your average negative feedback number is too high, your posts will get less exposure over time so it is paramount that you look at what posts are getting you negative feedbacks and when, as you can then use this information to adjust your content or marketing efforts accordingly.

Facebook Reactions

Several years ago, Facebook introduced a new feature called "Reactions' allowing users to show their love, anger, laughter, and more to a piece of content on Facebook. Facebook Reactions are counted the same as likes, however, you can see the breakdown of reactions on an individual post by looking at the Post Details. Doing so will give you a greater insight into what your audience thinks of your content. Take note of people who "love" your content -- they are likely good brand evangelists. And remember that an "angry" may not mean they dislike the content, but instead the subject matter.

Conversion

Another piece of important information to track is how much traffic that your page brings to the rest of your website. In other words, how many fans are converted into potential customers? If a significant number of website visitors were referred from Facebook, you know that your posts are generating interest in your products or services and are possibly helping to drive sales. Tracking this number is the true measure of your Facebook marketing ROI as even if you're generating traffic and leads from Facebook, if they're ultimately not turning into customers you may have to re-evaluate how much time and effort you're putting into Facebook as a social media marketing channel.

Likes and Unlikes

How quickly are your fans growing? It's not all about the numbers but, if you're attracting the right audience and they are engaging with your content, then of course you want to see some fan growth. Tracking the rates at which you are liked and disliked by others is an important metric to regularly analyse as it will show you when you have performed well and the times when you haven't allowing you to establish what you did at those times that could have made others follow you or unfollow you. Learning from this information helps develop a more successful strategy as it will show you the areas in which your audience responds to better and which areas they didn't, allowing you to learn what your audience wants and then applying it to your future efforts.

Engagement by Type of Content

Different types of content perform differently on Facebook and it is vital that you ascertain which formats (status update, picture, video upload, a link to video etc.) perform better or worse with your audience. If there are certain types of content performing well, you'll want to share more of this type of

content. Whilst it's always good to have a mix of content but you need to give more emphasis to the high-performing content.

Audience Profile

What type of audience are you building and attracting? You may have the most engaging content in the world but you could be attracting the wrong audience. It is vital to keep track of your fans and ensure they are the ones you want to target.

Audience Response Rate

How quickly are you responding to comments? The more engaged you are with your audience, the more engaged they will be with your brand and your content. You need to regularly check how quickly you are responding to the comments on your Page, and make sure you aim to have a fast and high response rate.

Facebook Maintenance Checklist

DAILY

- ✓ Respond to any interaction - new messages, tags, likes and comments i.e.
- ✓ Engage with and contribute to Facebook groups
- ✓ Post at least one status update with original, relevant and interesting business content being aware of the best time to publish
- ✓ Check relevant hashtags that present opportunities to interact
- ✓ Go through news feed and get updated on news and insights and add your thoughts and comments to any relevant discussions and/or share relevant content
- ✓ Share at least 3 interesting status updates you find.
- ✓ Running Facebook Ads? Review stats twice daily.
- ✓ Locate 3 relevant pieces of content your audience would like and schedule it.
- ✓ Review Facebook Insights. Look for trends and emulate them.
- ✓ Listen for and respond to every lead immediately.
- ✓ Look to see if any new connections from other social media platforms have Facebook and like their Page
- ✓ During the week gather information and sources for the following weeks post(s)

WEEKLY

- ✓ **Check Your Insights:** Your analytics will help you figure out what your audience likes and doesn't like, so you can plan your future content better. It'll also help alert you to any red flags early on. Regularly go through your analytics and look at What kinds of topics resonate best with your audience? What posts grab attention? Fan Growth?
- ✓ Actively find and 'like' any relevant other businesses and industry influencers

MONTHLY

- ✓ **Review Your About Page**: Is your About page up-to-date? If anything about you, your business, or any other content on your About page has changed since you published it, then you should update it.
- ✓ **Clean up Your Apps/Sidebar**: Regularly assess that all of the elements in your pages sidebar are still timely, useful, and relevant. Keep it clean and useful by deleting extraneous elements and placing the best content in a prominent position.

TWITTER

Twitter is one of the largest and most active social networks, with over 330 million active monthly users sending more than 500 million tweets a day. Often referred to as a micro blogging service as it limits your status updates to 280 characters, Twitter is a real-time information network that encourages its users to share and discover interesting content. Businesses have utilised the benefits of Twitter, recognising that it is one of the quickest ways to get a message out to people who may be interested in your products, services, ideas or events and also gives the chance to get real time feedback from customers. Perhaps the greatest feature of Twitter is the ability for your followers to share your tweets with their following at the click of a button, this is called a 'retweet' and is what cements Twitter as a successful word-of-mouth platform that can help your message reach an entirely new audience of prospective customers.

What's good about Twitter?
- The Twitter feed is public which can help give your business greater exposure in web search results
- The site is like a public forum, so it's easy to build a community of potential customers
- It is a quick way to share links to content to help spread your message to a wide audience.
- It is an open network so anyone can read your updates regardless of if they are a user or not

What's not so good about Twitter?
- It's sometimes challenging to create a meaningful post in only 280 characters
- Building an active following takes time and requires a daily commitment to sharing content
- With so many identical-looking tweets, it's hard to make a single one stand out
- Users are very vocal, so if they have a problem they will say so
- The lifespan of a tweet is very short

Which Businesses Should be on Twitter?

Twitter is very popular tool for use as way of speaking to people directly and for quick, snappy updates. From this, if you are a business that regularly and frequently shares breaking news, updates and likes to engage with fans directly then it is worthwhile having a Twitter presence.

Need to Know Facts, Stats and Tips about Twitter

- There are 330M monthly active users.
- A total of 1.3 billion accounts have been created.
- 80% of active users access the site via mobile.
- 707 is the average number of followers.
- There are 500 million Tweets sent each day. That's 6,000 Tweets every second.
- It took 3 years, 2 months and 1 day to go from the first Tweet to the billionth.
- 77% of Twitter users feel more positive about a brand when their Tweet has been replied to.
- 58% of top brands have over 100,00 followers on Twitter.
- 92% of companies Tweet more than once a day, 42% Tweet 1-5 times a day, and 19% Tweet 6-10 times a day.
- The average Twitter user follows five businesses.
- 80% of Twitter users have mentioned a brand in a Tweet.
- 54% of users surveyed by Twitter reported that they had taken action after seeing a brand mentioned in Tweets (including visiting their website, searching for the brand, or retweeting content).
- The last two years have seen a 2.5x increase in customer service conversations on Twitter.
- 60% of consumers expect brands to respond to their query within the hour, but the average is 1 hour 24 minutes.
- 76% of consumers are likely to recommend the brand following friendly service.
- Companies using Twitter for customer service see a 19% lift in customer satisfaction.
- Tweets with images receive 18% more click throughs, 89% more likes, and 150% more retweets.
- There are currently 330 million monthly active users on the platform.
- Twitter users send out 500 million tweets per day.
- 88% of social advertisers use it. This makes it even more popular than Instagram.
- Percentage of Twitter users on Mobile: 80%
- 24% of all internet male users use Twitter, whereas 21% of all internet female users use Twitter.
- 71% of Twitter users are reading news there.
- Twitter is the number one platform for government leaders
- 75% of B2B businesses market on Twitter
- Only 3% of customers will @ you when they complain.
- Twitter ads are 11% more effective than TV ads during live events
- 40% of users say they've made a purchase because of an influencer's tweet
- The half-life of a tweet is 24 minutes. In other words, a tweet gets half its interactions in the first half hour, and then starts a long, slow decline.
- Brands tweeted an average of 122 times a month last year
- The best time to tweet is 3 p.m. on weekdays.
- Tweets with a GIF get 55% more engagement
- 93% of Twitter videos are viewed on mobile
- Tweets with video attract 10x as much engagement

Why You Need Twitter For Your Business

Twitter might not be as large as Facebook, but it does have an extensive and constantly growing reach. Twitter places emphasis on sharing easily digestible newsworthy content and quick updates and exchanges. This makes it a refreshing social media platform that businesses have quickly utilized, using it extensively for making announcements, providing customer service and sharing online content.

Connect with Customers

Twitter is a great platform for connecting with your customers and providing customer service. It can be used beneficially for your business in that you can listen to and develop a relationship with your customers and gain feedback on how you can improve your product and services, both of which can greatly benefit your business in the future. In terms of providing value you can easily respond quickly and positively in real time to those that are interacting with you, showcasing your active customer service skills in responding to complaints, queries and general communications.

Keep Up To Date With Your Industry and Competition

Twitter will help you stay on top of your industry and market as it allows you to find out what people are saying in real time about a particular topic, enabling you to keep up to date with posts about your business, industry and your competition.

It Shows Your Personality

The internet can often be an impersonal place, however, using Twitter offers a real time, informal and chatty platform for your opinions, stories, humour and advice that gives your business a human face. People are more likely to purchase products or services from a business they feel like they already "know" and having a profile that you regularly update can help create a community and allow your followers to feel like they know your business.

Networking

Twitter is a great tool to use for networking as through the use of tweetups and general sharing of content you can meet and interact with many new businesses, customers and other individuals local to you and within your industry that will grow your network and potentially lead to new business opportunities and relationships.

Brand Awareness

Millions of people use Twitter actively on a daily basis and so it is likely that your existing customer base and potential customers and prospects are already users. From having the ability to display your brand

through a customisable profile together with being able to engage and directly interact with your followers who can easily share your content, Twitter becomes a powerful tool for helping small businesses to expand their reach and brand awareness across an active network.

Monitor Your Reputation

Knowing if people are talking about you and what they are saying is critical for your business and Twitter users are renowned for their frequent sharing of opinions (good and bad) about their experiences with businesses. Whether users are positive of negative about you on Twitter, ultimately you need to be there to address what they are saying either through a thank you or an acknowledgement of an issue and then a solution provided. By publicly responding to those that are talking about you, you tap into Twitters use as a powerful customer service tool and you build trust with others as responding to them shows you are listening and genuinely interested in what they have to say and acting upon it will help you to better your business and experiences of customers.

Still not convinced? Here are 7 more reasons why you need a Twitter account:

- ✓ Free to use, though paid advertising opportunities are also available.
- ✓ Users will follow businesses they have previously purchased from.
- ✓ Allows you to answer questions, provide support and give news updates.
- ✓ Highly news-orientated, making it perfect for promoting fresh content.
- ✓ An invaluable platform for competitive research.
- ✓ Increase brand awareness and find new customers.
- ✓ Gain even more exposure with the use of popular hashtags.

Creating a Twitter Account and Getting to Grips with The Basic Lingo

While unregistered users can visit your profile (so long as it's public), only registered users can share tweets and interact with other users. So to properly use Twitter, you have to first sign up for a profile. To sign up, you need to fill in your name and email address, create a password, and choose a username. Usernames, or @handles, are alphanumeric (meaning they can include letters and numbers), are case sensitive and can also include underscores. You can change your username at any time provided the @handle you want is not already being used.

When you sign in to your Twitter account, you are then taken to your home page. Across the top of the page is your navigation bar, where you can access your home page, notifications and messages, and browse the Discover tab. On the right-hand side is a search bar, along with your user icon (this will take you to your account and profile settings) and a Compose Tweet button.

Under the navigation bar, on the left-hand side, is a box that displays your profile's cover photo, your user icon, name and @handle, along with the number of tweets you've shared, the number of users you follow and the number of followers you have. Below that is the trends box, which shows you the top 10 trending topics and hashtags on Twitter at that given moment.

On the right-hand side, (or depending on the size of your screen and your screen resolution, this box could be on the left-hand side below the trending topics box) there is another box entitled 'Who to Follow' that displays suggested Twitter users and gives you the option to import your contacts from Gmail or connect to other address books.

At the centre of the dashboard is your Twitter feed. At the top of the feed is a box in which you can compose a tweet. The rest of your Twitter feed contains tweets from users you follow along with occasional advertisements. The feed is updated in real time and features infinite scrolling as users share tweets. From there, you can retweet, reply and favourite the tweets of others.

Customising Your Twitter Profile

Twitter doesn't give users a lot of customisation options, but it does allow for a little bit of personalisation. First, you need to upload a user icon. (Ideally one that is 400 pixels by 400 pixels and 2MB maximum). It can be photo or a logo it is up to you, just make sure that it is not left blank as the default Twitter user icon will be used which is an egg on a single-color background. Leaving it as such not only shows that you don't know how to use the platform, it also makes you look very unprofessional.

You can also add a header photo (similar to a cover photo on Facebook). This can be anything you feel represents you or your brand, just ensure it is a high-quality image, relevant/appropriate to your business and is eye catching. Twitter header photos should be 1500 pixels wide by 500 pixels high, and a maximum of 5MB.

Your Twitter page's layout can't be changed, but for a little added visual customization, you can choose a theme colour. The theme colour you select will appear as an accent colour on your profile, mostly visible in links and when you hover over the navigation bar. You'll also be able to see this theme colour from your home page, and not just on your profile.

When it comes to your profile information, you can create a short bio about yourself, which is limited to 160 characters. You can also list the city you're located in and include a link to your website.

Verified Accounts on Twitter

Have you ever seen an account with a little blue and white checkmark next to the name? That badge shows that the account is verified by Twitter, meaning that the user is considered to be a key brand or individual. In the case of celebrities, verification is a way to differentiate between fake accounts impersonating the user and the authentic account actually run by that user. The requirements for verification are constantly being updated, but the website doesn't take things like follower count or tweet count into consideration. You can't request to be verified — if Twitter thinks you meet the requirements, they'll find you and verify you eventually. Verified accounts benefit from access to special features, like filters in their notifications page, access to account analytics that include data about their followers and engagement with their tweets, and more.

Verified Twitter users can lose their verified status if they violate the Twitter rules or terms of service, change their @handle, or protect their tweets. In this case, Twitter will automatically review the user's account again to make sure it's still eligible for verification.

The Anatomy of a Tweet

Posting on Twitter is fairly straightforward. It's mostly text-based, with a strict 280-character limit that forces your messages to be short and to the point.

A tweet can also contain content formats other than just text;

- **Links:** Sharing links to your content or content from other websites that is relevant to your brand is a great way to make your Twitter feed more interesting and engaging. A top tip is to use a link-shortening service like Bit.ly when adding links to your tweets to save more room for text.
- **Images:** Twitter also allows you to share images in your tweets. Simply upload the photo or image(s) you want to share in the Compose Tweet box. As with adding links, adding photo(s) will take away from your available character count, so plan accordingly.
- **GIFs:** GIFs are essentially moving images taken from videos, and they're very popular and all over the Internet. Uploading GIFs in your tweets is a great way to incorporate meme marketing in your Twitter strategy.
- **Videos:** You can also share Vine videos and YouTube videos to Twitter, simply by sharing links. As with adding links or photos (or GIFs) to your tweets, adding a video takes up some of the character count available to you.
- **Polls:** Polls allow you to pose a question to your followers and track their votes. To add a poll to your tweet, click the Poll button at the bottom of the tweet composition box and fill in what you want the voting choices to be. Polls have a default of at least two choices, but you can add up to two more (for four choices total.) You can also fill out how long you want your poll to run for in days, minutes and hours.

Interacting With Others on Twitter

There are several ways to interact with other Twitter users, both publicly and privately.

- **@mentions:** The easiest way to reach a Twitter user is by tagging that user's @handle in your tweet. This will notify the other person, while other users who see the tweet can click on the @handle to see the person you're talking about. Top Tip: If you want to start your tweet with the other user's @handle, you need to place a period before the @ symbol if you want it to show up on your feed. This is not necessary however if you do not care if other users see your Tweet.
- **Likes:** If you like a particular tweet but don't want or need to respond to it, you can favourite it by clicking the heart button under the tweet. Your likes are stored in a list on your Twitter page that is visible to you and anyone who visits your profile.
- **Retweets:** Retweeting allows you to share what other Twitter users post so that your followers can see those posts as well. There are two methods of retweeting: You can click the retweet button under the original tweet, which will share the tweet in its original form on your feed, or you can quote the original tweet. When you retweet, it'll show up on your feed with the other user's profile picture and @handle. To quote a tweet or manually retweet, simply highlight, copy and paste the tweet into the compose tweet box, and write "RT" and the user's @handle before the tweet. You can also put quotes around the tweet, though some users do not. Quoting a tweet instead of directly retweeting it allows users to add their own thoughts to it or share it with other users by tagging their @handle in it.
- **Direct messages:** To privately interact with other Twitter users, the social network allows you to direct-message people (usually referred to as a DM on Twitter). Direct messaging used to be closed so that only users who were following each other could use the feature, but now everyone has the option to make their DMs open to the public.

Twitter Hashtags

A hashtag is, as defined by the Oxford dictionary "A word or phrase preceded by a hash sign (#), used on social media websites and applications, especially Twitter, to identify messages on a specific topic" and its first known use was back in 2008.

Hashtags are searchable on Twitter and therefore are a great way to make the content you share on the platform visible to users beyond your own followers. There are many highly popular hashtags that generally all active Twitter users are familiar with, like #FollowFriday (or #FF), which encourages your followers to reach out to other users you admire or work with, and #ThrowbackThursday (or #TBT), which encourages users to post vintage or childhood photos and memories. You can also create your own hashtags to draw attention to your brand.

Many Twitter users add their hashtags at the ends of their tweets, but you can add hashtags anywhere you want in the text. Just make sure the hashtags you use are relevant to your business and you limit their use to two or fewer per tweet. Top Tip: Do not be tempted to add as many as possible to increase your reach. This doesn't work — in fact, the more hashtags you use, the less likely people are to interact with your content because they'll find your posts spammy and it makes you look unprofessional.

BONUS SECTION: Using Hashtags on Other Social Media Channels

Hashtags may have started on Twitter but now most social media platforms support hashtags. Hashtags give your brand more exposure so you can spread the word about your product to a massive audience. In addition, when you use it on multiple times on different channels, people will easily remember your hashtag.

- **Twitter:** Using hashtags on Twitter is vital for growth. Posts with hashtags get twice as much engagement as posts without hashtags, according to Buffer. Tweets with two hashtags get the highest engagement, and engagement falls as the number of hashtags increase.
- **Facebook**: Use 2 hashtags on Facebook try one popular hashtag and one custom hashtag for your brand but proceed with caution, yes, they allow hashtags and yes, people use them. Way too much. In fact, three months after adopting the practice research that used EdgeRank information found that Facebook posts with hashtags had less engagement than those without.
- **Instagram**: It allows up to 30 hashtags, however keep it to no more than 11 per post for the highest level of engagement. Instagram is an outlier when it comes to hashtags. While the other sites give you a diminishing return if you use more than one or two, on Instagram the rule is the more the merrier. However, be careful not to use highly popular hashtags. Use niche hashtags revolving around your industry and limit your use of hashtags to 15-20 within a given hour.
- **Pinterest**: Use only 2 hashtags, it's a category of search so use your unique hashtag to help pinners to find relevant content.

Top Tip: Search the hashtag before you use it. Check each of the social media networks to make sure that your hashtag isn't being used for the wrong reason. Also, ensure that you don't choose something that can be interpreted in a different way. It is worth making sure that another brand isn't using hashtag specifically for their own promotion as well. Before using a hashtag, always you need to search to see if other people are using it and what they saying.

Trending Topics on Twitter

Trending topics are any topics that Twitter users are talking about at a very high rate. Often, these trending topics are hashtags, but they can also be words or phrases related to the subject. You can see the current trending topics on your Twitter home page in the trends box on the left-hand side.

When you click on a trending topic, it'll take you to a search page where you can view what people are saying about the topic, along with photos and related users. At the top of the page, you can select to view all of the tweets being shared, or just the top tweets — the ones getting the most interactions.

Twitter users can customise the trends box to show trending topics in different locations. For example, if you were in Birmingham, you could set it to only show you what's trending in Birmingham. You could also set it to show you trending topics in the United Kingdom overall, or around the world.

Topics become trending for a few reasons. Most commonly, trending topics result from breaking news or commonly talked about topics in the media. For example, if the UK election results were announced, you might see the candidates' names as trending topics.

Trending topics can also come about when large groups of Twitter users work together collectively to get a certain hashtag or phrase trending. For example, this is often the work of celebrity-obsessed fans, so it's not uncommon to see things about One Direction, Justin Bieber Taylor Swift in the trending section.

Done right, trending topics can be a great way for brands to get noticed. Only use trending topics in your tweets if those topics are genuinely relevant to your brand, and make sure you use them appropriately.

Twitter Lists

Twitter offers its users the ability to make lists of other users they find interesting. This gives users another way of tracking what people post, except with lists, you don't have to be following the users you include to see their posts regularly.

Lists are handy if you want to better organize your following list. For example, you might make a list of known people in your industry and name it "Industry Influencers," or if you had an interest in something like photography and want to track users in your area who tweet about those things, you could make lists of "Manchester Photographers.'

Creating lists is simple, just click your user icon in the top navigation bar so that the drop down menu appears and click Lists. From there, you can see two tabs: lists you're a member of (i.e., lists you've been added to) and lists you're subscribed to (the lists you've created). You'll see a Create List button below the Subscribed To and Member Of links. When you create a list, type in the name you want to give the list and a short description, and then choose whether you want the list to be publicly visible or private (visible only to you). If you make your lists public, the users you add to it will be notified. Once you're

done, simply click Save List. After the list has been created, you can add users to it by clicking the gear button next to the follow button on their page, selecting "Add or remove from list" and then selecting the list you'd like to add them to.

Live Tweeting

Live tweeting is when a user tweets his or her reactions to a live event as it is happening. Live tweeting most commonly occurs with TV shows and televised events, however. If you've ever been watching a TV show and seen a hash-tagged phrase overlaid on the bottom of the screen, it's because the programme wants to encourage its viewers to tweet about the show as they watch. It is also popular with brands when they throw events and want their attendees to live tweet while they're there, the brand will often create its own individual hashtag to use and share with the invite list so that others can follow around.

The same goes for major televised events like the Brit Awards. It's not uncommon during events such as these to see the trends box filled with related topics — for example, in the case of the Brits, it wouldn't be surprising to see the official awards show hashtag along with the names of celebrities that win major awards.

Twitter Chats

A Twitter chat is when several Twitter users get together online to discuss a specific topic. To do so, they create a hashtag which participants then incorporate into each of their related tweets. Twitter chats are a great way to engage followers and/or get a topic trending. Twitter chats are straightforward, but they do require a decent and active follower base to be successful.

Usually, one Twitter user will host a Twitter chat at a specific time and prepare specific questions and discussion points. The host will tweet out the questions and other participants will respond with their thoughts. Twitter chats usually last about an hour. They are a great way to show how active you are on social media and to get your followers (and their followers) engaged and asking questions or sharing their advice.

Questions to Help Form a Successful Twitter Marketing Strategy

Before you jump in and start tweeting there are several key strategic elements you must consider in order to create a Twitter marketing strategy that will ensure your Twitter profile is going to be in line with your business objectives and ultimately be a successful addition to your social media marketing strategy.

Why is my Business on Twitter? What are my Goals?

One of the first things you must do is determine what you want your Twitter profile to achieve for your business. Whether you want to use it to support sales by giving potential customers useful information in the form of relevant news updates or use it as an outlet for customer service or to build your brand by providing content that supports your offering, having clear objectives for your profile help optimise its reach and impact. Having clear goals and objectives will guide and dictate how to develop other parts of your Twitter strategy so it is vital that you pick realistic, achieve able and effective objectives for your business.

Common Twitter Marketing Goals

- Grow an Engaged and Relevant Following
- Generate Brand Awareness
- Generate Sales and Business Leads
- Customer Service Tool
- Establish Authority

Who Will be in Charge of Managing my Twitter Account?

Whether you will maintain your Twitter in house or hire an external social media manager or agency, you need to establish who will be maintaining your account and ensure that they are the right person who will present your brand well and effectively across Twitter. Part of this process is also ensuring the person running your account has a good understanding or your branding from the voice you want portrayed to how they interact and deal with queries/complaints etc. as they need to be able to confidently ensure they can represent your brand at all times.

Is my Target Market on Twitter, Who am I Going to be Tweeting to?

In addition to determining your objectives, having a clear idea of your target readers is paramount. Firstly, you need to ascertain whether your target market is actually on Twitter in the first place and also doing your research and knowing who you are tweeting too is key to being able to tailor your tweets around content that maximises interest and engagement from your readers.

What am I Going to Tweet? Have I Got a Content Strategy in Place?

Creating a content strategy is a key part of your success on Twitter as it will give you clear and consistent guidelines on vital aspects such as what to post, when and what voice you will portray. Deciding on what major content categories you want to include regularly helps you to stay focused and maintains a clear direction for your tweets to go in order to ensure your content is in line with your business goals and is targeting reader's needs. Having a clear understanding of the frequency you will be posting is also paramount in order to ensure it is in line with your wider social media strategy. An important part of the

content strategy development is also choosing the right 'voice' to portray for your business. Your tweets should reflect your personality as Twitter is a great way to show a 'human' side to your business that customers appreciate and prefer. It is important to have an idea of what voice you want for your profile as it needs to be consistently applied across all your posts, especially if your profile is going to be managed by several different contributors. In general, many find there are several key characteristics of successful tweets such as showing a personality and being contextually relevant that ensure tweets are as engaging and interesting as possible. Put simply, avoid generic corporate speak and replace it with your own unique voice and customers will be more drawn to and engage with you on Twitter.

How am I Going to Measure my Success on Twitter?

In order to measure the success of your Twitter presence you need a solid understanding of the initial objectives you want to achieve for your business from using Twitter. Whether you want to use Twitter as a customer service tool or to drive traffic to your blog or website, having a clear vision of why you are using Twitter will automatically shed light on what metrics and other data should be looking at in order to measure your success. An important part of measuring your success is also learning what works and what doesn't. As your strategy develops you may find you need to adjust your objectives so it is vital you don't neglect your analytics as they will help you to build a solid, successful and competitive Twitter presence.

Tweeting: What, and How Often?

Now it's time to start tweeting, there are several fundamental basics to follow to ensure you create powerful and engaging tweets.

With over 5,700 tweets posted every second and each one having an average life span of 3 hours, it can be hard to make your tweet stand out from the crowd. For small businesses without an already established brand this is an even more difficult task to manage. There are however several guidelines available to aid you in what to tweet, but always remember these four key things;

Never Go For The Direct Sell

When you first start tweeting it may be tempting to go with the direct sale approach tweeting information about how wonderful your business is and all of the things you sell or offer. This however is not a successful approach and in most cases will see you viewed as a spammer and will quickly lead to people unfollowing you or not following you at all. To avoid making this mistake you must strike a balance between subtle business tweets and ones centred on customer engagement, with a favourable emphasis on the latter.

Say Something Interesting and Useful

Write your tweets with your target audience in mind so rather than trying to appeal to a generic wider audience, write content that contains specialised information and analysis that those interested in your services or in your sector would read. For ideas simply think about questions you had when starting out in your industry or flag up interesting case studies or advice. By openly giving out advice and information you will become an online repository of specialist knowledge and this will attract the attention of your target audience.

Try to Include Some Form of Media Within Your Tweet

A common mistake made with tweeting is not including some form of media content such as a relevant video or picture that can lead tweets to look uninviting and not capture a reader's attention. To avoid making this mistake make sure to tweet insightful and valuable content that your readers will want to read and looks visually appealing also. Tweets with some form of media such as a photo or link always get more clicks so it is vital that you try to include some form of relevant media.

Be Creative

People always respond better to something that is new, fresh and clever so always brainstorm ideas in the mind-set of producing something that is creative and breaks the mould of other generic tweets. You are competing in the fast-paced and growing industry of social media marketing, so you need to make yourself stand out and give potential customers a compelling reason to choose you over your competitors.

> *Engagement on Twitter is reflected in five forms: retweets, favourites, clicks, lists and @mentions. Here are several ways to create the right type of customer engagement with your posts;*

The Humanising Tweet

Twitter offers an informal and chatty platform for your opinions, stories, humour and advice that gives your business a human face. These types of tweets, whether they are photos of staff, office celebrations etc., are designed to show your audience that there exists real people behind your brand and helps them to connect with you and get to know you and your story better.

The Promotional Tweet

By giving discounts or other benefits to your Twitter followers, you give them a reason to follow you and as a result acquire a new audience that will then see your other business updates. Common twitter promotions offer a free gift or service upon receiving a certain number of retweets or followers.

The Answering Replies Tweet

Twitter is a great tool for customer service but if you fail to monitor and reply to what is being said about your company, you're making a big mistake. Only when you engage with your customers and respond appropriately will you get the full value of Twitter as a customer service tool. This does not mean that you have to respond to every negative statement, but when there is a real issue or if a person has a specific question or wants to praise you, you need to address it quickly and honestly.

The Relevant Industry News, Trends or Events Tweet

To build your authority within your industry you need to act as a resource for people who come to you for relevant and up to date industry advice/news/ trends/ opinions and any other relevant articles that you know would be of interest to your target audience.

The Question and Participation Tweet

You will get a lot more out of tweeting if you enable and encourage your customers to respond to what you write. Beyond asking questions with your tweets, you also need to remember the conversation is two-way, so respond to the comments readers leave and you are likely to develop a community on your Twitter profile that can help turn your customers into fans who will promote your products and services and provide you with quality feedback.

The Get to Know the Business Tweet

Successful tweets often share something with followers that they can't get anywhere else, something that is interesting and beneficial that lets them know more about a business. People are more likely to purchase products or services from a business they feel like they already "know" and having a profile that you regularly update can help create a community and allow your readers to feel like they know your business.

The Relevant Resources and Links Tweet

If you regularly read industry news and find interesting articles, share them with your audience and add your own thoughts. This will go a long way in developing your reputation as a thought leader and as a source where people can come to find valuable and interesting industry insights.

The Fun Tweet

Sharing updates that are entirely business related all the time can lead to a monotonous twitter presence and may lead to unfollows as people think you are just trying to hard sell to them all the time. Instead look to strike a balance between business updates and ones that are fun, light and full of humour as you will attract followers and go a long way towards humanising your business.

Miscellaneous Tweets

There are many options for what information you can tweet to your followers and as you move forward you will find the content that works best for you and your target audience. Ultimately, share what you feel is interesting and relevant and will interest your readers and encourage them to engage with you and share your content. For example, many businesses use Twitter to tweet quotes that inspire them, promote a charity the business supports and to share the news if the company has won an award, received a great review, garnered some major press or has a great testimonial.

> *Although it takes some experimentation to find the best schedule for you, there are two things that should always be considered and will dictate your tweeting schedule; your company goals and what your audience wants.*

In general, 3-15 great content tweets per day are a good general amount to sustain an active presence on Twitter. This however may vary depending on what works best for your company, goals and readers so it is important to experiment to find a tweeting schedule that works for you. For example, if your goal is to become a cutting-edge information resource, you might be continually posting breaking news and events in your sector or industry, on the other hand if your main audience is mostly interested in technical or behind-the-scenes details, you'll probably tweet information less often. So the first step to determining your ideal tweeting frequency is to find the perfect balance of what you want and what your audience wants.

To maximise the benefits of having Twitter you need to ultimately ask yourself, Can you keep this schedule consistently? Can you always tweet high-quality content at this rate? And will you have enough content for this schedule? Once you've discovered the best times to tweet, being consistent with your publishing schedule has the benefit of encouraging new followers and the potential for retweets that will enhance your brand and impact.

How to Write an Effective Tweet

Twitter currently supports five formats that you can use to create your social media updates:

- Status Update
- Link Share
- Photo Upload
- Video Link Share
- GIF

While it took three years, two months, and a day to reach the billionth tweet shared, it now only takes one week to send one billion tweets. To help you get noticed among all this noise, take note of the following tips:

Start with a Relevant Following

The key to a successful presence and indeed tweet begins with you having built up a relevant and engaged following that wants to engage with you. If you only followed others in the hope of gaining an easy follow back or bought followers, then you are wasting your time as both of these types of followers are useless for your business as they will not engage with you and are likely to never become customers. Instead, look to build a relevant organic following by searching industry hashtags and follow those users that appear, include a follow me on Twitter link on your website and blog, tell your existing business contacts and customers you are on Twitter and utilise your other social networks to bring audiences over from your other networks.

Establish Your Objective for the Tweet

Every tweet you share needs to have a purpose. Whether you want to create interest in your latest blog post, promote a new product or service or generate engagement through a Q&A, knowing your objective will dictate and affect every aspect of what you include in your tweet from the links you'll include, where they go, the tone of the tweet, the CTA you include, right through to how you will measure the success of your tweet.

Create a Headline That Grabs Attention

At any given time, there could be hundreds of tweets in your target audience's Twitter feed and to ensure you stand out people need to be given a good reason to click on your link which is why creating a well-written, clear and attention grabbing headline is vital. Before you tweet simply ask yourself if you would share and click on that tweet based on its headline and if you wouldn't then you need to change it.

Keep the Tweet the Optimal Length

The limit for characters within your tweets is 280; however you do not have to use them all. Rather it is suggested that the optimal length for a Tweet is around 70-100 characters as this makes your tweet short enough to digest within a few seconds and is the right length for anyone who wants to retweet and add on a couple words for their own comment.

Include Some Form of Media

To make your tweets attract more attention it is recommended that you include some form of media content such as a photo or video as this makes the tweet more interesting and appealing. So make sure to tweet and share insightful, informative and valuable content that your readers will want to click on and looks visually appealing also.

Pay Attention to Spelling and Basic Grammar

You represent your brand with every tweet you post so don't leave your audience with a negative and unprofessional opinion of your business by not taking the time to proofread for spelling errors and not checking your general grammar. Ensure your tweet is clear, concise, the punctuation use is correct, you have correct spelling and you clearly spell out your words instead of using abbreviations to save characters as many followers may not be familiar with certain abbreviations.

Include a Clear Call to Action

Ensuring you include a clear call to action in every tweet you post ensure that each tweet will be purposeful for your business. Whether you want to direct the reader to a new blog post, a product page or to a newsletter signup page ensure you make it clear and concise to the reader what the next step is that you want them to take.

Utilise Relevant Trends and Hashtags

Hashtags are a great tool for connecting to a wider audience so ensure you utilise them within your tweets. For ideas you can relate them to the content you are posting to enhance the tweet or for content ideas you can do a search within your business community to see what is trending and if relevant, add your thoughts. It is important not to jump on and use any hashtag that is trending as many won't be relevant for your business, rather the key is to be selective and only utilise those that are relevant and will enhance your business in some way.

You can also create and promote a hashtag campaign yourself to help revive your community and spark conversation around your brand with both old and new customers. To start a hashtag campaign, decide on the goal of your campaign and how it will relate to your customers. Then research what your audience is talking about to come up with a hashtag that they'll identify with.

Using Links? Ensure They've Been Shortened

Using a link shortening tool such as bit.ly to shorten your URL's not only helps you easily gain more characters to use, it also provides valuable insights into how the link is being shared which is essential for future content creation and link selection.

Top Tip: Try placing links in the middle of the tweet. Dan Zarrella found that placing links roughly 25% through a tweet leads to a higher click through rate than including the link at the very end. This is probably due to the fact that most tweets include the link automatically at the end, so anytime there's a variance in a user stream, the tweet catches our attention more.

Actively Learn From the Tweets of Others

Be active in looking through your feed and looking at the tweets that stand out for you as this can give you valuable tips that can help guide you in creating better tweets in the future. To those tweets that stand out to you and made you click on them analyse why and look to what makes that tweet so good then apply it to your own tweets. By consistently looking at others and learning you will gain the necessary knowledge to know what makes a great tweet that your audience can't resist which in turn will make you gain more followers, respect, authority and ultimately make your Twitter presence more successful.

Optimize Twitter Publishing Times

The shelf life of a link on Twitter is only 2.8 hours. In order to get the maximum impact of each tweet, you need to publish your tweets at optimal times. According to recent data from Kevan Lee at Buffer...

- the most popular time to tweet: noon to 1 p.m. local time
- the early morning hours is when tweets receive the most clicks, on average
- the fewest tweets are sent between 3 and 4 a.m.

These are a general guide however as through your own testing and regular assessments of your analytics, you will come to learn the most effective publishing times for you.

Advertising Basics on Twitter

With hundreds of millions of tweets sent per day, it can be easy for your brand's Twitter marketing to get lost in the noise. Twitter ads can help you get your message in front of the users who are most likely to be interested in your business and its offering. Twitter offers very user-friendly ad formats, so it's a great time to consider running your first Twitter ad.

- **Expand your influence** - With Twitter Ads, you can get more likes, amplify your message, and get more people talking about your business

- **Connect with new audiences** - People on Twitter are looking for great content from the people, businesses, and brands they're interested in. Help them discover you.
- **Budget Control** - There's no minimum budget required for Twitter Ads. Pay only for the specific results you need, such as new account followers or sending traffic to your website.

Types of Twitter ads

Using Twitter is free, but if you'd like to pay to promote your account on the platform, there is a robust selection of advertising options available to you.

- **Promoted tweets:** Promoted tweets are simply tweets that an advertiser pays to display to people who are not already following them on Twitter. Like regular tweets, they can be retweeted, liked, and so on. They look just like regular tweets, too, except that they have a label that says "Promoted." Promoted tweets appear in targeted users' timelines, on user profiles, at the top of search results, and in the Twitter mobile and desktop apps.
- **Promoted Accounts**: Promoted Accounts (also known as Followers campaigns) allow you to promote your Twitter account to targeted Twitter users who don't yet follow you but might find your content interesting. Promoted Accounts are displayed in potential followers' timelines, as well as in the Who to Follow suggestions and search results. They include a Follow button and are clearly identified as Promoted.
- **Promoted Trends**: Trending topics on Twitter are the most talked about subjects on the social network, appearing on users' timelines, on the Explore tab, and on the Twitter app. Promoted Trends allow you to promote a hashtag at the top of that list. When Twitter users click on your Promoted Trend, they see an organic list of search results for the topic, with a Promoted tweet from you at the top of the list. As people pick up on your hashtag and start using it themselves, you can gain additional organic exposure that increases the reach of your campaign. Currently, Promoted Trends are not available for advertisers using Twitter's self-serve options. You can find out whether you're eligible to work with a Twitter Sales representative to purchase Promoted Trends by sending a direct message to @TwitterAdsHelp.

In addition to these options, Twitter has a host of other marketing tools designed to help advertisers improve their campaigns.

- **Twitter Amplify:** Twitter Amplify is a tool that allows advertisers to share real-time television content that they can integrate with their brand or sponsors. It is designed to help brands reach users beyond their current followers by delivering content to targeted audiences.
- **Promoted Video:** While Twitter Amplify gives brands the ability to share videos from TV programs and other broadcasts, Promoted Video opens up the possibilities to any kind of video. Promoted Video is different from sharing a YouTube video in your tweets — while both methods allow you to play a video in a tweet, Promoted Video content is hosted directly by Twitter and is only available as a paid marketing tool.
- **Mobile App Promotion:** This option lets advertisers target and reach their desired audiences via mobile devices to drive app downloads. Advertisers can create a custom image and app

description for use in the ad, and target users by their location, gender, language and mobile platform. The tool also features a unique measurement system so advertisers can see how their campaigns impact app installs, purchases and registrations.

BONUS TIP: Twitter Promote Mode

If you're new to social media advertising, you're not sure how much you can afford to spend, or you have a very small team with limited time, you might want to consider Twitter Promote Mode. Twitter Promote Mode costs a flat rate of £ 79 per month. Once enabled, all you have to do is tweet as you normally would and each day, Twitter will select up to your first 10 tweets that meet its quality requirement and promote them to your selected audience. Retweets, Quote Tweets, or replies will not be promoted. According to Twitter on average, accounts will reach 30,000 additional people and gain 30 followers each month but performance may vary.

How to Advertise on Twitter: A Step-by-Step Guide

Set up Your Twitter ads Account - If you've never used Twitter ads before, you'll need to set up an account. Just log into your Twitter account, then head to ads.Twitter.com. Enter your country and time zone, then click Let's go.

Choose Your Objective - Decide what you want your campaign to achieve whether it's to raise awareness of a specific Tweet, attract new followers, send traffic to your website, or increase engagement. With Twitter Ads, you can launch campaigns and tailor ads based on your business goals and what's happening with your brand right now

- Awareness - Promote your Tweets and maximize your reach.
- Tweet engagements - Promote your Tweets and get more Retweets, likes, and replies.
- Followers - Promote your account and grow your Twitter following.
- Website clicks - Promote your website and get more traffic.
- App installs - Promote your mobile app and get more downloads.
-

Define Your Ad Group - Ad groups are how you want to spend your money. Here, you can set budget, targeting, and placement for each of your campaigns. One campaign can have many ad groups and an ad group can contain one or more Tweets. For your first Twitter ads campaign, you are probably best sticking to one ad group. As you get more comfortable with Twitter ads, you can split up your campaign to target different audiences, use different creative, or test different budgets and timing.

Bidding - Twitter Ads run in an auction. Decide how much you will pay for each interaction, such as a new follower or a click to your website. If you want to control the bid amounts yourself, the interface will also show you suggested bids based on what others are paying. Or use automatic bidding, which determines the best bid cost based on your budget and goals. This is a good way for new Twitter advertisers to get started and learn how Twitter bidding works.

Define Ad Creative and Placement - Select the Tweets you want to focus on in your campaign. Twitter will show you a list of your existing tweets that you can choose to promote. If you prefer, you can choose to create a new tweet specifically for your ad. Include strong call-to-actions, like "sign up" or "start today." Avoid #hashtags or @mentions in your copy so that your audience does not click away from your ad.

Target Your Audience - Twitter offers a number of targeting options to help you choose the right audience for your ad and maximize your budget. Select geographic areas, the followers of a notable account, or target people's interests. The section called Audience features allows you to target based on specific user characteristics like events, interests, and behaviors, and even the specific keywords and TV shows users tweet about. To help guide you, the interface provides an estimated audience size that changes as you add more Twitter ads targeting options to your campaign.

Launch your campaign - Finally, review all the options you've selected, and click Launch campaign to launch your ad!

TOP TIP: Quick Promote is a great alternative method to employ if you already know which tweet you want to promote and you don't want to get into detailed targeting options. This easy alternative lets you set up a Twitter ad with just two clicks.

Tips to Get the Most out of Your Budget

- People scroll through Twitter quickly so you need get to the point fast. Don't assume you have to use all 280 characters—**short and to-the-point ad copy is a good way to go on Twitter!**

- **If you include a link, be sure it's clear what the link points too**: for example, an article, a product or a download. In doing so, you'll avoid paying for clicks from people who are not interested in the specific item you're linking to.

- You should also **make sure that your Twitter bio and profile page are up-to-date** and in good shape as users may click through to your profile before deciding whether to follow you.

- **The key to a great ad is a great call to action.** Make sure users know exactly what you want them to do. Try something short and snappy, like "follow us," "read more," "register now," or "download our free report."

- **Include Cards!** Cards are powerful tools that add extra functionality like website previews, app installs, and even conversations to your promoted tweets, making the tweets more engaging and interactive for users.

- **Test everything!** Twitter ads are a great way to learn what resonates with your audience—from ad format to length of copy and tone of voice. Test different formats to find out what works for you.

- **Choose a custom fit over one-size-fits all.** Campaigns with different goals need different creative. Even campaigns with the same goals should differ based on the specific offer or idea you're promoting at the time. Ultimately, the aim is to use Twitter's targeting options to ensure that your ad will only be seen by people who will find it relevant.

- **Use high-quality images and videos.** Your words are important, but visuals are what will grab the user's attention and allow your tweet to stand out. If you're using video ads, make sure they're sharp and compelling—use your video to tell a story that creates interest in your brand.

How to Build a Following and Amplify Your Impact

Writing your tweet is only the beginning. The next challenge is to promote your profile in order to get maximum exposure and attract attention. Rather than relying solely on search engines, there are several other key techniques you can employ to help get your content noticed.

Get Talking...

Central to building your followers is interaction and creating conversation. When your visibility increases, so do your followers. Asking questions is one of the best ways to get conversational on Twitter, but just as important is to participate in other people's conversations and provide information to them that they will find engaging, relevant and useful. The key to maximising your impact and gaining followers is to share ideas with and reply to those who have shared interests with you, therefore write your tweets with your target audience in mind rather than trying to appeal to a generic wider audience. Include content that contains specialised information and ideas that those interested in your services or sector would read. Be conversational about topics that will be of interest and provide value to others and this will

encourage your followers to reach out to their own networks and help spread your message and build your brand following.

... And Stay Talking

Building an active following takes time and requires a daily commitment to sharing content. There are more than 9,500 tweets posted every second, according to Internet Live Stats. Posting valuable content is the only chance to break through the noise. It is therefore vital that in the very beginning you figure out a comfortable tweeting routine that works with your editorial calendar, be it tweeting 5 or 20 times daily, and stick to it in order to maintain consistency and maximise your impact.

Use Your Followers to get More Followers

Create tweets that encourage your followers to retweet. A common method is to announce that you'll offer a discount or some other benefit to everyone who retweets your offer, but only if you get a certain total number of retweets. Offer your customers a reward if they mention your business — a discount, free trial, or extra service, whatever is relevant for your business. It's also a good idea to include a link to the terms and conditions of your offer in the Tweet.

Promote Your Twitter @username

Anywhere your customers interact with your brand is an opportunity to encourage them to follow you on Twitter. Once you begin tweeting, remember to promote it across all your other social media platforms and that includes mentioning it on your e-newsletter, your email signature, business card, product packaging and anywhere else your customers will see it. This also applies if you're an active participant in a forum or membership site, placing a signature with your Twitter link will direct more attention to your page.

Use Twitter Directories

Directories categorise Twitter users into areas of interest and expertise allowing you to easy find, follow and interact with industry influencers and other similar business owners and businesses relevant to you. Not only does this allow you to connect with quality people on Twitter it opens you up to the potentially valuable information that they share and also opens you up to their audiences if they interact with you and share your tweets.

Utilise Relevant Hashtags and Trends

Ensure that you actively pay attention to relevant trends and hashtags and act when you can see an opportunity that you can utilise. Things that are popular at a certain time creates a great opportunity for you to attract new followers so whether it's a person or event that is trending and relates to your

business ensure you jump on board and share a piece of content that fits in as you will stand a good chance of gaining some of the traffic and attention that comes with a trending topic thereby opening you up to a new audience and potential new followers.

Go to Tweetups

Tweetups are a great way to connect in person with those that you follow and interact with on Twitter. Whether you attend an already established Tweetup or you create your own remember to extend the Tweetup invite to the networks of your followers as this has potential for greater reach and audience which is a great way to network with others leading to new relationships and potential future business opportunities.

Go live with Live Video Tweets!

Research has suggested that 80% of the people who view a video on Twitter tend to remember it. Posting live video broadcasts can be the best way to make a real-time appearance on social media and to promote your brand!

Optimise and Refine Your Twitter Bio

Your Twitter bio constitutes one of the most important aspects of your profile as your bio is crucial in persuading or dissuading another user from following you. Users will often make a snap decision based on what you have written so it is crucial to present yourself in a professional, targeted and interesting way. Your bio should clearly tell people what you do, what updates they should expect from following you, and why they should follow you. In order to attract and encourage your target audience and the people in your niche to find and follow you, you need to include the right keywords and details

Stay Human!

The key to success on social media is to remember that you are dealing with people, and people respond to people! To encourage engagement, deepen relationships and attract attention it is vital to present yourself as a 'real' person through a relaxed, approachable and 'human' tone. One of the worst things a business can do on Twitter, and any other social media, is to be 'automated' and 'salesy' and provide boring updates rather than actively engaging their audience with informative, engaging and entertaining content. Make yourself attractive to social media users by letting them know there exists a 'real' person behind the brand by sharing your brand story, making them laugh and encouraging engagement through create content.

Be Active and Post Consistently

When someone checks your Twitter profile, they are able to see how active you are and when you last posted. There is nothing worse than for them to see an irregular posting schedule or no postings at all, as they will immediately make the decision that you are not worth following. Being regular with your Twitter activity shows others that you are interested in interacting and engaging with a community which encourages others to follow you and join in. People are on social media to be informed, engaged and interact with friends, family and their favourite brands etc. so show them you are interested in what they have to say by joining in with, encouraging and utilising the conversations others are having online.

Include User Handles for RTs

Give your tweet the best chance of getting retweeted by including the handle of the contributor(s) of the original content that you are sharing or some other relevant user that you want to target.

Tag Users in Photos for More Retweets

With Twitters limiting character constraints, it's not always easy to include all the user handles you would like to in your tweets. A great tip is to upload a photo to Twitter, as you can tag up to 10 people in that photo. All the people tagged will be notified and so it helps get more potential users to retweet your content. You can frequently use this tactic to include tagging post authors, brands mentioned, or simply the people in the photo.

Link to Problem-Solving Content

One way to grab your followers' attention is to provide content that is valuable to your target audience and will help improve their lives in some way. To identify what content might be valuable to your audience, read through your followers' profiles to discover their likes, dislikes and current influences. Select a common issue that they're dealing with then create content that presents a solution to their problem and promote it on Twitter. It is important that you do this in a genuine and non-self-serving way as your audience will quickly see through your deception. Genuinely look to provide value to their lives and you will find doing so is a great way to integrate your brand into their lifestyles and help you build more genuine customer relationships.

Run a Contest

People love giveaways, so running a Twitter contest for a chance to win free stuff is a good way to encourage engagement. You will also benefit from all of the social mentions as they will boost brand awareness. Choose a giveaway that is relevant to your audience with a contest theme that resonates with your followers. When deciding how people will enter the contest it's important to keep a low barrier to entry to make it easy for people to participate. Make sure you promote the contest on multiple social media channels.

Offer Personalised Encouragement

Customers are thrilled when you show them respect and appreciation by devoting the time to interact with them. Give your fans words of encouragement. Identify tweets that announce major milestones (such as a new home, baby, running a marathon, getting or married) then craft a short message of encouragement. You can make the message more personal if you don't use any hashtags.

Share Your Followers Tweets

Retweet your followers to show you recognize the value of their content and that what they're saying or posting online matters. When retweeting your followers, be sure to choose relevant tweets that align with your brand values, add a comment to the retweet to contribute something to the conversation and that the user's profile is a real person. How often you retweet is up to you; some experts recommend 20% of your tweets should be retweets whilst others recommend a 50/50 split. Find out what works best for your industry and your audience and go from there.

Use IFTTT to Curate Twitter Lists Automatically

When you add people to a Twitter list, it shows to them that their tweets are valuable enough to you to be put in a specific category and as such, the people on your lists are likely to reciprocate the favour by following your account. While adding users to a Twitter list manually takes time, a great tool for making it easier to automate the process is IFTTT. To create an account with IFTTT head to their website and create an account or login, then connect your Twitter account. Next, create a 'recipe' that tells your Twitter account that when a new tweet is posted with a hashtag you determine, it should add that user to a one of your lists. Now, whenever people tweet with the hashtag in your recipe, they will be automatically added to your list. Some people will follow you immediately after this, so be sure to send out a tweet to thank them. Connect with the others on your list with a tweet, saying that you added them to your list because you find their content valuable.

Respond to Tweets From Big Brands

It's good practice to get into the habit of replying to relevant tweets posted by influential accounts with hundreds of thousands or millions of followers. When you tweet actively and consistently, your tweets and account are more likely to get noticed and followed. Responding to a giant in your industry is a prime opportunity to engage with a bigger audience. Once you respond, your tweet is attached to their tweet and everyone else can see it. Just remember to do it in a genuine way when you can truly add value to the conversation.

Thank People Who Engage With You

Thank and engage with people every single time they engage with you, whether they ask a question, offer a suggestion, mention you at an event, favourite one of your tweets etc. Not only will this help you

keep followers, it also prompts them to share your content even more with their network, helping to increasing your visibility. People really appreciate brands who listen to what they have to say and respond to them. Getting in this habit is a great way to organically build an engaged Twitter community.

Tweet Those You Quote

When you write a blog post that includes a Twitter user remember to @mention those you include. People love to see their names published so tweet directly to them and tell them about it and they'll want to read what you said. From this, they will be likely to reply, retweet and follow you back. If they are particularly influential and have hundreds of thousands of Twitter followers, they may retweet and respond which increases your visibility greatly to their audience and could add numbers to your following.

Embed Tweets Into Blog Posts

A great method to increase the visibility of your tweets is to embed them into your blog posts. Write a blog post then embed some of your own tweets, as well as tweets from other experts, to help beef up the content. To embed a tweet into your blog, simply click the three little dot below the tweet on your Twitter desktop version. Then hit Embed Tweet to get the code. This a also a great tactic to entice readers to follow you as this shows your readers some of your tweets, and gives them great examples of what they'll get if they follow you.

Install Twitter Buttons, Widgets and Apps

Visitors to your website will often look for different ways to follow you on social networks, so make sure your website is primed and ready with follow buttons and widgets in prominent places. If you sell products, give away free downloads or have an email subscribe option on your website and include follow buttons on your thank-you pages. Be sure to also add a Twitter widget to your website and a Twitter app on your Facebook fan page to show your fans your tweets. This is a sleek cross-promotion method that gives fans a taste of your tweets and encourages them to follow you.

Participate in Twitter Chats

A Twitter chat is a live event that focuses on one subject and is moderated by an individual or brand. People in the chat use a single hashtag and respond to the questions or comments coming from the moderator and/or interviewee. Getting involved in Twitter chats is great for increasing your visibility and gives you the opportunity to share your expertise with new people. Interact with other chat attendees and gain more organic followers along the way.

Share Other People's Content

To develop valuable relationships and start the cycle of reciprocity on Twitter, actively share content from others. Find blogs, news articles and opinion pieces that involve your niche and broadcast their posts to your Twitter followers taking care to include the author's Twitter handle, as well as the blog's Twitter account. The author will get a notification you shared the post and is liable to reply, retweet and maybe even follow you.

Have Fun!

Whilst most of your content needs to be in alignment with our brand, every once in a while, it pays to give yourself and your fans a break. Brighten up your followers' feeds with a Twitter "coffee break," so instead of the usual articles, links or niche-based content you post share some fun material, whether it's interesting facts or statistics, cute videos, adorable pictures, tips or jokes. Fun tweets like this can get you a lot of engagement and sharing. However, do take care to not post anything offensive or completely irrelevant to your business.

Tips for Success

Use Hashtags Judiciously

Do not overload your tweets with hashtags to try and gain visibility. While hashtags can be helpful and open up your content to relevant audiences, Twitter itself says that including more than two hashtags in a tweet is likely overkill. This is supported by a Salesforce study that found tweets with 1-2 hashtags receive 21% higher engagement than those with 3+ hashtags. Stick to a couple of relevant Hashtags per tweet to keep it focused.

Upload Photos in the Correct Size

You need to ensure the images you upload are optimized for the correct dimensions. Most people assume that a perfectly square image is the best dimension for Twitter, but the most engaged with Twitter photos are the horizontal ones that render nicely in a user's horizontally structured stream. The ideal dimension therefore is 440 x 220px.

Answer Customer Calls for Help

Twitter is a great place for you to strengthen customer relationships by showcasing your customer service skills and helping to solve your customers' problems. You can give your Twitter followers one–on–one assistance through direct messages and/or engage with the customer's tweet and then move the

conversation to direct message. It's important that you strive to respond to customer concerns in a timely manner and state your customer service hours of operation in your profile. If you don't, people will assume a service representative is on duty 24/7.

Utilise Keywords in Your Tweets

Choose several keywords that accurately and best describe your business and industry and strategically use them within your tweets. Doing so gives each of your tweets a purpose as you will show up in search results relating to your keywords and get found by a new, relevant audience.

Connect and Interact With Relevant People

One of the most important parts of a successful Twitter strategy is following and interacting with quality, relevant people not just anyone who you think will follow you back. You need to be selective and targeted with those you choose to follow as you need them to be the right people who will be interested in your content and from whom you can build a relationship with. Importantly, you need to actively and regularly seek out relevant people through directory searches, influencer twitter lists and through looking at who others are following and then listening to, starting and joining in with conversations with them. Remember to also show your excellent customer service skills by regularly searching for anyone who talks about your brand and interacts with you and interact with them back. Also actively listen to conversations surrounding your industry and by adding your thoughts to the conversation you can establish yourself as an authority within your sector. Doing this will get you more noticed by others and increase your brand exposure resulting in a successful Twitter presence.

Be Social

If someone has taken the time to connect with you, start a conversation or retweet you then remember to reciprocate and interact with them back. Twitter is a powerful tool for helping spread the word about your business so it pays to deliver a good, personal customer service for all those who are looking to interact with you. A simple retweet can go a long way towards helping another business in your community so when relevant look for great content from others to share with your audience and you will be rewarded with greater exposure and develop a genuine rapport within your Twitter community. Remember the purpose of using social media is to be social so look to get to know others on Twitter by actively looking for great content that you can share and comment on, conversations that you can join and by encouraging engagement and fostering good relationships.

Stay Relevant and on Topic

One of the important aspects of having a clear strategy is that is keeps you focused on what content you share with your audience and what kind of content is acceptable to retweet etc. Without a strategy it is easy to share and retweet a broad range of content that may not always be relevant for your business, so to ensure you are developing a quality audience that is relevant to you and also in order to help develop

yourself as an authority within your sector it is vital that you stay relevant with what you post and ensure the content is tailored to meet the needs of your target audience.

Don't Be Tempted to Automate Everything

There are many tools available to help you automate your posts on Twitter which is an attractive option for a very busy business owner. However do not be tempted to automate everything as this defeats the purpose of using a social network as you deliberately miss out on the vital social aspect. From this, you need to be real and post in real time as this is the only way engage in real conversation within your community and show them that you are genuinely there to give value to them and interact with them. In addition if you automate everything you potentially open up yourself to an embarrassing event of one of your scheduled tweets being no longer relevant or cause offensive/ thoughtlessness etc. if events happen outside of the online world that may affect your tweet.

Keep Your Profile Updated and Optimised

Your Twitter profile represents your business in the online world and as such you need to ensure it represents you accurately. This means you need to regularly check your profile to ensure all information is updated and optimised, from an informative bio to a good headshot of yourself and a Twitter Header Image that is consistent with your branding and contains your contact details. Part of this process of staying relevant is to look to tailor your background image and/or profile picture to coincide with national holidays and other special events that are relevant to you.

Stay Updated on News and Changes of Twitter

As Twitter evolves it is likely to make important changes that you as a business need to be aware of. Remember to follow the official Twitter business page and subscribe to their blog to make sure you are aware and up to date with Twitter's business updates.

Be Visual

Tweets that contain visuals such as photos, infographics and videos get the highest amount of engagement on Twitter, so you need to actively and consistently incorporate visual elements into your tweets. Photos and videos are more visible and take up more space on a user's feed than a simple text based post so look to include high-quality, eye catching and relevant visuals and you will encourage your audience to interact with and retweet your content.

Include Strong Calls to Action

By ensuring you include a clear call to action in your tweets, you are making sure that each tweet is purposeful for your business. A call to action could be asking for a retweet, directing the reader to an

external site or simply asking a user to interact with you, whatever your call to action is you need to ensure you consistently form tweets that encourage the reader to continue the interaction with you.

Create and Share Curated Lists

Twitter lists are a great tool to utilise for filtering information. With Twitter lists, you are able to categorise Twitter users into areas of interest, characteristics and expertise allowing you to easy find, follow and interact with industry influencers and other similar business owners and businesses relevant to you. As you follow more people, your feed gets noisy and crowded with tweets which may result in you missing important messages. To make sure you never miss an important message utilise Twitter lists and categorise the most important people you follow so you can easy see their messages and they don't get lost in the noise of everyone else. Not only does this allow you to connect with quality people on Twitter, it opens you up to the potentially valuable information that they share and also opens you up to their audiences if they interact with you and share your tweets. Another great feature of Twitter lists is that you can set them to be private or public. This allows you to be able to do a range of important tasks from 'secretly' monitoring your competitors with a private list or show off and share your impressive roster of brand advocates in a public list. By creating and sharing lists you position yourself as an authority in your field and are able to grow your Twitter community as people begin to trust you to curate the information they are seeking.

Reply to the Right Audience

Many users assume that every tweet they send appears in every one of their followers' feeds; however this isn't actually the case. If you begin a tweet with a @username only that user and any followers you both have in common will see the tweet in their feed, which limits a tweets visibility greatly. Whilst limiting the visibility of a tweet can work in your favour, for example if you are responding to a user about a particular bad customer service complaint, by starting your replies with the @username you decrease the number of people who will see the potentially negative conversation. On the other hand, in most cases you want your tweets, especially your positive ones about recommendations, new product launches, customer testimonials etc., to have as much visibility as possible. In this instance you do not want to start a tweet with @username, instead you can use the common method of starting your tweet with a period then the username: .@username or the other method you can apply is to move the username further into your text, for example, "Thank you very much @username! We're glad you love our product."

Don't Just Tweet Article Headlines

Simply retweeting an article or sharing an article without modifying the headline is a common mistake seen on Twitter. It not only makes the user seem lazy and boring, it shows a missed opportunity for you to engage others. So instead of simply tweeting or retweeting the article using the headline already generated automatically for it, put in more effort into it by adding your thoughts and opinions based on the article, taking a retweetable quote from the article, pose questions about the article (e.g. "Have you

tried this new tactic?") Or ask your followers for their opinion (e.g. "Has this marketing tactic worked best for you too?") to get people curious about it. This also has the added benefit of not only encouraging engagement but shows yourself as an authority in your sector as you are sharing with your community valuable and trusted information and adding your valuable thoughts and creating debates. The added benefit of sharing content in this way, especially if it is your own article you're sharing, is it also allows you to use all three methods to tweet about the same article multiple times. This is a great way to promote an article several times, each in a different way, without spamming your followers' feeds.

Show Your Personality and Remember to Be Yourself!

The most successful businesses on Twitter are those that show the real people behind the brand. Twitter and social media in general offers an informal and chatty platform for your opinions, stories, humour and advice that gives your business a human face and it is through this great ability to humanise your business through the content you tweet that ultimately makes your business appear more engaging, relatable and trustworthy to others. Ensure you utilise this opportunity for your customers to get to know the real you better, so whether you are sharing industry expertise, reviewing a product or sharing an aspect of your brand story, each post gives your customers helping them to better understand who you are, what you do, and ultimately tells them why they should care about you.

Don't Give Up

After months of marketing efforts, you may still see a low follower count on your Twitter profile which can be disheartening. But don't give up because real success takes time and patience. The key is to stay consistent with your tweeting, add your own unique voice and views, engage with people who resonate with you and continually read up on it so you become better. Like any marketing tactic, it takes commitment, time and patience to become proficient at it.

Test Paid Marketing

Twitter, like many other social media networks, is free for users but offers a good selection of advertising options. Similarly to Facebook, followers you have may not see all of your organic posts and even the best campaigns with great potential are derailed if no one sees them, so it's best to reserve some funding for sponsored Twitter content to help boost your profile and keep your brand moving forward.

Get Happy

The science behind going viral and sharing contagious content lies in emotional content that pulls at the heart strings. Strive to consistently creating uplifting, positive content and you will be more likely to hit the viral sweet spot. Babies, kids, cute animals and everyday hero stories are always great for pulling at the heart-strings to connect on an emotional level.

Strike a Balance

On the one hand you need to engage your audience and interact with your followers, but on the other you don't want to become a nuisance account with it or you will quickly lose followers. Don't retweet every mention you get, or tweet too often. You want your followers to view your updates as valuable and worthwhile, not be turned off by a constant onslaught that dominates their Twitter feed. If you learn from best practises and by looking at your analytics and what your audience tells you Twitter can one of the most powerful tools in your marketing arsenal if it's wielded correctly.

Be Real

Nothing is more attractive on a digital platform than a personality and the great thing about Twitter is that it allows you to be real in real-time, but in bite-sized chunks. Don't be afraid to be you on social media so if you have an original thought about a current event, a movie, a trending topic, an element of your industry, a brand, or a product then share it. You might be surprised at how many other people agree with what you're saying and want to engage with it. You will however make missteps, everyone does. After some time and with regular practice, you'll become more comfortable expressing yourself in 140 characters or less.

Link your Tweets Together

From time to time you might have thoughts that take up more than 140 characters and the good news is you can beat Twitter at its 280 character game by linking your tweets together. Linked tweets appear nicely connected in your followers' feeds and so this feature makes it easy for your followers to read a series of your tweets about the same subject, instead of having to fumble through their feed looking for your related tweets. Linking a tweet is simple, if you reply to your tweet and then delete your handle that automatically pops up at the beginning of the reply tweet, these linked tweets will appear seamlessly.

Pin a Tweet

A pinned tweet is a great introduction to your Twitter presence and a great chance to make a good first impression. Choose a tweet that performed particularly well, one that really expresses who you are, or announces something you want people to know about. The pinned tweet effectively announces your presence so make it a good one.

Common Mistakes to Avoid

Only Tweeting About Yourself

The essence of social media marketing is about creating social engagement. Therefore you need to encourage interaction from your followers by sharing valuable and informative information and comments and listening to and joining in with conversations. Whilst you have a presence as you will ultimately want to drive sales, your tweets should not blatantly reflect this, you need to instead focus on making people love your brand by sharing stories, responding to interactions and sharing and retweeting information they are going to find useful and interesting. A successful Twitter presence is one which is achieved through social interaction and not through pushy sales promotion tweets.

Begging for Followers

The more people that follow you results in the more reach you have for your tweets. This leads many businesses to beg for followers rather than earning them through posting engaging content, interacting with others and giving incentives to encourage people to follow. Begging for followers affects your businesses reputation online as it makes you appear untrustworthy and desperate.

Randomly Retweeting

Retweeting is a great practice for businesses to get into however many businesses make the mistake of using retweets as a way of replacing their own content and randomly retweet any content with no real thought to whether the content is relevant to them or their own audiences. Don't make this mistake by ensuring the content you are retweeting is relevant to your audience and in line with your own overall branding and marketing strategies.

Using Too Many Hashtags

Hashtags are a great way to gather traffic and attention by utilising relevant trends and highlighting keywords, but only if they are used correctly and effectively. The maximum number of hashtags to use per tweet is 3 as anymore can make it unclear to the reader what the main focus of your tweet is in addition to general making your tweet look unprofessional and demonstrates someone that doesn't really know how to use Twitter effectively. By making sure you have a clear goal and message for each tweet you will ensure you know where to clearly put your hashtag to maximise effectiveness.

Rapid Tweeting

It is clear when a business has no posting strategy as a look to their feed shows days go by without a tweet then there will be a sudden, rapid surge of tweets on a particular day. Do not let your business fall into this approach as not only will you lose and fail to attract new followers you also make it clear to

people that you do not understand how to use Twitter making you appear unprofessional. There is no rule as to how often you should be tweeting as this is different for each individual so to ensure you are providing a consistent and effective tweeting schedule for your followers you should actively check your engagement rates to gauge the responses from your audience as this will show you what type of and how many tweets are the most effective.

Choosing a Long and/or Irrelevant Twitter Handle

Your Twitter handle needs to be clear and representative of your business. If your handle is too long then you're losing valuable space and if it is irrelevant then you come across as unprofessional and the lack of a handle that is clear to the brand may mean potential followers may miss out on finding you as it is not clear with your Twitter handle who you actually are.

Using Automatic Direct Messages

Sending an automatic direct message to followers is a common occurrence and one that reflects badly on your business. Don't make your first impression a negative one for the reader by sending an automatic and impersonal direct message. This makes you appear like a robot and often leads to unfollows and an overall general bad impression for your business.

Not Checking Your Tweets for Spelling and Grammatical Errors

You must remember that you represent your business with every tweet therefore it is vital that you review each tweet carefully before you post. A tweet that is grammatically incorrect, incoherent or riddled with spelling mistakes will affect your reputation negatively so ensure you double check your grammar, spelling and ensure your tweet is clear and concise before you post it.

Only Tweeting 9-5

Just because your working hours are only 9 – 5 doesn't mean that your audience is only going to be online and interacting at that time. Therefore you need to take the time to monitor your account at several points throughout the day, respond to any interactions from others and find out when your audience is most active on Twitter.

Connecting Your Facebook and Twitter Account

Connecting your Facebook and Twitter feeds, whilst appealing to a time-strapped business owner, is not recommended as each platform requires a tailored use of content and has a best time to post, therefore you need to treat your Facebook and Twitter accounts as separate entities and share your content individually by tailoring them to each one as opposed to having Twitter automatically tweet the same message you posted on Facebook.

Don't be an Egg!

In the age of authenticity, where you need your brand to show a human side, you've got to treat your Twitter account as a customized digital representation of your personality. This means not leaving your profile picture as the default egg. Make sure you upload and choose a high-quality picture that is professional, relevant and representative of you and your brand.

Don't be Self- Serving

Don't be network-y in the sense that you openly act/express that the only reason you're on Twitter is for sales purposes. Many businesses on Twitter employ a tactic of pushing continual sales messages that offer little or no engagement and interaction. This is a very damaging approach. Instead you need to prove yourself to be part of the community, and the networking and leads will come in time naturally. If you engage, interact and provide value in the form of good content and a consistent presence, people will eventually find and follow you and importantly people won't follow you back just because you've asked them to. Twitter is a powerful and successful tool for those who approach it from a connecting and communing building point of view through active participation, not idle expectations and self-serving content.

Measuring Success

Like any other marketing strategy, the success of your Twitter profile must be measured against your business objectives. Analysing your Twitter metrics will show you a wealth of information and insights and help determine whether your profile is having a measurable impact and whether the data is reflective of the overall goals of your business Twitter profile. Twitter's Analytics Dashboard provides a pretty good overview of what's working and what isn't for your business. Displayed monthly from your Twitter analytics dashboard, these account metrics provide a snapshot of standout activity.

Accessing your Twitter Analytics dashboard will show you monthly highlights and help you get to know your Twitter followers. You'll be able to see:

- Your follower growth
- Your followers' interests
- Your followers' demographics, such as language, gender, and location
- How many people have seen your Tweets, visited your profile, mentioned your @username, or followed your account
- Your top Tweets and follower with the largest network in any given month

- **Top tweet:** The tweet that earned the most impressions for a given month.
  Since this tweet reached your largest audience, it's a good example of what you're doing right. This can be any number of factors from tweeting at the right time of day, hashtag use, to content that resonated, or all the above. You may want to consider promoting this tweet.
- **Top follower:** The top follower of the month, with the highest number of their own followers. Your top followers hold the greatest potential to broaden the exposure of your tweets through retweets and favourites. They are also good connections to have when it comes to finding influencers.
- **Top mention:** A tweet with the most impressions in which another Twitter user has tagged your username.
  This Twitter is one to consider reaching out to or at least keeping them in mind for the next time you're running an influencer campaign.

Follower Growth

Tracking your follower count is important as it shows you whether your Twitter strategies and campaigns are worthwhile and you are successfully attracting people to your profile and business. If your following remains constant over time, this could indicate that you're not utilising Twitter as well as you could and show areas in need of improvement. Your goal should always be to increase relevant followers so you can grow your reach as greater reach results in more visibility of your tweets that could potentially lead to more leads and customers.

Follower Quality and Engagement

Engagement is about gauging how much people interact with you and the number and quality of retweets, favourites, @mentions, and lists and link clicks are a good way to measure engagement. Tracking these metrics on a regular basis offer the biggest returns in helping you grow your audience so it is vital that you utilise what each individual metric is showing you as using this information will help guide your strategy and ensure you are targeting your readers needs and encouraging interaction and engagement.

Conversion

Another piece of important information about your Twitter success that can be taken from your analytics is how much traffic that Twitter brings to the rest of your website. In other words, how many Twitter followers/readers are converted into potential customers? If a significant number of website visitors were referred from Twitter, you know that your tweets are generating interest in your products or services and are possibly helping to drive sales. Tracking this number is the true measure of your Twitter marketing ROI as even if you're generating traffic and leads from Twitter, if they're ultimately not turning into customers you may have to re-evaluate how much time and effort you're putting into Twitter as a social media marketing channel.

Link Shares

Particularly if you are sharing a lot of links from your website or blog, a metric you should be analysing is how many times your content has been shared on Twitter. An easy way to do this is by using a URL Shortening tool such as bit.ly as this tool not only shortens your link creating more character space for you in your Tweets, it also helps determine what types of content are most popular which will ultimately allow you to see which type of content you should focus on creating in the future.

Lists

Creating lists enables the user to filter the Twitter 'noise' and focus on what and who is important to them on Twitter. Therefore if you have been added to a relevant list then it shows you that you have been considered influential and that user wants to ensure that they always see your tweets. This is good indicator to you that the content you are posting resonates well with others which goes a long way to show you as an authority within your sector.

Twitter Maintenance Checklist

DAILY

- ✓ Post several original tweets sharing blog posts, tips, news etc.
- ✓ Engage with targeted people, prospects and industry influencers
- ✓ Search for tweets mentioning your business, product or service
- ✓ Search for and monitor hashtags and keywords relevant to you and/or your local area
- ✓ See who competitors, industry influencers etc. are following and if appropriate follow them too
- ✓ Respond to any interaction - new direct messages, favourites and mentions.
- ✓ Check relevant hashtags trending that present opportunities to interact
- ✓ Go through feed and get updated on news and insights and add your thoughts and comments to any relevant discussions and/or share relevant content
- ✓ Running Twitter Ads? Review stats twice daily.
- ✓ Listen for and respond to every lead immediately
- ✓ Look to see if any new connections from other social media platforms have Twitter and follow their account
- ✓ During the week gather information and sources for the following weeks post(s)

WEEKLY

- ✓ **Check Your Insights** - Your analytics will help you figure out what your audience likes and doesn't like, so you can plan your future content better. It'll also help alert you to any red flags

early on. Regularly go through your analytics and look at what kinds of topics resonate best with your audience? What tweets grab attention? Follower Growth?
- ✓ Actively find and follow any relevant other businesses and industry influencers
- ✓ Go through your follow lists and unfollow anyone who is inactive

MONTHLY

- ✓ **Review Your Bio** - Is your bio up-to-date? If anything about you, your business, or any other content on your About page has changed since you published it, then you should update it.

LINKEDIN (FOR PERSONAL USE)

LinkedIn launched in 2003 and is currently the third most popular social network in terms of unique monthly visitors -- right behind Facebook and Twitter. LinkedIn is the world's largest professional online network, with over 590 million users spanning more than 200 countries. The network is primarily centred on careers and network building and is highly popular with business-to-business users. It enables users to connect and share content with other professionals, including colleagues as well as potential employers, business partners, and new employees. It is also beneficial for those looking to share and discover industry news and knowledge and for those looking for jobs.

What's Good About LinkedIn?
- It is reflective of 'the six degrees of separation' theory as the nature of the site allows you to reach out to new people through your existing connections
- It allows for questions and answer inquiries to be addressed with a professional slant
- It is useful to look up background information on people before a meeting or interview

What's not so Good About LinkedIn?
- People use the site for purely professional purposes, so marketing messages and sales are not always welcomed
- More used for business purposes and thus doesn't play as active a role in people's daily lives as with other social networks such as Facebook
- LinkedIn is essentially a closed network meaning that you can only interact with users who have given permission to do so. The result of this means your network will not grow without active networking on your part.

Who Should be on LinkedIn?

The business nature of LinkedIn means that all professionals should have a presence on LinkedIn including freelancers, bloggers, designers, marketers and any other service providers. There are also opportunities for professional businesses to be on LinkedIn, allowing businesses to develop themselves as authorities in their sector and keep their networks informed with business updates by sharing relevant industry opinions and analysis.

Need to Know Facts, Stats and Tips about LinkedIn

- LinkedIn now has 590 million users with 260 million of them being active on a monthly basis.
- LinkedIn performs 277% better than Facebook and Twitter when it comes to generating visitor-to-lead conversions.
- It's also the platform most used by salespeople to engage with their clients/prospects. 73% of B2B companies said they use it for this purpose.
- 80% of social media B2B leads come from LinkedIn.
- The three major platforms—Facebook, Twitter and LinkedIn contributed to 90% of social traffic to B2B blogs and sites. And the platform was responsible for half of that traffic.
- 91% of executives believe that LinkedIn is the top choice for professionally relevant content.
- 89% of B2B marketers include LinkedIn in their digital marketing mix.
- 56% of professionals access the platform using multiple devices.
- 62% of LinkedIn members engage with content on the platform because they found it educational or informative.
- 61% engage with content because it's relevant to them.
- Percentage of users that use LinkedIn Daily: 40%
- Number of New LinkedIn New Members per Second: 2
- 70% of LinkedIn users are from Outside of US.
- There are 57% of male users and 44% female users on LinkedIn.
- After US, India, Brazil, Great Britain and Canada has the highest number of LinkedIn users.
- 13% of Millennials (15-34 Years old) use LinkedIn.
- 28% of all internet male users use LinkedIn, whereas 27% of All Internet Female users use LinkedIn.

Why You Need a LinkedIn Profile

Knowledge

Having a readily available network of other business professionals means there is a resourceful knowledge base where you can learn, discuss and stay on top of industry news. This means you can better expand your knowledge of your business sector and learn tips and tricks from other industry professionals, all of which can benefit you and your business greatly.

Industry Connections and Networking

LinkedIn offers a great platform for connecting with other professionals in your industry. Within the Groups area you can have professional discussions centred on a topic or industry that allows you to share ideas with peers, pick up tips to help your business grow and connect with people who share similar passions. By sharing your expertise and content with customers, members and prospects in a more social environment, you can not only stay in touch with your connections, you can also make it easy for others to share the things you are posting online with their colleagues.

Authority

Through group discussions and general engagement, there is plenty of opportunity for you to demonstrate your expertise and show yourself as an authority through the content you post. By regularly contributing to LinkedIn with valuable, interesting and relevant industry analysis and comment, it shows that you have a deep interest in your sector and are more informed than the average participant; giving potential clients a compelling reason to choose you over competitors. Moreover, those customers will continue to visit and spread the word to others of your valuable and interesting industry knowledge.

Personal Branding

Whenever you meet a person at a networking event to promote your business, the next step that person will take is to look you up online. A professional LinkedIn profile provides you with an opportunity to be easily found and to showcase who you are and why you are a valuable connection to have. Think of your profile as a compelling presentation of your professional self that compels the viewer to connect with you.

Extended Sales Arm

The people in your LinkedIn network could aid your next sale. The potential power of LinkedIn for your business lies in the people in the network you have built and the connections you have made— vendors, colleagues, business partners and the people you meet along the way at events. It's not only about who you know; it's about who they know. LinkedIn provides a great tool in its advanced search capabilities that allow you to know exactly which companies you need to connect with and who in your existing relationships/ connections might provide an introduction to them. That's what makes LinkedIn a very powerful tool to have in your arsenal, that is, the ability to tap into that connection and grow your brand through word-of-mouth.

How to Create an Effective LinkedIn Personal Profile

The Profile Summary

The summary area of your LinkedIn Profile constitutes the most important part of the entire page because it is the first thing readers' scan after reading your name and tagline. For this reason your summary must be compelling. Here are some suggestions that will improve your summary:

- ✓ Write it in the first person 'I am' etc. as it shows an authenticity that you miss out on when writing in the third person.

- Write your Summary in the Who / What / Goals format. Clearly stating who you are, what you do with the final section providing information about your professional goals and aspirations.
- Read your summary and keep asking yourself 'so what?' as this will help you to pin point areas for improvement.

Optimise your Profile for SEO Benefit

Suggestions for optimising your LinkedIn Profile for SEO benefit include:

- Customise the URL for your public profile
- Embed keywords strategically throughout your profile
- Try to list up to the maximum of three links in the billboard area (e.g., your business website, your personal website, your blog). When entering the anchor text for the hyperlink, embed as many of your keywords as possible.

Fill Out Every Section Fully

- **Emphasize Your Professional Skills**
  LinkedIn showcases your top 10 skills based on endorsements so people know where you excel. Make sure you fully optimize and fill out as many specific keywords you can to help you get quick endorsements from your connections for those skills.
- **Promote Your Projects**
  Promote and highlight your products, services and projects in the Projects section. Directly link each project to your website and include team members when applicable.
- **Link to Your Publications**
  The Publications section is perfect if you're an author, regular contributor to top publications, have eBooks, white papers and other company content that you want to promote. You can directly link each publication to where visitors can buy your books, link to author profile pages and also to landing pages for your content.
- **Share Your Honours and Awards**
  This section is where you can highlight notable lists and mentions you've received from recognized authorities and publications in your industry.
- **Showcase Specialized Certifications**
  The Certifications section allows you to showcase your specialised educational achievements within your industry. If your business has received a certification for your industry, promote and showcase it here so people can learn more about it.
- **Highlight Industry-Related Coursework**
  If you've taken any courses that are relevant and apply to your business, you can list them in the Courses section. This can include coursework you completed at university, on-the-job training course and those offered by recognised organizations in your industry.
- **Feature Your Professional Memberships**
  If you belong to professional organizations in your industry, use the Organizations section to highlight your membership and the position you hold/have held.
- **Demonstrate Language Proficiency**

Demand for people who speak several languages is on the rise. Therefore, if you are fluent in multiple languages, include that information in the Languages section.

✓ *Highlight Your LinkedIn Groups*

When you join LinkedIn groups, you have the option of listing them on your profile, as shown in the Groups section below. You should utilise this opportunity as this can benefit you three-fold:
- People who want to get to know you can do so by joining the groups you're in and engaging with you there.
- If you run groups for your business, you can display them on your profile to help increase membership.
- Joining groups related to your industry means you can add more keywords to your profile

✓ *Publicise Your Interests*

When you follow businesses, news channels, publishers and influencers found on LinkedIn Pulse, they will appear in the Following section of your profile. Use this section to optimise your profile for specific keywords, highlight publications that you may contribute to and showcase your customers.

✓ *Support Your Causes*

One in five hiring managers has chosen a candidate based on his or her volunteer experience so add the Volunteer section to your profile to show others that you also care about helping others. For non-profits, this is also a great way to promote your organization and cause.

Keep Your Network Posted with Status Updates

Keeping your network posted with status updates should be a routine procedure. It gives you the opportunity to share valuable information with your network about what you're doing. Done right, status updates can engage your followers, create leads, and facilitate customer conversion. Here are some tips on how to optimise your status updates:

- ✓ Leverage the power of status updates by embedding special keywords when posting
- ✓ Focus on sharing informative and useful updates as that is the information members expect from connections they follow on LinkedIn
- ✓ Post status updates encouraging your followers to interact with you and this includes using a clear call to action within your post
- ✓ Post regularly and consistently and you will reach more of your audience and extend your reach.

Use Your Profile as a Central Hub

When searching for someone on Google in most cases their LinkedIn profile is seen on the first page with the vast majority appearing in the first five results. This means that you need keep your profile current and up to date to highlight your experience and expertise and in addition requires that your profile needs to become a central source for connecting all of your other social media platforms. LinkedIn has many available tools for you to utilise that can link your profile with your Blog and Twitter feed among others so is a great way to support and drive attention to your other sites.

Add Rich Visual Content to Your LinkedIn Profile

Throughout your profile LinkedIn provides you with the opportunity to visually enhance your profile so you need to leverage this opportunity. Add some oomph to your profile by adding some up to date, rich, visual content and you will help yourself and your profile to stand out from the rest and get noticed. Embracing the visual in social media marketing is highly important so utilise this and share with your audience creative, informative and engaging visual elements such as pictures, SlideShare presentations and videos. A key thing is to also remember not to just create and then forget your newly visual profile, rather, actively update and refresh your profile with current, fresh and valuable content such as examples of new work, recent articles and features in the press.

Connect with New Contacts in Groups and Answers

Joining and contributing to LinkedIn Groups helps to locate people with shared interests and establish valuable new connections. In addition to the benefit of increased traffic to your profile page, participating within a Group has the added benefit of learning from others and participation in a group or within the LinkedIn Answers section allows you to highlight your ideas and insight. The more you participate, the more you'll build credibility and trust within your industry. If you're contributing valuable content, you will soon improve your own reputation as an invaluable resource on select topics by other industry connections.

Give and Get Recommendations

Recommendations from colleagues, business partners and satisfied clients go a long way in establishing your value and credibility. As either an employee or a business, a recommendation can carry a great deal of weight in the eyes of future customers or employers as they essentially act as solid examples of a good experience with you in a personal manner. If you want to get recommendations, use LinkedIn to give them to people you've worked with and who have done a great job for you and they will likely reciprocate. Similarly with the new Endorsement feature, if you endorse someone, they'll be notified and you're likely to get a reciprocal endorsement in return.

Add, Remove, and Rearrange Entire Sections of Your Profile

LinkedIn enables you to reorder entire sections of your profile in any way that you prefer. This is a great feature to help you optimise your profile as you can place your most important sections in prominent places and delete any that are not relevant to you for example. Simply go into edit mode, hover your mouse over the double-sided arrow in each section. Your mouse will turn into a four-arrowed icon, at which point you can click, then drag and drop to another position on your profile.

Edit Your Public Profile Settings

You want to ensure that people can find your profile when they do a public search. You ideally want to show public viewers as much as possible to convince them to click to view your full profile and make a connection. Locate the Privacy & Settings option on your LinkedIn homepage and click Manage. To access your public profile settings, click your profile image and select the Privacy & Settings option. On the next page, click Edit Your Public Profile to see what items are displayed on your public profile. The right side of the page shows a list of items that are displayed on your private profile and you can choose which items to show on your public profile. You can choose to share only a few sections of your profile with public viewers or be fully transparent and show all sections. Just ensure that you enable the setting that allows anyone to see your public profile. You may feel uneasy about showing your entire profile but it is important to do so as your public profile will never display rich-text media like videos or full-text recommendations, therefore, your description of your job experience is the most important part of your profile.

Consider Upgrading Your LinkedIn Account

The goal of improving your public image on LinkedIn is to get high-quality connections. With a premium plan, you gain access to additional features such as seeing people who viewed your profile, requesting and making introductions and mailing other users from within LinkedIn. These are features that could greatly benefit your business so consider upgrading your account if you are in a position to do so.

To ensure you get yourself noticed in the competitive world of business, you need to present yourself online in a way that impresses and builds confidence in your skills, products, and services. Use the checklist below to ensure you create a powerful LinkedIn profile that sells who you are and why you deserve to be noticed.

LinkedIn Professional Profile Checklist

- ✓ **Professionally Taken Photograph**
  Your LinkedIn profile is your digital introduction and first impression with your reader. It's important to look your best and a professionally taken photograph will ensure you are portrayed in the best light.

- ✓ *Professional Name*
  You need to present a name that is professional, relevant and representative of what you want to present yourself as to others. Remember to stay away from cheesy and gimmicky names.

- ✓ *Attention Grabbing Headline*
  The headline needs to be powerful and draw a reader in and compels them to read on. Use this area to clearly and professionally show to others how you can help them and encourage them to want to find out more about you. Remember to present yourself in a positive and articulated way staying away from overtly selling yourself.

- ✓ *Customised Profile URL*
  LinkedIn provides you with a default URL which you need to customise. Not only will this aid your SEO efforts, it looks more professional especially as you are likely to include your LinkedIn URL in your email signature or on your business card.

- ✓ *Compelling, Interesting Summary*
  Your LinkedIn Summary needs to stand out as this is your chance to demonstrate to potential business connections and employers that you are an expert and someone who deserves to be noticed. Your professional headline served the role of initially drawing visitors to your profile and so your professional summary must expand upon and support this further by supporting what you say in your headline. You need to craft well written paragraphs that convince the reader that they need to work with you and want to initiate contact. From this, remember to finish this section with a clear call to action as it's important to tell your reader how to reach you once they've finished reading your LinkedIn summary.

- ✓ *Complete Experiences that are Keyword-Rich*
  A powerful LinkedIn profile includes your past experiences which is an area that is highly sensitive when it comes to SEO. By including keywords that people are using to find someone like you, you are ensuring that your LinkedIn profile performs well in search and that you will be found. You need to ascertain which keywords that you would like to appear under in LinkedIn search results and when you do a search for those keywords look at the profiles of those that appear in the top few results, taking the time to examine how they have placed their keywords and then use that knowledge and apply it to your own profile.

- ✓ *Embraces the Visual*
  LinkedIn gives you the opportunity to add visual elements to your profile so you need to leverage this opportunity. Embracing the visual in social media marketing remains highly important so utilise this and share with your audience creative, informative and engaging visual elements such as pictures, memes, presentations and videos.

- ✓ *Easily Contactable*
  Take a look through your profile and ask yourself 'how contactable am I'? If you are looking to LinkedIn to foster business opportunities then you need to make sure that it is easy and clear throughout profile how you can be contacted. Remember to include your contact details such as your email address or and/or phone number and links to your website and other social media accounts. It is vital that you don't make it hard for someone to get in contact with you if they want to as if you do they are likely to move on and contact someone else.

- **Member of Several Relevant LinkedIn Groups**
  Being a member of several relevant LinkedIn groups to your industry has several important benefits including being a powerful help towards getting noticed. LinkedIn Groups also present great avenues for potential business opportunities, keeping up to date with industry news and also encourages and fosters relevant debate and conversation with others with similar interests. Therefore be active within your groups and you will likely be rewarded with increased contacts, knowledge and the potential for business opportunities.

- **Credible Recommendations**
  Recommendations go a long way towards establishing your credibility as they act as concrete examples that others have worked with and have been impressed by their experience with you. This will ultimately act a powerful persuader in the eyes of future customers or employers looking to potentially work with you.

- **Completed Profile**
  Your LinkedIn profile extends far beyond the summary section. Work Experiences, Volunteer Experiences & Causes, Certifications, Education, Interests, and Groups and Associations are just a few of the additional sections that need to be fully completed in order to have a powerful LinkedIn profile.

Tips for Success

Easily Find New Connections - or Connect With Old Ones!

The Connections tab in the top navigation offers a variety of other tools useful to help you grow and connect with contacts in your professional network. By clicking 'Add Connections' in the drop-down menu you can import contacts from your email accounts and get suggestions for other connections. The Find Alumni feature allows you connect with other alumni in addition to the Keep in Touch feature that helps you stay in touch with current connections, keep track of your communications, and get notifications when contacts in your network change jobs or have birthdays for example. LinkedIn has a connected mobile app so you can take advantage of these features and interact easily on the go.

Leverage the Perks of LinkedIn Groups

There are many 'hidden' perks of LinkedIn Groups that many people do not know about. For example, did you know that if you're a member of the same group as another user, you can bypass the need to be a first-degree connection in order to message them? Provided you've been a member of LinkedIn for at least 30 days and a member of the particular group for at least 4 days, LinkedIn allows you to send up to 15 free 1:1 messages to fellow group members per month (across all groups you belong to). In addition, group members are also able to view the profiles of other members of the same group without being

connected. Join more groups to take advantage of this ability to enable more messaging and profile viewership capabilities.

Create a Profile Badge for your Personal Website or Blog

If you have your own personal website or blog, you can promote your personal LinkedIn presence and help grow your professional network by adding a Profile Badge that links to your public LinkedIn profile.

Take Advantage of Advanced Search Options

LinkedIn's Advanced Search feature provides a much richer search experience. For example, if you want to find out if you're connected to anyone who works at a specific company, type the company name in the company field in Advanced Search, then filter the results by "Relationship" to see if you have any first- or second-degree connections to any employees.

Leverage @mentions in Your Status Updates

Make use of the ability to tag or @mention other users and companies in status updates by include the @ symbol immediately followed by the user's/company's name in your status update. This will ensure that user/company will get alerted that you mentioned them, and their name will also link to their profile/page in the status update itself.

Proofread Your Profile

Your profile represents you in the professional world therefore always remember to check your copy for correct spellings, punctuation and grammar as your LinkedIn profile is an extension of your corporate persona so simple errors could damage your authority, reputation and appeal. This also extends to checking your profile thoroughly to ensure what you are saying is effectively and clearly communicated to the reader and the layout is visual appealing with short sharp paragraphs. It is beneficial to ask someone external to read through your profile to check for mistakes and also to see whether they understand clearly all what you are saying within your profile.

Do Not Lie About Anything

In an age where it is easy to check information on the internet such as your education or job experience it is neither worthwhile nor appropriate to lie within your profile. In doing so you risk a very public 'outing' if you are found out that instantly makes you look unprofessional and untrustworthy which will likely affect your potential for future business.

Utilise LinkedIn Badges on Your Website

LinkedIn has available several types of profile badges that can help you promote your LinkedIn profile. By using the HTML code you can attach a badge to your blog, website or any other forums you are active on and when users click on these badges, they'll be automatically directed to your LinkedIn profile, helping you expand your connections.

Personalise Your LinkedIn Connection Requests

When attempting to make a connection with a fellow professional, always tailor and personalise your request email rather than using the default message. Personalising the message makes it look as if you have made the extra effort to connect and as such you reduce the risk of those people ignoring you who will automatically do so when they see the default message appear. Review LinkedIn's suggested connections at least a few times a week and make it a goal to find people in your industry or niche and personally connect with them, aiming to connect with two or three people each time. When you send a connection request, personalise it in some way for that individual person as doing so will increase the chance that they will approve your request and give you a better shot at landing a new connection.

Leverage LinkedIn Applications

LinkedIn has several applications which you can use to enhance your profile. Examples include the WordPress app which lets you sync blog posts with your LinkedIn profile or the SlideShare application that enables you to embed videos in your profile. The aim on LinkedIn is to create the most eye-catching profile so adding relevant applications that help you show your skills off is going to help you attract attention.

Keep Your LinkedIn Profile Up to Date

Make sure at least once every 3 months you assess and update your LinkedIn Profile. Check all information is still relevant and correct and remember to always update your profile every time you receive an award, achievement or any other relevant information.

Synchronise Your LinkedIn Profile and CV

Take the extra time to be sure that extracts from your professional CV match perfectly with the information shown on LinkedIn's Experience section. This is for consistency but also avoids the potential embarrassment of getting tripped up in an interview or when meeting with a potential client when it is discovered that what you claim on your CV does not match up with your LinkedIn Profile.

Keep It Professional at All Times

LinkedIn is considered the most professional social media platform therefore it is expected that you conduct yourself professionally when you are interacting with others and sharing updates. Before you post a comment or share something remember that you are representing yourself in a business environment so if it isn't relevant or could cause offence do not risk your reputation and post it.

Turn Off Notifications When Updating Your Profile

When you are updating your profile with a lot of changes remember to temporarily disable notifications. The reason for this is it can become quite annoying for your connections to receive a stream of updates in a short period of time as you change and update your profile.

Regularly Connect with Your Connections

Once you have a new connection don't simply forget about them, make an effort to reach out and create and maintain a new relationship. This can be as simple as leaving a positive comment on their update or sending them a link to some information they might find useful. Not only is this polite and shows you are genuinely interested in maintaining your connections, it also makes yourself active in their mind and so they may instantly think of you for new business opportunities that arrive.

Introduce Your Connections to One Another

If you have a connection that could provide value or be a useful contact for one of your other connections, then introduce them to one another. This is a great way for you to develop relationships and gain referrals for yourself.

Connect Offline

With so much networking and interacting conducted over the internet, it's easy to get used to only interacting with others online and forget that the people we're connecting with are not just a name and picture on our screen, they actually exist in the 'real' world. Online conversations however are not sufficient enough on their own to truly build relationships, networks and to get results. Rather, you need to make sure you get the most out of your new connections and make a good impression by putting in an effort to meet offline and talk with and meet the people who you've connected with.

Utilise LinkedIn Sponsored Updates

Using Sponsored updates is a way of putting your content in front of key influencers and audiences on LinkedIn, ultimately helping you to build your credibility as an expert in your industry and helping you gain more exposure to those people who are not in your network. With sponsored updates you have the ability to narrowly limit the audience for your update by targeting your update by location, company

category, job title, schools attended, LinkedIn groups and more. The comprehensive analytics that are provided also lets you determine just how effective your paid updates are, allowing to you make the most of your investment. The Metrics you are able to analyse range from Impressions, total spent, Clicks, to CTR (click-through rate) and CPC (cost per click). You also have the very useful ability to compare the effectiveness of your sponsored against non-sponsored updates on your company page's analytics page. Metrics that you can track here range from the level of Interactions, Impressions, Clicks and Engagement. Looking at which can help you determine the rate at which your sponsored updates perform than your non-sponsored updates. The key to remember with sponsored updates however is that you need to sponsor posts that are highly valuable, engaging and informative to your target audience, to ensure you have a positive return on investment and help establish yourself and business as a leading thought expert in your industry.

Offer Value in Discussion Groups

Being a member of relevant groups on LinkedIn allows you to interact with and participate in relevant discussions with other members who are in your industry or are of interest all within in a professional setting. LinkedIn discussion groups provide a valuable opportunity for marketers to establish themselves as thought leaders, learn more about their community and target audience and not to mention helping to generate leads. Make it a priority to stay active and contribute regularly in order to enrich discussions with valuable, informative and engaging content that engages and targets your audience's needs. In doing so you help establish yourself as a valued and trusted source of information to your industry, help foster new connections, learn new and relevant news and could ultimately lead to new business opportunities.

Focus on Developing Relationships Rather Than Adding Connections

You will get a lot more out of LinkedIn if you start to periodically reach out to your connections in your personal network in order to get to know them better and importantly develop relationships. Look to collaborate and share information with them, talk to and learn about them and their skill set/knowledge and ask questions to generally get to know them. The reasoning behind developing relationships is that once you both develop a bond and trust element between each other you become a trusted advisor to one other making it more likely that if an opportunity presents itself where you can help one another, recommend the others product or service you're the first person they turn to. From your point of view, you have a specialist in an area to answer your questions on a topic, provide potential business opportunities to or to collaborate with on projects and in turn, you become the same for your connections. Ultimately, treating each individual as a human and getting to know them can develop into something greater from simply a new friendship, collaboration to even new business.

Don't Treat LinkedIn as an Online Version of Your CV

Whilst LinkedIn is a platform for showcasing you and your skillset, you should not treat it like an online version of your CV. Instead of creating your profile in the bog-standard format of talking about yourself

in a general sense like 'here is where I went to school' 'this is the business I work for' 'this is what I do for a job' etc. Look to instead craft your entire profile in way that clearly and concisely addresses, targets and fixes your target audience's needs, making them have to take notice of you and is compelling enough to get the point across of why no one else but you can be the saviour to their problems/needs. For example in the job section don't just simply state what you do in a generic sense, mould your answer to your specific target audience and instead write your section in the format of "I help [Insert Target Audience] achieve [Insert Their Desired Outcome] by providing [list product, skills and/or services you offer]."

Post Status Updates Daily

It's important to be active on LinkedIn, and that starts with posting status updates every day. Think of your LinkedIn updates the same way as any social media post. Make sure they add value, talk about your business and include a call to action. When you consistently stay in the feeds of your connections, there's more opportunity for them to comment, like and share your posts. This interaction gets you introduced to their connections and gives you one more way to grow your network. When people are sharing and commenting on your stuff, it's social proof that you're an expert in your field.

Engage With Your Connections' Updates

Review your wall regularly and share, comment on and like other people's updates and long-form posts. Start relationships with new connections by commenting on their updates. Build an audience by joining the conversation on popular posts in your niche. This interaction lets people know you exist and gives you more visibility. Some of these people are likely to want to know more about you, leading to new connections.

Leverage Local Networking Groups

If you belong to a local networking group, look through your membership directory and send LinkedIn connection requests to individual members. Even if you don't remember meeting someone in person, use your shared real-world connection to personalize your connection request and start to get to know that person online. For example, you could say something like "We're both members of (local group name), and I would love to connect here, too." Then head to your next networking meeting newly armed with great networking info. Search for local group members in LinkedIn groups. You may find them there, too.

Post Content and Develop Authority With LinkedIn's Publishing Platform

LinkedIn has a publishing platform that is a great, powerful tool to help you publish professional, attractive looking posts (three posts are displayed with images at the top of your profile page) and help you build momentum and establish yourself as a thought leader in your industry or niche. One of the key benefits of the publishing platform is that your posts are seen by the entire LinkedIn community, not just

your connections. Getting noticed by this broader audience will help you build your network, increasing your exposure. Those who normally wouldn't see your profile in search results will now have a chance to find out what you do and how you can help them. Keep your content fresh and current by making sure you publish at least a few times a month. Write articles about your own business and industry expertise or career experiences to differentiate yourself and stand out. Share your unique perspective and insights. The frequency of your posts will also make a difference in growing your visibility, reach and engagement. To see the best results, make a commitment to publishing content consistently on LinkedIn's platform.

Here are four reasons to jump on the LinkedIn publishing platform:

- ✓ Position yourself as an industry expert. Sharing how you think and providing insights and guidance through your LinkedIn posts can position you as the go-to expert in your industry.
- ✓ Increase your reach. As you publish more posts on LinkedIn, you will earn more followers (which are different from connections). Your followers can see your published posts and share with their respective networks.
- ✓ Give you SEO a Boost. Your LinkedIn posts will also be indexed by Google search and can be discovered across the social web outside of LinkedIn as well.
- ✓ Generate new leads. In every LinkedIn post you publish, include a simple call to action either within the post or at the end in your bio section.

Learn Valuable Info From LinkedIn Publisher Stats

The new LinkedIn Publisher stats offer amazing insight into very useful information such as how many people are viewing each post, reader demographics, the top four industries, job titles, locations and traffic sources that showed interest in your posts and the people who engage with your posts. You can also see who engaged with your posts by liking or commenting on them, which includes people you are not directly connected to so it makes it an excellent opportunity to find potential prospects or partners.

To see your stats, go to the Who's Viewed Your Posts tab, which is located under Profile in the main navigation under Who's Viewed Your Profile. Click on any post to see a graph that shows the number of views by the last 7 days, 15 days, 30 days, 6 months or 1 year. Regularly review these numbers, as well as the elements of the posts themselves, to see patterns that will tell you what topics, format and length your readers are most interested in.

Market Smart

They key to success on LinkedIn is to consistently market smart. Here is a simple but very effective 3-point plan to boost your build authority and trust and see your leads skyrocket. It's a simple as researching and engaging with new users and groups before reaching out directly with appropriate and targeted content. When you do reach out and post something, you need to ask yourself when crafting your post: "Why am I doing this post, who benefits and what would I like them to do next?"

- Research, find and join relevant groups in your niche.

- Join the conversation. Engage with posts and comment with useful insights and note what's trending/popular.
- Reach out directly and connect with new people via profile email or InMail. Share valuable, engaging and useful articles and insights. Create content that you can also place on your blog, video channel, podcast or in a LinkedIn post. Where possible, drive your visitor back to your preferred online asset. (Website, eBook, landing page etc.)

Common Mistakes to Avoid

Listing Skills that LinkedIn Doesn't Recognise

When you start typing a skill on your LinkedIn profile, make sure it appears in the dropdown menu. If it doesn't it is not a frequently searched item so make sure you stick to the thousands of skills LinkedIn already has in the system and your profile will pop up more often in search results.

Not Personalising Your LinkedIn Public Profile URL

Many people leave the default mess of letters and numbers at the end of the URL. You need to change this to your name or as close as it you can come to it as it will make you appear more professional and enhance your personal brand.

Having No Photo or An Inappropriate Photo

One of the biggest mistakes on a LinkedIn profile is to not use a photo or using one that is inappropriate. LinkedIn is a professional networking site so your photo should reflect your general industry and your personal professionalism. Ensure your picture is representative of you by being up to date, clear and good quality. Never make the mistake of failing to use a photo at all as this can easily lead to missed connections.

Sending Spammy Messages and Over Posting

Remember to always share updates in the mind frame of helping and providing value to others. This means avoiding posting spammy and self-serving messages to your connections and especially not posting high quantities of updates a day.

Asking For or Giving People You Don't Know Recommendations

You should never ask for a recommendation or give one to someone that you don't know and can't personally vouch for. The reason being that if you give someone a recommendation that is actually a poor worker then it reflects badly on you for recommending them to others, similarly if someone gives you a recommendation that has a poor reputation this also will appear negatively on you.

Criticising and Commenting Negatively In Groups

LinkedIn groups are a great place to make new connections and interact professionally with others, however if you act negatively posting rude, critical or offensive comments you harm your reputation and will miss out on potential business opportunities.

Posting Self-Serving Content in Your Groups

LinkedIn Groups are to be used to share relevant, informative and interesting updates to other members, not for spamming your self-serving content. If you have a genuine piece of information that you know other members will find useful but is self-promoting in some way then you need to craft it in a way that ensures that the aim of the content is to provide value first.

Asking New Connections or People You Don't Know To Endorse You

It is very easy to give and receive endorsements from others on LinkedIn without thought and this is primarily why endorsements do not hold as much respect as recommendations do. So do not be tempted to go and endorse as many connections as possible in the hope that they return them to you. Rather only endorse those you can personally vouch for and preferably create a personal recommendation.

Treating LinkedIn Like Other Social Media Platforms

LinkedIn etiquette is very different from other social media platforms such as Facebook and Twitter. It is widely accepted that LinkedIn is the most professional platform and as such you need to act as though you are a professional environment. This does not mean that you shouldn't show a personality; rather just remember who your audience is as they are not likely to receive a meme of a cat for example in the same way as an audience on Facebook will.

Not Including Past Jobs or Volunteer Work

Your profile needs to be a robust and complete picture of you in a professional setting, so even if you have changed fields you still need to include past examples of your work and the skills you acquired whilst there as it all works together to create an account of you and your skills. Similarly volunteering

work can tell a potential employer or business prospect a lot about you as a person, your interests and what extra skills you have acquired outside of work so it is important that you include it within your profile taking care to elaborating on tasks you completed and skills acquired.

Lurking

Many people set up a profile and assume that is enough to get you noticed. Rather, to truly get the most out of LinkedIn you need to make a conscious effort to be active in your groups, share content that engages your connections and maintain an up to date profile.

Not Utilising LinkedIn Groups

LinkedIn groups are a great resource for building your knowledge base and connecting with individuals in similar industries. There is much to gain in terms of knowledge development, new connections and business opportunities by joining and being an active member of LinkedIn Groups, so make the effort to join groups that are relevant to you and your interests so you don't miss out on these important benefits.

Not Making Sure Your Profile is 100% Complete

Always make sure that your profile is 100% completed. If you fail to do so you will not only be harder to find on LinkedIn, you could potentially miss out on business opportunities and connections the result of which means you don't get the full benefit of being on the network.

Never Modifying Your Profile

You should always pay attention to the numbers at which people view your profile and how often you come up in search as if these numbers are low it shows you that you need to recapture the attention of others. You can do this by potentially updating your titles and your headline and revitalising your descriptions every so often to try and attract attention and capture additional search traffic.

Not Knowing the Difference Between a LinkedIn Profile and a LinkedIn Company Page

There are two ways you can choose to have a presence on LinkedIn as a business owner. If you choose to create a company page you will be communicating as your business to others that have chosen to follow you and get updates from you to learn more about your business. With a LinkedIn Profile you will be communicating as an individual rather than as a business, allowing you to connect with clients, colleagues, and other members of your professional network.

Not Being Selective About the Connections You Accept

The people who you have connected with on LinkedIn are a representation of you and shows to others the kind of professionals you associate with. From this it is important not to just accept and connect with anyone just to appear more popular, instead look to connect with people you can genuinely learn from or be a benefit to and make sure you know who they are and what their credentials are.

Not Sharing a Variety of Rich Media in Your Posts

It is critical to embrace the visual and be creative with the updates you share by posting a variety of content types such as videos, infographics and SlideShare documents to engage and interest your connections. If you post unappealing, self-promoting content continually you will not attract the critical attention you need from others and will inevitably damage your reputation.

Not Promoting Your Profile to Others

You could have put together the perfect LinkedIn profile but if you fail to tell others about it then you miss out on connecting with new prospects. So remember to promote your profile across all other social media including a badge on your website, putting a URL on business literature and packaging and including it on your e-newsletter and email signature.

Not Considering Your Search Optimisation (SEO) Efforts

You need to consciously optimise your profile for SEO looking to at the very least have a completed profile and strategically place keywords throughout your profile. If you neglect your efforts and your profile is not SEO friendly then you risk losing crucial visibility and being highly ranked in search and seen by others.

Measuring Success

Like any other marketing strategy, the success of your LinkedIn profile must be measured against your business objectives. Analysing your LinkedIn metrics will show you a wealth of information and insights and help determine whether your profile is having a measurable impact and whether the data is reflective of the overall goals of your LinkedIn profile page.

LinkedIn Profile Views

LinkedIn will provide you with the number of people who have accessed your LinkedIn profile in the last week. Looking at these stats will give you a good idea as to whether you are growing your LinkedIn presence.

Your Network Size or Total Connections

You are only as visible as the size of your network, so having a large number of valuable connections is a good indication that you are expanding your influence and visibility on LinkedIn.

Level of New Invitations

Counting the amount of new invitations is a good way of tracking that your network is continuing to grow. If you get a good level of new invitations every week then you know that you are growing your influence and potential value from your LinkedIn efforts.

Level of Interactions on Updates

Posting regular and valuable updates is a great way to build a presence and looking at the level of interaction your posts generate, is a good indication that readers are finding your posts insightful and are engaged with what you have to say. Potential employers and businesses looking to connect will search for influential people in their industry and the level of interactions is a good measure of such influence.

Total Number of Recommendations

When a member of your network recommends you, this acts as a confirmation that the skills you claim you have are genuine. Recommendations from colleagues, business partners and satisfied clients go a long way in the eyes of potential customers and business connections so having a large number of genuine recommendations is a good indication that you are establishing your value and credibility.

Number of Business Leads

If you are on LinkedIn to generate new business, then measuring the number and quality of leads generated is essential. Keep track of how may requests for business you have had and make sure you establish the value and quality of these requests.

LinkedIn Maintenance Checklist

DAILY

- Share a status update with relevant business content
- Check and respond to any messages, invitations, notifications and respond where appropriate
- Engage with and add your thoughts to relevant discussions in your groups
- Send at least 5 new connection requests a day by looking for other members in your groups and the 'people you may know' section. Ideally, tailor your 'invitation to connect' message
- Go through news feed and get updated on news and insights and add your thoughts and comments to any relevant discussions
- Review what your connections are up to or sharing on the activity feed and interact. This can create an opportunity to start a conversation and strengthen a connection., whether congratulating someone on a promotion or commenting on a link they've posted,
- Review new recommendations.
- Check out who viewed your profile. This is a great way to get intelligence on who is out there – including possible new connections.

WEEKLY

- If you blog, post your blog post in relevant LinkedIn groups
- Look to see if any new connections from other social media platforms have LinkedIn and connect with them
- Actively look for relevant groups you can join
- Follow 3 new companies
- Ask for 1-2 recommendations per week
- Connect with 2-5 new people per week
- Regularly include your LinkedIn URL everywhere you insert your contact information (i.e., email signatures, marketing collateral, business cards, etc.)
- Create/Import at least 2 relevant blog posts (via RSS feed) into the News section of your groups and ask for feedback
- Spend 10 minutes reviewing discussions on your most relevant groups
- Promote your Groups online at least once per week
- Invite 1-3 co-workers, colleagues, and customers to join and start discussions in your groups
- Regularly monitor the Q&A section for questions you are uniquely qualified to answer

LINKEDIN (FOR BUSINESS USE)

Creating a LinkedIn company page can bring a wealth of benefits to your business. At a basic level, you can use this platform to educate others of the basics of your business and operations. However you can take your LinkedIn marketing to the next level by utilising the many features LinkedIn offers for companies, in raising brand awareness, promoting career opportunities and the ability to showcase products and services to your potential customers. Whether you're just starting your business or already deeply establishes, LinkedIn is a trusted network by small businesses, so don't miss out on the ample opportunities it has to offer you and your business.

Why LinkedIn Company Pages?

LinkedIn company pages, when done well, can be an important tool for increasing brand awareness and developing yourself as a thought leader through regular engagement with followers and through sharing rich, quality updates. Not only can it be an essential tool for brand visibility, but you are also presented with an invaluable opportunity to tap into a rich network of professionals in your industry that you can develop into a community who can be a captive audience for your business messages.

LinkedIn Pages empower your organization to engage the world's professional community;

- ✓ Engage your people and join the conversations that matter
- ✓ Post and respond on the go with the LinkedIn mobile app
- ✓ Share PowerPoints, PDFs and Word Docs
- ✓ Associate your Page to trending hashtags
- ✓ Discover content trending with your target audience
- ✓ Monitor activity with visual analytics
- ✓ Drive specific actions with a customizable call-to-action button
- ✓ Re-share your employees' best LinkedIn posts
- ✓ Re-share member posts that mention your company

Free Marketing

Think of your LinkedIn company page as a free and effective marketing tool that's used to drive people to your site. You are presented with a great opportunity to connect with potential customers, increase brand awareness, and establish yourself as an industry influencer through the content you post. An added benefit of having a LinkedIn company page is that through the use of strategically placed keywords, you can use your page to boost your presence in search engine results.

LinkedIn's Hiring Capabilities

The biggest mistake a small business can make is not taking advantage of LinkedIn's free small business offerings. If you're trying to attract potential candidates, LinkedIn is the first place where all the top talent will be looking. When you're actively hiring, LinkedIn allows you to publish job postings, as well as the ability to use LinkedIn's search to find potential candidates. By proactively searching you'll be able to find candidates that fit your hiring needs, reach out to them directly, and drive them to your job posting.

Still not convinced? Here are 8 more reasons why you need a LinkedIn company page

- ✓ Allows you to showcase your brand in a professional capacity
- ✓ Allows you to directly reach out to other professionals in your industry
- ✓ Is an invaluable resource for finding and recruiting employees
- ✓ Allows you to secure recommendations and endorsements of your brand
- ✓ Provides groups that you can use for research, networking and more
- ✓ Helps to amplify your brand to potential business partners and customers.
- ✓ Helps you to build up trust and authority in your niche
- ✓ Allows you to leverage your employees with professional profiles

Need to Know Facts, Stats and Tips about LinkedIn Company Pages

- 57% of companies have a LinkedIn Company Page.
- 50% of B2B buyers use LinkedIn when making purchasing decisions.
- LinkedIn is the most-used social media platform amongst Fortune 500 companies.
- LinkedIn is the #1 channel B2B marketers use to distribute content at 94%.
- LinkedIn makes up more than 50% of all social traffic to B2B websites & blogs.
- 91% of marketing executives list LinkedIn as the top place to find quality content.
- 92% of B2B marketers include LinkedIn in their digital marketing mix.
- 59% of B2B marketers say LinkedIn generates leads for their business.
- 38% of B2B marketers say LinkedIn is generating revenue for them. More than 1 in 3 B2B marketers say LinkedIn generates revenue for their business. That's 3x more than Twitter, 4x more than Facebook & 19x more than Instagram.
- 46% of social traffic to corporate websites comes from LinkedIn.
- 65% of B2B companies have acquired a customer through LinkedIn.
- Only 0.59% of posts from B2B marketers come from company pages, but over 10% of leads generated come from them.
- 1 out of every 3 LinkedIn group posts that converted included a question mark in the subject line.
- The average length of a post that converts is 248 characters.
- The use of LinkedIn company pages grew from 24% in 2015 to 57% in 2016.

Who Should have a LinkedIn Company Page?

LinkedIn is not only a resource for companies in B2B industries. Provided that the platform is approached and managed in the right way, many small businesses can profit from having an active LinkedIn profile, whether it's to find prospective employees or to forge new connections.

Setting Up Your LinkedIn Company Page and Getting to Grips with The Basic Lingo

Setting up a company page on LinkedIn is a similar process to creating a business page on other social networks, the difference being that a more professional approach to its content and available assets is important. After all, your LinkedIn marketing goals, and therefore the way in which you develop your presence, should be to attract other professionals including industry leaders, potential employees, partners and more serious customers.

You'll need a standard user account in addition to having already made some business connections on LinkedIn, before you can create a company page. Once you have the necessary prerequisites, you'll be able to find the Companies option in the 'Interests' menu at the top of your LinkedIn homepage. In the next step, you'll need to provide your company name and email address. Once you have verified your email address, you'll need to add a short description of your company and its mission as well as a logo and banner image with 646 by 220 pixels of space to work with.

Understanding the Basics

LinkedIn isn't tended to be used by people as intensively as is the case with Facebook or Twitter. LinkedIn's features and abilities are more reflective of a professional following, and as such businesses should take advantage of this.

Connections: While Facebook has 'likes' and Twitter has 'followers', LinkedIn has 'connections'. LinkedIn aims to enforce strict rules governing how you can build up the number of connections to your company page, recommending that you only invite people that you know personally, not at the very least because they will have access to the email address that you provided when signing up. When you invite someone to join your network, they will become a first-degree connection, while those who are connected to your connections are described as second-degree connections.

Groups: LinkedIn provides a groups area in which professionals can collectively join and share relevant content and establish meaningful relationships with one another in a professional capacity. Groups can be formed around individual brands, support groups, causes, publications, skills or industries. With almost 2 million groups on LinkedIn, there will likely be many groups that you take an active interest in and join. Likewise, you can also create your own groups.

Recruitment: LinkedIn provides a range of job search and recruitment features, and thanks to the network's high credibility and ease of use, many businesses are encouraging prospective employees to reach out to companies using the network.

An Introduction to Paid Advertising on LinkedIn

LinkedIn's various paid advertising opportunities often get overlooked but provide some of the best targeting options of any paid online advertising solution. Paid advertising with LinkedIn works in much the same way as it does with Facebook or Google AdWords, its uniqueness lies in its ability for a greater focus on targeting a professional audience. With LinkedIn's advertising options you'll be able to target a very specific and relevant audience by choosing from a range of options based on the professional information included in their profiles, such as job titles, skills, interests and employers.

You can create paid advertisements through the Campaign Manager section of your account. There are two options available: An ad featuring text, image or video content that will reach a targeted audience, or you can sponsor one of your existing posts to reach a wider audience in a similar manner to Twitter's Promoted Tweets feature.

When creating a targeted ad, you are provided with a wide range of targeting options, affording you a far greater degree of control over most other paid advertising platforms online. Therefore you will need to have a thorough understanding of your target audience as the extensive range of advanced options allow you to specify everything from the type of skill to the age group of your target audience, With targeted ads, you'll also be able to choose from two pricing models: pay-per-click or pay-per-impression. You also have the ability to set a minimum daily budget, though it is advisable to set your budget high enough for at least 100 clicks per day.

LinkedIn offers several different self-service advertising solutions. Here's a quick overview:

- **Sponsored content:** is a LinkedIn Page update that is promoted to a broader audience in the LinkedIn newsfeed across both desktop and mobile, helping you raise awareness, build relationships, and drive quality leads.
- **Text Ads:** These are pay-per-click or CPM ads that appear on the LinkedIn homepage, profile pages, Groups pages, search results pages, and more.
- **Sponsored InMail:** Similar to email marketing, but within the LinkedIn ecosystem. Sponsored InMail allows you to send personalized ads to LinkedIn members' inboxes. Messages are only delivered when members are active on LinkedIn, making them likely to be noticed.

TOP TIP: Combining two different methods of advertising on LinkedIn will help create a sales funnel to guide your customer along the way.

Sponsored Content Tips

- Write ad headlines that are under 150 characters. Concise headlines lead to more engagement.
- Keep descriptive copy under 70 characters.
- Embed larger images instead of standard thumbnails. An image size of 1200 x 627 pixels is recommended. Content with larger visuals tend to get up to 38% higher CTR (click-through rates).
- Feature a clear CTA (call to action), so your audience knows how to act on their interest.
- Be specific with ad targeting, but not so specific that you narrow your audience.
- Analyse industry news instead of just sharing it. This will keep your content from feeling generic and help establish thought leadership in your field.
- Use rich media (like video, audio, or other element) by incorporating YouTube, Vimeo, and SlideShare videos. They play right in the LinkedIn feed, so your audience can engage organically.
- Include human interest stories that connect to your brand, and you will help your audience establish an emotional connection.
- Every 1-2 weeks, pause the ad with the lowest engagement and replace it with new ad creative. Over time, this will improve your ad relevance score.
- Install the LinkedIn Insight Tag on your website, so you can track conversions and enable demographic reporting on your website visitors.

Sponsored InMail tips

- Keep your message concise. Body text under 500 characters has a 46% higher CTR (click-through rate).
- Be personal and relevant. Sponsored InMail allows you to add macros such as first name to personalize your message to each recipient.
- Make your message interactive by adding hyperlinks. Messages with links in the body text have been shown to lift CTR by 21%.
- Use friendly, low-pressure language in your CTA. The top 5 performing CTAs for Sponsored InMail are: Try, Free, Today, Click and Apply.
- Try CTAs that are 1 or 3 words. These word lengths for CTA buttons show a 13% higher CTR.

Questions to Ask Before You Get Started Using LinkedIn for Business

Who is Going to Set up and Maintain my Business Page?

Before you begin, you need to have a clear idea of who is going to be creating and maintaining your LinkedIn business page. Whether you assign the role to an existing member of staff or hire an external social media manager you need to ensure that the person that will be in charge of representing your business on LinkedIn is capable, with the knowledge and experience of how to successfully utilise LinkedIn and ultimately make it a successful addition to your marketing strategy.

How Should I Portray my Business?

Like with any other public platform you need to consider how you are going to portray your business to others and how you are going to link it with your other marketing efforts. As part of this consideration you will need to address areas such as how you are going to tie your branding to the overall typography and visual aspects of the page to what type of voice you want to portray within your status updates and of course what your overall objectives are for the page. Making sure your business is presented in a representative and appealing way is crucial so you need to ensure you have a clear understanding of how you want your business to appear to your audience and how and what you can utilise to help you achieve it.

What Images and Resources can I Utilise?

LinkedIn allows you opportunities to utilise the visual on your page. From the large cover image to allowing a variety of content types to be shared within updates, it is vital that you pull your resources and utilise these areas to help make your business inform, engage and stand out from the crowd. So look to see what visual aspects of LinkedIn you can use to your advantage, remembering to choose attention-grabbing images that reflect your brand and draws people in to learn more about your business. You also could and should explore the use of different types of content within your updates, from podcasts to eBooks and using brand videos. Mixing up the types of content you share grabs attention and keeps people engaged so pull the resources you have at your disposal, from customer testimonials, product demonstrations videos, to webinar footage and behind-the-scenes pictures and share them with your audience.

Have I Got a Clear Content Strategy in Place?

Posting status updates lets you reach out to and share news with LinkedIn members who have chosen to follow your business page. From this you need to utilise this connection and form a content strategy that provides value to and resonates with your target audience. You will come to learn what content formats they prefer, what content they interact with most, at what times and how many updates you need to post daily or weekly to maximise effectiveness. Just remember to always share content that is going to entertain, inform and be relevant to your audience and you are likely to be rewarded with engagement and a two-way conversation with your followers that can create business opportunities, help you learn more about your customers' needs and other beneficial information that can aid your business in the future.

How am I Going to Promote my Page?

You need to consider how you are going to let others know about your page which will involve utilising opportunities both online and offline. Online you can use a variety of methods from using your other social media platforms to encourage others to visit your page, to adding a LinkedIn "follow" button to your business website and putting your company page's URL email signature and your e-newsletters. You can also encourage your employees to create their own LinkedIn profiles and ask them to interact

with your business page by sharing statuses and directing connections to the page. Offline you can verbally tell others of your page in any conferences, meetings in addition to putting the URL on your business card, packing and anywhere else your customers/ prospects will see it.

How am I Going to Measure the Success of my Page?

How you define the success of you page will depend on what your overall objectives are for your page. LinkedIn provides a range of analytics that show everything from who's visiting your page to what types of content they click on, like and share and at what rates so remember to continually analyse these analytics to see whether you are meeting your objectives for you page and what if any areas are in need of improvement and revaluation.

How to Build a Branded LinkedIn Company Page that Gets You Noticed

Your Company Page serves as the foundation of your business's presence on LinkedIn making it crucial that you develop and utilise this platform and its features in order to enhance your marketing, brand awareness and hiring and recruiting efforts.

Know Your Audience/Competitors
Thoroughly researching both your target audience and your competition on LinkedIn are crucial as they will help inform and dictate how you position your page. One of the first things you must do before you form your company page is to understand the audience you are trying to target, finding out important factors such as where they spend their time online, how they like to digest content and other important general demographics. The same level of research also needs to be applied to your competition. Look to find out what is and isn't working for your competition on LinkedIn, in what areas they perform well and where they don't so you can then apply the lessons learnt to your own strategy.

Establish Your Presence
Essentially, your company page acts as a central informational hub for visitors looking to learn more about your business. Creating a page is simple, to get started you just add your business logo, a banner image, description, specialties, industry, website, amongst other important aspects that help tell you and your brand story. The more difficult but highly important part of creating your page is the consideration you need to direct towards you're your SEO efforts and writing with language that will attract and target the audience that you want. In terms of SEO, LinkedIn itself is very SEO friendly and there are plenty of opportunities to insert keywords throughout your page. Enhancing your SEO and indeed attracting the right audience however is very much dictated by the language and keywords that you use throughout your page. Therefore it is fundamental that you use rich, descriptive language

embedded with powerful, keyword-rich phrases that clearly and concisely tells your readers who you are, what your visions are, your purpose, expertise and the skills/value that you offer.

Foster Relationships

LinkedIn provides businesses with a platform to reach the world's largest professional community. Whilst members are primarily there to discuss business, recruit new hires and inform others on products and services, the real value to businesses lies in using LinkedIn to foster relationships and working on interacting and engaging others in the community. Businesses that genuinely seek to get to know their audiences and provide valuable, informative and engaging content outperform those that seek to sell and broadcast to others.

Attract followers

After you have established and optimised your business presence on LinkedIn, you need to start attracting an audience. There are several simple and effective strategies to ensure your page is perfectly optimized to be findable and attractive to your target audience.

- ✓ **Get your staff and colleagues engaged on your page** – Announce to your employees that you now have a LinkedIn company page and if they have LinkedIn themselves, to engage with and share your Company Updates. To amplify your efforts you can also encourage them to add a link to your Company Page to their email signatures.
- ✓ **Tell your customers and business partners about your page** – Once you have created and optimised your page you can utilise your existing contacts and drive traffic to your page by announcing your page in a compelling blog post, newsletter or email announcement.
- ✓ **Add a "Follow" button to your website** – On LinkedIn's website developer.linkedin.com there is a host of widgets that you can assess and use to enhance your LinkedIn marketing. A popular and effective strategy is to implement the "Follow" button on your blog or website to attract the traffic from those sites and compel them to follow your company page easily with a single click.

Engage Followers and Share Great Content

If you have positioned and developed your page effectively, people will follow your company page as a way to engage and interact with you. Whilst LinkedIn is a professional space, you still need to realise it is a social network so actively and regularly facilitate that engagement by making the effort to communicate with your followers through asking questions, replying to comments, providing valuable updates and other engagement strategies. One of the most effective and important ways of creating relationships and engaging your followers is to encourage conversation, with your Company update being the perfect tool for starting those conversations.

Essentially, LinkedIn members want content that is valuable, informative, insightful and encourages engagement. As such every status update you post should embody these characteristics.

LinkedIn currently provides four ways to launch your social media updates:

- Status Update
- Link Share
- Photo Upload
- Video Link Share

✓ **Don't be sales-y**: Overly promotional content with heavy emphasis on product promotion is not received well on LinkedIn. You can post business-related news or product announcements but you must make sure they are delivered in a way that provides value and has a specific benefit to your followers.

✓ **Post Once per Weekday**: Developing a consistent posting schedule encourages engagement, fosters familiarity and through providing valuable content regularly you can help develop yourself as an authority within your sector.

✓ **Post at Optimal Times**: Generally updates posted are most effective during the common business hours of 9-5. However you should experiment to see what works best for your company.

✓ **Include Links to Great Content**: Company updates that contain links have been found to have up to 45 percent higher follower engagement than updates without links. Therefore ensure you share links to great and informative content and remember to write a compelling sentence to describe and accompany the link to encourage members to click through.

✓ **Tailor your Content to Specific Audiences**: Content that is customised and targeted to a follower's interests and needs is going to resonate best with them so ensure you write your updates with your target audience in mind. You can take your targeting further by using LinkedIn's Targeted Updates that allows you to match your message to an audience effectively. Targeted updates are a feature to help you promote content more effectively. After you have created a status update you can choose whether to share it with all your followers or a targeted audience that you can dictate based on geography, job, industry, company size amongst other factors.

✓ **Provide Content That Solves Problems for Your Audience:** LinkedIn offers you the opportunity to enhance your updates with rich content. Therefore you should utilise this and team it with providing expert content that solves problems for your audience. From white papers, videos, how-tos, to blogposts and case studies, you can share a whole host of rich content to inform your audience. The savvy business will also put consideration into their SEO effort by include SEO-rich keywords throughout the content updates as this will add to the findability of your page when members search for keywords and will also help in your general SEO efforts since company pages are extremely SEO-friendly.

✓ **Ask Questions**: to amplify your efforts you need to encourage engagement with your followers and the best way to do that is to ask questions to your audience and let them have their say as on average, status updates that contain questions receive almost 50 percent more comments. They will embrace to chance to have their voice heard and to respond to questions about industry trends, their views on business developments, new products/services and more which not only benefits your brand awareness but you also get to know more about your audience

- **Respond to Comments**: Your input doesn't end after you have clicked post on your status update, rather, you need to then respond efficiently and in a way that shows of your excellent customer service skills to the conversations that develop from your status update.
- **Listen to Conversations Outside of LinkedIn to Help Create Content**: By listening to relevant conversations outside of your LinkedIn page on your blog posts, forums etc. you are able to collect findings that show what types of content that are most popular and resonate best with your audience, which you can then take and apply to your own LinkedIn content marketing efforts. By posting content that directly addresses your audience's interests and solves their problems your followers will find your updates interesting and hopefully share them within their own personal networks, which goes a long way in attracting an audience and establishing yourself as a thought leader within your community.
- **The Most in-Demand Content is Industry Insights:** According to numbers from LinkedIn, 6 out of every 10 LinkedIn users are interested in industry insights—the most-demanded type of content among LinkedIn members. Second to industry insight, company news which appeals to 53 percent of LinkedIn members. New products and services are the third most popular content, with 43 percent interested in this kind of update. From this, you need to always strive to share your informative expertise, be helpful and transparent when you post and you will appeal to the majority of your audience and meet the expectations your audience expect from you when they followed you on LinkedIn.
- **Help your Employees Help You:** Engagement on your profile can be a big help to those who happen to stop by, and it turns out that your own employees could be Employees are 70 percent more likely to click, share, and comment on an update than a typical LinkedIn user. Making them a great asset to build engagement on your page. From this, you need to take advantage of this and make it easy for employees to engage with your content. Send notifications and links every time you post or when particularly important updates go live and ask them for engagement.

- **Share Links for Engagement and Share Images for More Comments:** A study by QuickSprout found that including a link in your LinkedIn posts drives 200% more engagement. That same study also revealed that posting images on LinkedIn results in 98% higher comment rate.
- **Keep Link Titles <70 Characters**: When you're uploading these engagement-driving links directly to your LinkedIn Company Page, if the original post has a lengthy title, be sure to click into the title to edit it. Any title above 70 characters gets cut off when posted on your Page.
- **Keep Link Descriptions <250 characters**: The description associated with your status update is given 250 characters before it's cut off with an ellipsis. So similar to the link title limitations, ensure you shorten your Meta description for it to properly display on LinkedIn.
- **Generate Leads With Offers:** A HubSpot study found that LinkedIn is 277% more effective for lead generation than Facebook and Twitter. Take advantage of this by highlighting your great offers and including call to actions in your posts.

✓ **Learn and Optimize From Your Engagement Percentage:** Engagement will show you where to improve, grow, and change the way you update to your LinkedIn profile. By regularly reviewing areas such as the category of content you posted, who was targeted, and the day of the week and time of day that you posted you can help craft even more optimized posts the next time you update. Logged-in admins can find the analytics by clicking the dropdown menu from the blue Edit button in the top right of your company profile. From the main insights page, you can view general information about the visits to your profile, including helpful demographic info that can show you the locations of visitors, seniority, industry, and even how many visits came from your own employees. To dig deeper, click on the analytics link at the top of the page, and you can view the complete stats for the updates you share. Engagement percentage measures the total number of interactions, clicks, and followers acquired for each update you post to your account. In other words, engagement percentage can tell you how many people, of those who saw your update, truly engaged with it.

Learn, Analyse and Refine

As with any other of your marketing efforts and campaigns, in order to determine your success you need to measure your performance and use the data you collect to inform and develop your future efforts to optimise your campaigns and maximise their effectiveness. LinkedIn's analytics provide you with a wealth of data that you can explore to see vital insights into how your campaign is performing, from what content resonates best with your audience, to the best times to post and much more. In order to be successful on LinkedIn and get the most out of using it for your company you therefore need to regularly assess your analytics, listen to what they tell you and ultimately understand what that means you need to do in your future campaigns to ensure you are maximising engagement, driving brand awareness and maximising your ROI.

Tips for Success

Write a Compelling Summary

The home page on a LinkedIn Company Page provides you with plenty of areas to showcase your business, from the cover photo to your company updates and importantly, an area for you to include a great description of your business. A visitor has come to your page to find out about who you are, what you have to offer and whether you're worth following or not, so it is vital that you create a clear, concise and compelling summary about your business that describes who you are, what you do, why they should take note of you. Ensure within it you also include strategically placed keywords to boost your SEO efforts and help people can find your LinkedIn Company Page through relevant searches.

Utilise the Cover Image

The cover photo appears it a dominant position at the top of the home page of your LinkedIn Company Page so it is an important tool to utilise to showcase your business. Ensure you choose a photo that is good quality, visually appealing, capture's people's attention and entices them in to take a closer look at your Page content and what else you have to show throughout your profile.

Promote Your LinkedIn Company Page

Your LinkedIn company page can be full of great content and ground breaking ideas and services, but it you fail to promote your page and announce to the world that it exists, then chances are no one is going to see it. From putting a link to your page on your business card, email signature, to displaying it on your packaging and corporate literature, anywhere where your customers will see it is where you should display and advertise your page. You should also explore and utilise the widgets available on LinkedIn's website such as the LinkedIn Company Follow button that makes it easy for people on your website or blog to follow your company on LinkedIn with just one click. Don't miss out on the areas offline that you can also utilise to promote your page, from telling those you meet at meetings of your page, to having a find us on LinkedIn sticker in your shop window.

Use Featured Updates to Highlight Important Content

LinkedIn offers the featured updates tool to help you highlight important content. So whether you want to promote an event, hype a sale or promotion, or draw attention to a specific piece of content, you can set any update that you publish as featured and it will then be highlighted at the top of your page. This is a great feature to utilise to direct attention to content that you want more people to see.

Utilise the Rich, Visual Content to Capture Attention

Using visual media throughout your profile is a very important aspect of your marketing as it make your LinkedIn company page visually appealing to visitors and grabs their attention, making it more likely they will consume and share your content. From using a compelling image in your LinkedIn Company page banner, to enhancing your updates with videos and photos, there are plenty of opportunities for you to provide rich, visual content to your audience to capture attention.

Make Your Updates Short and Sweet

Your status updates show up in the news feed of a user's home page, so you want to ensure that you grab attention with your post and compel the user to click on your update and consume your content and potentially share it with their network. One of the best ways to grab attention is to post updates that are concise, include a high-quality and relevant piece of visual media (image, video etc.) and contains a compelling description of the link or content you are sharing that lets readers know what to expect when they click through, yet is enticing enough without giving away the whole story.

Create Showcase Pages

Enhance your LinkedIn presence by using showcase pages. LinkedIn showcase pages are an extension of your company page and enable you to highlight certain products or services on a separate page from the company page. This allow you to customize your messages to highlight and separate content for different customer segments. LinkedIn users can follow showcase pages for topics or products that they're interested in. This means that the content they see in their news feeds will be more focused and relevant to them, which is likely to result in higher engagement. Before you begin page should ensure you have three optimised and high-quality graphics – a cover photo, a logo and then a thumbnail. Once you create a showcase page, boost your impact by promoting it across any other social networks you are using. You can also add follow buttons and sponsor your posts to extend the reach of your showcase posts beyond your network.

Take Advantage of LinkedIn Groups

Groups are great tools for prospecting as you search for groups around certain industries and interests, so they are already segmented. Meaning that going in, you already know your audience. Choose several core members of your team to become involved in LinkedIn groups for certain segments. Prepare a strategy and guidelines for posting and interacting to make sure they feel comfortable and know exactly how establish and portray your business effectively within the groups. Over time, these team members will help position your company as a thought leader in the groups, hopefully resulting in when other members of the group are looking for a new product/service, you will be the first they think of.

Boost Your Content with LinkedIn Ads

LinkedIn targeting is a powerful tool for B2B, because it's so simple to target by job, industry, seniority, education, etc. Start with a consideration of your KPIs and they will guide which advertising option you utilise. For example if you are looking for exposure, use pay per impressions. Or if you are looking for a sign up or a download, then paying for clicks is the best route to take.

Effectively Manage Your Company Page

The new LinkedIn Company Page Notification Center streamlines how you manage your company page, while allowing you to better understand which updates and content are performing the best. Access the new Company Page Notification Center dashboard, and you:

- ✓ Get an overview of how many likes, comments and shares you've received on the updates on your company page
- ✓ See how often your company has been mentioned by LinkedIn members on the platform
- ✓ View every publicly shared mention of your company on LinkedIn
- ✓ Comment and like as a company representative in response to mentions about your company
- ✓ Gain greater insights into how the content and messaging on your LinkedIn company page is performing

Keep Track of Industry News Using LinkedIn Pulse

Pulse is a great section of LinkedIn where you can discover popular articles and trending content tailored to your interests. It can be found under Interests in LinkedIn's top navigation. Browse Top Posts to monitor the most popular content on LinkedIn Pulse, or click the Discover more link found via the hamburger menu to find and follow specific influencer contributors, publishers, or topic-related channels. You can sign up for daily or weekly email summary notifications of Pulse news or instant notifications when influencers you're following post something new.

Check out LinkedIn's Content Marketing Score & Trending Content Resources

If you're a LinkedIn Business Solutions customer, you can learn how impactful your organic and paid LinkedIn content is with the Content Marketing Score and Trending Content resources. Your Content Marketing Score measures user engagement with your Sponsored Updates, Company Pages, LinkedIn Groups, employee updates, and Influencer posts then provides recommendations on how you can improve your score, and thus the effectiveness of your LinkedIn content. LinkedIn's Trending Content resource also provides you with a sense of which types of content are most popular on LinkedIn in your industry, highlighting the most popular content being shared on LinkedIn for various audiences and topic segments. Monitoring this will help you to understand what content your company should be creating and sharing on LinkedIn to generate the most engagement. Business Solutions customers can contact their LinkedIn account executives any time to learn more about these resources.

Use LinkedIn to Generate Leads

A study by HubSpot found that traffic from LinkedIn generated the highest visitor-to-lead conversion rate (2.74%) of the top social networks, almost 3 times higher than both Twitter (.69%) and Facebook (.77%). LinkedIn can help you generate leads. To get the most out of LinkedIn for lead generation, aim to promote and share links to your blog posts and landing pages in your Company Status Updates, LinkedIn Groups, on your Showcase Pages, and in calls-to-action placed in posts you publish via LinkedIn's publishing platform, Pulse.

Create your Own Industry LinkedIn Group

In addition to joining already established groups, consider creating a LinkedIn Group of your very own. Create a group based on a relevant industry-related topic and become a LinkedIn Group administrator. You can then use this group to establish yourself as a thought leader in your industry, grow a community of advocates, generate new marketing content ideas, and help generate new leads.

Email Your LinkedIn Group

One of the perks of managing a LinkedIn Group is the fact that you can literally email the members of your group -- up to once per week. These emails take the form of LinkedIn Announcements, which are

messages sent directly to the email inboxes of group members (if they've enabled messages from groups in their settings). This is a prime opportunity for generating leads from LinkedIn, particularly if you've built up a robust group of users.

Recruit New Talent via LinkedIn Careers

Looking to fill a position on your team? Build the Careers section of your Company Page, which you can use then to promote your available job openings. There are more robust customization options available for this section, if you purchase a Silver or Gold Careers package. There are several benefits of doing this, firstly it enables dynamic, customizable modules (that display different version of the page based on viewers' LinkedIn profiles), analytics about who is viewing the page, direct links to recruiters, video content, etc. In addition to allowing you to add a large, clickable cover image that can be transformed into a call-to-action. This image can direct users to a specific job, a list of jobs and opportunities located on your website, or examples of your company's culture. The overall look and feel of your Careers page will depend on what information and images you choose to include, such as a list of jobs, recent updates, people at your company, a summary section for your careers, and what employees are saying about working at your company. If you're actively recruiting candidates with specific skills and expertise, don't forget about LinkedIn's Advanced Search feature.

Add the Company Follow and LinkedIn Share Buttons to your Website/Content

Promote your company's LinkedIn presence and help grow the reach of your Company Page by adding the Company Follow button to your website and to your various content assets like blog posts, emails, and landing pages to extend the reach of your content to LinkedIn users.

Analyse and Learn With Your Company Page Analytics

Use the Analytics tab for Company Pages to evaluate the performance of your Company Page. Access your page's analytics by clicking the Analytics tab in the top navigation of your Company Page. This tab offers very useful data about the effectiveness of your page's reach, status updates and engagement, as well as information about your page's followers, where they came from, how your following has grown over time and how your data compares to other companies, etc.

Measuring Success

Lead Generation and Conversion Rates

Ultimately you are on LinkedIn to generate leads and potential buyers so it is vital that you measure the rates at which you are driving both. By analysing the rate at which your updates are driving leads and by tracking conversions you can ascertain whether you are maximising your ROI with your current efforts. If you fail to see leads or conversions generated from your content then you need to revaluate your strategy.

Performance of Updates

LinkedIn analytics allows you to see impressions, clicks and engagement rates for any given update. Analysing these metrics for each update you share helps inform you on what content resonates best with your audience which you can take and apply to future content creation efforts, ensuring that you are targeting your audience's needs and interests with every post you create.

Engagement Rate

Engagement on LinkedIn is reflected in many forms from the amount of times members have clicked, liked, commented on and shared your content. Measuring engagement rates is an important process as it shows your performance in terms of your audience and whether you are successfully attracting and engaging them with your updates. By gathering a better understanding of what content draws most comments, likes or shares, and similarly what content doesn't you are helping to better your campaign as the lessons you learn can be adapted and applied to your future efforts.

Follower Demographics

By analysing who the people that are following your page you can gather important insights into whether you are attracting the right type of targeted audience with your currents efforts. Regularly take the time to assess your audience demographics: where are they from? What industry do they work in? What is their occupation? These are just some of the many characteristics you should be looking at. If you find that the people you are attracting are the ones you are targeting and match your ideal buyer persona then you know your current efforts are working, similarly however if you find you are attracting an audience that is not relevant to you or one you want are not targeting then you need to explore what areas you need to change, whether it's the content you are sharing to how you have described your page, whatever the reason is, analysing your audience demographics is an important part of measuring your success.

How You Compare to Others

Another way of assessing how well you are performing is to do a comparison of others on LinkedIn that are similar to you and compare your efforts. If you find your competitors are using LinkedIn company pages then look to see important figures such as their total followers growth over time, to their engagement rates and what content they post that is received well (through interactions, comments etc.) as looking it this information will help you better your own campaign for example, if you see areas in which they appear to perform well then you can apply that to your own efforts.

YOUTUBE

YouTube is the most popular video hosting and sharing platform with over one and a half billion active users. Businesses have utilised the benefits of YouTube, recognising that with the power of video, YouTube's massive audience, and AdWords' targeting tools, you have the ability to reach and impact potential customers all around the world. Having the ability to embed a YouTube video player on your website or blog also means you can easily share your video on Facebook, Twitter and other social media network making it easy to efficiently share your story and build your business online.

What's Good About YouTube?
- A great tool for improving search engine rankings
- It is a free platform for advertisements

What's Not so Good About YouTube?
- Not useful for businesses where videos are not relevant or useful to them
- A successful YouTube channel needs a consistent uploading schedule so is not suitable for companies without the time or resources to keep producing quality videos

Should your Business Have a YouTube Channel?
If your target audience and customers are watching videos on YouTube related to your industry, then you need have a YouTube channel to attract that audience. YouTube is great for businesses that are innately visual and regularly produce videos that are product informative, demonstrations of products or services and generally informative and entertaining content that will be valued by a certain group. The sheer audience size of YouTube attracts many businesses to YouTube but with a lot of competition to face businesses should only use YouTube if they can regularly and consistently produce good quality, varied, fresh and entertaining videos.

Need to Know Facts, Stats and Tips About YouTube

- Over one billion hours of videos are watched on YouTube every day.
- YouTube has over 1.9 billion monthly active logged-in users.
- On mobile devices alone, YouTube reaches more adults aged 18-49 during prime time than any cable network does in an average week.
- 75% of adults report watching YouTube on their mobile devices.
- More than 70% of YouTube watch time is generated from mobile devices.

- YouTube mobile ads are 84% more likely to hold attention than TV ads.
- Over 50,000 years of product review videos have been watched on mobile devices over the past two years.
- In 2018, YouTube was the most popular IOS app.
- 46% of millennials (25-34-year-olds) have increased their YouTube usage since last year.
- 70% of millennial YouTube users watched a YouTube video to learn how to do something new or learn about something they're interested in.
- YouTube is the world's second largest search engine.
- YouTube is the second most trafficked website behind Google.
- YouTube users collectively watch over 46,000 years of content each year.
- 68% of YouTube users watched a video to help them make a purchase decision.
- 80% of YouTube users who watched a video to help them make a purchase decision said they watched the video at the beginning of the shopping process.
- 95% of the most popular YouTube videos are music videos.
- 47% of on-demand music streaming was listened to on YouTube.
- There are twice as many small- and medium-sized businesses advertising on YouTube since 2016.
- Four times as many people prefer watching video on YouTube rather than on social media platforms.
- YouTube users watch more than 180 million hours of content on TV screens every day.
- YouTube users are three times more likely to prefer watching a YouTube tutorial video compared to reading the product's instructions.
- "Relaxing" and "feeling entertained" are the top two reasons viewers watch YouTube.
- Relaxation videos like soap cutting and slime playing experienced a 70% increase in watch time in 2018.
- Comedy, music, entertainment/pop culture, and "how to" are the four most popular content categories on YouTube.

Why You Need YouTube for Your Business

Brand Awareness

Videos are a powerful branding tool and if done right can leave a lasting impression on an audience. The vast audience of YouTube together with the easily sharable format that comes with a video means the potential for your video reaching a new and extensive range of potential customers is a powerful benefit of YouTube.

It's Free and Very Popular

YouTube is a free channel that millions of people view every day. Together with the fact that it is the second most popular search engine in the world and the third most visited website in the internet, your business could greatly benefit from having a channel where you can reach millions of people and benefit from free promotion.

It's Great For SEO

YouTube is a great resource for improving search engine rankings. Video is a highly sharable content format and is shared easily across social media networks and between people so look to optimise your channel with SEO friendly wording and embed videos onto your website with targeted keywords and you will likely benefit from an increase in Google's search results and attract natural traffic to your website over your competitors.

It Shows Your Personality and Creativity

The internet can often be an impersonal place; however having a YouTube Channel offers a creative platform for you to share your brand story that gives your business a human face. People are more likely to purchase products or services from a business they feel like they already "know" and having a channel that you regularly update can help create a community and allow your viewers to feel like they know your business.

Creating Your YouTube Account and Getting to Grips with The Basic Lingo

All YouTube accounts need to be directly tied to a Google+ account. If you already manage your business Google+ Page, you can use that to create a YouTube account for your business. If you don't, you will need to create a Google+ account.

Creating an Account With a Current Google+ Page

Whilst there is another way, this is by far the most efficient way to create a YouTube account for your brand. Once you've logged into your Google+ page, to create a YouTube channel you will need to;

- Make sure that you're logged into the Google+ account you want to attach to a YouTube page and go to YouTube.
- Go to the top right corner where your page's thumbnail is and click the dropdown.
- When you click the page you want to make a channel for, you'll see a page that says create a channel for _____. Simply click ok.
- YouTube will take you through a quick tutorial, then you're ready to start building your channel and posting content.

Your YouTube Channel Page

Your YouTube dashboard is filled with a whole host of tabs. The first two tabs that are you need to fill out with information are the "Home" and "About" tabs.

Home Tab

Your profile photo will default to the one you're using on your Google+ account, so if you ever want to change it you'll need to do so there. YouTube also has the option for a cover photo. To upload your photo, click the "Add channel art" button in the middle of the cover photo area. Alternatively, with your mouse, hover over the photo space to reveal an edit button in the upper right corner to open a drop-down menu. Select "Edit channel art" and then either upload or drag the image you want to use. The recommended file size is 2,560 x 1,440 pixels, but bear in mind that not all of that file will appear on your profile.

About Tab

After you have got the visuals in place, click the "About" tab on your channel's home page. Three buttons will appear in this section to guide the further development of your YouTube account.

- **Channel description:** In this text box, enter a description of your brand and/or the type of content that you will be sharing.
- **Links:** This section helps you connect YouTube to your other online profiles. You can select whether to display links overlaid on the cover photo and how many links will appear there. You can also decide whether or not to show when you created the account and how many views your channel has.
- **Add Channels:** Use this area to highlight your partners, your different departments, or your individual employees. If you don't know of any other YouTube channels you want to feature, you can leave this section blank and update it as you get acquainted with the platform.

YouTube Creator Studio

After personalising your channel, head over to the "Creator Studio" to create content and manage your page. There are several different tabs on that dash.

Dashboard: The customizable YouTube dashboard is the place to go to quickly scan what's going on with your page. There are 5 different widgets that you can add, remove or rearrange to help you quickly get a high level view of your page.

Video Manager: The video manager is the place to go to manage all of your content. There are also a few unique features that can be found on this page.

- The ability to live-stream a life event
- A tab to access your search history

- A tab that shows you all of the videos you've liked
- A place to go to create video playlists

Top Tip: As you upload more videos, be sure to take advantage of the ability to create playlists. Navigate to the Video Manager, which is in the same drop-down menu as the Dashboard. Mark the videos you want to include and then click on the "Playlists" button. In this menu, you can opt to create a new playlist or add on to an existing one.

Community: YouTube is just like any other one of social media platforms in that you develop an online community that you need to maintain and manage. As your presence continues to build, it's important to continue to engage with your audiences and build relationships.

Channel: There are a ton of features in the channel section that help you personalise your page. An important feature of this is to decide whether or not you want to monetize your site. If you upload a lot of high quality content that you think will get a lot of views, this could be something for you to look into as a means of generating revenue.

Analytics: YouTube has a robust analytics suite and just as you use analytics in every other social media platform you use to marketing your business, you should actively use this data to help guide the kind of content that you produce. Some of the key things to look at are:

- Audience Demographics
- Playback Locations
- Traffic Sources
- Devices Watched From
- Audience Retention

Now that you have the basics down, it's time to start creating some content. The first clip you'll want to upload to the network is a punchy trailer for your channel.

7 Key Questions to Help Form a Successful YouTube Strategy

Before you jump in and start uploading there are several key strategic elements you must consider in order to create a YouTube marketing strategy that will ensure your YouTube channel is going to be in line with your business objectives and ultimately be a successful addition to your social media marketing strategy.

What are my Objectives for my YouTube Channel?

Having well-defined goals and a clear vision of your objectives for your YouTube channel is imperative for many reasons. It not only influences the type of video content you'll share but also impacts on what analytics you will look to in how you measure your success. Whether you want to use YouTube as an outlet to showcase new products, drive sales or boost your website traffic, having clear objectives is crucial to how successful your presence on YouTube will be.

Common YouTube Marketing Objectives

- Brand Awareness
- Increase Authority
- Product Support and Advice
- Supporting PR efforts

Who am I Going to Target With my Videos?

In order to have the chances of a well-received video, you need to have a clear idea of who you are going to be targeting with your videos. It is vital you take the time to gather important facts about your target audience ranging from their average age to what styles and formats they prefer to receive their information, as this will help ensure you create videos that are directly tailored towards them and are likely to resonate with them therefore improving the likelihood of success.

What Am I Going to Upload?

One of the most vital aspects of YouTube marketing that you need to know is that people come to YouTube to be informed, educated and entertained and not to watch boring sales adverts. The key is to provide video content that is going to interest, inspire and entertain your target audience as well as enhancing your business image and brand. Whether you will shoot your own videos or hire an external business, remember to share good quality videos that someone in your industry or sector will be interested in viewing. You can upload videos of anything from behind the scenes, product demonstrations to a day in the life of a member or staff, anything that you feel will enhance your brand and interest your viewers. Just remember to pick a niche, be consistent and give the viewers what they want.

Do I Have a Clear Content Posting Strategy in Place?

Having a well-developed uploading schedule is an important step towards building a repeat audience and subscriber base and also impacts greatly on how well you build a successful YouTube channel. The two things that will dictate your publishing schedule are your business goals and resources and what your audience wants. So whether you upload a new video once a week or every fortnight, ensure each time it is consistently good, targets your viewers' needs and is reflective of your brand.

How am I Going to Promote my Channel?

There are many resources you can utilise to help you promote your YouTube Channel. From embedding your YouTube videos and playlists to your business's website and blog to putting your YouTube URL link onto your corporate literature and business cards. Remember to also cross promote on your other social media channels by sharing a direct link to every new video you upload across all of your business's social media networks.

What are my Competitors Doing?

Knowing what types of videos your competitors are producing and how their audience responds to them are both key pieces of information that you need to know. It is by looking at how well (or how badly) they are performing on YouTube that you can get valuable information that you can apply to your own strategy. If they are performing well then find out why and apply that to your own efforts and equally if you see areas in which they are performing badly, then see these as opportunities for you to improve on with your own channel. Additionally, if you find that none of your competitors are using YouTube you have to ask yourself why, are they missing an opportunity? In which case you need to establish yourself on YouTube first or are they doing the right thing in not having a presence on YouTube? And if that is the case then you need to establish whether you really need to be on YouTube yourself.

How am I Going to Measure my Channel's Success?

To measure your success effectively you need to first establish your objectives for your YouTube presence as this will dictate what analytics you will measure. Analysing your YouTube Analytics on a regular basis will show you a wealth of valuable information from how many people watch your videos, how they discovered your videos, how many subscribers you have, as well as how many likes, dislikes, comments and shares each of your videos has received. Tracking these metrics will help show you what types of content resonate with your viewers that will help guide your future video content creation.

Uploading: What, and How Often?

With over 300 hours' worth of video uploaded onto YouTube every minute, it can be hard to make your videos stand out from the crowd. Below are several ideas for powerful and engaging videos that you can create that will generate engagement and ensure people are actively searching for them.

Video Interviews and Thought Leadership

You can display your business as thought leaders in a specific industry by offering free information that demonstrates your skills and intelligence and provides genuine value for users. This can be done either by presenting strategic, academic content such as speeches or seminars, interviews with industry influencers or by offering tips about a given field of knowledge.

How-To Videos and Tutorials

YouTube is a great place to find how-to videos as many people prefer to get instruction from a video rather than a text-heavy article. If you have specific and uncommon knowledge within your business that others would likely benefit from learning about, simple tutorials can be a valuable asset.

Behind the Scenes Video

Behind the scenes videos are often successful because they are of interest to your customers and show them something that cannot get elsewhere. For ideas you could post a video of how your product is made or interesting insights from those who work in the back end of your business. A behind-the-scenes video can highlight the hard work and dedication you and your employees put into your business and show a part of the process that customers may not witness from their end.

Testimonial Video

Many customers use reviews in their decision to make a purchase. By sourcing video testimonials of past customers with great reviews, you will add an extra dimension to your reviews section that will show you are offering a really good product or service as happy customers have taken the time to document how happy they are. You can invite your best customer advocates in to make the video at your location, or you can ask them to record and upload videos themselves.

Special Events Coverage

If you are attending a special event such as a conference, trade show, ball or dinner, be sure to bring your camera so you can post event photos and record footage of the event that can then be shared with your audience.

Site & Facility Tour

For businesses that strongly rely on their business space to attract and keep customers, for example hotels, restaurants and art galleries, a video site and facility tour can be a great way to boost your brand image.

Media Highlights

If your business has been in the news recently, a video recap of your media highlights can show your authority, show your product/ service off in a new light and remind or show those that may have missed the original broadcast. Remember to attain any necessary rights to the video footage to avoid copyright infringement and video deletion.

Webinars

Webinars are a great marketing tool, so if you already have regular webinars where you discuss anything from general news and insights surrounding your industry to demonstrations of your product, record and utilise them by repurposing them for use on your YouTube Channel and share them with your audience.

Promotions

When you have a new promotion running, from an offer, to a discount or freebie giveaway you can use promotional videos on YouTube to attract attention to your channel and potentially get your offers seen by a wider audience.

Product Showcases and Demonstrations

If you have a particular product you want to put in the spot light or show off a products great use or indeed how to use it then creating a video is a great way to inform your audience.

> *Although it takes some experimentation to find the best publishing schedule for you, there are two things that should always be considered and will dictate your posting schedule; your business goals and what your audience wants.*

How often to upload videos is different for everyone, for those that have a lot of special effects in their videos they may only upload once a week due to time constraints or others that upload less technical videos may be able to upload several times a week. What is important for being successful on YouTube is that you make an uploading schedule and stick to it. Scheduling is not only important for your audience; it's also needed to help keep yourself on track. If you know that you have set a goal to upload a video to YouTube once a week for example, then you will make sure to get it done. If you don't have a schedule then it is easier to put of the work and neglect your channel and it will not become a successful addition to your social media presence. Ultimately how often you upload will vary depending on what works best for your business, goals and audience so it is important to experiment to find a posting schedule that works for you. So the first step to determining your ideal posting frequency is to find the perfect balance between what you want are capable of and what your audience wants.

To maximise the benefits of having a YouTube channel you need to ultimately ask yourself, Can you keep this schedule consistently? Can you always publish high-quality content at this rate? And will you have enough content for this schedule? Once you've discovered the best times to post, being consistent with your publishing schedule has the benefit of expanding your reach and drawing in an audience.

How to Create a Branded YouTube Channel that Gets you Noticed

Always Create Great Content

The key to building an audience and maintaining a successful presence is to always provide content that is valuable, relevant and entertaining to the viewer. YouTube provides you with a great platform to showcase your visual creativity and show that you understand and care about your audience enough to consistency produce a variety of videos that address consumer needs and genuinely interest and provide value to them.

Make Your Videos Easy to Find

YouTube is very heavily saturated with videos making it harder than ever to get your videos noticed. Simply uploading your video and waiting for people to come across it will not suffice. Rather, you need to make it easy for the right audience to discover your videos by applying several key factors in your videos;

- Use relevant keywords and search categories to attract your target audience
- Embed your YouTube videos onto your website
- Share your videos across social networks
- Include your website URL in the video description

- Ensure your video is categorised and tagged correctly and relevantly
- Consider advertising to give your videos a boost

Appeal to your Target Audience

With so much choice for the consumer, getting your video noticed can be a difficult task. The key to ensuring you stand a better chance of getting noticed is to do your research and find out exactly what your audience is watching and searching for on YouTube and then apply this knowledge to your own efforts. You will better reach your audience if you know what type of content resonates best with them and directly provide solutions for them or answer their questions and queries with your videos.

Thoroughly Brand your YouTube Channel

Your YouTube channel needs to act as a hub of your brand making it clear to the viewer who you are when they arrive on your page. Ensure you fully utilise the customisable features of your channel from the background to the video cover image to ensure that you create a branded environment for your audience where they trust that it is your brand page and where they are welcomed and encouraged to interact. There are several key areas to utilise to ensure you don't miss any branding opportunities on your page;

- Include links to your website
- Effectively and clearly communicate your brand and purpose in the description
- Ensure all creative aspects (colours, graphics, typography etc.) reflect your brand.

Know Your Limits

Maintaining a successful YouTube presence takes a lot of consistent and continual effort. From uploading content to creating titles, responding to comments, tracking analytics and general promotion, maintaining your account can easily become a very time-consuming role. From this, ensure the person who maintains it has the time, talent and expertise to run it effectively as you are publicly representing your brand to a vast audience online, so you do not want to give them a negative impression by ineffectively using YouTube. If you find yourself or the person running your account is struggling, then strongly consider outsourcing to a specialist who has the adequate skill set to represent your brand well. Your business can only benefit from you knowing your limits and realising when the time is right to get a professional on board.

Listen to and act on What Your Analytics Tell You

Track your videos performance through your analytics will help you to understand your audience, how they interact with your videos and what content resonates best with them. Armed with this information, you gain a very advantageous position where you can use this information to help you optimise your

future videos to ensure you are directly addressing your target audience needs, making them more likely to keep coming back to your channel and share your content with others.

Be Sociable and Engage Your Audience

To fully utilise the benefits of YouTube for your business you need to embrace the social aspect of the social network and continually interact and engage with your audience and other users. You need to be actively dedicated to your page looking for opportunities to interact with others and respond to comments and feedback on your videos. YouTube has very much developed into an active online community which you need to be a part of and participate in. There is much to gain in engaging with users and audiences from potential business opportunities, partnerships with other users and by listening to your audience you can get to know them better helping to create better content that is going to attract them in the future.

Keep Your Channel Updated and Fresh

Once you have set up your channel, developed a solid posting strategy and perfected your channel design you are well on your way to a strong YouTube presence but your work is by no means finished. In order to keep the attention of your audience and attract new ones you need to actively keep your channel updated with fresh content and continually analyse your analytics to gauge your audience response to your videos to ensure you are consistently targeting their needs with your videos. Continually look to see how you can better enhance your audience's experience with your videos and act on what your analytics tell you, positive and negative about your efforts and respond accordingly.

Be Aware of YouTube's Future Trends & Updates

As new technology emerges and YouTube grows and develops it is likely to make changes that can affect your business marketing. Ensure you stay aware of changing trends and utilise any new developments within YouTube and a broader technical sense to help better your videos and audience video experience.

How to Build a Following and Amplify your Impact

Uploading your video is only the beginning. The next challenge is to promote your YouTube channel in order to get maximum exposure and attract attention. Rather than relying solely on search engines, there are several other key techniques you can employ to help get your content noticed.

Make Your Video Easy to Find

You need to ensure that your videos are easy to find both within YouTube and externally in areas such as search results. To make your videos easily searchable you need to focus on several key areas and optimise them. Firstly you need to ensure you title your video effectively, by strategically placing target keywords and clearly telling your audience what your video is about. Secondly you need a well-written description for your video ensuring you are as descriptive and keyword-rich as possible. You will also need to include a URL that directs traffic onto a page you choose. Finally don't forget to utilise tags for your video being sure to include any and all related keywords in the tags field. There are many other factors that will affect how easily get found from the number of page views to subscribers, however the above factors are the easiest for you to control and utilise so ensure as a basic start you optimise them as fully as you can.

Use YouTube AdWords

With YouTube AdWords, you can promote your video to potential customers on YouTube and across the web exactly when they're searching for your product or service. You simply create your Ad, set your budget and choose options that speak to your target audience and AdWords will automatically position your video in front of the people who are reading, searching for, or watching online content related to your business. You will only pay when someone actually watches your video and you can also choose how much you want to pay per view. This means you can control your costs while promoting your business around the world.

Embed Your Video on Your Website

By embedding your videos onto your website you provide your website viewers with a direct view of your YouTube channel making it easier for them to subscribe to your channel and increase your video views. Also look to enable video embedding on your videos that allows other users to post your videos to their websites; this will give you an extra avenue for a potential whole new audience.

Leverage Your Other Social Media Platforms

One of the easiest ways to promote your videos and build an audience for your YouTube channel is to leverage your existing social media platforms and share regular updates linking to your videos across them. Every time you upload a new video share it across your other networks such as a Facebook, your

blog and Twitter using a keyword-rich title and make sure your descriptive post includes appropriate and complementary content. Also take the time to add a link to your YouTube channel in your social network descriptions. You should also promote your channel across your other assets from including your YouTube URL in your email signature and business cards to your packaging and other corporate literature.

Send Your Videos to Others You Know Will Find Them Useful

Whether it's a past client, a friend or an owner of a website you found through a search or directory, if you feel that your video can be useful or relevant to someone then share it with them. Many viewers discover YouTube videos through other sites, blogs and word of mouth, so make sure you target those website owners or clients that will be likely to find your videos interesting and informative and thus share it with their own audience. The traffic you can generate from this could become a significant source of views for your videos.

Promote Your Video Offline

Leveraging your offline assets is an easy and effective way to promote your YouTube channel. Anywhere your customers or clients interact with you is a place where you should have a link to your YouTube channel. From adding a link to your channel on your traditional advertising, a YouTube playlist on a monitor in your store or office and across your corporate literature there are plenty of ways for you to promote your channel beyond the online world.

Encourage Engagement and Interactivity

By creating an online community who actively get involved by sharing their views, commenting, interacting and sharing your content you will successfully utilise the social aspect of the network and be rewarded with a band of loyal fans who will help you better your business through constructive opinions and suggestions as well as helping you build your fan base as they are likely to recommend you to others and share your content. There are many ways to encourage engagement from your audience from asking them questions, to running contests and promotions and by creating high quality content that naturally gets people talking.

Work with Other YouTube Users

Other YouTube users are not all to be seen as just your competitors. Rather, by collectively working with other users you will help build your network and gain exposure to new audiences. Look to support other users and look for opportunities where you can work together and help promote one another. From sharing their content to collaborating on an upcoming major event, there are many ways for you to give a boost to other businesses and get one in return. You will ultimately get a lot more out of YouTube as a marketing channel if you realise and utilise the social community-based aspect of it.

Ask for Subscribers

One of the most basic ways to increase your subscriber count is to ask for people to subscribe in your videos. Ensure each video you create contains a compelling call to action that directs and encourages the viewer to click on the subscribe button right above your video. A simple formula commonly used for this means is too clearly and compellingly state to the viewer 1. What you want them to do 2. How they are to do it 3. Why they should it. As an example you can say "Make sure you stay up to date with my latest videos and effective marketing tips by subscribing to my YouTube channel by clicking the button above this video."

Add a YouTube Widget and More to Your Website and Blog

If you already have a website and/or blog that is attracting traffic, you already have a great opportunity to leverage those visitors to encourage more subscribers to your channel. The best thing is that by simply adding a widget to those pages, those website and/or blog visitors can also subscribe to your YouTube channel at the click of a button. Make sure you explore your blog and website features to see what widgets you can utilise.

Consistently Interact

In order to be successful and see results on YouTube, you need to not see it simply as a place to host your videos and instead realise that it is a community filled with brands and people that are wanting to be informed, entertained and interact and engage with other users. Therefore regularly and actively take the time to interact with and support other members of the community, this means both in terms of interacting with your audience and customers but also in terms of supporting others in their YouTube marketing efforts. In doing so you also utilise one of the best ways to build a following of subscribers as by leaving real and genuine comments on channels and videos and by liking and subscribing to those channels that you have found valuable to you, you are likely to be rewarded with reciprocations from other channels which can open you up to their followings and subscribers.

Add Cards, Bumper ads, and Watermarks to promote your channel

Cards, bumper ads, and watermarks are clickable CTAs you can add to your YouTube videos. These are effective because they're relatively unobtrusive, offering minimal disruptions to the viewing experience.

- **Cards:** small, transparent CTAs that expand when clicked. Use these to direct viewers to your website, purchase pages, or even other videos on your channel.
- **Bumper ads:** six-second video ads appearing at the start or end of a video.
- **Watermarks:** Custom subscribe buttons visible only to non-subscribers. You can use a branding watermark to embed your channel logo across all videos on your channel. When you add a watermark, viewers can directly subscribe to your channel if they hover over the watermark when using YouTube on a computer. It won't show to users who are already subscribed to your channel.

Follow YouTube's video specifications

Start by uploading video footage that's optimized for YouTube. Fortunately, the platform has a range of video specifications to suit a variety of needs.

Recommended sizes: 426 by 240 pixels (240p), 640 by 360 pixels (360p), 854 by 480 pixels (480p), 1280 by 720 pixels (720p), 1920 by 1080 pixels (1080p), 2560 by 1440 pixels (1440p) and 3840 by 2160 pixels (2160p)

- Minimum size: 426 by 240 pixels
- Maximum size: 3840 by 2160 pixels
- Supported aspect ratios: 16:9 and 4:3
- Recommended specs: .MOV, .MPEG4, MP4, .AVI, .WMV, .MPEGPS, .FLV, 3GPP, or WebM
- Maximum file size: 128 GB
- Maximum length: 12 hours long

Add End Screens to Videos

End screens are a powerful tool which can help extend watch time on your channel by directing viewers to something next at the end of your videos (e.g. They can be used to point viewers to other videos, playlists or channels on YouTube; to call for subscriptions to your channel; and to promote your website, merchandise and crowdfunding campaigns.). You can add them to the last 5-20 seconds of a video and they appear on both desktop and mobile. It's important to note that your video has to be at least 25 seconds long to have an end screen. Other interactive elements, like card teasers and branding watermarks, are suppressed during the end screen. To add an End Screen;

- Open the Videos page in YouTube Studio beta and select a video.
- From the left-hand menu, select Editor.
- Select Add an end screen.

Note: There are times when end screens may be skipped, such as when your video is playing in background mode. Also, end screen size and placement can vary based on the dimensions of the screen so try to avoid pointing to an exact place on-screen.

Tips for Success

Quality Over Quantity

When it comes to uploading videos, it is always quality over quantity. You will need to thoroughly invest time and effort into the quality of your videos and if you find yourself struggling to keep producing quality videos and end up uploading just for the sake of it, you need to reassess your publishing schedule and make it more realistic for you. Your business will not benefit or gain a positive reputation if the content you produce is not engaging, well presented and consistently good so always make producing high quality and engaging content your priority.

Don't Overlook Tags

YouTube's content is organised on a tag word basis therefore it is key that you take the time to attach the correct tags to your videos. This will ensure that your videos will be attracting the right kind of traffic and attention.

Choose Your Featured Video Wisely

First impressions are everything therefore make sure the video you select for your featured video has an eye-catching title and is high-quality, engaging and relevant. Remember to switch the featured video regularly in order to keep your channel fresh and appealing.

Pick a Niche

To become an authority and a valued source of information it is best to create content that lets you thrive in a specific niche rather than trying to appeal to a generic wider audience. Focus on your specialty within your industry and position your channel to project that clearly, showing your audience that your channel is the best place to receive valuable, informative and relevant information that is targeted to their needs.

Brand Your Channel

It is vital that your channel is representative of your business so you must apply your branding strategically and consistently. This consistency also applies to other aspects such as the voice you portray so ensure in the beginning you create a YouTube video marketing plan that works in conjunction with and enhances your overall online and social media marketing plan. This will ensure you have a consistent image portrayed across all your online social networks.

Strategically Place Keywords

To make yourself more easily found in search results you need to pick your keywords and strategically place them throughout your channel. Put them in your title, description and tags and beyond YouTube place them in the supporting content you post when sharing your videos across your other social networks. YouTube video marketing is a great tool for helping your SEO efforts so spend the time to choose the most appropriate and effective keywords and utilise them.

Choose a Good Thumbnail

A thumbnail is one of the things that can catch the attention of a viewer and acts as a first impression of your video therefore it essential that you choose a thumbnail that is eye-catching and representative of the content within your video.

Don't Forget to Use Call to Actions

You can place call to actions strategically throughout your channel, from End Screens on your videos to links within your video description. It is vital that you encourage the viewer to take the next step after they view your video from encouraging them to subscribe, directing them to your blog or website or simply to encourage them to leave a comment. Ensure you utilise effective calls to actions by making them simple, clear and concise.

Keep Your Video Short & Sweet

Keeping your videos short and sweet will help keep the attention of viewers and make them more likely to watch your video until the end- an important factor if you choose to put your call to action at the end of your video. Ensure you share consistently good content in every video you post and utilise your analytics and comments as they will show you important aspects of your videos from what makes people stop watching them at a certain point to how well the subject matter has been received.

Be Innovative, Fresh and Clever

YouTube has become a heavily saturated channel for marketing, so you need to make your videos stand out and demand attention. Take the time to break the mould of generics business videos and look to inject humour, fun and creativity into every video that you share.

Utilise Every Opportunity to Make a Video

Every video you upload is part of your story that you share with your audience. Everything from your ups and downs, your proudest achievements, to your charity work and the people behind your business are all areas in which you can document on video and share with your viewers. So whenever you launch a new product, attend a conference or find a new way to use one of your products, look to see if it is an event that you can document on video and produce an engaging and fun video from it.

Common Mistakes to Avoid

Choosing a Poor Title

Your video can be full of valuable and interesting information for your target audience but if you fail to attract their attention by choosing a poor title you risk them not seeing your video at all. You need to make the title of your video appeal to your target audience by making it concise, eye catching, include utilised keywords and make it descriptive of what your video is actually about.

Choosing a Poor Description

If you fail to provide enough information or fail to evoke interest with your description you could essentially discourage that potential viewer from watching your video. You need to make your description compelling enough to draw viewers in and make them feel they cannot go away without watching your video. Within your description you should include a relevant call action and be clear and concise with what information you share.

Using Weak Tags

Using weak tags that are not relevant or representative of your video won't encourage the people you are targeting with your video to find it. Therefore you need to fully optimise your videos and make them easy to find within search results with appropriate tags playing a considerable role in this.

Only Uploading Videos to YouTube

Once you upload a video you need to promote your video and utilise every promotion tool and resource you have available. The more places you promote it, the more potential audience you have so share your video on all your social media platforms, send it to others who may find it useful and promote it across all other promotional tools you have available.

Ignoring Comments

You need to remember the social aspect of YouTube and make sure you are open to and respond to comments, positive and negative, as this shows you have a vested interest in what your audience thinks about your content. If you fail to respond to those who take the time to comment then you miss out on vital interactions from others that could have led to potential business opportunities. So make sure you encourage your audience to leave comments on your videos and respond and engage with people when necessary.

Having Unrealistic Expectations

Many business owners have the expectation that their video will be an instant success and go viral, but you need to understand that there is no overarching formula for going viral. Whilst having millions of views is brilliant, realistically it may not happen to you so make sure you realistically define what you are hoping to achieve from using YouTube for your business and work to those objectives.

Uploading Inconsistently

Your YouTube channel will not enhance your marketing efforts if you do not maintain a consistent posting schedule. In the beginning you need to create a posting schedule that is consistent and works for you and your audience and will help you avoid rapid uploading then months of no activity on your

channel. Being consistent allows those who subscribe to know when to expect a new video from you which will keep your channel active and attract new viewers.

Ignoring Analytics

Not taking the time to analyse important information about your videos such as your viewer retention, likes and comments means you fail to see what is working with your videos and what isn't. You are making videos for your audience so it is vital that you look at your analytics and see how your audience responds to them as this will help show vital information that can help guide future video creation and ensure that you are directly targeting your audience needs with every one of your videos.

Measuring Success

Like any other marketing strategy, the success of your business YouTube channel must be measured against your business objectives. Analysing your metrics will show you a wealth of information and help determine whether your channel is having a measurable impact and whether the data is reflective of the overall goals of your business page. Below are several key metrics you need to analyse to measure your video success.

Total Views

Whilst relying solely on views as a form of measurement is not advised, looking at your videos views can provide you with some important information. You can use this metric to determine what type of content resonates best with your audience and looking at your average number of views per video can help you gather a clear understanding of what video content performs well and which doesn't that will help guide your content creation in the future. Treat your video views as the basic foundation on which to analyse each of your individual video's success.

Significant Discovery Events

Having a clear understanding of how traffic was driven to your YouTube videos is essential as it shows you insights into which marketing channels drive traffic to your videos over others that will help you learn how to drive relevant viewers to your videos in the future. Looking at the videos significant discovery events will show the noteworthy referral sources of viewers to a video so whether it is a certain website or social network that is sending you the most traffic, you can actively focus your efforts and adjust your video promotion strategy accordingly.

Audience Demographics

By viewing the demographics of your viewers you are able to gain a deeper understanding of who is watching your videos and whether they are right demographics and therefore, relevant viewers you are targeting with your videos. Look at each individual video to understand who is watching and try to draw conclusions from it such as whether your audience changes over time and whether they represent a certain segment as analysing the data in this way can help you make informed decisions for future content creation and marketing strategies.

Ratings, Comments and Favourites

Analysing your audience feedback will help give you a greater understanding of what content resonates best with your audience as these actions require more of an effort from your audience than them simply watching it and so is often a greater indication of engagement than just the views of your videos. Looking at the feedback from ratings, to likes and comments will show you what videos your audience are engaging with which can help you understand what your audience needs and wants from a video that will help guide what type of content you need to continue to produce in the future.

Audience Retention

Examining your audience retention metrics will help you to see vital information such as how long viewers watched your YouTube video and at what point your viewers stopped watching your video. Whilst these metrics can't tell you why they stopped watching as this can vary due to many factors including the videos content, length and more, they can shed light on the weaknesses in your video content. For example, if your metrics show all of your viewers stop watching your video at the same point you can attempt to understand why and look to see whether it's the videos content, length or subject matter that turned them off which can help prevent you having the same issues in the future for the later videos you create.

Video Shares

The amount of shares across social networks each of your videos receives is a big indicator as to which videos are popular and perform well allowing you to take this information and apply it to future videos.

Subscriber Rates

Monitoring the growth of your subscriber base will help you understand the reach of your YouTube content and whether you are continually interesting viewers with your videos. By analysing the subscribers you have gained or lost on every video you can get a sense of what content resonates best with your audience and as such you can use this information to make your videos more effective in the future. This will encourage more subscribers which translates to more people who have the potential to see your channel's video content on their subscriptions stream on their YouTube homepage.

PINTEREST

With over 175 million active users, Pinterest is one of the fastest growing social networks. It is essentially a collection of virtual pinboards allowing you to 'pin' images of products, places, services etc. you like or want onto your own boards. The visual aspect and appeal of the site has captured the interest of many businesses, from retailers to designers who are using it as an online portfolio or product catalogue. A pin could be a gift, recipe or even a quote and has become very popular with people who use it in lots of different ways from planning their weddings, decorating their homes to organising recipes. Business that are visual based have recognised the benefits of Pinterest learning how adding the Pin It button to your website is a great way of driving sales and a great tool for SEO as people can then pin and repin those images on Pinterest and then click to your website to buy your product/service.

What's Good About Pinterest?
- Pinterest is visual based so is perfect for businesses who want to showcase their products and services through pictures
- Users want to grow their presence on Pinterest by pinning and in doing so they act as marketers on your behalf

What's Not so Good About Pinterest?
- Not useful for businesses in certain industries who don't require the visual appeal
- The demographics are gender biased, women make up 85% of the user base

Which Businesses Should be on Pinterest?

Businesses that naturally lend themselves to visual marketing should have a presence of Pinterest. From food shops, restaurants, photographers, DIY stores to wedding and fashion related businesses you can appeal to a wide audience and showcase your products and services through your striking photos or videos.

Need to Know Facts, Stats and Tips about Pinterest

- Total Number of Monthly Active Pinterest Users: 175 million
- Total Number of Pinterest Pins: 50 billion+
- Total Number of Pinterest Boards: 1 billion+
- Total Number of Pinterest Users who save Shopping Pins on Boards Daily: 2 million
- 81% of Pinterest users are Females.
- Men account for only 7% of total pins on Pinterest.
- Millennials use Pinterest as much as Instagram.
- Median age of a Pinterest user is 40, however majority of active pinners are below 40.
- 87% of Pinners have purchased a product because of Pinterest.
- 72% of Pinners use Pinterest to decide what to buy offline.
- Over 5% of all referral traffic to websites comes from Pinterest.
- Pinterest said 80% of its users access Pinterest through a mobile device.
- 93% of active pinners said they use Pinterest to plan for purchases and 87% said they've purchased something because of Pinterest.
- Two-thirds of pins represent brands and products.
- Food & Drink & Technology are the most popular categories for men.

Why You Need Pinterest for Your Business

Traffic and SEO

One of the most beneficial marketing benefits Pinterest offers is the ability to drive more traffic to your website. Pinterest provides you with plenty of optimisation opportunities on which to boost your SEO. From giving your pins descriptive names, to incorporating hashtags and including a reference link back to your business website, all of these factors work together to ensure you get seen in search results.

Showcase Your Products

Displaying products through interesting and engaging boards gives customers a shopping experience that can influence purchase behaviour. By showcasing your products and services through good quality and eye catching pictures and videos you present to a wide audience an interactive guide of what you have to offer.

Build Your Brand Identity

The images pinned on your board should represent the personality and values of your business. With an image you are not only showcasing a product, you are portraying a lifestyle that can and should be used compel and inspire potential customer to want to get involved and buy your product/service.

Interact with Customers

Pinterest is about creating conversations. It can be a powerful word of mouth tool, generating interest in your company and get people talking about all things relevant to the brand, with the opportunity for content to be shared virally amongst members.

Creating Your Pinterest Account and Getting to Grips with The Basic Lingo

To use Pinterest, you first have to sign up for an account. Importantly, using the main sign-up page creates a personal account and for businesses, it's really important that you make sure you specifically sign up for a business account. It's important to make this distinction because business accounts, whilst remaining free like personal Pinterest accounts, give you access to great features to help your business thrive on the platform, one example is the analytics tools.

To sign up for a business account, you need to sign up at specific business sign up page and enter your email address, a password, the name of your business and your website (though this last one is optional). You also need to select what type of business you run from a drop-down menu. From there, you will then be directed to set up your profile.

When you log in to your Pinterest account, you're taken to your home feed. This is where the most recent pins from the other Pinterest accounts you follow are displayed and features endless scrolling for seamless browsing.

Across the top of each page you visit on Pinterest, there is a large search bar. To the left, you'll see the Pinterest logo (clicking this will take you back to the home page), as well as menu options for Ads and Analytics. To the right, there is a drop-down menu, which displays links to all of the categories you can browse through on the platform.

Alongside that, you'll see a "+" button and a chat bubble button. The + allows you to quick-add a new pin or create a new ad, and the chat button pulls up a drop-down menu with three options: News, You and Messages.

- **News:** displays trending pins and other information such as updates
- **You:** shows your notifications from when other users interact with your pins
- **Messages:** displays your messages with other Pinterest users.

Clicking on your profile picture will show a drop-down menu with options to go to your profile to see all your boards and pins, access your settings, billing, ads support, the platform's Help page, and to log out of your account.

Pinterest is all about pins and boards... so what exactly are they? Simply put, **Pins** are the content you share on Pinterest, and **Boards** are how you organise and categorise that content. Before you can start pinning anything, you need to create your boards.

Creating Your Boards

To create your first Pinterest board, go to your profile and you'll see a red Create Board button. Once you click, a box will pop up with the information you need to fill in. You can enter a name for your board and a description of what your board is about (these are optional, but by no means leave them blank), and select a category for it (also optional, but again do not ignore this). In addition, you can choose to keep your board secret, so that only you (and any others user(s) you choose, if any) have access to it.

At the bottom of the box, you'll also see an option entitled "Collaborators," with a text box where you can invite other Pinterest users by username or email to contribute pins to the board. Adding other users to your board creates a group board, which will show up on both your profile and the other users' profiles.

Once you're done filling out your board's information, click Create and you're done. From there, you can start adding pins.

To create subsequent boards, simply go to your profile page and in the space to the left of your existing boards, you'll see a rectangular grey space with a Create a Board button. From there, simply follow the same steps.

Adding Pins

You can add pins to your Pinterest boards in several different ways. To add your own content to Pinterest, go to the board you want to pin to (or use the + button from the top of the page) and click the Add a Pin button. A box will pop up with the options to add a pin from the Web or from your computer. If you decide to add a pin from the Web, Pinterest will prompt you to enter a link to the page you're wanting to pin from. Once you enter the link, you'll be taken to a page that shows all of the images from that website, as well as existing pins that were created by others from that website's domain. You can then select the picture you want to pin by hovering over the image and clicking the Pin it button. This will open a box that allows you to enter a description and choose a board for your pin. You can also create a new board to pin it to and choosing this option will let you name your new board and select whether or not you'd like to add collaborators or keep the board secret. You'll have to go back into this board later to edit it if you'd like to add a description and choose a category. When you're done perfecting your pin, click the Create button. Pinning content from the Web will ensure that your pin links back to the website it came from.

If you choose to add a pin from your computer, Pinterest will prompt you to select and upload an image file. From there, the process of adding a pin is the same as above. Regardless of the way you choose to add your pins, you can always go back to specific pins at a later date to edit their descriptions, move them to different boards or delete them altogether.

To pin from the mobile app, go to your profile tab and click the + button. This gives you the option to create a new board or pin from your phone's photos, the Web, your clipboard or to pin your location if you use the maps feature (part of Pinterest's "Rich Pins").

All pins must include an image or a video in order to be added to Pinterest.

You can also "re-pin" content from other Pinterest users, in addition to adding your own content, and it's good to do a mix of both. Re-pinning is an easy way to be more active on Pinterest when you don't have your own content to share, plus it can get other Pinterest users to notice your brand. To find content to re-pin, you can browse through your home feed, look in specific categories or search certain keywords in the search bar. When you want to re-pin an existing pin, hover over the image and click the red Pin It button. You'll then be prompted to select or create a board, and you can either leave the previous user's description or write your own.

Rich Pins

Rich Pins are a type of organic Pin format that provide more context about an idea by showing extra information directly on the Pin. Rich Pins are a free product available for anyone on Pinterest. You can identify Rich Pins by the extra information above and below the image on close-up, and the bold title in grid.

Types of Rich Pin

Rich Pins add extra details to Pins and update important information from the websites they came from. If something changes on the original website, the Rich Pin is updated to reflect that change. There are four types of Rich Pin: product, article, app and recipe. Product Rich Pins show the most up-to-date price, availability and product information directly on your Pin. Article and Recipe Rich Pins will be updated to reflect any edits you make on your site. App Rich pins show an install button so people can download your app without leaving Pinterest.

Apply for Rich Pins

- If you have product, article or recipe content on your site, mark up these pages with rich meta tags
- After adding meta tags to your web pages, validate one of your correctly marked-up content pages in the Rich Pin validator
- If the web page you are applying with is correctly marked up, an 'Apply' button will appear
- Click the button to apply for Rich Pins
- Once you apply, Pinterest will process your application within 24 hours.

When your site is enabled for Rich Pins, all content that contains correct meta tags on your site will start appearing as Rich Pins when added to Pinterest. Existing Pins that link back to pages with rich meta tags will also start appearing as Rich Pins.

Interacting with other Pinterest users

Pinterest is, unlike other social networks, much more focused towards sharing content than it is about interacting with other users. Having said this, it is still a social network, and as such offers users ways to connect with other people.

- **Likes:** Liking a pin is the easiest way to interact with another Pinterest user (and to save a pin for later, if you don't have time to pin it right away). Simply hover over the pin you want to like and click the heart-shaped button. Doing so will notify that user, and you can access your liked posts from the "Likes" tab on your profile page.
- **Comments:** To add comments to other users' pins, click on the pin you want to comment on and this will pull up a larger window with the pin and more information about it, under the pin, you'll see a comment box where you can type in and share what you want to say.
- **Sending Pins:** You can also send pins you want to share with other users (or non-Pinterest users, even) by hovering over pins and clicking the send button. A box will pop up that allows you to search for other Pinterest users by username, or type in an email address to mail the pin to.
- **Tagging Users:** Just like on Twitter, you can tag users using the @ symbol on Pinterest. When you're writing a description for your pin or adding a comment to someone else's pin, just type in the @ symbol and the username of the person you want to tag, and they'll be notified.
- **Messages:** You can send private messages to other Pinterest users by clicking the Messages option in the notifications box at the top of the page. Simply select "New message," type in the user you want to talk to, and hit "Next." This will open a small chat window at the bottom of your screen where you can drag and drop pins and send instant messages.

Hashtags on Pinterest

Pinterest users can use hashtags when sharing their pins, as with other social networks like Twitter, Facebook and Tumblr. However it is worth noting that there is a lot less emphasis placed on the importance of Hashtags on Pinterest and they are really only to be seen as a bonus on Pinterest, rather than on Twitter for example where they can make or break how successful your posts are.

Pinterest has its own unique search system and hashtags are not the most effective way to make your content searchable on this social network. Hashtags on Pinterest only work in pin descriptions, so if you put them elsewhere, you'll only waste your time and look like you don't know how to use the platform. Hashtags are more effective if you use your own, brand-specific hashtags, and less effective if you were to share a pin with the hashtag #recipes, for example. What's more important on Pinterest is that you use proper keywords when describing your pins and boards, keep your boards organised and categorise your boards correctly.

Personalising your Pinterest Profile

Unlike other social networks, Pinterest does not give you many profile customisation options, allowing you only being able to upload a profile picture, use a custom username, and write a summary about you or your business. Whilst you can't change the layout of your Pinterest page like you can on Tumblr or upload a banner image like on Facebook or Twitter, there are other ways to make your profile unique and to stand out from the crowd

You can name your pinboards with clever phrases and keywords that are both searchable and relatable to your brand. You can also enter a short description of each board that explains what that board is about and how it aligns with your brand. Additionally, you can choose cover photos for each board that relate back to your brand and are visually stimulating. There may not be much you can customise about your Pinterest profile, but you can still successfully represent your brand with the options the platform gives you if you are clever enough and get creative.

Trending Topics on Pinterest

To see what's trending on Pinterest, click on the drop-down menu in the search bar and select "Popular." if you're on mobile, go to the search tab and select the same category. The Popular page will show you a feed of the most popular pins on Pinterest at that time. Above the popular pins, you'll see a banner of the top interests on Pinterest at that time. You can click these interests and see the popular pins in those topics in addition to related topics. Knowing what's trending on Pinterest can help you decide what types of content to pin. Any time you can relate trending topics back to your brand, you make your business more discoverable on Pinterest.

Advertising on Pinterest

Promoted Pins are a paid advertising option for businesses. Promoted Pins are just like regular Pins, only you pay to have them seen by more people. In doing so, you can target specific audiences, choose to pay for either pin engagement or visits to your website, and track how your ads are performing. So far this feature is only available in the United States so for now, to access Promoted Pins, you'll have to sign up for the wait list.

Pinterest Analytics

To access your account's analytics page, simply click Analytics at the top of the page. This will pull up a drop-down menu with three options: Overview, Profile and Audience.

Selecting Overview takes you to a dashboard where you can see several boxes containing statistics about your profile, audience and more. In one box, you can see data on your profile's average daily impressions and viewers; and in another, you can see your average monthly viewers and average monthly engagements. You can click More in either of these boxes to see graphs of all your data. Selecting Profile or Audience will take you directly to this data as well. Below those boxes, you'll see data on how many impressions your pins are receiving. Through Pinterest analytics you can learn valuable

things about your audience demographics, like gender, location and other interests, what devices visitors to your page are using, along with what your most popular pins are. All of which will help you guide your future Pinterest strategy to maximise its effectiveness.

Creating a Pinterest Strategy for Your Business

What Does my Business Want to Achieve on Pinterest?

Whether want to use Pinterest to help launch new products or as a catalogue for your products, having clear objectives for your presence is crucial as it will dictate and influence several key areas from which types of Pinterest boards to create and how you will measure your success on Pinterest.

Common Pinterest Business Objectives

- Drive Traffic to Your Site
- Strengthen Brand Identity
- Increase Your Brand Authority
- Expand Your Reach

Have I Built Customer Personas?

To have an effective Pinterest plan, it is vital to understand your audience. When you know your followers, you are better able to create engaging Pinterest content that connects with them. Want to know your audience better? Just ask. Do basic research by sending out surveys to your customers. Another option is to study your followers' profiles or review Pinterest analytics. Then create user personas based on the data. When you understand who follows you and when, you are better able to provide them with tips and tricks that speak to them. This will definitely help you stand out from the competition.

What Kind of Boards Should I Create?

Deciding on what boards you are going to create will depend on a number of factors, from what industry you are in to what your objectives are for your page. Ultimately however, the boards that you will create will stem from a clear and strong strategy that you need to develop in the beginning, being especially clear on what you want your boards to represent about you and what you want your audience to feel when they look at your boards. In general, you could start with pins relating to your products and services and develop ideas as you go along from what inspires you to customer testimonials, product demonstrations and general pictures of your office. Just always remember to use good quality visual images and support them with quality keyword rich descriptions.

What Visual Resources Do I Have That I Can I Utilise?

Pinterest is centred on the visual and is the perfect platform for you to showcase the visual resources you have for your business. So look to see what is relevant to share with your audience from your product and services, to eBooks, blog posts and images of staff events – the opportunities to share engaging and informative are only restricted by your own creativity.

How Am I Going to Promote My Boards and Page?

There are many ways for you to promote your page to others from utilising your other social media platforms, to ensuring you have included relevant hashtags and keywords to your pins that can help people find your images when searching Pinterest. You will also need to add Pinterest's follow button to your business website that will alert your web visitors to your Pinterest boards. Anywhere where your audience will see it is the place to alert them to your Pinterest profile so this includes adding your URL to your e-newsletter, business card, packaging and anywhere else that is relevant for your business.

How am I Going to Measure my Success?

As with any other marketing campaign, what you are going measure in order to define your success will depend on what the initial objectives are that you have for your Pinterest presence. Whether you want to use is as an outlet to boost sales or to show others your brand identity, remember to continually look and analyse your analytics and act on what they show you.

What Should You be Pinning?

> *Pinterest helps people discover things in a simple, visual way. People are on Pinterest to share with others their interests, hobbies, tastes and passions. Therefore, as a business on Pinterest your job is to provide inspiration for these interests by making sure each of your boards tells a unique, genuine story about what interests you, what/who you are and have to offer. What types of boards you should create should also be based around your Pinterest marketing goals.*

Valuable Information, Tips and Advice

Successful boards often deliver something valuable to the reader, whether that is entertainment or information. Create your boards around information that will be valuable, useful and engaging for consumers. Tips and advice are popular on Pinterest as they engage and give value to your audience and therefore makes them more likely to interact. Look to create content within your boards that can inform, teach and provide value to your audience.

Feedback for Your Business

If you are thinking about launching a new service or product or looking for opinions about how a particular aspect of your business is being received, then creating a Pinterest board that acts as a virtual focus group can help you to directly connect and engage with your customers and get valuable feedback. You can find out important information about your customers likes, dislikes and preferences that can greatly help your business efforts in the future.

New Products or Services

You can draw attention to a new product or service launch by dedicating a board to it. Pin information about the features and benefits, suggested audiences and uses, and special deals, testimonials, etc. After the release, you can also post customers' comments, media reviews and photos of clients using the product or service.

Showcase Your Company Culture and Employees

You can also generate greater customer engagement by showing your audience an inside look at your business through boards that showcase your business style, projects, ideas, motivations and other commitments. You can also feature photos of your office and employees that will humanise your business and make people feel like they know you. Customers are more likely to interact with a company they feel like they know, so showing a personality will draw people to your page.

Showcase Your Customers

There are many ways you can involve your customers in your content, from happy customer testimonials, pictures of customers using your product/service to a pin of a customer's own business. Maintaining good relationships with customers and continually engaging with them is a great way to encourage them to recommend you to their connections and cement yourself as a personable and genuine business with great customer service.

Competitions

If you run regular giveaways, pin those up onto a Competitions Board. Popular competitions run on Pinterest are based on people having to pin something (usually related to your product/ service) to win

something. This encourages user engagement and interaction but also directs traffic to your website if they are requested to pin something directly of it.

Humour

Incorporating humour is an excellent way to engage with current and potential customers on Pinterest. When you utilize humour in your Pinterest marketing, especially funny material that speaks to your fans and followers, it grabs attention and improves clicks and engagement. Look to create a specific funny board that acts as a way to put a humorous twist on your content.

Share User-Generated Images

Sharing real-life photos is very effective in engaging clients and building lasting relationships. This helps your followers feel like they are part of your business, and they are more likely to engage and interact with you. Share real-life photos from your business and encourage users to do the same. Great examples to get you started with are creating a "behind the scenes' board and a user board, and go from there.

Showcase Product Hacks

Pinterest is known as a place for DIY, tips and life hacks. Take advantage of this by using Pinterest as a platform to educate your audience with tips and tricks that relate to your product. This is something you can do regardless of your industry. Just make sure it's relevant. Think of some great tips to share, then create and curate the content to go with it. Your customers will appreciate this valuable and informative content and will show it through likes and repins.

Repin Other Users' Content

When marketing on Pinterest, it may seem tempting to have the lion's share of your pins be for your own products. After all, the main function of your account is to promote your brand. However, only pinning your own promotional content is a big faux pas. A top tip is to build an overall mood around your product, and one way to do that is to repin relevant content from others. For bonus points, you can team up with partners/local businesses to turn this pinning strategy into a competition for your pinners or simply run a completion of your own. A great illustration of using this strategy is by Next and their 'Style by Colour' Competition. This encouraged users to create a board that reflects their style and favourite autumnal colour, actively encouraging them to pin pins reflective of autumn and actively encouraged pinners to pin from other sites. Once done users were requested to tweet Next with the hashtag #myawcolour with the competition winner getting vouchers to spend at Next. Be sure to do this carefully however and avoid spreading content that is from an irrelevant source or a direct competitor. Rather, repin content from users with interests and quality content that complement your brand and products. This approach not only provides excellent supplementary content for your followers, but it also

helps foster beneficial relationships with other users. The simple act of repinning can lead to partnerships with influential pinners.

How to Build a Following and Amplify your Impact

Pinning images is only the beginning. The next challenge is to promote your Pinterest page in order to get maximum exposure and attract attention. Rather than relying solely on search engines, there are several other key techniques you can employ to help get your content noticed.

Engage with Other Pinners

One of the key elements of building a community on any social media network is engaging with your audience. On Pinterest following other users, especially influencers, is a great way to get your content noticed and spread across a much larger network of people. By following other users and engaging with their content, you increase the chances that they will follow you back, repin, like, and comment on your images, and give you greater exposure to their large followings. Once you start to build your network, don't forget to be social and remember to continue interacting with and engaging your existing fans.

Promote your Pinterest Page

Anywhere your customers interact with your brand is an opportunity to encourage them to find you on Pinterest. Once you begin pinning, remember to promote it across all your other social media platforms and that includes mentioning it on your e-newsletter, your email signature, business card, product packaging and anywhere else your customers will see it. Adding a Pinterest "Follow" and "Pin It" Button on your website is also a great way to drive traffic to your page and encourages your customers and readers to pin your products.

Create and Inspire with Interesting Boards

The key to a successful Pinterest presence is to create and showcase a range of boards that enhance your brand, engage your audience and host a range of varied content that inspires and interests your audience. Your boards need to be a reflection of your business values and interests so be creative and remember that people can pick and choose which boards they follow, so not every board has to appeal to everyone. It is important that you also consider the overall look of the board taking care to give your board's names and descriptions ensuring they are keyword rich and clear. Choosing an eye-catching cover pin for each board is also important as you want to compel your audience to click on and see your board and you will also need to ensure that each board is filled with enough quality pins to make it feel substantial. Utilise seasons and special observances with your boards also by putting your most relevant boards at the top of your profile to coincide with the seasons and other national events.

Host Competitions

Competitions on Pinterest can help drive a lot of attention to your profile. "Pin It to Win It" competitions are very popular with businesses and if done well can really boost sales and traffic. You can generate attention and engagement with competitions that get your fans involved by pinning images from your website onto their own boards, just make the competition interesting and gets others talking about your brand with a great prize also.

Pin Your Deals and Offers

Creating a board that houses your latest deals and offers is a great way to attract attention. If you want really utilise the community you can create an exclusive board for Pinterest members only and encourage them to share them with other users that will potentially get your offers seen by a wider audience.

Comment on Popular Pins

Take advantage of the popular pins section of Pinterest and use this opportunity to add your thoughts and comments on popular pins to generate conversation. Always leave a thoughtful and meaningful comment and this will encourage others to check out your profile and opens up the potential for new interactions with potential new customers.

Highlight Your Individual Boards

If you have boards that are particularly popular then place them highly on your profile to promote them and gain more followers. You can also tailor your board layouts to coincide with seasons and events and promote them to gather attention.

Add a Pin It Button to Your Website

You can easily drive referral traffic from your website to Pinterest by utilising hover buttons that are effective calls to action. Install the hover Pin It button on images on your website and this will act as a visual reminder to your visitors that you have a Pinterest profile and it also makes it easy for users to pin images from your site onto their own boards.

Invite Others to a Group Board

A great way to collaborate with clients and prospects on Pinterest is to create a group board and invite others to pin onto the board. As the creator only you can moderate the board and remove inappropriate

pinners and pins leaving a great canvas for others to contribute and add their pins and comments. This helps create a social and engaging group that will attract more attention to your profile.

Follow and Interact With Other Businesses

Connecting with other businesses on Pinterest is a great way to build your following and increase attention to you and your profile. Look to see if businesses you have dealt with in the past have profiles and also businesses that are similar to you in industry and location. If you follow other businesses on their other social networking sites such as their Twitter or blog then look to see if they are on Pinterest and connect with them also. By connecting with and interacting with other businesses you have the potential to be seen by their audiences which can open up the opportunity for potential new customers and visitors to your profile.

Refine Your Boards

Successful boards on Pinterest are often crafted by users who put great efforts in making their boards as niche as possible so that they stand a better chance of being found and subsequently followed by a target audience. Look to see if any boards that you have are labelled with a generic title that covers a broad area and actively look to refine it, seeing if you can split that broad board into several more refined ones. For example if you have a board called 'Weddings' that contains lots of different wedding related pins look to refine it and create several different boards such as 'Wedding Dresses' 'Wedding Invites' etc. By refining your boards you not only organise your page better, you always ensure they become more relevant to the people who are the most interested in those specific topics likely increasing your chances of getting more of the right followers.

Utilise Trends

Ensure that you actively pay attention to relevant trends and act when you can see an opportunity that you can utilise. Things that are popular at a certain time make for a great opportunity for attracting new followers so whether it's a person or event that is trending and relates to your business jump on board and share a pin that fits in as you will stand a good chance of gaining some of the traffic and attention that comes with a trending topic.

Ensure You Tag Users

If you are following at least one of a user's boards, you have the ability to tag them. By placing an @ symbol in front of the users name within a pin description or comment the pin will then feature their name and also link to their profile page. Tagging other users is a great opportunity to grab their attention and encourage engagement and interaction, both of which can go a long way in attracting new followers.

Ensure Every Pin is Perfectly Optimised

One of the fundamental factors for a successful Pinterest presence is to ensure that every pin you share is optimised in 4 key areas;

High Quality Image - Great pins at the very basic level need to start with a high-quality image. Look to ensure your image has no pixilation, is large, high resolution and generally good quality. It is also advisable to avoid pinning cheesy generic stock photos as Pinterest users want to be inspired with your beautiful and informative images so ensure every image you share is tailored towards providing value and is beneficial to the viewer in some way. Part of choosing a good quality image is also ensuring that your image supports the accompanying text and links and is reflective of the link you are sharing. Essentially, make sure that people know what's inside the pin so they feel compelled to click it. If you feel that your image isn't doing so on its own then add text to it as this can make the difference between the viewer clicking on your pin or not.

Succinct, Snappy SEO-Rich Description - A pin's description is a prime example of an SEO opportunity. When trying to build your presence on Pinterest you mustn't forget and overlook this commonly neglected area as your description has a big impact on your results. Ensure that your image description is clear, concise and enticing to the viewer, all with a consideration of using key SEO-friendly words to describe the content behind the pin so your pins can successfully rank highly in search engines.

Call-to-Action - Call to actions are a very powerful tool that you need to include on your pins, whether you place it on the image itself or within your pins description it is fundamental that you have included one. Whether your call to action is to encourage someone to comment, repin the image or move onto view a product on your website you need to make it clear to your followers what you want them to do so make your call to action clear and concise.

Attribution - Lastly you should always consider both protecting yourself from content theft on Pinterest but also on the other hand correctly attributing others credit for their own content. It is easy to get content stolen on Pinterest, so you need to ensure you always credit the work of others that you use and also protect yourself from others who will not do the same for your content. Giving credit to others is easy and involves a simple acknowledgement to them in the pin description. In regards to protecting your original pins there are several key elements to utilise, from adding your logo or website URL in the photo to using your key branding elements in the image design or even consider using a watermark on all of your images. Whatever elements you use ensure they are applied consistently as not only will it protect you from content theft it, having your logo or other brand elements on your pins is beneficial for your brand recognition.

Ensure Your Page is Optimised

The best way to convince visitors to follow you is to optimize your Pinterest page. Here are some key areas to focus on.

- **Profile**
  For the business name, use your company name or your name if it's for your personal brand. Upload a relevant, high quality profile image, such as your company logo, a professionally taken

headshot or an image with your company's name. Match your username with your business name. If the username is already taken or is too long, choose something similar to it or use an abbreviation. Take the time to write a convincing and compelling bio in the 160 characters you are given. Help attract local followers by adding your town or city and other location details. Don't forget to add your website and social media accounts. This information will be displayed right below your profile image. You can add your Facebook account only if it's a personal page as the option to add a Facebook business page isn't available yet.

- **Boards**
Make sure that your page has at least 10 boards. Place your most important or popular boards in the top row. That way they're displayed prominently above the fold, and people will see them immediately when they visit your brand page. Optimise your boards by adding good and keyword rich board names, descriptions and cover images. **Top Tip:** Create a few secret boards so you can save images to pin publicly later on.

Participate in Pinterest Group Boards

Pinterest group boards are a great collaborative tool to utilise in order to get your pins seen in front of a larger, targeted audience. Essentially a group board is where a select group of pinners pin items and collaborate towards creating a large pin board that is focused around a subject that the board's creator has chosen. You can be invited by another user to pin onto a group board which if it is a relevant theme to you, can be a great tool for getting your pins seen by a large and relevant audience. If you can't find a group that matches your interest or chosen theme then you can by all means start one of your own and then invite any pinners you follow and who also follow you to become part of the group. This is also a great way to collaborate with the community and get yourself established towards being a thought leader in your industry.

Partner With Influencers and Power Pinners

One of the best ways to advertise and promote your product is to get someone who is already established and is a well-known industry specialist with a large following to give you a helping hand. Word of mouth marketing and getting social proof from others goes a long way towards attracting attention and brand awareness therefore actively look to find those in your industry on Pinterest who are seen as power users and look to partner with them or at the very least interact with them and comment and share their pins in the hope that they will reciprocate and pin some of your content to their own following.

Design Content to Support Goals

Before you can determine what to pin, think about your goals. They might be to drive engagement, build an audience or to drive traffic. Once you choose your goals, you can determine what to pin by reviewing your Pinterest analytics. To access this data, click the gear icon and choose Analytics from the drop-down menu. Look at your Pinterest analytics to see what content resonates with your target audience. Your analytics page has three sections: Your Pinterest Profile, Your Audience and Activity from Your

Website. In the Your Pinterest Profile section, find out how your pins are performing. Your pins are categorized depending on the impressions, clicks, repins and likes they've received. Depending on your goal, choose the category you want to view. If you want to drive engagement, for example, look for pins that have been repinned and liked most. If you want to drive more traffic, take a look at clicks. It is also recommended that you visit the Your Audience section to look at your followers demographics and interests. Click the Interests tab to find out about their interests, the boards where most of your pins are being pinned and businesses that your audience engages with. Write down all this information and use it brainstorm ideas about what to pin.

Design Skinny Images

A Research by Curalate found that tall images with aspect ratios between 2:3 and 4:5 get 60% more repins than very tall images. You can get photos for free from sites like Pixabay, Pexels and Unsplash or you'll find affordable illustrations and icons on sites like Creative Market. It is highly recommended however that where possible you try to create your own images. You can do this easily with free tools like PicMonkey and Canva.

Test Various Pin Times

The best times to pin, according to Social Marketing Writing is from 2 pm to 4 pm and 8 pm to 1 am with the best day to pin being Saturday. This is only a general guideline however and you may come to find your optimal posting times are different. The important thing is the test various pins times to work out what is most effective for your business. To save you time, there are many online tools you can use to schedule pins. Use Viraltag, for example, to simplify the process of creating and importing images; it integrates with Canva, Flickr, Facebook, Picasa and Instagram. The tool's Image Enhancer makes it easy to edit your images. When you're scheduling pins, use a combination of your content and content from others. Where possible, include the handle of the creator of the image or content in your description.

Always Serve Complementary Content

Followers look to you and your business for be informed with valuable content. Show you know your industry and develop powerful relationships with loyal clients by providing your audience with Pinterest boards filled with helpful and engaging content. Always seek to know what your clients want and need, and create and serve them complementary content that helps them view you as a trusted resource.

Create Multiple Boards

A way to strengthen your brand presence is to vary the types of boards you create. Create multiple boards to give your followers a variety of topics covering a huge selection of relevant content. That way, you speak to multiple facets of your audience thereby increasing your appeal and reach. Remember when pinning to only include content that remains relevant to and strengthens your brand. More boards and topics will lead to an increase in followers.

Experiment With Promoted Pins

Promoted pins offer the option to pay for additional exposure for your content. As with all advertising, its best practise to experiment with different options. Test different images, copy and even categories, and then choose the ones that work best for you.

Collaborate With Popular Pinners

Group boards allow you to invite contributors to add their own pins to a common board. When contributors are chosen carefully, these group boards greatly benefit marketers by leveraging the contributors' influence and following. In the end it all boils down to an understanding that to be successful on Pinterest you need to create and foster a genuine and involved community and recognise the power of collaboration by inviting others into the conversation.

Design a Recognisable Style

The average Pinterest user follows nine brands, which means not only are you competing with individuals for attention, you're also competing with other companies. Even once someone follows you, there's no guarantee they'll notice your pins. One way to set your pins apart from the rest is to develop a recognisable style. Your signature style can be as bold as adding your logo or other identifying mark to all of your pins, or as subtle as sticking to certain aesthetic markers like lighting, angles or typography. All of these considerations work towards one central aim: to make it easy for users to recognise your pins as they scroll through their feeds.

Optimise Pins for Mobile Devices

According to the latest usage data from Pinterest, 75% of all users access the platform from a mobile device. That means it's absolutely necessary to optimize your images for mobile and any deficiency in your images is going to cost you dearly. To optimize your images for mobile devices, make sure they're large enough to view on a small screen. This is particularly important for images that include text. The most effective way to know whether your post is a fit for mobile is to simply preview all of your images on a smartphone and see how they look before you post them.

Tips for Success

Add Your Logo/Website to Your Images

When pinning original content, consider adding a watermark of your website or logo to your image this is to preserve pin integrity and ensure that the image will always stay connected to your website and will continue to promote your brand.

Verify your Account

When you create a business account make sure to have it verified. This can add authority and trust to a profile and can also make it stand out from other profiles within a search.

Engaging Board Cover Photos

One of the important things to consider when you begin creating boards is to select an engaging cover photo for each board. When a visitor lands on your Pinterest profile, you want the content to stand out and you can do this very easily by carefully selecting the cover photo for each board.

Make your Website Pinterest Friendly

To motivate your customers to share your content you need to optimise your business website to make it easy and compelling for them to do so. The Pinterest Goodies page found on Pinterest plays host to several widgets that you can download and utilise on your website to make pinning your products and following your profile simple for fans to do. From a follow us widget, to a Pin it widget and even a widget that's lets you showcase a specific board or your pins right inside on your site. Whatever widgets you choose to use, ensure you clearly display them on your site so that you can help turn your website traffic into potential new followers for your Pinterest profile.

Pin Consistently

Pinning consistently will come naturally if you have a well-developed pinning strategy. Consistently with your pinning goes a long way towards helping people discover your pins and increasing the number of followers you gain. As a basis look to pin/repin at least 5 – 10 images daily and stick to that routine, don't pin aggressively for several days straight and then neglect your profile for a week as this will not keep you in followers home pages which will not help you grow your following.

Pin at Optimal and Different Times of the Day

There are users all over the world on Pinterest all pinning and viewing at different times throughout the day. Therefore to help you potentially get seen by a new and global audience you should look to use response data to determine the best times to pin on your boards.

Convert Your Pinterest Personal Page to a Business Page

Although there's no visual difference in a personal and business page, if you are using Pinterest as your business you should convert to using a business page as this allows you to access certain features such as analytics that personal pages don't which is key to measuring your business success on Pinterest.

Bias Business Specific Boards and Not Get Carried Away With Casual

It is very easy, especially without a clear strategy, to get carried away with the casual aspect of Pinterest and eventually lose sight of the opportunity to create boards that are representative of your business. So just remember to be clear you're your strategy and stick to creating boards that both interest your audience and are representative or related to your business and industry.

Utilise Your Brand Assets and Create a Board For Them

Whilst some industries are more visual than others, there is a need nowadays for all industries to embrace the visual and utilise the many business resources that can be easily repurposed for use on Pinterest. From brand videos, to corporate literature such as white papers, e-books and photos of corporate events there may be a lot more assets available to you than you realise that together will make a strong Pinterest board collection.

Use Keywords Strategically

By strategically using keywords across your profile you are helping to make you profile more discoverable via search and therefore open to traffic and new interactions. Take the time to optimise all aspects of your profile with strategically place keywords from your business description, board name to your description for Pinterest search and you'll get higher placement in results.

Share Different Types of Content

Many have the perception that Pinterest only allows the use of images and therefore one of the greatest features and one of the most underutilised by many Pinterest users is posting varying types of content. From audio from Sound Cloud to videos from YouTube and slideshows from SlideShare Pinterest allows users to share a whole range of rich and varied content so utilise this feature and help your business stand out from the crowd.

Vary Your Board Positions with the Seasons & Special Observances

As national observances are celebrated and seasons change so too must your boards and their positions. These special events are a great time for your business to place your seasonal boards at the top of your profile to attract more attention and followers. As you plan new Pinterest boards, look for widely celebrated events and plan your board display accordingly placing an emphasis on encouraging interaction from your audience that will drive traffic at these crucial times of year for sales.

Don't Neglect Your Business Description

You have up to 200 characters to describe your business in the about section and it is important to craft them wisely. Have your keywords in mind and make it easy to read with a clear, interesting and relevant description to take advantage of SEO on Pinterest.

Optimise Your Page for SEO

As with any other social media platform you need to consider your SEO efforts when marketing on Pinterest. There are many ways to optimise your page for SEO including, optimising your about section and pin descriptions with descriptive keywords, including links back to your website and ensuring the images you pin have descriptive file names and relevant hashtags you can also include a reference link back to your website to drive traffic.

Stay Informed of Pinterest's Business News

As Pinterest evolves it is likely to make important changes that you as a business need to be aware of. Remember to follow the official Pinterest business page and subscribe to their blog to make sure you stay on top of Pinterest's business updates.

Take Note of Your Pinterest Followers

It is important for you to look at your Pinterest followers to find out important information such as who is looking, commenting and sharing your pins. Finding out this information can help you gain vital feedback about when your followers repin, the comments you gain and if you see the same people frequently repinning and interacting with you it shows you your potential brand ambassadors. Additionally, the information about who is interacting with you can also shed light on important potential opportunities to engage with individuals and businesses that may not have been an intended target in your Pinterest strategy.

Keep Your Pinterest Boards Fresh

Updating your followers Pinterest feed with fresh content regularly is key to a successful presence. Pinterest users love fresh content as it's something new and they get a first look especially before it becomes spread across Pinterest. From this you should actively look to pin original content from a variety of sites and sources as this will attract attention from other users and gives them a reason to follow your boards as they know you will provide them with regular, fresh and interesting content.

Keep Your Boards Organised

Organised boards are fundamental for not only your own general ease of use of Pinterest but also go a long way in gathering followers. Your organisational skills need to be applied to everything from your

board names, what boards you generate, how many boards you generate, to ensuring your pins are always placed in the appropriately named board. In addition, you will also need to ensure each board cover has the best pin and that your boards are arranged in an order that best represents you or your brand. Whilst it may seem a lot of effort, you will be rewarded greatly in the long term as organising your boards keeps them user-friendly, easily searchable for your audience and will ensure your Pinterest presence is as fully optimised as it can be for attracting followers and building your brand awareness positively.

Include Price Tags

Users on Pinterest are not only there for creative inspiration but are also there to find new things to buy. Whilst it is great to have a profile filled with value and inspiration, you as a business and marketer are ultimately on Pinterest to drive traffic to your website and inspire purchases by others. Therefore it is up to you on your profile to influence and compel buyer behaviour and one of the most important ways to drive traffic and increase revenue is to include a price tag and information on the pins that you create as research has found Pinterest pins with prices get 36 percent more likes than those without. It is important to remember however that your Pinterest profile isn't simple seen as purely a sales driven platform where you simply broadcast your products, rather you need to provide value to your community with a mix of rich, quality pins that inspire, inform and excite your audience.

Create a Board for Your Blog

Cross promoting your content across your social media platforms is a vital task that you can utilise to increase your brand awareness and drive traffic to your sites. If you have a blog, ensure that you create a board on your Pinterest profile that is solely a place for your followers to find all your blog posts and place it in a prominent position. You also need to consider your SEO efforts by naming your boards and pins using relevant keywords, making it easier for followers to find them in search engine results. On every new blog post you publish, you then need to add it to your blog board on Pinterest and look to include a clear, concise and key word rich summary of the article, a relevant high-quality image (ideally not a generic stock photo) and a link back to the blog post itself.

Think of Pinterest as a Search Engine

Despite Pinterest being a visual platform, text plays a very important role and as such, you need to approach Pinterest in the mind set of it being a visual search engine. From your board's names to pin descriptions and what you name your image files, you need to consider your keyword research and strategically place those words throughout your pins and profile to ensure you attract your target audience and increase your visibility in Pinterest search results.

Regularly Explore your Analytics

Pinterest Analytics shows you a wealth of important data that you can and should regularly analyse. From your pin impressions, the quantity of repins to clicks, what content resonates best with your audience and much more, you should regularly keep track of what your analytics tell you as it will help you make informed choices for future content creation and distribution. A monthly check of your analytics is enough to show you a wealth of important information that will inform and help you adapt your Pinterest strategy to ensure it is as effective as it can be moving forward.

Optimise for Mobile

With ever increasing numbers of people accessing Pinterest from their mobile devices, it is vital that you optimise your profile for mobile users and give them a mobile friendly experience. Therefore you should test and experiment with your images to see how they look on both your desktop and a variety of other mobile devices to ensure you provide a seamless experience for those visiting your Pinterest page no matter what device they are viewing it from. When assessing your site from different devices, you should check for several key areas such as; are your images pinnable? Are the social media sharing buttons clearly positioned and working properly? If text is used, it is readable on a small screen? And importantly, do the images appear on the mobile version of your website? The time you spend too perfect your profile from your desktop should also be spent on making your site work for mobile too, if you fail to do so then you could lose not your pins but crucially, traffic and sales also.

Like Other People's Pins

If you come across pins that you like but aren't necessarily useful to your audience or be something that you want to pin to one of your boards, you may want to consider liking them rather than repining them. Anytime you like someone's pin, it will show up in their activity feed. This may grab their attention and get them to follow you.

Use Keywords For Search Results

Hashtags are no longer necessary on Pinterest as the search functionality looks for keywords in pin descriptions. When writing your pin descriptions, make sure you are using the keywords most people would use to find your content. For example, if you want to be found under the keyword 'Golf', you would obviously use the word "Golf" somewhere in your description. This makes it easier to be found and will create more followers leading to more exposure.

Use Pinterest's Browser Extensions for Easier Pinning

Pinterest offers browser extensions for Chrome, Firefox, Internet Explorer and Safari. Downloading the extension gives you a pin it button right in your browser's toolbar. This is a great way to seamlessly pin interesting things you see whilst surfing the Internet. Once you the extension is installed, you will be able

to simply right click, choose Pin this Image from the drop down and be able to choose the board that you want to pin it to. Not only will it pin the graphic but it will link back to the originating source.

Pin Videos

Pinterest doesn't just allow you to pin images...you can also pin videos! Pinterest allows you to pin videos from sites like Dailymotion, TED, YouTube and Vimeo. In order to pin a video, you have to make sure you have the 'share' URL of the video; not the URL where you watched the video, or the embed code. On YouTube, for instance, you'll find this link under the video under 'Share'.

Use Pinterest's Mobile App

It is recommended you download Pinterest's mobile app. It will allow you to easily browse, pin, repin and even take photos to pin right from your phone which is perfect for growing your page and interacting on the go.

Repin for a Few Minutes Each Day

To get noticed on Pinterest, you need to pin and repin regularly. Even taking around three minutes each day to curate and repin to your Pinterest boards can have a profound effect on your profile. To find relevant content to repin simply enter keywords for your niche or industry in Pinterest search. Remember to check the links on any pins to make sure they're active and relevant before you share them.

Follow Relevant Pinners

For successful Pinterest marketing, you must actively follow pinners in your niche. Find pinners relevant to your niche through a Pinterest search and look to follow three to five new pinners every day, being careful not to follow just anyone. Once you find potential pinners to follow, review their profiles and check their Pinterest activities to see if they'll add value to your Pinterest marketing.

Comment on a Pin a Day

Keep your eyes open for relevant pins on which you can offer input. If a pin inspires you, add something to the conversation, aiming for one comment at least a day. Your comments can be as short or as long as you'd like, just make sure it is relevant, pertinent and not self-promotional.

Create Pinterest Images in Batches

Save yourself a lot of time by getting a good image creation tool such as Canva and creating images of your own to pin to your Pinterest boards. A pro tip is to do this task all in one sitting. If you aim to create a fresh image to pin each weekday, that means 7 images a week. One image should take about 5 minutes minimum, so this should only take around 35-minutes. The Ideal size for a pin is 735 x 1102 pixels, however on Canva you can choose the default Pinterest graphics layout that is already optimised for size so all you need to do is focus on creating your design.

Follow Analytics to Generate Content Ideas

To find inspiration for original pins, review Pinterest Analytics each week. Evaluate your repin, impression and click progress over a period of time, as well as individual pin performance. Jot down the best pins and boards and this will help you understand which boards and images are getting the most attention from your followers. Then apply what you've learned when you create pins for the next week.

Common Mistakes to Avoid

Not Strategically Placing Your Boards

Newly created pinboards fall into place after those you created first. As time passes, the boards you most want your followers to see may be lowest on the page. To avoid making this mistake you need to edit your profile so that your most important boards are in the top row of pinboards. Additionally, you should adjust your boards to coincide with seasons and other national observances placing those most likely to get attention at the top of your page.

Using Bad Quality Images

Images and videos are central to Pinterest so it's vital to represent your brand with good, high quality photos. Low quality photos aren't just visually bad quality they are also ones that are bland and uninspiring so to ensure you are successful on Pinterest you need to evoke a response from your audience with images that make an impact and inspire people to learn more about you.

Pinning Only Your Products or Services

Rather than using Pinterest as a blatant sales tool by only pinning your products and services, you need to embrace the social aspect of Pinterest and engage with your audience. Pins that illicit an emotional response with your consumer and inform, inspire and entertain are going to be the ones that get repinned, so focus on giving your audience what they want as opposed to old-fashioned pushy sales tactics.

Not Completing Your Pinterest Business Profile

As with any other social media platform it is important to make sure you complete your profile. A well-presented business Pinterest account will make your business look more professional and credible, so ensure you complete all the sections in the business profile, including links to your other websites, a good quality brand logo so you are easily identified and a clear about section that contains your detailed business information and represents your business effectively.

Not Including Prices on Your Images

It is widely known that Pinterest pins with prices get more likes than pins without them. So remember to either include the price in your description on every product pin you post or incorporate the price in the image you pin.

Not Linking Your Pins to Product Pages

A Pinterest user does not have to visit your Pinterest homepage to engage with your posts, they simply can just repin from others, so it is vital that you link your product pins back to a product landing page to ensure you don't miss on a good marketing opportunity.

Not Including a Description on Your Images

If you fail to include descriptions on your pins they will not show up in a Pinterest search which makes you less discoverable. So ensure that every time you utilise the pin description and create a well-written and clear description of your product with strategically placed keywords and relevant hashtags. You can write up to 500 characters within a pin description so make the most of this and craft a description that effectively tells the viewers about your product and where appropriate, link back to your website, other social networks or your blog to drive traffic to your business.

Not Using Pinterest Analytics

If you fail you explore your analytics you miss out on the chance to learn important information that can affect your Pinterest marketing strategy. Analytics are there to help you make your boards more effective so regularly analyse your analytics and respond accordingly to what the information is showing you.

Neglecting or Abandoning Your Pinterest Profile

Having a neglected profile that is no longer updated is harmful to your social and business reputation. If you find you no longer use your profile you need to go back to basics and look at your marketing strategy to understand what went wrong and what you are going to do to ensure Pinterest becomes an effective

tool in your marketing strategy. If you still struggle you need to evaluate whether Pinterest itself is actually a profile your business needs to have a presence on at all.

Not Engaging With The Community

The nature of Pinterest is based on social collaboration and you need to utilise the social aspect of Pinterest by monitoring, listening and responding to what your fans are saying and doing. Actively look to connect and interact with those who follow you and other businesses similar to you as being social goes a long way towards establishing your reputation as a credible and genuine business as well as making others more likely to interact with you and tell others they know about you too which has the potential for new business opportunities.

Pinning or Repinning Inappropriate Items

Your Pinterest page is an extension of your business persona so don't harm your reputation by pinning or repinning images and other items that are inappropriate and not representative of your business.

Not Choosing a Category for Each of Your Boards

For each new board you create, you can and should choose a category to place it into. By placing your board into an appropriate category you will make your content more searchable by others.

Not Having a Pinning Strategy

Without a pinning strategy it's easy to visit your profile every so often and repin anything that catches your eye leading to boards that are filled with random images and doesn't really enhance or represent what your business is trying to convey on Pinterest. The key is to remember that as a brand you are trying to show others what your business is all about so strategically plan out your boards and have in mind what message you want the audience to get when they look at each of your boards.

Not Promoting Your Business Pinterest Page

No one will know your Pinterest profile exists if you fail to promote it. So utilise the networks and resources you already such as your other social networks, your website and word of mouth to help spread the word.

Measuring Success

Accessing your Pinterest analytics will show you a whole host of important information. You will be able to see what people like from your profile, what they save from your website and data about your audience, too, so you can learn what your customers really want. With Pinterest Analytics, you can learn;

- What Pins and boards from your profile people love most
- What people like to save from your website
- Who your Pinterest audience is, including their gender, location and other interests
- What devices people use when they're Pinning your stuff
- How adding the Pin It button to your website leads to referral traffic from Pinterest

Pins From Your Website

One of the most important metrics to consider is the number of pins created from your websites content. By analysing this metric you can help determine the important factor of whether the visual content on your website is interesting enough for your website visitors to pin to your boards. By looking at this metric over time you can also assess what visual content is most engaging for your audience and similarly show you areas where your content isn't attracting attention therefore highlighting what content you should show in the future to engage your audience and encourage more pins.

Number of Visitors and Visits to Your Website

A big indicator as to the success of your Pinterest presence is the level at which your audience on Pinterest was driven to your website. When looking at this metric you should also look to see the number of new visitors as this will help you determine whether you are successfully expanding your reach into new audiences and therefore potential new customers. Looking at the level of returning visitors via Pinterest is also worthwhile as it shows you whether you are continually attracting and engaging previous visitors successfully enough that they have want to and are given a reason to return to your website.

Most Repinned Content

The most repinned metric is fundamental in understanding what content is being repinned the most, therefore showing your business what content is resonating best with your audience. Reviewing the pins that get repinned the most helps you identify the key aspects of the type of content that works for your Pinterest audience which will better inform your future content creation efforts to ensure future pinning success and effectiveness.

Most Clicked Content

Understanding what content on Pinterest drives the most traffic to your website is highly important as it will show you essentially what content compels people to visit your website, giving you more understanding of the potential to generate revenue. Ensure you explore which pins drive the most traffic to your website and use this information in your future content creation. Analysing this metric can also show you whether the Pin it button on your website is driving engagement as if the same content that has a pin it button appears in the most clicked report then you know the pin it button is a successful aspect of your Pinterest marketing as it is helping to drive engagement on Pinterest which could translate into potential revenue for your website.

Pinterest Maintenance Checklist

DAILY

- ✓ Go through Pinterest home page and pin any relevant images to boards
- ✓ Using the search bar type in keywords, relevant words and words associated with your boards to find more images and try to pin at least 1 new image to each of your boards
- ✓ See who has followed you and respond accordingly

WEEKLY

- ✓ Think of any ideas for new boards you can create. Think of boards your target audience/current clients etc. would like to see.
- ✓ Go through boards and make sure everything is organised
- ✓ Look to see if any new connections from other social media platforms have Pinterest and follow them
- ✓ Create batches of original images for use within the week

INSTAGRAM

At its most basic, Instagram is a social networking app made for sharing photos and videos from a smartphone. From a marketing perspective, Instagram makes a strong business case with over a billion users. When compared among the major social networks, only Facebook and YouTube have more people logging in each month. Instagram provides a huge asset for visual content, which we all know is driving social like none other and has developed itself into a fully-fledged, global platform that allows brands to humanize their content, showcase their products, inspire their audience and promote their brand all in a friendly, authentic way without directly selling to your customers.

What's good about Instagram?

- ✓ One of the best attributes about Instagram is that it greatly accomplishes its original goal: **fast, easy, and efficient photo-sharing**. Not only this but photos shared via Instagram are reaching a huge audience, thanks to steady user adoption. People engage better with visuals rather than words. It's widely known that photos rule when it comes to marketing as photos make an emotional connection in a way that text cannot. They make your company and brand more relatable and of course, are fun and engaging.

- ✓ **No Character And Caption Limit.** While there are some limits when it comes to the bio and username, unlike some social media platforms like Twitter, Instagram does not have a character limit when it comes to the image caption. The description of every post can be as long as you want it to be.

- ✓ Despite being one of the most popular and highly used social media platform after Facebook, the number of local businesses making use of Instagram is still limited – which is great as it means **competition is still considerably low**, unlike in the case of other social platforms like Facebook.

What's not so good about Instagram?

- ✓ Since Instagram is a visual tool, you need to have appealing content to share to stand any chance of success on this platform.

- ✓ Instagram is a service that is designed to be used with mobile devices, such as tablet computers or smart phones. It has very limited functionality on desktop computers.

- ✓ Instagram is only an iPhone and Android app. If you have Windows mobile or Blackberry, it won't work. That means you won't be reaching all your target audience.

Need to Know Facts, Stats and Tips about Instagram

- The number of monthly active Instagram users has grown to 1 billion
- Instagram continues to attract a younger audience with 72% of teens saying that they use the platform.
- Even in terms of engagement, Instagram is ahead of Facebook with a median engagement rate of 1.73% per post for brands.
- But among marketers, Instagram still takes second place to Facebook with 83% of them using the platform.
- Users upload more than 100 million photos and videos on a daily basis.
- 2 billion Likes occur on the platform every day.
- Thursday is the best day to post on Instagram for brands across all verticals.
- Instagram Profiles saw a follower growth rate of 17-33% during 2018.
- Videos get 21.2% more interactions compared to images and 18.6% more interactions compared to carousels.
- Instagram Stories Daily Active Users: 300 million
- Number of Businesses on Instagram: 25 million
- Number of Instagram Likes per day: 4.2 billion
- Number of Photos uploaded per day: 95 million, up from 70 million last year
- 68% of Instagram users are Females.
- More than 40 Billion photos have been uploaded to Instagram so far.
- 200 million Instagrammers actively visit the profile of a business every day
- Posts with at least one hashtag average 12.6% more engagement.
- More than 400 million accounts now use Instagram Stories every day, according to Instagram.

Why You Need Instagram For Your Business

From the boom in popularity of Instagram Stories, to the very impressive stats of user adoption engagement and the recent expansion of advertising opportunities—it's a good time to be using Instagram for business. Only if your business can thrive in this creative and inherently visual platform though.

How to Create an Instagram Business Account and the Basic Lingo

1. **Download the Instagram App**

   The very first thing you need to do is to download the Instagram App which is available for free in both the Apple App Store and Google Play. At Current, Instagram does not have a desktop version that includes all the functions of the mobile app. For example, you can view content on Instagram's website, but you can't upload content via your desktop.

2. **Create an Instagram Account**

   Once downloaded, it's time to create your account. When you open the app, you'll have two choices -- Log In With Facebook or Sign Up With Phone or Email. Whilst it is in tempting to use the Facebook option, from a business perspective you need to sign up with a business email to ensure your profile isn't linked with your personal Facebook account. Next, enter your details. Your Full Name is the name that will be displayed on your profile so be sure to enter your actual business name so your profile is recognizable to visitors.

3. **Pick a Username**

   You'll then be prompted to choose a username. In a similar way to Twitter, your username is unique to your profile and allows other accounts to find, connect and engage with your brand. Pick a username that is recognizable, easy to find and -subject to availability- it would ideally be your exact business name. Should your business name already be taken by another user, try to create a username that is as close as possible. You can update your username later in your account settings, so don't worry if you want to change it in the future.

4. **Choosing the Right Profile Photo**

   Your profile picture is one of the first things people see when searching for and visiting your profile so keep your image in line with your logo, branding or visual elements. Be aware that Instagram displays your profile photo in a circle format and will automatically crop your photo to fit inside the circle so be aware of this and leave room around the corners of your image.

5. **Your Instagram Bio**

   Instagram bios have a 150-character maximum so you'll need to be direct and concise in telling the audience who you are and what you do. Your bio is the only place where you can feature a clickable URL and drive traffic to an external site so you need to take advantage of this. It's common practice for businesses to use this to showcase their website, feature their most recent

post, or a landing page for a competition. Don't worry about trying to stuff keywords and hashtags into your description as they aren't searchable on your bio. You can edit your profile photo, profile name, username, bio, or URL. at any time by clicking on the "Edit Profile" button on your profile.

6. Managing Your Settings

In the upper right-hand corner of your profile if you click on the small gear (dots if you're using an Android) icon this will take you to your settings. There you'll be able to manage all your profile settings such as changing your password, see posts you've liked, enable notifications, and much more. To boost engagement, there are a few settings you should check out right away:

Comments: Having people engage with your content is great but sometimes you may come across certain comments that are negative, offend your audience or go against your brand values. Instagram can automatically hide comments that contain certain keywords or phrases (for example expletives) To do this, you must turn on the feature and enter your chosen specific words and phrases into your Instagram settings.

Switch to Business Profile: Business profiles make it easy for your audience to contact you, provides more in-depth insights and makes it easier for you to promote content. Importantly, to switch to an Instagram business profile your business must have a Facebook business page and you must be a Facebook page admin to connect the two platforms. To switch to a business profile, view your profile, and click on the gear icon in the upper right-hand corner to view your settings. Scroll down and click on "Switch to Business Profile." Log in with Facebook and allow Instagram to manage your Pages. Select a Facebook Page to connect with your Instagram profile. Instagram will automatically import relevant information from your Facebook page for you to edit.

Private Account: Instagram will automatically set your profile to public and you should keep it this way! If you're a business, you need users to be able to automatically see your posts and follow your business without any obstacles.

Story Settings: You can manage who can see and reply to your Instagram Stories in your "Story Settings." You should allow all your followers to see and reply to your Stories to increase brand engagement and awareness.

Adding Additional Instagram Accounts: If you manage multiple accounts you can add up to five accounts so you're able to quickly switch between them without logging in and out. To add an account, click on the gear to reveal your settings. Scroll to the bottom and click "Add Account." Enter the username and password of the account you'd like to add. To switch between accounts, go to your profile and tap your username at the top of the screen. Simply click on the account you'd like to switch to.

The Basic Content

Instagram allows users to post photos and videos to their Instagram feed as well as Instagram "stories" and live videos.

How to Add a Photo

To post a new photo, tap the add (camera) button on the bottom of your screen. This will open your phone's camera, and you can choose either to take a new photo or video or select one from your camera roll. Click Next, and you'll be taken to a screen with multiple options, including Instagram's filters and an Edit button, which will allow you to adjust the photo by changing the brightness, contrast, structure, warmth, saturation, colour, fade, highlights and shadows. You can also add a vignette or tilt-shift the picture. Once you've edited the photo, click Next. This gives you two options: You can post the photo to your public feed or send it directly to a friend/friends. If you choose to make it public, write a caption to describe the picture, add a location to geotag it, add several relevant hashtags, tag people and share it on multiple platforms. You have the option to turn off comments, found at the bottom of the Advanced Settings page. If you choose to send the picture directly to someone else, simply compose a caption and send it to one or several friends. If you want to change or add something after you've published a post, tap the ellipses (...) button on that post and select Edit to update the caption or add a location or tags. Here you can also share the post on other social networks or delete the post entirely.

Instagram Stories

Instagram Stories are pieces of content that disappear after 24 hours. At the top of your home page is a horizontal bar that has your profile photo with a plus sign. When you select the photo of yourself, it opens another screen, with the option of live video, an option called Normal (which takes a photo), Boomerang (which creates a GIF) and Hands-Free, which records a video without requiring you to hold down the record button. You also have the option to draw on the photo or video with the pen icon on the top right, add stickers with the sticky-note icon, or add text with the "Aa" icon. To add more content to your story, click the camera icon located on the top left.

Instagram Video

On Instagram users can either share a video that remains on the profile or take and stream a live video that disappears. If you're looking to take video that remains on your Instagram feed, you can upload video you've taken or take video directly through the app to post. If you choose to take or upload video, you can still add filters and change the cover. You also have the option of whether to include sound. The Live Video option offers you the benefit of giving customers content in a fun and different way such as a live look behind the scenes of interesting aspects of your business or a live Q&A through the comments. Once the live video has ended, it is no longer available anywhere, which sets it apart from Facebook.

Interacting with Other Instagram Users

There are many ways to interact with other users on Instagram. For instance, you can tag other users in your photos, comment on content or privately message people.

- **Liking:** Liking is the basic way to connect with other users. To like a photo, either double-tap the image or tap the heart button under the post. To view a list of photos you've liked, go to your profile, press the gear button on the top-right corner and select Posts You've Liked.

- **Commenting:** Next to the Like button is a Comment button — just tap it and the app will take you to the Comments page for that photo, with a text box where you can enter what you want to say. Just press Send when you finish typing.

- **Mentioning:** As on Twitter, you can use the @ symbol to tag other users in your Instagram comments or post captions. When you type the @ symbol, followed by the first letter of a person's username, it will bring up a list of people to select from; or, you can simply finish typing out the person's username on your own. If you want to reply to another user's comment, you need to tag the person this way, or else that user won't get a notification.

- **Tagging:** Instagram allows you to add tags before you post an image or video. To do so, tap the Tag People option before sharing your photo, and then tap where in the photo you'd like to add a tag. The app will then prompt you to type in the person's name to search for his or her account. Once you've tagged other users in your photo and shared the image, other users can tap on the photo to see the people who are tagged.

- **Direct messaging:** To access Instagram Direct, go to the home page and tap the button in the top-right corner. Here, you can send private instant messages, photos and videos to other users. To send a new direct message (DM), tap the "+" button in the top-right corner, and select Send Photo or Video, or Send Message. Once you've sent the message, you and the recipients can message back and forth. Users who are not already following you will be asked whether they want to allow you to send them photos and videos before they can view your direct message.

How to Create an Instagram Marketing Strategy

Many businesses feel pressured to be on every social media platform without thinking through their strategy, especially when it's the new exciting platform that all the millennials are using! However, since Instagram is very different from other popular social sites it requires a different marketing strategy.

1. **Determine Your Objectives**

First thing's first, you need to lay the foundation and establish what you want to achieve on Instagram. Whether you've never published a single photo or you're an Instagram pro, it's important to start with clear goals in mind. Consider the following the questions to help build a solid foundation to your Instagram marketing strategy:

- Why are you using Instagram?

- How can Instagram assist you in achieving your overall marketing goals?
- How does Instagram offer you something different to other platforms?
- Who is your target audience and which members of your audience are active on Instagram?
- How will Instagram integrate with the other networks in your social media strategy?
- How much time or budget can you commit to Instagram?

Depending on your industry, brand and key performance indicators, your Instagram marketing strategy should ideally target several objectives. Here are some common ones that businesses tend to choose:

- Increased brand awareness
- Showcase your team and recruit new talent
- Increase customer engagement and brand loyalty
- Showcase products and services
- Share company and industry news/updates
- Connect with influencers
- Drive sales through traffic
- Showcase your company culture and values
- Advertise to potential customers

As you continue to create your strategy, these objectives will guide you in determining the best approach to each part of the process.

2. Determine Your Instagram Audience

Marketing is all about delivering the right message, to the right people, at the right time. Just like on any other social media platform, you need to determine the audience you want to reach before you begin marketing on Instagram. Don't know where to start? Some helpful factors to consider when narrowing down your target Instagram audience are age, location, gender, income, interests, motivations, and pain points. If you already have other marketing strategies in place, you can draw from those to help. Some other tips include, taking a look at your competitor's followers and monitoring popular event and interest hashtags that are related to your business then find out who's using and engaging with the hashtags and check out their profiles.

3. Competitive Analysis for Instagram

After you determine your Instagram audience, do a competitive analysis to see what other marketers in your field are posting as the information you gather from this audit will serve as a benchmark as you

start growing your own account. If you already know your top competitors, start with searching for their Instagram profiles. If not, try searching for terms related to your business or industry to find similar, relevant accounts.

Conduct a quick audit of those accounts looking specifically at;

- What types of posts are getting the highest amount of engagement?
- What popular hashtags they are using
- What kinds of captions they are writing
- How often they are publishing
- How quickly they are growing
- Are there any marketing opportunities they might have missed?

4. Choose Your Content Strategy (More on this Later)

Instagram is an inherently visual social platform and the content you share with your audience is the back bone of your marketing campaign. It should be relevant, valuable and engaging for your followers whilst at the same time being consistent with your brand and strategy.

Common Types of Content

- **Product Based Content:** This is a popular Instagram marketing strategy focusing all your posts on your products in a straight forward marketing campaign. All your followers receive pictures and videos of your products exclusively.
- **User Generated Content:** Another effective marketing strategy is to rely on user generated content. The aim is to create campaigns focused on attracting a large audience who are willing to get involved with the brand's channel and hashtags and upload their own content. For example, upload themselves using the product etc.

Successful brands use a mixture of both on Instagram. Once you have decided on the type of content for your strategy, you Importantly need to think about the hastags you will use to supplement and enhance the content. Hashtags are sometimes just as important as your brand image and they will help you grow followers exponentially if used correctly. You can use popular hash tags in order to get more chances to be discovered through search engines but at the same time, you can choose to use less popular tags if they are properly targeted inside a specific niche. By all means you can create your own user generated hashtags to build your brand awareness, and for competitions you are running etc.

5. Setting Up an Editorial Calendar

On average, brands post about six images per week on Instagram which adds up to over 300 posts per year! With that many posts, it can be difficult to keep track of all the content you need to post as well as what you've already posted. Instagram does not reward quantity but if you are consistent and able to deliver quality content frequently, your followers will reward you with a higher engagement rate. Creating an editorial calendar is a helpful way to cut down on the amount of time required to manage

your Instagram presence and is also a great place to record any key events you want to highlight on your Instagram account such as new product launches, national holidays, special observances or special offers. Ultimately, your content schedule and the frequency of your posting depends on two things your available time/resources and what your audience wants. This is why after the first couple of months, you should look to study your audience and try to find out vital insights such as when to post in order to get the most engagement as this will guide your strategy going forward.

6. Building a Consistent Brand on Instagram

It's clear when a business on Instagram doesn't have a consistent brand strategy as their content is random, sporadic and disjointed, which will do nothing but confuse their audience and will likely cause an account to lose followers. To avoid this, it's important to maintain a consistent brand aesthetic across your Instagram account. To determine what yours looks like, start by thinking about your brand personality. What are your brand values? What's your brand personality? Are you bold and adventurous with a bright colour palette? Or are you sensible and regal and use a lot of purple in your brand? Ideally, someone should be able to see a picture in their feed and instantly know that it's from your brand just by looking at the photo.

7. Utilize Paid Advertising

You can create a successful marketing strategy on Instagram without paying for ads but only to a certain point. If you want to be sure of your future success, you need to capitalize on this feature and leverage the opportunities available to you to boost traffic, sales and awareness. It's important to note that at current, the advertising feature on Instagram is linked with Facebook ads and cannot be used independently. In a nutshell this means, you will have to create a Facebook account as well in order to use them, in case you don't have one already. Whilst it might appear to be somewhat annoying to have to do this, it's actually of tremendous benefit to you as Facebook has access to more user data than any other social media or advertising platform. Therefore, you can be assured that you are getting the best ad targeting option available for marketers with great results in the long term.

Here are some top tips for maximising advertising campaigns on Instagram:

- **Use eye-catching images:** Ads are not intrusive and are shown in users' feeds just like any other posts, therefore your ads need to be as attractive and persuasive as your regular posts. This means that you need to focus on great imagery, professionally quality photos and attention-grabbing captions.
- **Target your ads precisely:** To maximize your gains from the advertising campaign you must target your ads precisely. This means carefully studying your followers, potential customers and your competition to identify specific segments of your targeted population and deliver your ads to them. The more you can narrow down the pool of potential customers, the better the results will be.

Creating a Content Strategy for Instagram

Visual content is at the heart of Instagram. The 100 million photos and videos shared daily to the platform are the reason more than 300 million people visit the app every day. Instagram is a powerful platform for marketing and advertising purposes and creating quality, engaging content should be at the core of your strategy, but what should you post about?

There's no definitive rule for the best strategy to take when it comes to your content — it'll vary from business to business. What's important is to focus on creating content that resonates with your audience and is aligned with your goals. This first step to defining what this content is starts with defining themes for your content.

Create Your Content Themes

Content is the foundation of your Instagram presence. Every business, no matter its size or industry has access to a wealth of potentially brilliant content to share on Instagram. Whether it's new products launches, behind the scenes access, a feature in the local news or a meet the team segment, there's a whole host of subject opportunities you can utilize for your videos and photos. Based on your target audience and objectives, the key to success is to develop a plan to deliver eye-catching content to your audience on a consistent basis. To start, review your objectives and determine what aspects of your brand to showcase in your Instagram content. Products, services, team members and your local community all offer rich potential for subject matter. Once you have a list of specific content themes, brainstorm possible subjects for your images and videos. Building content themes around what you know works is essential to success, a quick Instagram audit will tell you everything you need to know about what content is resonating best with your audience. Once you have your data, develop your content themes around that style of visual, whether it's photos with animals, brightly-coloured images or videos of your product.

Examples of popular content themes:

- Behind the scenes content
- User generated content
- Product demos / showcase
- Educational
- Humanising Content
- Fun/Meme/Humour
- Customer Stories
- Meet the Team

Creating content themes can be a fun, creative and interactive task for you and your staff and can be as simple as starting with a pen and paper and throwing around some ideas. Start with your key company

values and write down everything that comes to mind from it, including associated visuals including brand colours. From these notes, you can then start to formulate ideas for your key content themes. Once you have your content themes in place you can pull them all together to create a content plan. Included in this plan should be a consideration of the style and aesthetic feel of your posts, alongside your posting frequency.

Determine Content Types and Strike a Balance

Instagram started as a photo-sharing app, but its creative users now publish everything from graphics and videos to Boomerang videos. Quality matters on Instagram so when you put together your content for your social media schedule consider a striking a balance of content types that will work best for the resources you have and the engagement you want from your audience. For example if your audience loves a high-quality video that tells a compelling story about your product, work them into your content more often. Beyond simply uploading a simple snap, Instagram has matured and offers several supplementary apps that help you get even more unique and creative content with your posts. Some of those include;

- **Hyperlapse:** This app allows users to shoot stop-motion time-lapse. While the camera moves a short distance, the action between each shot is rapid.
- **Layout:** Combine photos and videos together in a single Instagram post through custom layouts and features like mirrored landscapes.
- **Boomerang:** Similar to a GIF, Boomerang plays a short cut video forward, but also backward, repeatedly to create a nonstop motion.

No matter how great your content, there will be always room for more when it comes to social media marketing. Beyond settling for the basic, a good strategy will benefit and indeed take advantage of the additional and more advanced content options available.

- **Instagram Stories:** This feature allows you to interact with your followers by sharing posts without the worry of over posting. You can share as many images and ideas you want throughout a day and create stories that will disappear from your profile grid or feed after 24 hours. This is a great way to grow your audience because every time you post, you get on top of your followers' feed.
- **Instagram Live:** This feature is most effective when you have a significant number of followers. Just like stories, videos from Instagram live appear at the top of your followers' feeds and are a great tool to showcase new products or engage with your fans.
- **Consider Contests:** Contests are a great, proven way to attract more followers. Example popular content types include;

    The comment contest: Ask your followers to post comments on one of your posts in order to enter the contest.

    Photo contest: Ask your followers to post images with a brand specific hashtag you've created.

Live Content: Engage with your followers in a live session, ask them something and the first who are answering in the comment section will win the price

Establish Posting Frequency and Schedule Content

To establish and maintain an active presence on Instagram you need to determine a constituent frequency with which you will post. Developing a content calendar that integrates your themes key dates and campaigns in advance is a great way to ensure you are consistently seen by your audience and maximising opportunities for engagement. Whilst some of the best content for Instagram will occur spontaneously, scheduled Instagram posts work to fill in the gaps in between and always ensures you are getting the messages out that you need to. You will come to find using your insights what post frequency works best for your audience. So take what you learn and apply it to future content calendars.

Establish Clear Guidelines on Team Roles, Style Guide & Workflow

Even if only one person is responsible for managing your business Instagram account, there's so much more to consider than just what filter you are going to use for your photo. To ensure your brand is consistent and unified on Instagram it's a really good idea to establish clear guidelines on important factors such as visual composition, filters, location tagging, hashtags and captions. Planning and maintaining a brand aesthetic and style in advance is key to maximizing the potential of each Instagram feature and functionality.

Top Tip: Depending on your team and objectives, you might divide responsibilities into content creation and publishing, community management, discovery and analytics, and assign them to team members with different strengths.

Start by reviewing the existing visual representations of your brand: your logo, website, graphics, photography and other collateral. Do you have an established colour palette? A tone in pictures? Your Instagram content, and everything you choose between should reflect the same branding in order to create a sense of visual harmony when a user looks at your profile. Consider creating a social media style guide to maintain consistency.

How to Create Your Instagram Style Guide

Style guides contain all the necessary information for a piece of content to ensure consistency across all marketing channels and throughout every piece of content you produce. From the design and layout of post to the copy and hashtags that accompany it. When it comes to Instagram you should consider the following items: Composition, Colour, Fonts, Filters, Captions and Hashtags.

Composition: Composition refers to the placement or arrangement of visual elements or ingredients in a work of art, as distinct from the subject of a work. Define a few quick composition rules which can include things like: Solid background colour and main focus of the picture to the Rule of Thirds.

Colour Palette: Having a palette doesn't mean that you have to strictly only use these colours, but it will help your posts have a familiar, consistent and focused feeling.

Fonts: Keep things consistent with your brand by choosing the same fonts you use on your website or other marketing materials.

Filters: Instagram filters are a great tool as they enhance photos with just a few taps, making you feel like a pro! Filters can drastically change the look and feel of a photo or video, so it's important to use only a few that you feel best represent your brand — and stick to the few you've chosen.

Captions: Instagram captions are limited to 2,200 characters and are a great way of enhancing your content further. They are regularly used as a place for sharing stories, micro-blogging, asking questions and encouraging replies.

Hashtags: Hashtags are a uniform way to categorize and discover content. Research from Track Maven found that posts with over 11 hashtags tend to get more engagement. When it comes to choosing the right hashtags for your content, it's best to do your research and see which hashtags people in your market are using and which are most active.

Put Effort Into Your Captions

While captions are limited to 2,200 characters and truncated with an ellipsis after three lines of text (so try to include the most important part of your message within those first three lines!), they are still an important part of your post. You have the space to say something engaging, inspire action and feed your brands story so make sure your captions are put to use! After all, a great image alone is great, but one with a story is even better.

Learn to Love Hashtags

To see the most success out of your Instagram hashtags, make them easy to discover, remember and read. It's always best to use hashtags to connect with new followers and increase engagement on your posts.

Try Social Sharing Across Networks

Instagram allows you to connect your profile to accounts on Facebook, Twitter and Tumblr amongst others. It's simple to automatically push your Instagram posts to various network so determine whether you want to cross-post or promote your Instagram content in this way and take advantage of the simplicity if you do!

How to Craft Instagram Posts That Drive Sales

Instagram allows you to post several types of content including photos, videos, and Stories. Below are several different Instagram post types and some best practices for encouraging engagement.

Images

The most common type of post on Instagram is an image post. When creating image posts, it's important to post a variety of different photo content types. Instagram users are looking for genuine posts from brands not overt advertisements so avoid posting too many photos of your products/service. As you start to explore the platform, you'll see there are many kinds of images you can post to your account, what's important is to take note of any concepts or styles you come across when connecting with other and monitoring your competition, that you think would work well for your brand – and get creative! To get you started, below is a list with some of the most successful Instagram image types.

- **Behind the Scenes Posts:** These posts are designed to humanise the brand by offering a glimpse into a part of your business or brand that people don't normally see.

- **Repost From Employees:** Sometimes you don't need to look any further for great content than your own employees. Reposting great photos from your employees is an easy way to curate authentic content and help humanize your business.

- **Educational Posts:** These type of posts offer quick tips on how to do or make something – often related to your product or industry.

- **Influencer Posts:** Tap into an expansive audience by piggybacking on the fame of a celebrity or well-known public figure to draw attention to your brand. These posts often include a visual of the influencer using or interacting with your product.

- **Motivational Posts:** A motivational post usually combines a simple visual with some kind of uplifting text or quote overlaid on top. They can be a great way to motivate your audience but be careful not to appear cheesy.

- **User Generated Content:** User generated content is curated content from your fans and followers. Take a look at your tagged photos or posts using your brand hashtag and consider reposting high-quality images that are particularly positive. Remember to @mention the original poster in the caption as this gives a nice shout-out to the fan showing you care, but also has the benefit or boosting your brand.

- **Special Observances:** Join in with relevant fun observances like National Hamburger Day and National Sibling Day to reach a wider audience and tap into potential great engagement. Just ensure the observances are relevant to your brand and not just for the sake of joining in.

Top Tips for Images

- ✓ **Instagram Photo Sizes:** Square (classic): use a high quality 1080 x 1080 pixels image. You can use the same resolution 1080 x 1080 pixels also for the videos. Landscape (horizontal): A great choice for panoramas, "large" photos and HD videos. Use a high-quality image 1920 x 1080

pixels wide. For Landscape Videos use a format of at least 1200 × 673 pixels in full view or retina display if you don't have an HD video. Otherwise, prefer the 1920 x 1080 pixels full HD format. Portrait (vertical): The format here is 1080 x 1350 pixels. Instagram Stories (vertical): Prefer the 1080×1920 pixels format both for videos and images. Remember the video should be compressed into an mp4 format.

- ✓ **Follow the Rule of Thirds:** When composing your photo, you should aim to place your subject at the intersection of one set of vertical and horizontal lines. By placing your subject off centre, it creates a slight imbalance that will catch a viewer's eye. To switch the grid on in an iPhone, go to "Settings," choose "Photos & Camera," and switch "Grid" to on.

- ✓ **Focus on a Single Subject:** Try to focus on a single subject in each photo and remove distractions by cropping them out or finding a clean background to shoot against.

- ✓ **Take Advantage of Negative Space:** Negative space is the empty space around your subject. Allowing for empty negative space around your subject ensures attention is focused on the desired focus of your image and prevents it from looking crowded.

- ✓ **Show Different Perspectives:** People are used to seeing the world from eye level. To create interesting and fresh photos, share shots from different perspectives to break up the monotony e.g. (birds eye view). Experiment with different angles to find new perspectives on common sights.

- ✓ **Symmetry and Patterns:** The human eye is naturally drawn to symmetrical shapes and objects. Similarly, people are also drawn to patterns. Sometimes a pattern could be man-made, such as a tiled floor, while other times it could be natural, such as petals on a flower.

- ✓ **Use Natural Light:** Try to use soft natural light to prevent harsh shadows that can create unwanted dark and light areas in your photos.

- ✓ **Adding Filters and Editing Photos:** Thanks to Instagram's built-in tools and filters, editing photos is simple, only taking a few minutes and can have a huge impact on the quality of your photos. Each Instagram filter has its own personality that can drastically change a photo. Simply Press the "Edit" button to adjust your photo's alignment, brightness, contrast, structure, and more. Press "Next" when you're done to add final details and publish.

Videos

Instagram also lets you upload videos up to 60 seconds in length. You can download videos from your computer for upload or you can film and edit together videos yourself using mobile apps such a Splice which is a free popular editing tool that allows you to cut together multiple clips and add titles and music. Keep in mind that Instagram videos begin playing without sound so ensure your videos don't need sound to be understood.

- ▪ **Boomerangs/GIFs:** Boomerangs and GIFs allow you to put a quirky spin on traditional video by adding repetitive, looping motion. A Boomerang post takes a burst of photos and then converts them into a perfectly looping short video that plays over and over again. These kinds of posts are great for anything with repetitive motion like someone jumping or toasting glasses.

- **Hyperlapse:** An app from Instagram that allows you to condense lengthy videos into shorter, engaging content. To create your own Hyperlapse videos, download the free app onto your mobile device. When prompted, allow it to access your camera, tap the circle once to begin recording, and again to stop. Once you're done recording, you can choose a playback speed between 1X and 12X. Save the final Hyperlapse video to your camera roll to upload later.

- **Stories:** Instagram Stories allow users to post at a higher frequency without worry of over posting. While your profile feed should feature high-quality polished photos, Stories can be a little more raw which have the benefit of making you appear more authentic. Stories are a helpful tool to showcase live events your business hosts or attends, give a behind-the-scenes look at your brand or showcase your company culture. Like Snapchat Stories, your Instagram Story disappears after 24 hours. **How to Post to Your Story:** Instagram offers three options for posting to your Story. You can tap the camera in the upper left, tap the Your Story + button above your feed, or just swipe right. Take a photo by tapping the shutter button or press and hold it to take a video. You can and should add some personality to your content by selecting one of the pens to add a doodle. To choose a precise colour, press and hold one of the colours. Press the "Aa" symbol to add text or an emoji with your keyboard and the smile icon to add stickers. You can then swipe to the left or right to add a colour filter.

Instagram also allows you to tag another account in your Story which is a great way to connect with other businesses and marketing partners. To tag someone, type the "@" followed by the username of the person or brand you'd like to mention. When someone views your story, the username will appear underlined indicating that they can tap it and be directed to the profile. You'll receive a notification if you've been mentioned in someone's story. When you're ready to publish, press the Your Story + icon or save it to your camera roll to publish it to your Instagram account. Stories appear at the top of the Instagram feed and in your profile picture. To see who viewed your content, swipe up when viewing your Story.

- **Instagram Live:** Instagram also has a live video option to share content with your audience in real time. To start a live video stream, open up the camera within the app, select the "Live" option from the menu at the bottom of your screen, and click the button to "Start Live Video." Once you start the live video, any of your followers who are currently on the app will receive a notification so they can watch. Live viewers can also comment on the the live video using the built-in chat feature. Live videos are a great tool for showcasing exciting, real-time content or engaging moments like Q&As. Just remember to not overuse this function and save it for special events/moments.

How to Write an Instagram Caption

Instagram has recently changed its algorithm so that a user's feed is curated based on what they'll likely find engaging. In a nutshell, this means the visibility of your posts will depend on the number of Likes and comments it receives. This puts pressure on you as a business competing online to create content that is designed to delight and engage your audience. The maximum character count for a caption is 2,200 characters, but remember, users will only be able to see the first 3-4 lines of the caption before they are prompted to view "more." Ensure you put your most important phrases at the beginning of the caption but don't be afraid of creating long captions as Instagram can be a great way to share you brands

story. Use the caption wisely to direct people to a desired action whether that's to take part in a competition, read your latest blog post, discover a latest product or simply as an encouragement to your audience to "like" your photo, comment on it, or share it with their friends. Instagram also allows you to add a link to your bio. Brands often use this to encourage customers to check out a new product or blog post, regularly changing the link to make sure it corresponds with their most recent posts/competitions etc. A top tip is to use shortened tracking links in your URL so you can see how much of your traffic came from your Instagram account.

The most important tip is to experiment find your distinctive Instagram 'voice.' What works on LinkedIn will not translate to Instagram for example. The key is to try experimenting with emojis and other creative tools/apps to give your brand a distinct, light hearted, authentic tone. It can take a while to develop your brand's voice, so don't give up if you don't get it right the first time. If you're ever struggling in doubt about what to write, just keep it short and simple and allow your visuals do the talking.

How to Find Your Best Frequency and Timing on Instagram

Maintaining a consistent and frequent publishing schedule helps your audience learn when to expect new content from you and has the added benefit of making sure you maximize frequent engagement as you have less chance of hitting any lulls or stretches without updates. A study by Union Metrics found that most brands post to Instagram daily with the average number of posts at 1.5 posts per day. At the very basic, it is recommended that you aim to post at least once per day on Instagram and experiment with additional posts to find what level works best for you.

What Time Should you Post to Instagram?

Timing is one of many elements considered by Instagrams algorithm when it decides what content to show you. From this, it's important to post at the times when your content is likely to pick up the most engagement. A recent study showed lunch time from 11am-1pm is the best time to post on Instagram, followed by evenings from 7-9pm. However it is best to treat those times as guidelines since the best time to post rely on a bunch of factors and vary from profile to profile. Just experiment and find out what works best for you and your audience.

How to Ensure Consistent Posting on Instagram

Once you've determined your content themes and the frequency at which you'd like to post to Instagram, one of the best ways to ensure you stick to your strategy is to create a content calendar that tracks which posts will be shared and when. Using a calendar lets you step away from the task of creating just one piece of content to see an overall view for the weeks even months to come. It also provides more time to create specific content pieces that contribute to a larger goal for the company. Consider using Excel or Google Sheets, or whatever tool is best for you and consider:

- The type of content you want to publish: What image/video will resonate with your followers and attract potential new followers?

- What do you need to do to create the above chosen content? Canva? Filters? Eternal Apps?
- Who is your target audience? Define who your demographic is and who would be most interested in the visuals you have to offer.
- Will you use location tags? What about hashtags? (Top Tip: Store a variety of hashtags in your phone's notepad feature to easily cut and paste)
- Caption your image: Populate this in your social media calendar.

How to Use Hashtags on Instagram

Hashtags are a keyword or keyword phrase that are used to categorize and reference anything from events, entertainment, breaking news, conferences or reoccurring themes and are a great way to make your content more visible. With 95 million photos shared every day on Instagram, it can be difficult for your account to get noticed. Hashtags are a great tool to utilize to get you noticed as they work by connecting posts from users who aren't otherwise connected into a single feed. Basically means that if your account is set to public, anyone searching the hashtags you used can see your post. Just remember, your account must be public for your posts to appear on hashtag feeds.

Instagram's hashtag feeds are very simple to navigate and make it easy for users to find related content. They're split up into three parts - top posts, most recent posts, and related hashtags.

- **Top posts:** appear at the top of a trending hashtag or location feed and feature nine posts that have seen a lot of engagement.
- **Most Recent:** posts feature a live stream of every post that has used that specific hashtag in chronological order. If you're using a popular, trending hashtag, your post will quickly get pushed down the queue!
- **Related Hashtags:** are a great way to find other hashtags people are using to discuss a topic. For example, if you're planning on tagging your post with #Tea, you may want to tag related hashtags like #Cuppa, #Brew or #Teabreak to broaden your post reach. Using hashtags is easy! Simply create hashtags using characters, numbers, or emojis and add up to thirty to your post's caption or comments.

Choosing an Instagram Hashtag

If you're searching for what hashtags to use from the beginning, brainstorming keywords and researching trends is easiest in the Instagram app itself, your best option is to start in the "Explore" tab. There you can click on popular posts to see what hashtags were used. If you already have a hashtag in mind, you can also use the "Explore" tab to find popular, related hashtags. To do this, click on the magnifying glass at the bottom of your app and type the hashtag in the search bar. Filter your results by "Tags" to see how many posts have used that hashtag and other related hashtags. You should aim to pick a mix of general, popular hashtags and more specific hashtags to increase your post audience, relevancy and 'shelf life'. In some cases, you may want to create your own branded hashtag. Businesses have created their own hashtags for many great benefits, for example to roll out a new product or Instagram campaign, promote an event, and much more. If you're planning on using your own hashtag,

be sure to do some research to make sure it's not being used for another purpose, by a competitor or has negative connotations associated with it and once you have found a good one for your business, encourage your audience to use it.

Where to Place an Instagram Hashtag into Your Content

Great news, you have a wonderful piece of content and you've chosen the perfect mix of hashtags - all that's left to do is figure out where to incorporate those hashtags in your content. The major rule is that Hashtags should feel natural in your caption so don't spammy. If you're struggling to fitting your hashtags into the language of your caption naturally, you can put them at them at the end of your caption or in the first comment. Don't feel pressured to incorporate them directly into your caption copy -- they work the same no matter where they're placed.

How to Get More Followers on Instagram

As with all social media platforms, whether you're an established business with thousands of followers or you're just starting out, growing your following takes consistent time and sustained effort. You may be tempted by the many ads out there that offer you the easy way out and give you the offer to buy followers - don't do this. Purchasing followers won't get you any future engagement, which is exactly what you need to make sure your posts are seen in a user's feed. Luckily, there are a few easy to implement things you can focus on to start gaining more followers the right organic way.

- First and foremost, get the basic rights and **make sure your username is recognizable and searchable**. It's simple, If people can't find you, they can't follow you! You also need to craft your bio so it's direct and entices the user to follow you. It's one of the first things someone sees before they make the decision to follow you so be sure to include who you are and what you do and a strong call to action.

- Once your profile is optimized**, start posting**! It's a good idea to get a solid number of posts up (15 or so) before you really start engaging people and working hard to get followers. If users visit your profile and find it empty, they likely won't follow. So make yourself 'likeable' by having a profile that's filled with high quality unique, original, content that's in line with your brand visual image and values. Make yourself a 'must follow' account in the eyes of your target audience.

- After you've posted some content, **start following accounts that interest you and relate to your business**. Think of Instagram like a community and look for other businesses in your area or influencers who might enjoy your product/service. After you follow an account, interact with their content as this is the most natural way to engage the community and draw attention to your own Instagram account. Remember to appreciate your followers by responding to their comments and engaging with their content.

- Next, **encourage others to share your content**. Invite brand ambassadors to share your account and tap into a wider relevant audience by collaborating with similar accounts. For example if you are a dog groomer, you can team up with a dog clothing shop and offer exclusive discounts to each other's audiences.

- **Promote your Instagram on other channels**. Include an Instagram social share button on your website or encourage your followers on another platform to follow you on Instagram. Sometimes the fastest way to gain more followers is to simply ask for them!

- **Make your content discoverable by using other influencers** as that will help you build your community. Influencers will certainly amplify your reach if they share your posts with their followers. You can contact them directly and ask for a collaboration or sponsorship or simply tag them into a particular piece of interesting content you have shared and share under some of their tags in order to get noticed and forwarded.

- **Explore the Instagram community:** Instagram has introduced the Explore tab, "making it faster to find people you want to follow". At the bottom of your screen, there is the Explore icon. Open this feature in order to see 4 tabs: Top, People, Tag and Places. The People tab will help you find new and interesting accounts you may follow or contact. You will soon master the art of Instagram and amass a large, active following by choosing to be a part of the Instagram community. Instagram is a social network and this is why, it will work best for your interest, if you use it as such. Form relationships with your followers and other relevant companies and participate in active discussions and link or comment other peoples' photos or videos. Once they are aware of your presence, they will most likely share your content with their own audience if they find it valuable.

- **Post on other social media channels as well:** Whilst some of your potential customers will see your posts on Instagram, in order to have a successful marketing campaign and attract as many Instagram users as you can, you should also consider posting on other social media platforms. This tactic works well with Facebook as the two platforms are interconnect anyway. You stand a great chance of reaching two audiences this way as some of the Instagram users who are not able to see your posts on this platform may see them on Facebook and follow you over on Instagram as well.

- **Make sure your content is discoverable.** You can use the Explorer tab to also make your posts easier to be discovered by Instagram users. In order to do this you should research the most popular hashtags and use them in your posts. The more people are searching for a hash tag you have included in a post, the more likely is to be discovered by them and grow your audience. There are a few things to avoid here however, firstly don't overuse these hashtags and don't obsess over your branding. You shouldn't force you brand name on every post as this will be seen as pushy and spammy, and at the same time, there is no need to include irrelevant hash

tags. Don't jump on a hashtag for the sake of it just because it's trending, content should be relevant, consistent and valuable in order to attract more attention.

How to Convert Instagram Followers into Customers

Once you've worked hard to establish a dedicated follower base you can start to convert those followers into paying customers. There are several ways to do this, here are a few top tips.

- **Charity:** According to a recent survey, 81% of millennials expect companies to make a public commitment to giving back. Doing so can build love for your brand and help turn followers into customers. It's no secret that brands that team with charity's and put out content that 'pulls at the heartstrings' have a greater chance of going viral.

- **Teasers:** Instagram is a great platform to show your audience glimpses of new products before they become available. While you don't want to spam your followers' feeds with only product photos, a few images can build excitement. You can go the extra mile and team this tactic with Promotions and Contests.

- **Promotions:** Deals, discounts, BOGOs, and other promotional offerings are a great way to drive first-time sales with your Instagram audience. Be sure to mention exactly what is needed to receive the promotional offer and include when the offer expires to create a sense of urgency.

- **Contests**: Promote contests by asking users to follow your account or post content with a specific hashtag to enter.

- **Launch a Product Live:** To give certain launches and extra special buzz, it may even make sense to showcase a new product or service using Instagram Live. You can quickly drive users to purchase by including a purchase link in your bio.

How to Optimize Your Instagram Profile to Increase Your Growth and Engagement

Your Instagram profile is essentially your homepage on the platform. It provides you with space to share a little information about your business and also gives you the chance to drive some traffic back to your website. There are several ways to maximize your Instagram profile and drive as much value as possible from it, here are a few top tips.

- **Your bio:** What you choose to share in your description here should be representative of your business and show your followers what you do as a company. As the very basic level, most businesses tend to include a brand slogan or tagline and an outline of who you are and what you do. With a 150 character limit, your Instagram bio should focus on what's important about your brand and direct the user to a desired action. If you have one, here would be a great place to include a branded hashtag to inform users how to share and find additional content related to your brand. You have just one link you can include in your bio, and only advertisers can share live links outside that space, so make it count and point it to something valuable.

- **Your profile picture:** is one of the most important parts of your Instagram profile and when someone views one of your posts or clicks on your profile, it's ideal if your brand is instantly recognizable. For many brands this tends to mean using one of three options: Logo, Logomark (the logo, minus any words) or Mascot.

- **Your link:** Unlike many other social networks, Instagram doesn't allow you to add links to every post. Instead, you only get one link, and as mentioned that's the one in your profile. Most businesses tend to use this link to drive traffic back to their homepage, to campaign-specific landing pages or individual pieces of blog content.

- **Embrace user generated content:** Curating content from your followers is a win-win scenario as it will help you to build a vibrant and engaged community and can also encourage your audience to share their own creative ways of interacting with your products, services or company.

- **Include some faces in your posts to boost engagement:** Here's something to think about - A study from Georgia Tech looked at 1.1 million random Instagram pictures and discovered something really interesting - Pictures with faces get: 38% more likes and 32% more comments.

- **Experiment with Instagram ads:** 95 million photos and videos are shared on Instagram per day and as more and more brands join Instagram, the feed becomes more competitive and it can be harder to stand out. With Instagram ads, you can reach the specific groups of Instagram users you want to connect with, engage them, and convert them into customers.

- **Follow Industry Accounts & Instagram Influencers:** For example, if you're a clothing retailer, you'd want to follow top fashion bloggers. By following top accounts in your industry you can easily keep an eye on interesting content, find other accounts of note to follow in the industry and even find inspiration for your own feed. After you follow, Instagram will recommend other accounts to follow. Importantly though, don't just follow anyone and everyone it suggests, whether it's competitors, political figures or random influencers be sure to vet and inspect anyone you follow to ensure they're appropriate to your brand and audience.

- **Monitor Brand Keywords & Misspellings:** Another way to see who's talking about your brand, even if they aren't mentioning your handle, is to monitor branded keywords and commo misspellings. To make sure you never miss a beat, actively make the effort to regularly search for your brand name, common brand misspellings, products names, services or events and terms related to your brand.

- **Use Instagram Stories to Test Content**: Stories are a safe way to publish in-the-moment content. Users have a different anticipation for content when it comes to Stories, whilst you can 'plan' to provide links or call to actions to specific landing pages, users respond best to raw spontaneity. It's therefore highly recommended to make this content easy to read, view and understand so users don't skip you the next time you publish a story. You should explore the feature and test some more "tame" content ideas through Instagram Stories to see what sticks. Just make sure to keep your Stories consistent and in line with the rest of your content and Instagram marketing strategy.

- **Analyse Your Results:** Tracking how well your content performs and your follower growth will allow you to adapt your Instagram marketing strategy going forward. By regularly acting on what your analytics tell you, this allows you to develop more successfully and deliver more content your audience will respond to whilst helping you optimize for future campaigns. As you develop and implement your brand's Instagram marketing strategy, you will learn to find what types of content, posting frequency and engagement practices work for you. Building your brand and growing a following on Instagram is challenging and very much trial and error but learning from your mistakes and avoiding common pitfalls will help you to build a strong brand presence that tells a powerful story and encourages engagement.

How to Increase Sales Using Instagram

- **Have a Plan of Action:** To be successful on Instagram you need to know from the beginning what it is you want to achieve on the platform and focus everything from the types of content you use, to what Call to Actions you include in your captions on those objectives. Doing so ensures that everything is working as hard as it can for you to achieve your goals. As discussed earlier, have a plan however basic it may be, to ensure you don't end up posting irrelevant content with no consistency and no aims.

- **Eye-catching Pictures with High Quality:** You might not be a professional photographer, but keep in mind that picture quality is crucially important element of a good and successful brand on Instagram. If you are not good at taking pictures yourself, know your weaknesses, bite the bullet and let someone else do it for you, or if your budget doesn't allow an extra pair of hands, then simply read some tips and tricks that can improve your skills.

- **Don't just Rely on Instagram**: Whilst Instagram is a great mobile marketing tool to have in your arsenal, it is not the only tool. By design, Instagram works best in conjunction with other sites and especially visually friendly content sites like Pinterest, and Facebook, as these sites also offer the best viral impact for sharing and discussing photos. Instagram can be connected to other social networks very easily, so take advantage of this great feature to give the opportunity for all of your audiences on all of your different social networks will be able to view them.

- **Get Involved With Your Community:** If you really want to interact and engage with customers, Instagram is one of the best ways of doing it. Providing customer service through social media has quickly become an expectation of users online and providing great customer service to your community and solving your customers problems should always be at the forefront of your efforts. Additionally, such as any social media campaign, you should live by the saying that "no man is an island" meaning you should reach out and interact with your community by liking and commenting on the photos of others too - especially if they mention your product or brand. You should also look to foster engagement and reward your community by regularly hosting contests, scavenger hunts, and other promotions that encourage your community to display your brand on their photo feed and on their other connected social media networks. This is a great way to ensure followers will participate and talk about your brand, it gives them a continued reason to follow you as well as importantly giving them a reward for being connected to you.

- **Geo-Tag Instagram Photos:** This - brilliant for businesses- feature puts a place on a literal map. Geo-tagging allows you to add your location to your photos when you post them, and if you use this feature, the service will create a photo map of your posts. This shows you, on a map, where all of your photos have been taken, so this is especially useful if you have a brick and mortar location like a store, office, restaurant, salon, or studio. Adding your location to your photos displays that location above your photo in each post that has been geotagged. People can click on geotagged locations and see all of the posts in that area, so this can be another great way to gain followers and interactions as followers who live or work nearby may be more likely to interact with you or do business with you if they see that you're nearby. Beyond these initial benefits, using geo-tags can help you promote your event or your participation at an event in a great way. Restaurants, retailers, and any other brand can promote their location and their products in use using and promoting geo-tagged Instagram photos. In another example a company could make a scavenger hunt out of geo-tagging for contests and other promotions. Importantly, You can toggle your location on and off before you post an image. This comes in handy if you want certain posts to be added to your map but want others to be left off.

- **Attract New Customers:** Don't make the mistake of starting a new Instagram account and thinking your business will automatically surge, because unless you're a big celebrity, in reality that's just not going to happen. The way it actually works is that as you build followers, more and more of them will begin to take interest in your content and offerings. Over time, this growing list of potential customers will develop - and it will because Instagram is fun, addictive and easy- Only with time and consistently good engagement and content will you build a loyal

following. This will then open up valuable branding opportunities, new sales and an army of loyal brand advocates who actually share your content.

- **Create Your Own Hashtag and Engage People that Use it:** Creating, using, promoting, and monitoring your own hashtag has many great benefits. For starters, people can easily find photos related to you or your brand, it's easier to interact with your community and is brilliant for brand awareness. A lovely little piece of important information is that when a user likes a photo on Instagram it appears in their News Feed on Facebook! Not only that but if one of their friend's clicks on that liked photo they immediately go to Instagram's hosted picture and can see all of the comments and your hashtags! They can also share the photo from there as well… what a fantastic trio of benefits you should definitely utilize for your business.

Getting Started With Instagram Advertising

Instagram advertising offers a unique and brilliant opportunity for brands to engage with their audience. Since Instagram ads appear in the feed like any other post, they aren't as obvious or disruptive as typical ads seen online and across social media. They provide a natural way to encourage users to learn more about your business or product.

How Create an Instagram Ad

Creating an Instagram ad is easy. In fact, if you've ever set up a Facebook ad you're almost there already! This is because even though your ad will run on Instagram, the setup is all done through Facebook's ad platform. To begin creating your ad, select the post you'd like to boost in Instagram or create a new one in Facebook Ad Manager. If you haven't run ads through Facebook before, you'll be prompted to set up an account. You'll also need to claim your Instagram Business account to link it to your Facebook page. To claim your Instagram account, go to your Business Manager and, on the left side of the page, hover over the menu to click "Instagram Accounts." Then click on "Claim Instagram Account." Add your account information and click "Next." Next, pick an objective and name your campaign. While Facebook offers many different objective choices, only a few include Instagram advertising as an option. To ensure you're on the right track, pick from any of the following options:

- Brand Awareness
- Reach
- Traffic
- App Installs
- Engagement
- Video Views
- Conversions

Once you've selected your objective, you'll be prompted to name your ad set. Next, you can target your ad using a range of demographic and psychographic factors, including age, gender, location, language, work, financial status, behaviours, and connections. You can also load previously used custom audiences. After you're done selecting your target audience, select "Edit Placements" under the placements options and select "Instagram" under the available platforms. **Don't forget this step! Otherwise your ad will only show up on Facebook.** After you select Instagram as your placement, you'll be asked to set the budget and schedule for your ad. You can set a daily spend budget or a lifetime budget for the ad and indicate start and end dates for your campaign. If you do not set a start and end date or a lifetime budget, your ad will continue to run indefinitely with the daily budget you allocate. You can also access more budget and scheduling options under the "Advanced Options" drop down. Here, you can do things like scheduling your ad to run only during certain hours of the day or set your ad to generate results as quickly as possible using the "Accelerated" delivery type. This option is useful for ads focused around timely events.

Next, you'll be promote to set up the content of your ad. You can boost an existing post or upload a new image and caption to run as your ad. Instagram allows you to create ads using a Single Image or Video, a Carousel Ad, or a Story Ad that runs as a sponsored ad in Instagram stories. To maximize ad delivery, Facebook recommends using images that are at 600 px X 600 px for square format ads, 600 px X 315 px for landscape ads, and 600 px X 750 px for vertical ads. Facebook recommends avoiding too much text on the image or video thumbnail. Once your ad creative is uploaded, you're all set!

How Much Should You Spend on Instagram Ads?

The total amount you should invest in Instagram advertising campaigns should be tied to your campaign goal, and of course your allocated budget. No matter what your goal, it's important to monitor and optimize your Instagram ads to make the most of your budget and make sure the ads are working as hard as they can for you.

A Quick Guide to Instagram Analytics

One of Instagram's few flaws lie in its lack of an in-depth analytics platform built into the app the same way Facebook or other social media platforms have. Once you switch your account to a Business Account, you do gain access to some limited analytics like follower growth, impressions, reach, and engagement by clicking on the "View Insights" option below your uploaded images and videos. You can also track impressions, spend, and engagement on ad campaigns through Facebook's Ad Manager. Whilst all very helpful, these metrics are limited to individual posts and campaigns and certainly don't give you the full picture of how your presence is performing.

The good news is that you can access more in-depth Instagram metrics with a range of third-party apps. Simply Measured and Iconsquare are (paid) popular tools that allow you to track additional metrics such as followers and engagement over time, optimal post time based on previous posts, and your performance compared to selected competitors. It's worthwhile taking advantage of the free trial that both services offer to see if their analytics offerings are right for you before you make the investment.

Although the individual metrics you track on Instagram will vary depending on your objectives, some basic key metrics to keep track of are engagement levels of your content (Likes and comments) and number of followers over time. As you progress with your Instagram marketing strategy, you'll begin to notice some trends such as what types of content resonates best with your audience, your audience growth, and the number of likes and comments your posts receive. All of this data shows you what's working and what isn't which you can learn from and act on going forward to improve the results of your Instagram marketing.

To gain access to Instagram Insights for your Instagram account, you'll have to convert your Instagram profile to a Business Profile. Once you have converted to a Business Profile, you'll see a graph icon in the upper-right corner of your profile. That's the button for Instagram Insights. Note: Instagram Insights is only available in the mobile app.

Tips For Success

- **Utilize Stories!** Instagram Stories are highly engaging (and because they require a user to seek them out), they make a very effective platform for advertising. With over 300 million people using Instagram Stories every day, it comes as no surprise that one-third of the most viewed Instagram stories actually come from businesses. Stories enable you to post a mix of photos and images in a single post that disappears after 24 hours. There benefits last much longer for your reach and engagement rates though, pushing up your chances of appearing in the Explore section and helping you gain new followers in the process. Crucially, followers are automatically notified of any new pre-recorded or live Stories. Live Stories are ideal for capturing attention because they're happening in the moment, whilst pre-recorded Stories are perfect for in-depth coverage of your products, quick-fire promotions, or sharing narratives.

- **Find an Interesting Angle:** Find a creative angle for a photo to showcase your product in an interesting way. Think about whether you should show the entire product, frame the shot a certain way or include another item to accompany the product. Whilst you should experiment with different content, once you find the most effective angle for your products, make sure you prioritize that approach in your content calendar to maximize engagement opportunities.

- **Explore the full range of Instagram video formats.** Instagram recognizes the power and popularity of video and offers a suite of video options for businesses to deploy. From Instagram Stories that can mash up videos and stills into a single ad, to standalone 60-second videos ideal for long-form features, make sure you use the strengths of each video format. Relating to this, its certainly worthwhile to look into Instagram's video ad formats to promote your business. Instagram offers three key video formats to create Instagram ads: single video ads offer the opportunity to create up to 60-second commercials, 'carousels' enable followers to swipe across for additional images or videos, and Instagram Stories offers a vertical full-screen format where images and videos can be spliced together to create visually-arresting ads.

- **Convert Instagram followers into email subscribers.** Email remains an imperative channel for building deep customer relations. Ensure you implement the following 3 prong approach. First, create a clickable incentive in your Instagram post, for instance, consider offering free content or a discount. Second, once the audience clicks through, ensure you have a strong landing page waiting for them when they get there that features a call to action linked to an email submission form. Third, create a mailing list!

- **Drive traffic to your website by adding a link to Instagram Stories.** Businesses can add a link to their Story as long as they have 10,000 followers or more. To add a link, you'll need to upload your photo or video to Instagram then tap the link icon at the top of the screen. Type in the link, do a quick preview to check all is well and hit 'done'. A simple but essential option!

- **Use emojis effectively.** Nearly 50% of comments or captions on the platform feature emojis. Critically, these are searchable—users can seek out posts that include specific emojis. With over 2,623+ emojis available, it is essential to create a strategy on how to use emojis that captures your brand without looking too informal.

- **Focus on Lighting:** The lighting in a photo can tell a story about your brand so whether photos are taken indoors or outdoors, good lighting is crucial. Even with careful tweaking, Instagram's editing tools often can't fix a photo taken with poor lighting. Therefore it's vital to get this basic photography skill nailed down in every photo before you even think about using the advanced filters.

- **Use a Filter:** Each filter has a unique story and feel that it communicates. There is an array of filters at your disposal to communicate a particular mood for your brand and products. Whilst a 'normal' photo is the most popular choice people use and indeed there is an immensely popular #nofilter hashtag dedicated for that purpose, using artistically edited photos can add a lot to your photo. To use a filter, once you've taken or uploaded a photo or video Tap Next, then tap the filter you'd like to apply. Tap the filter again if you want to adjust filter strength up or down using the slider. The simply tap Done to save your change. The most popular way to upload an image or video is without any filter at all. But for those who do like to use them, Clarendon is the most popular option followed by Gingham, Juno and Lark. The Most-used Instagram Stories Face Filters are Puppy, Bunny, Koala, Genius and Love.

- **Tell a Story With the Caption:** You can give life to a photo with the caption and it's important to learn what type of description resonates best with your audience.

- **Create a Hashtag Campaign:** User-generated content is one of the best ways to promote your community and products. Create a brand-centric hashtag campaign for your followers to use in their posts. Remember that engagement is a two-way street so follow and interact with your

followers that are using it and like the posts that are positive and aesthetically aligned with your brand.

- **Use a Call to Action:** Ensure every piece of content has a purpose by adding a call to action to it which prompts customers to do something. It could be as simple as "Shop Now!" or "Download our app." Whatever you choose, make sure the action is relevant to your post as this is a great way to gain new followers.

- **Partner With Influencers:** Consider partnering with influencers to create compelling content to promote your products and increase your reach. Influencers already have built-in distribution lists with large groups of followers and are trusted for their opinions on what products to purchase. By working with influencers, you harness their popularity and tap into their vast and relevant audience which will expand your own follower count and boost sales.

- **Best Times to Post:** Instagram is a mobile App so users are on the platform at all times of the day. However, there are a few studies out there that have found the optimal times to post on Instagram for peak engagement to be Mondays and Thursdays at any time except between 3:00 p.m. and 4:00 pm and overall, users tend to engage with more content during off-work hours on weekdays. Simply think in the mind frame of your audience and work out when they are most likely to be looking on their phone. For example, if your target audience is a Teacher for example, they are most likely to be active during the evening when they are back home as opposed to during the day when they will be busy teaching.

- **Link Instagram to Your Facebook Page:** One of Instagram's unique features is that it allows you to share your content seamlessly across other social networking sites. Linking your Instagram to your other social accounts like Facebook will increase the number of eyes on your posts and allows you to benefit from targeting both audiences. Be careful however as its not recommended to automatically link you Instagram to every one of your other social platforms as what works on Instagram probably won't yield the same results on other channels and it's important to tailor your content to each platform. Note: Your Facebook Page will already be linked to your Instagram if you set up an Instagram business profile. To link your Facebook page to your Instagram account, start in your Instagram profile by going to the gear in the upper right corner. In the "Options" menu, scroll down to "Settings" and look for "Linked Accounts." If you're not already logged into Facebook on your phone, you'll be prompted to do so, and then you'll need to pick the Facebook Business Page you'd like to link. Next, you'll be directed to the "Share Settings" menu. The Facebook logo should be blue to indicate that sharing is on.

- **How to See Posts You've Liked:** This is more of general useful little tip, but handy nonetheless! You can easily check out all the posts you've Liked in the "Options" menu of your profile. Press the gear icon and select "Posts You've Liked." Then scroll down until you find the photo or video you're looking for.

- **How to Reorder Instagram Filters:** To save precious time when uploading photos, Instagram lets you reorder filters so you can position the ones you use most often at the beginning of your options. To reorder or hide filters, begin editing a post like you normally would. Scroll to the far right in the filter options and click the "Manage" gear icon. Hold your finger down on the three grey lines and drag the filter up or down. To hide a filter, uncheck it on the right side of your screen.

- **Hide Posts You've Been Tagged In**: If someone tags your brand in a post, it will show up when you click the person avatar in right icon on your profile. To remove a tagged post, click the three dots in the top right corner and choose "Hide Photos." Select the posts you want to remove and click "Hide Photos" again. This won't remove the posts from Instagram, but it will remove them from your profile. If you don't want to have to remove tagged posts, you can manually choose just to include the ones you do like. Click the three dots again and press "Tagging Options." You can then choose to "Add Manually." From here on out, you'll be notified when someone tags you in a photo. When that happens, tap on the photo you were tagged in and choose "Show on Profile."

- **Utilize Available Tools**: There are several useful Instagram marketing tools that will help you get the most out of your marketing campaigns.

Ones for Planning, Editing, Scheduling

Sprout Social: A complete social media management tool that offers access to a range of very useful areas from managing multiple Instagram accounts, to robust analytics and planning and scheduling capabilities. You can also communicate easier with your customers, monitor hashtags and track posts from Instagram locations.

Hootsuite: One of the most popular platforms for social media management. You can plan campaigns, schedule posts and analyse results of marketing campaigns for multiple social media platforms all in one handy place.

Ones for measuring performance and selling products

Crowdfire: This tool help monitor your account, providing useful insights such as those of your new followers or recent unfollows, it will also find the best moments of the day to post and the best and most suitable hashtags for your campaign.

INK361: This tool gives you a complete package that allows you to manage and analyse your account, as well as delivering useful statistics based on timing, hashtags, location, number of likes and comments.

Websta is a free analytics tool for Instagram that will help you grow your account, understand your audience, customize your Instagram feed, follow posts chronologically, explore hot brands, users and hashtags and engage with your followers.

EXTRA RESOURCES

Useful Social Media Links

Social Media News and Resource Websites

Social Media Quickstarter	http://www.socialquickstarter.com/
Mashable	http://mashable.com/social-media/
Social Media Today	http://socialmediatoday.com/
Social Media Examiner	http://www.socialmediaexaminer.com/
Hubspot Blog	http://blog.hubspot.com/
KISSmetrics Blog	http://blog.kissmetrics.com/
Econsultancy Blog	https://econsultancy.com/blog
Constant Contact Blog	http://blogs.constantcontact.com/
Content Marketing Institute	http://contentmarketinginstitute.com/
Danny Brown Blog	http://dannybrown.me/
Jenn's Trends Blog	http://jennstrends.com/
Top Dog Social Media Blog	http://topdogsocialmedia.com/blog/
Wishpond Blog	http://blog.wishpond.com/
Boom Social Blog	http://kimgarst.com/blog/
Jeff Bullas Blog	http://www.jeffbullas.com/
The Marketing Donut	http://www.marketingdonut.co.uk/
Socially Stacked	http://www.sociallystacked.com/
Buffer Social	https://blog.bufferapp.com/
Peg Fitzpatrick	http://pegfitzpatrick.com/blog/
RazorSocial	http://www.razorsocial.com/blog/

Rebekah Radice	http://rebekahradice.com/blog/
The Social Media Hat	https://www.thesocialmediahat.com/
John Loomer	http://www.jonloomer.com/
Unmetric	http://blog.unmetric.com/
Socialmouths	http://socialmouths.com/blog/
Seth Godin	http://sethgodin.typepad.com/
Pam Moore	http://www.pammarketingnut.com/blog/

Blogging

Getting Started with Wordpress http://learn.wordpress.com/get-started/

Wordpress Blog http://wordpress.org/news/

Facebook

Getting Started with Facebook Business Pages

https://en-gb.facebook.com/business/overview

https://www.facebook.com/help/364458366957655/

Facebook Page Guidelines https://www.facebook.com/page_guidelines.php

Facebook Blog http://blog.facebook.com/

Twitter

Getting Started with Twitter

https://support.twitter.com/articles/215585-getting-started-with-twitter#

Twitter Blog https://blog.twitter.com/

Pinterest

Getting Started With Pinterest http://business.pinterest.com/en/getting-started

Pinterest Blog http://uk.blog.pinterest.com/

Pinterest Business Blog http://business.pinterest.com/en/blog

YouTube

Getting Started With YouTube

https://www.youtube.com/yt/about/en-GB/getting-started.html

YouTube Blog http://youtube-global.blogspot.co.uk/

LinkedIn

LinkedIn Blog http://blog.linkedin.com/

Getting Started with a LinkedIn Business Page
http://business.linkedin.com/marketing-solutions/company-pages/get-started.html

Getting Started With a LinkedIn Personal Profile
http://www.marketingdonut.co.uk/marketing/internet- marketing/social-media-and-online-networking/get-started-with-linkedin

Instagram

Instagram Blog https://business.instagram.com/blog

Getting Started With Instagram https://help.instagram.com/454502981253053/

MONTHLY CLEAN UP AND REFRESH OF SOCIAL MEDIA PLATFORMS - CHECKLIST

In order to keep your social media platforms fresh, relevant and effective there are several monthly maintenance jobs you need to complete. By regularly monitoring your pages and making it a habit to assess your settings, competitors and other important aspects, you ensure that your social media marketing is highly effective helping you to maximise your ROI.

- ✓ **Update Your Bios and Descriptions**: Are your descriptions on your platforms relevant and up to date? Ensure you regularly update your bios with and new key information, links, messages or any other important information such as a new email address or website link.

- ✓ **Update Your Logos, Cover Images, Banners and Backgrounds:** Are your logos and other visual identity covers up to date and relevant? By updating your social media logo and cover images to represent the current trends, seasons and any other important info like offers, sales and promotions, you keep your pages feeling fresh for your fans and followers.

- ✓ **Organise your Followings**: If you follow a lot of blogs or have a large Twitter following it is worthwhile getting organised with up to date lists that contain the content and people you want to be able to find easily. On Twitter itself you can create lists based on interests or organise the updates from important users and influencers, if you already utilise this feature then ensure it is kept up to date and organised. If you don't use Twitter lists then it's worthwhile that you start.

- ✓ **Assess your Competitors Pages:** Regularly examining what your competitors are doing on their social media platforms can reveal a lot of useful information to help you inform your own strategy. Explore keys are such as which social media platforms they are using, How engaged their fans are, what types of content they share, which types of content draw the most engagement, are they doing anything new? And are they using any social media platforms that you aren't?

- ✓ **Review Page Permissions and Privacy Settings:** It is important for security purposes that you review who has access to your social media pages, both people and third-party applications and

update these permissions accordingly. Ideally if a person who knows your passwords has since left your business you should change all of your passwords immediately. As a general rule of thumb however you should look to update your passwords on a quarterly or every few months basis.

- ✓ **Explore New Options and Keep up With Trends and Developments:** Every month you should look at any emerging trends and developments in your industry and social media platforms that you need to be aware of and that you can utilise. Regularly check to see if you're missing out on any new network features that could benefit you by checking the official websites and blogs of your social media platforms. You should also be up to date on industry trends, developments and any new emerging social media platforms by regularly reading articles and following industry influencers.

- ✓ **Revisit and Assess Goals**: Key to your success is meeting your social media goals and objectives so ensure you regularly take a look at your analytics across your social media platforms to ensure you are meeting all aspects of them. As time progresses you may find your strategy and goals need to change or adapt therefore it is important to regularly assess your goals and ensure they are still the ones you want to aim for.

83 ENGAGING IDEAS FOR YOUR SOCIAL MEDIA CONTENT

Never be stuck for social media content ideas again with this list of 83 ideas guaranteed to keep you inspired for a long time!

- **Explain How You do Something:** if you have a unique way you make your product, handle complaints or welcome new customers then share it and describe your process.
- **Staff Profiles:** help to humanise your brand by sharing staff photos and information.
- **Personal Stories:** People love to see the humans behind the brand and read what they get up to, so if you have just graduated from university or you have just had a baby and you are happy to tell your audience, then share your stories.
- **Show Your Charity/Community Work:** If your business supports a charity or gives back to the local community, document and share what you do.
- **Join or Create a Debate:** if you feel you can add value to a relevant debate then join in, likewise if you want to hear someone's opinions then create a debate yourself.
- **Create a Regular Feature:** regular features are a great way of drawing readers back to your page, your regular feature can be anything from a 'customer of the week' spotlight to a monthly collection of useful online articles that will benefit your audience.
- **Useful Tips and Advice:** Providing useful and informative tips and advice always generates interest.
- **Create a How-To:** how-to posts are great for informing your audience and promoting your products uses. If there is more than one way to use your product or service? Or a way of using your product that no one has thought of? Then describe it in a how-to post.
- **Industry Experts or Celebrity Interviews:** If you have an industry expert that is of interest to your customers or are lucky enough to have celebrity contacts then a quick and easy interview post with them can generate a lot of interest.
- **Keyword Research:** Use Google Analytics or similar tools to see what search terms bring prospects to your site. You can then form your next post around those keywords.
- **Write a Series:** if you would like to go into great depth into a topic or teach your audience something complicated, then break the topic into several parts.
- **Conduct Market Research:** conduct market research and get your customers involved to share their opinions on your new product/ service etc.

- **Create a Contest:** Contests always generate engagement and interest just be sure to make the prize relevant and worthwhile to your audience.
- **Take a Reader Poll:** if you want serious questions answering or just simply for fun, polling you audience can be a great way to gather useful information and engage your audience.
- **Create a FAQ:** compile a list of the most common questions you get asked, write the answers to them and share them.
- **Create an Award:** Giving awards such as a "best of" is guaranteed to gather attention.
- **Share your Customer Feedback:** customer testimonials can go a great way in terms of gathering attention, if you get a great testimonial then ask permission to share it.
- **Reveal Industry Secrets:** People are always drawn to information that reveals secrets they wouldn't normally find out. Therefore exposing secrets from your industry will be sure to get attention.
- **Tell your Story:** everybody loves to read about other people's dreams, aspirations and challenges, so write about why and how you started your business.
- **Add your Thoughts to a Popular Post:** if you feel you can add value to a popular debate or post then join in and add your thoughts.
- **Share Relevant Breaking News:** if you know that a current event is going to interest or affect your customers or audience then share it with them.
- **Ask Questions:** is there something you want to find out or know about your customers? Then ask them and let your readers create the content.
- **Talk about Relevant Trends:** sharing relevant trends helps you convey authority within your industry.
- **Create a Podcast:** Record a quick interview with an expert, or just give a few of your own useful tips.
- **Create an Infographic:** Infographics are highly popular on social networks so create and interesting and fact filled post and it's guaranteed to get shared.
- **Report on a Conference:** if you have visited a conference and gathered lots of useful information that your audience will find useful then share it.
- **Show Behind the Scenes:** People love to see behind the scenes as it shows them an aspect of your business that they wouldn't normally see. Take shots of yourself and your work day, your employees, or a picture of your office or workspace.
- **Review Books and Articles:** if you've read a book or an interesting article you think your audience will find valuable and relevant, review it.
- **Review a Product or Service:** If there is a product or service that is relevant to your customers then write about it.
- **Compare Products or Services:** you could go beyond simply reviewing one product or service and compare two or more instead.
- **Post a Video:** videos gather a lot of attention if they are inspiring and provide something valuable to the viewer whether that be information or entertainment.
- **Share a Highlight:** document what the big milestones are in your business history and tell your audience about those important moments and how they changed your business.
- **Share your Passions:** telling personal stories and aspects about you help to humanize your brand and inspire your audience.

- **Share your Visions:** if your company philosophy is unique and you offer something different from your competitors then share it with your audience.
- **Share Something Inspiring:** people like to feel inspired so write about what inspires you and keeps you positive.
- **Compile a Useful Resource List:** having a resource list full of information such as good links, websites or good books related to your business, can be a very valuable resource for your customers.
- **The Story Behind One of Your Products/Services:** if there is an interesting story behind one of your products or services then share it with your audience.
- **A Day in The Life:** Day in the life posts work similarly to behind the scenes posts as they offer the reader an aspect of your business they wouldn't normally get to see. Give customers an hour-by-hour account of a typical day at your business from the viewpoint of one of your employees.
- **Offer Something Special:** if you have a special event planned or simply want to announce a new product then make sure you write about it. For extra attention make if you want to run a giveaway along with your special announcement then only make it available to blog subscribers for example.
- **Anniversary Posts:** If you launched a product or service a year ago or had a milestone in your business then do an anniversary post a year later to describe what has changed since that event.
- **Round up The Best of Your Blog:** if you have blog posts that are buried in your archive but you know is some of your most informative and interesting work then do a round-up at the end of the year and compile your 10 favourite blog posts for example.
- **Upcoming Events Your Business is Involved in or Attending:** If you are attending an event then be sure to take photos and document what you do. Even if the event is not directly related to your business, taking photos and sharing them still has the added benefit of humanizing your brand.
- **Profiles of Businesses You Work With:** if you work with some other great businesses then give them free advertisement and tell your customers about them. The likelihood is that the other business will return the favour.
- **Make a Prediction:** share your opinion on what you think the future holds for an aspect of your industry.
- **Discuss Your Future Plans:** give readers a sneak peek at what you have planned for the future to start generating interest.
- **Share Quotes**: Whether they're funny, inspiring or motivational quotes always perform well.
- **Share Statistics or Data**: Show yourself as a cutting-edge industry resource by share new, relevant industry statistics
- **Link to a Guest Post**: Share a link to a post you contributed to another site.
- **Product Photos:** You could share a photo of brand-new product look, an employee using the product or a customer-submitted photo etc.
- **Humor:** Some lighthearted humorous memes, images, gifs or videos can go a long way towards showing the personality of your business.
- **Giveaways:** Giveaways are a great way to not only generate excitement and brand awareness but they also act as a way to say "thank you" to your fans and brand advocates.

- **Host a Chat:** Engage your community by hosting a Google + hangout, Facebook or Twitter chat.
- **General Trivia:** Share interesting industry trivia by sharing a regular 'Did you Know' feature.
- **Create a Free eBook:** Share your interesting knowledge for free in an eBook and be rewarded by a free and easy way to capture contact information and generate new leads.
- **Create an Events Calendar:** Encourage your readers to subscribe to your events and keep up to date with what's happening in your business.
- **Show of Your Customer Service:** Customer service through social media is quickly becoming an expectation of consumers. So grab the chance to show off how much you care about your customers by actively responding, engaging and helping your audience with anything they need.
- **Show of Case Studies:** Show your worth and entice readers with a visual case study of your best work.
- **Ask for Reviews or Testimonials:** Build social proof by asking (nicely!) for reviews and testimonials.
- **Provide a Recommendation:** Give back and share the love by recommending a business you have worked with.
- **Celebrate Odd Holidays:** Did you know today is 'Draw a Picture of a Bird Day'!? Use a tool like Days of the Year to find out what today's bizarre/wacky holiday is and if it is relevant to your business then celebrate it with your audience to generate engagement and show your personality.
- **Thank Your Fans:** Remind your fans you appreciate then by offering a simple thank you. This can go a long way to building connections with your fans. (If you really love them you can combine this thank you with a free giveaway!)
- **Post Teaser Content:** Do you have something exciting and special coming up like a new product launch? Tease your audience with small clues to boost engagement and awareness.
- **Link to a Blog Comment:** if someone has left a particularly interesting, controversial or helpful comment on your blog, post a link to it and get your fans and followers to weigh in.
- **Ask Your Fans for Content Ideas:** Generate content that your audience wants to see by asking them what they want and need.
- **Use Your Website Analytics to Find Content ideas:** Look through your analytics to find out which topics generate the most interest from your audience and make those topics the focus for your next blog post etc.
- **Hold a Q&A Session:** Give your fans the chance to ask you anything by hosting a live Q&A.
- **Recommend a Book:** if you have read a book you think your audience can benefit from, tell them about it.
- **Demos:** Demos are like a show-and-tell for your product or service and are particularly powerful when combined with user-generated content.
- **Opinions and Rants:** Controversy is one of the ways to publish viral content. Opinion pieces have the potential to be interesting and provoke a lot of interest. Take a stance on a popular belief and turn it on its head.
- **Failures and What Not to Do:** Just as successes are fun for your audience to read, outlining techniques that don't work well is also interesting—particularly when your product or service solves the challenges presented from the failed techniques.

- **Worksheets:** Worksheets are perfect for turning the actionable advice from guides into printable materials for note-taking, brainstorming, and ideation.
- **Checklists:** Checklists are a type of worksheet that helps your audience follow a step-by-step process to achieve a desired outcome.
- **Templates:** Templates may combine information from guides, worksheets, and checklists all into one type of content to walk your audience through a step-by-step process. These are great as free downloads in exchange for email addresses to help you build your email list.
- **Diagrams:** Sometimes, a complex pattern is best told in a visual way as a symbolic representation of information.
- **Photography:** Stock and personal photography can work well to complement written content. Custom-taken images for your brand are even better, showing the faces and places where you work and the humans behind the scenes at your company.
- **Memes:** When you want to show a little personality in content like a blog post, memes get the point across with a little humour.
- **Comics and Cartoons**: Not all comics or cartoons need to be funny, necessarily. Hand-drawn or even computer-generated cartoons can also help tell a step-by-step story.
- **Illustrations:** Illustrations create visual interest in your content and make for some very shareable graphics.
- **Hand-Written Notes, Sketches, and Brainstorms**: Some solo marketers may not have the luxury of a designer on hand. There are times when images of sketches, written notes, and brainstorms work well to illustrate your concepts.
- **Courses**: Courses are a type of long-form content typically delivered through emails containing exclusive content dedicated to education. These an excellent way to grow your email list while building a community around your brand.
- **Event Replays**: Record your webinars and virtual events to provide videos of the content after the events are over. This is a great way to repurpose your hand work to help get the most bang for your buck.
- **Live-Streaming Video**: For any event, new tools like Meerkat and Periscope help marketers bring the events live to online audiences.
- **User-Generated Content**: If you do/host something like a Twitter chat, Facebook or LinkedIn Group, for example, collect the responses and publish a recap. The answers will all be advice from your own users—people from your chat.

HOW TO BEST INCORPORATE SOCIAL MEDIA CHANNELS ON YOUR WEBSITE

There is no one-size-fits all approach to integrating social media into your website: however, a combination of the following strategies are sure fire ways for any ecommerce brand to really start leveraging the power of the social sphere.

Homepage Feeds

Homepage social feeds represent an incredibly powerful means of bringing your product to life on-site. Such feeds can help your site feel more human and less like a sales pitch. If you decide to integrate a social feed into your website, keep in mind that you need to ensure that your feed only contains high-quality images and content worthy of your homepage versus unrelated selfies or advertisements. Feeds are a form of social proof, arguably the most important psychological trigger when it comes to drawing in new customers.

Social Buttons

Social buttons are an absolute must do for any brand, this is especially true in today's world where customers are spending a bulk of their time on Facebook versus on-site, it's incredibly important that you make following your business via social a one-click process versus forcing followers to try and find you. You can also use social media buttons on your website to increase sales: such buttons can promote your brand's social media channels as a way for visitors to hear about contests or promotions you may be running. Regardless of where you place your buttons, you should keep the following in mind before rolling them out:

- Make sure that your buttons mesh with your site's layout and colour scheme.
- Only highlight the social platforms that you're active on: if you're only active on Facebook, Instagram and Twitter, for example, don't bother linking to your dead Pinterest page.

Hashtags

There's perhaps no easier way to encourage social sharing than by creating a hashtag. Not unlike social buttons, hashtags can be implemented throughout your brand's visual content to provide customers

with a hub of discussion and sharing for your brand and its products. Beyond coming up with something unique, keep the following in mind as well:

- Keep your hashtag short and sweet (the ideal hashtag length is said to be under 11 characters)
- Be prepared to curate your hashtag in order to avoid spam or potentially irrelevant images
- Pick something that you can use for the long-haul: the more you use your hashtag throughout your marketing, the more likely it is to catch on.

Product Pages

Social media represents the modern word of mouth: buyers want to show off and share to others about their purchases. To feed into your customers' needs to share, ensure that you have social sharing enabled on your product pages. Be careful however as it's crucial that the social buttons on your product pages should not interrupt the buying process, but rather provide a way for customers to receive one-click feedback on their next purchase. Keep the following principles in mind as a means of optimizing your products for shares:

- Do not use the same social buttons on your homepage and product pages: your product buttons should be smaller and stylized differently.
- Only offer sharing to the social networks where it makes sense: Facebook, Twitter and Pinterest are much better than somewhere such as LinkedIn.
- Make sure that your plugin captures your product's image and description appropriately as it's shared
- Don't forget about the importance of your customers' experience once they've landed. Give them a chance to share their experience in the buying process: you may be surprised at how many of them are more than happy to sing your praises.

Social Sign Ins

Did you know that 73% of users prefer to log in to a site with social login, as opposed to providing an email address and creating a new account? Improve your website visitors' experience with social login and increase your website registration conversions and retention. The benefit of social sign-ins are two-fold: visitors can browse your site without the annoyance of creating a new account and they can comment on your blog with ease.

Include Share Buttons

If you sell a product or run a full-fledged eCommerce site and you haven't added share buttons to your product pages, you are missing out on a whole host of potential social impressions. Share buttons should enable website-goers to seamlessly share or recommend a product. Two broad tools that can help with this are AddThis and ShareThis. Both provide efficient and easy-to-use solutions for social media sharing across eCommerce sites with the added benefit of analytics to see how the content is getting shared.

Social Proof

With 79% of consumers trusting social proof as much as personal recommendations, it's important you integrate the proper social widgets on your website to increase sales and website conversions. One way to do this is to use one of Facebook's social widgets, such as the "Like Box". This feature shows your visitors that you're a credible source, their friends also like your Facebook page, and that you're a legitimate product or brand. As an added bonus you'll also be able to increase your Facebook likes with this social media integration.

Making Social Part of the Retail Experience

There are many other ways to integrate social media to improve conversions, streamline customer services and drive repeat business and referrals.

- Improve your post-purchase page with a range of social cues (i.e. Share your purchase) to enhance the customer experience, and to spread the word about your business.
- Add a simple sharing section which allows a user to send a tweet or a Facebook status with a link to the product they just bought.
- The post-purchase page can also include quick links to your social media channels, email newsletter and links to access customer services too. This is also the place, as well as in order communications, to share any referral discounts you offer for customers who share with their friends.

Reviews and Ratings

Social customer service is just as important as other functions like contact forms, call centres and live chat, so make sure you offer a good service that customers can access. Reviews help reassure customers, improve SEO and encourage repeat business. Linking social sign-in to your reviews set up will more than likely lead to more reviews from customers, as it just makes everything easier and more streamline. Make your social customer service easy and obvious to access by displaying it prominently on your help pages.

POWERFUL CALL TO ACTION PHRASES YOU NEED TO USE IN YOUR SOCIAL MEDIA CONTENT!

Having thousands Facebook Likes or Instagram followers is great, but it doesn't mean anything if those followers never take any action. Whether it's a tweet, blog title or text in your ad, every word you share in an update needs to inspire people to do something beyond just reading it. Words are very powerful and for social media to be a successful addition to your marketing strategy you must learn how to right copy that converts!

What Does a Call to Action Mean?

A call-to-action (CTA) is an image or text that prompts your visitors, leads, and customers to take action. It might be signing up for your email list, buying a product, investing in a service, or following you on social media.

Call-to-Action Statistics

- Almost 90 percent of website visitors read headlines and CTA copy. Many of them don't read anything else.
- Full-screen CTAs, such as exit popups you create through Hello Bar, perform better than any other position for CTAs (up to 25 percent conversion rate).
- Color can make a huge difference in whether or not people click on CTAs.
- More than 90% of visitors who read your headline also read your CTA copy. (Unbounce)
- Emails with a single call-to-action increased clicks 371% and sales 1617%. (WordStream)
- Adding CTAs to your Facebook page can increase click-through rate by 285%. (AdRoll)
- By forcing visitors to watch an informational video on their services before presenting a CTA, Kimberly Snyder increased conversions by 144%. (QuickSprout)
- For KISSmetrics, a CTA within a video gets 380% more clicks than their normal sidebar CTAs. (QuickSprout)

CTA Phrases to Persuade

If your intent is to persuade people to choose your product/service, here are several phrases to try incorporating into your call to action:

- **"Try it free now"** or **"Start your free trial now"** Everyone loves a freebie. This CTA is good because instead of straight up asking a prospect to hand over money for your product/service, you're offering a free 'test drive.'

- **"Join now and get…"** Here you're simply asking your audience to reply to your message to get something of value in return. It could be an e-book, a free sample, or a template, just make sure it's relevant to your audience.

- **"Start now to get…"** or **"Your Journey to X Starts here"** or **"Start now"** infers to your prospect that they are about to begin an exciting process — with the rest of the CTA telling the user how he or she will benefit.

- **"Talk to an expert now"** This is a great CTA to use for an online chat opportunity or when you want the prospect to call. Telling your prospect that you are a team of experts, will automatically make them feel safer in your hands.

- **"Learn more about us at…"** Prospects at the top of the sales funnel are collecting information, learning about brands and your industry without knowing exactly what they want yet. Using a CTA that invites people to learn more about your business can be extremely effective at building brand awareness. When prospects decide they're ready to buy, they'll have your business name at the top of their mind.

- **"Please don't hesitate to call us"** Let your customers know you don't mind talking to them over the phone. These types of CTA's belong on every page of your site.

- **"Order now and receive a free gift"** If you can tempt prospects with a free gift, they're more likely to buy the original product. The free gift on offer doesn't have to be physical, it could be a discount off a future purchase or a downloadable template for example.

- **"Get yours now"** A personable CTA subtly telling the consumer that you want him or her to have something valuable — something other people might want.

- **"Request your FREE quote today"** Giving a free quote costs nothing but time to you, but once you have the prospect communicating with you it may just turn to a sale!

- **"Click here to get free shipping"** Use this popular CTA to overcome one of the chief barriers to buying products online - shipping costs!

- **"Money-Back Guarantee offer here"** When you offer a money-back guarantee, consumers feel more confident trying out your product or service.

- **Activate X Today!** Using a CTA like this one puts the prospect in the driver's seat and motivates them to act. These call to actions work well if you're offering a discount on products or a free demo of your service.

CTA Phrases to Create a Sense of Urgency

Creating a sense of urgency encourages customers to act now instead of holding off making the purchase. Here are some effective call to action phrases that you should consider using as the sooner you can get people to take action, the better!

- **"Download here immediately."** Or **"Download here right now"** Strong adjectives promote urgency and encourage click-throughs.

- **"Act quickly or you might lose it"** Loss-aversion is a common psychological principle that is proven to work! Get the point across that if they don't act now, they might lose something valuable.

- **"Reserve your spot now"** Same principle as above! Tell your prospects that if they don't sign up and reserve their spots, they run the risk of leaving it too late.

- **"Order now while there's still time!"** Urgency is often a key element in effective call-to-action phrases. Subtly pressure consumers into acting now rather than waiting until the opportunity passes them by.

- **"In a hurry? Call…"** Call-to-action phrases like this one let the consumer know that you're willing to respond to their needs right away. A perfect CTA to use if you offer out-of-hours or emergency services.

- **"It's very important that you respond promptly"** With this CTA you're telling the prospect that if they don't respond right away then they might lose out on something good.

- **"Offer expires very soon"** A powerful, snappy CTA that clearly states there's an offer on the table, but if you don't snap it up, you'll miss out.

- **"For a short time only"** This CTA is popular during sales or clearances. It's clearly stating that here is a chance to buy a limited-edition product, take advantage of a big discount, or get some other benefit. But only if you act now.

- **"Limited availability"** a great CTA as it creates urgency and infers your product is highly popular. A win-win for you as it serves as a form of social proof as well as an incentive to act quickly.

- **"Expires at midnight tonight"** It gives a definitely end point to the sale, so your prospects know they have to act quickly as the clock is ticking.

CTA Phrases to Imply Exclusivity

A very effective way to make people act is to imply exclusivity with whatever you're offering. Try these phrases out to get people taking action and jumping at the chance to be a part of your product or service to not get left out of the group.

- **"I invite you to…"** Everyone needs to feel wanted and special —foster that sense of belonging by giving the impression that you're personally inviting your prospect to do what you want.

- **"Join X Other [Category] as Subscribers to My Email List"** A great CTA for social proof. This CTA comes in many forms for example "Become one of the X people who subscribe to my emails." Or "Join the club! Over X request my emails. You could, too!"

  - **"Request an invitation"**

  - **"Members Only"**

  - **"Only available to X"**

  - **"Pre-register/Pre-order"**

  - **"Exclusive access"**

USEFUL TOOLS AND APPS TO HELP YOU MARKET SMART

Updating Facebook, creating images for Pinterest; posting a stream of Tweets and or crafting your weekly blog post – all of these tasks can easily eat away at your day until there is little or no time for anything else. Those with the budget can hire a dedicated social media manager to do all this for them, but for a cash-strapped start-up with no budget for a freelancer, it can feel like a struggle to get your marketing successfully off the ground. Be thankful therefore, that there are a huge variety of great tools available that are all specifically designed to address these issues. Utilising the readily available tools to help you manage your social media presence will make the whole process significantly more streamline and free up your day for other important tasks to growing your business.

- *Canva*
  Visual content is vital in your social media marketing. Turn to Canva to help you easily produce high-quality, eye-catching mages for free or if you have a budget, gain access to thousands of graphics and photos. They offer numerous templates that help your images look like a great designer has done them (but in the fraction of the time and cost!).

- *Buffer*
  Buffer makes allows you to create a posting schedule for your Twitter, LinkedIn, Facebook, Pinterest and Google+ pages all in one place, which makes posting your social-media content across multiple social media accounts is a whole lot easier.

- *Brand24*
  Brand24 delivers real-time information on what's been said as well as what is going on with your competition. This continual insight not only saves you having to search around for what people are saying about your brand, but it will help you effectively respond to positive and negative comments across your social-media platforms, so you can stay engaged with your audience and utilise any potential sales opportunities.

- *Cyfe*
  Cyfe is a cloud-based service that allows you easily monitor and share all of your vital business data from one single location in real-time. It delivers detailed reports related to SEO, Google

Analytics, AdWords and brand mentions. Cyfe can also help with industry and competitor research as a business intelligence tool, helping to turn data and trends into actionable insights.

- *Social Clout*
  Social Clout is a social media monitoring and analytics tool, that looks at where you can make significant improvements in engagement, campaigns and keywords. It delivers reports on demographics and social-media results, providing data on multiple social-media accounts to help you track the progress and be able to note the differences in responses across platforms.

- *AgoraPulse*
  If you use Facebook and Twitter for business, this tool enhances what you can do with both social-media platforms, allowing you to manage all Social Media messages in one place, schedule and publish content. It also offers solutions for customer relationship management, applications, analytics reports, contests and more.

- *Follower Wonk*
  Follower Wonk helps you find, analyze and optimize your social-media efforts solely for Twitter. You can get richer data about your followers, where they are located, and when they tweet plus the ability to locate new influencers and optimise your own tweets.

- *Inkybee*
  This social-media tool provides a way for you to locate and connect with influencers (bloggers, social-media celebrities etc.) in your industry who can elevate your brand and help open you up to and attract more potential customers.

- *Sendible*
  A popular and powerful social-media tool, Sendible brings together all aspects of your social-media management responsibilities. From gathering all posts and comments into one dashboard for analysis, measurement and engagement. To publishing, collaboration, mobile tools and customer relationship management.

- *Openr*
  This tool lets you add a relevant, targeted promotional message to any page you share on your social-media profiles. The result is more leads and traffic while helping you learn more about your audience.

- *Socedo*
  Socedo automates the lead generation process by bringing in relevant social prospects through social media into your sales pipeline. The platform matches users' interest with your defined criteria and engages prospective customers, automatically using a customisable workflow. This tool also provides insights and analytics and insights allowing you to fine-tune the workflow in order to get better quality leads.

- *Hooks App*
  The Hooks app is an alert system to use on your iPhone allowing you to stay up to date on anything through push notifications. There are hundreds of channels, including music, weather, sports scores, weather, stock prices, shipping tracking and even a channel to let you know when a concert from a certain artist is upcoming. Think of any channel, then think of anything you want to be notified of on that channel, whether it's every time a certain person tweets or when a website is down. For example, to do a Twitter alert, just set up the app, go to Twitter search and plug in the hashtag. You will then get an alert on your phone every time someone tweets that hashtag.

- *TwitShot*
  TwitShot is a free tool that's a combination of a website, Chrome extension and iOS app that simplifies the way you find images for your tweets. With TwitShot, you can easily drop photos into tweets. Simply drop in a URL for whatever piece of content you want to tweet, and TwitShot will scrape the site and find all image options. This is much more efficient than downloading and re-uploading an image when you want to tweet.

- *Google Trends*
  Google Trends is a free service that provides you with on-demand insight into what people are searching for and whether it's increasing or decreasing as a trend. Simply type in a couple of keywords and compare their interest activity. Google Trends tracks activity on these keywords all the way back to 2004, and shows if activity is increasing or decreasing, relative to the other search term. You can do this worldwide, but or search by country and get insights into what people are searching for, see whether the trend is moving up or down and more.

- *Firefox Web Shortcuts*
  If use the Firefox web browser, there are some cool tricks you can utilise. For example, hold down Cmd+Opt+M (for Mac) or Ctrl+Shift+M (for Windows) to see how your site looks on mobile. By holding down Cmd+Opt+Q (Mac) or Ctrl+Shift+Q (Windows) you can also see how your web page loads and what's slowing it down. This is great way to test and troubleshoot your website.

FINAL WORDS

Thank You!

Hopefully you have enjoyed reading this guide and start to see great improvements in your social media marketing by implementing the material that has been covered in this guide. I appreciate you taking the time to buy this guide, and if you've got a moment, I'd love to hear what you thought about it. Share your thoughts with me via email on info@scarlettdarbyshire.co.uk or let me know what you thought over on social media.

If You Get Stuck!

I'm only an email away, just give me a shout! I can always be reached on info@scarlettdarbyshire.co.uk or on Twitter. My handle is @ConsultScarlett. My passion lies in helping small businesses just like yours, so do not be afraid to reach out and ask.

Follow me on Twitter @ConsultScarlett

Connect With Me On LinkedIn: Search for Scarlett Darbyshire

Pin With Me On Pinterest: Search /ConsultScarlett

Keep Going!

Social media is more like a marathon than a sprint, but anything that's worth doing takes time. Just remember to keep at it and you will be glad you did a year from today!

All information was correct at the time of writing (Jan 2018)

Printed in Great Britain
by Amazon

Rewild Yourself: Becoming Nature is ;
helping us to turn our thinking aroun
experience and fully use all our sense
connected to everything around us. Tl
wild and inspirational book, ensuring
I absolutely Love it!

GLENNIE KINDRED, author of *Letting In the Wild Edges*

When you weep from the profound beauty of a sunset, listen to the symphony of the forest or drink water that gushes from the earth a part of you relaxes and you begin to remember. You remember who you truly are - a wild being with an indigenous soul within a spiritual ecology. Rachel Corby helps ignite this memory in her latest book, *Rewild Yourself: Becoming Nature*, as she reminds us that our resilience, depth perception and ability to adapt, crucial skills during these times, are directly linked to our wildness, that part of our self that never left the Earth.

PAM MONTGOMERY, author of *Partner Earth; A Spiritual Ecology* and *Plant Spirit Healing; A Guide to Working with Plant Consciousness.*

ReWild Yourself: Becoming Nature articulates the historical roots of modern cultures separation from Nature as well as the resulting cascade of contemporary afflictions and ailments, the continual rise in the use of anti depressants to dull awareness of and pain from the deep chasm separating humans from the place we belong in Nature, with Nature and as Nature. That place we abandoned long ago. We stand as a culture on the brink of collapse. Our spirit is diseased. Society is sick. Fear is rampant. We look across the separation growing ever deeper and wider while reaching for solutions "out there," if we reach at all.

ReWild Yourself: Becoming Nature guides the reader to workable solutions that are within reach of each of us, from inside. "…this path is within each of us but our minds and our modern lives have obscured it from plain sight."

With a voice of fierce passion, Corby unapologetically charts a map for our return to the territory of wildness inside and out.

JULIE MCINTYRE, clinical herbalist, educator and ceremonialist. Author of *Sex and the Intelligence of the Heart; Nature, Intimacy and Sexual Energy.*

Rachel Corby writes beautifully as always, here eloquently expressing the seriousness of our need for the Wild, for the deep and true medicine of nature. A compelling read and a wonderful reminder that the earth is powerfully alive and magic is afoot all around us even under the tarmac.

PIP WALLER, herbalist and plant spirit medicine practitioner. Author of *Holistic Anatomy – an integrative guide to the human body, The Domestic Alchemist, The Herbal Handbook for Home & Health.*

Also by Rachel Corby

The Medicine Garden
20 Amazing Plants & Their Practical Uses

*Re*Wild *Yourself:*
Becoming Nature

Rachel Corby

AMANITA FORREST PRESS

Published by Amanita Forrest Press, Stroud, UK. 2015.

Copyright © 2015 Rachel Corby

All Rights Reserved. No part of this publication, including text or illustrations, may be reproduced, stored in a retrieval system, or transmitted, in any form or by any means, electronic, mechanical, photocopying or otherwise, without prior permission of the author, Rachel Corby, www.wildgaiansoul.com

ISBN-13: 978-1512155723

Book designed and set into type by Raúl López Cabello
www.itsasunnyday.com

Cover and illustrations by Wendy Milner
www.wendymilner.co.uk

DISCLAIMER

When undertaking the exercises outlined in these pages, your wildness, the connection to nature, and the feelings and physical manifestations that arise as a result may not happen exactly as I describe them to you. We are each wired differently, living in different circumstances and faced with different opportunities.

I have written with safety in mind, but when following any exercise, or in any work with diet or entheogens, the reader should proceed with due care and caution. I in no way encourage any reader to participate in any illegal activity, and will not be held accountable for any action taken by a reader based on information presented in this book.

This book has been written for anyone who has ever felt lost and alone, who has ever felt different, for anyone who has ever wondered why, or what is the point to this life. It is all of you to whom I dedicate this book. And of course to the wild, the wildness that runs through and connects all things.

CONTENTS

ACKNOWLEDGEMENTS 10

PROLOGUE 11

PART I: The Wild Path 16

1. WHAT IS REWILDING? 18

    1.1 The Need For Communication 19

    1.2 Introducing Gaia 21

    1.3 Recognising the Intelligence in Nature 22

    1.4 About This Book 23

2. CIVILISATION'S CURSE - Orphans, aliens and other lonely beings . .25

    2.1 Our Physical Separation From Nature 25

    2.2 Our Mental Separation From Nature 29

    2.3 Separation From Natural Landscapes And Loss Of Identity 32

    2.4 The Cycle Of Life 33

    2.5 Our Separation From Other Humans 38

    2.6 The Price We Pay 40

3. RENDING THE VEIL OF ILLUSION 46

    3.1 The Health Benefits of Nature 48

    3.2 Nature Therapy 51

    3.3 The Ever Pulsating Universe 53

    3.4 Connected By Light 54

    3.5 Expanding Outwards 58

PART II: Wild Heart 62

4. WHEN EVERYTHING'S ALIVE - Acknowledging the livingness

of the world 64

    4.1 The Life in our Immediate Environment 66

    4.2 Urban Environments 68

    4.3 Beyond The Urban Fringe 68

    4.4 Developing Our Ability To Communicate 70

5. FEELING BEFORE THINKING 73

6. REAWAKENING YOUR WILD HEART .76

    6.1 Embracing The Wild 77

7

PART III: Wild Body 88

7. THIS SENSUAL WORLD - Awakening your senses 90

   7.1 Hearing 92

   7.2 Sight 96

   7.3 Touch 100

   7.4 Smell 103

   7.5 Taste 109

   7.6 Fully Inhabiting This Sensual World .111

8. EATING YOUR BODY WILD 116

   8.1 Water 116

   8.2 Our Relationship To Food 118

   8.3 Local And Seasonal Foods 120

   8.4 The Evolution Of Food Production 122

   8.5 Wild Foods 125

   8.6 Wild Medicine 130

   8.7 Raw Food & Remedial Work 132

   8.8 Eating With Awareness 137

   8.9 The Flesh Of Earth Becomes Us 140

9. YOUR OWN SWEET PIECE OF NATURE 141

   9.1 Self-Massage 141

   9.2 The Importance Of Movement 142

   9.3 Hosting Other Lifeforms 143

   9.4 Whole Body Intelligence 146

PART IV: Wild Nature 148

10. FINGERS IN THE EARTH - Skin on skin contact 150

   10.1 Gardening 150

11. DEEP NATURE IMMERSION 154

   11.1 Facing Fear 156

   11.2 Metamorphosis As Nature Claims You 157

   11.3 Vision Quest 158

   11.4 Deep Immersion Activities 162

   11.5 Finding It Where You Can 163

PART V: Wild Spirit 168
12. ENTHEOGENIC PLANTS AND CONNECTION TO SPIRIT 170
   12.1 What, Why, Where? 171
   12.2 Entheogen Etiquette 177
   12.3 Plant Wisdom 182
   12.4 Integration 184
   12.5 Developing Life Long Relationships 186
   12.6 To Imbibe, Or Not To Imbibe? 188
   12.7 A Few Words Of Caution 189

PART VI: Wild Future 192
   13. TOWARDS AN HARMONIOUS CONVERGENCE 194
   13.1 Where Civilisation Is At 195
   13.2 The Wild Utopian Dream 199
   13.3 Wildness Pervading 200
   13.4 Where I'm At 202
   13.5 The Last Word 206

NOTES. 208

BIBLIOGRAPHY 216

ABOUT THE AUTHOR 223

ACKNOWLEDGEMENTS

The words of the following writers have opened up new avenues of thought for me and inspired me to ask more, I owe them deep gratitude; Jeremy Narby, Terrence McKenna, Michael Talbot, Graham Hancock, David Wolfe. Many of the ideas I have expanded in this book were seeded by Stephen Harrod Buhner and the work I did whilst apprenticing with him, thank you always. I am also forever grateful to both the genus loci of Pen-y-Fan for cradling my form and the autumn fruiting flora that cover her lower flanks who have so generously shared their wisdom and guidance. To John Perkins for helping me see the flow of pure energy more clearly and completely than ever before. To Andrew Cox for words of wisdom and encouragement, a man for whom the green fingers of Gaia have fully penetrated his heart and mind. To Deborah Coulson who has shared much of this adventure into plants with me, and even sponsored some of my investigations. To Nathanial Hughes for allowing me to teach from his beautiful turf roofed wooden apothecary and all the friendship and encouragement offered along the way. To Jon Cousins for great conversation which inspired some of the thoughts that I expanded in Chapter 3. To my husband, Stephen for nuggets of inspiration. To Sue Melton who encouraged thousands of young people from Hertfordshire in the 1980s and '90s to adventure into the wilderness within the structure of the Duke of Edinburgh's Award Scheme. To my wonderful friends Kevin Byrnes, Kamaldeep Sidhu, Tony Cardew and Emma Morgan for reading through the rough drafts and giving invaluable help with regards to grammar, attention to detail, and general flow. To Wendy Milner for your beautiful illustrations. To Raul Lopez Cabello for page setting and conversion into print and ebook formats. To P.N. for introducing me to the one who became my plant ally. To my dark angel for teaching me the value of disillusionment and for directing me towards some shadowy corners inside myself that, until then, had remained untended. To my light angel for infinite possibilities. And finally to all the wonderful people who have attended my workshops and walked away glowing, with sparkling eyes, as their wildness and Gaia connection have been re-ignited; encouraging me and reaffirming the power and importance of this work.

PROLOGUE

I know enough to know that there is no such thing as a normal upbringing; each life is unique and different. Even siblings in the same
home will have experienced different things at a single point in time,
so let me tell you my story. In my early years my mum stayed at home
to raise me and my siblings. She made many of our clothes and along
with my gran knitted all of our woollies. Our home was warmed with
the smells of mum's delicious cooking and baking. My dad grew beans
and rhubarb in the back garden. He took us for long walks on weekends, rubbing nettle stings with dock leaves and occasionally collecting
fragrant elderflowers for making wine. I remember secretly planting a
ring of daffodil and tulip bulbs with him in the middle of our lawn, to
surprise my mum with a splash of colour in spring. Our family holidays
involved exploring the rugged wild beauty of the British coastline. My
winter evenings were spent imagining fairy worlds rise and fall in the
crackling embers of our open fire. A cosy picture; but even so, I was born
into a world dislocated from nature. My home was cleaned, decorated
and furnished with products containing synthetic chemicals. Snuggled
in alongside the home knits and baking, I slept between viscose sheets,
was clothed in man made fibres and ate factory processed foods. The
rush for modernity in the 1970's somehow closed the door to nature,
firmly.

Even as a young child I was often troubled, angry and confused. I
felt like an alien, as if I had been dropped onto this Earth, abandoned.
I felt different, misunderstood. Some of my happiest memories from early
childhood were the times I spent playing with my secret friends. Those
friends resided on the compost heap in my parents back garden. They
included discarded egg shells, earthworms and the little round smelly
seeds of the towering Leylandii trees that screened my play place from
the world. I could spend hours at a time collecting them up, arranging
them and talking to them. However, those halcyon days did not last.

As the years passed I found myself struggling, never understanding
the sadness, the feeling of loss, that grew inside of me. I was mourn-
ing, but for what I did not know. My experience was not unique. For
an infant life is enchanting, even a tissue can amuse and entertain for
hours as it flutters when thrown in the air. Then there is the touch of it
on your skin, the smell and, of course, what happens when it inevitably
gets explored by a gummy toothless mouth. As we get older there is a

growing sense of disenchantment and alienation. As we enter our teens the search to fill the emptiness begins in earnest whether it is through shopping, food, TV, sex, drugs...

What was lucky for me was that instead of finding ways to mask the ennui, numb the disappointment with life, the door to another possibility, another truth, began to open. I began trekking in wild nature, in the national parks of Wales and Scotland. In those places of wildness, whilst camping and walking, I could feel a metamorphosis occurring inside; it was as if until this point I had spent my life half asleep. I sat out late, watching myriad stars twinkling against a dark velvet sky; I flung my head back in wind and rain to catch sharp arrows of moisture at the back of my throat; I plunged my cold hands into icy streams and splashed my face with vibrant life source; I saw patterns in rocks and whole worlds in patches of moss. The wildness and simplicity of outdoor life struck deep in my heart. I had never before felt so alive. This world felt more real, made me feel more real, than anything I had known since my earliest days of wonder.

I fell deeply in love with the natural world. I studied geomorphology and ecology, so that I could understand the processes that shape the landscapes we live amongst. I roamed the planet, often working with the land, learning more and more about different habitats and their different life forms, systems and processes. Whenever I spent time immersed in nature it felt wonderful; the wilder the place, the stronger the feeling.

Our ancient ancestors existed in a state of full nature immersion. They had an in-built intimacy with their environment, with every part of it. Not just with animals but with stones, plants and rivers, the wind. It was essential for their moment to moment survival, being able to read the signs whether of poisonous plant, presence of predators or extreme weather event looming. Their fate was married to their ability to read and understand the world. We would not be here now if they had not been such wonderful experts at it. However, during the last millennium or so, a separation has increasingly arisen between humanity and the rest of nature. The relationship of reciprocity with the animate natural world has slowly and silently disintegrated. We find ourselves no longer an interactive part of nature, instead separate and distanced from it.

That which I discuss and recommend in the following pages is

nothing new, just forgotten. I will trace the route I have followed, the route back to the love of Earth, to the remembering of wild Earth and my wild self. This journey, this path, is within each of us but our minds and our modern lives have obscured it from plain sight. To find our wild nature we must rediscover from where we came. There is a memory of this in the unexplored parts of ourselves, so when we begin opening up there is a flow, a momentum, that carries us home. To remember and explore the wild nature of the Earth is to remember and explore our own wild nature; the two are inseparable. The illusion of separation brings only sadness, deep pain and loneliness.

It is the same with any life. Imagine one secluded day struck out of it, and think how different its course would have been. Pause you who read this, and think for a moment of the long chain of iron or gold, of thorns or flowers that never would have bound you, but for the formation of the first link on one memorable day.

Charles Dickens

The following is the recollection of my defining moment, of a moment and experience so intense, so surreal, that it has coloured and directed my every moment since.

Walking in the bright warm spring sunshine I am suddenly aware of the presence of my plant ally. There is a tsunami of colour building and knowing that wave when it rushes over me will blind me I rapidly make for the shade of a small, gnarled, moss covered, hawthorn tree. I curl up at its wizened roots as the swirl of otherworldly colour overtakes me and sweeps me away into another reality. Overwhelmed by the presence of my plant ally, tears begin to flow in awe of its beauty.

My humanness fades to a vague, distant, memory, barely registering as I feel my physical body meld with the Earth

*that is cradling my form. It seems my body is disappearing
into a mess of ectoplasmic goo as I merge with Other. At this
point, half digested, I discover I can look into both worlds. The
human material world of mountainside, moss, stream, sheep,
tree and cloud; but also the Other, like looking through Alice's
looking-glass into Wonderland. The backdrop to Other is
black but the interest lies in the movement, the vast networks
of fast moving squiggle lines of colour, like a highway of
light, of energy. The coloured lines are all very fine, moving
independently of each other, many in the yellow spectrum
although the whole rainbow is represented. I understand
the traces of coloured light to contain information, they
are constantly moving, updating, connecting - they are
information super-highways. I can see the outlines of the
forms I recognise in the material world - trees, grasses –
within these moving streams of light, all interacting with each
other, constantly exchanging, sharing, adjusting. Everything
is connected by these endless living, pulsating, golden light
streams. In this moment I come to recognise them as the
source that is all things, all life, all knowledge and all being. I
realise that this is how life is for my ally, how it perceives and
experiences the world, and I have the feeling that it's how most
of life, other than humankind, also perceives and experiences
the world. What a revelation. What an honour to be privy to
this, to see and feel it. Euphoria engulfs me.*

*My heart beat has slowed immeasurably. The memory of my
human form suddenly kicks in, it is weak but enough for me
to remember who I am. I can feel my human life fading away.
My nose is clogged with ectoplasm and moss, obstructing
that which in part anchors me to human form, my living
breath. I have a choice, my ally lays it out before me. I can
join for all time, be a never ending movement of light in this
extraordinary realm of purity and energy, or I can return
to my human life. This is the hardest and saddest decision of
my life, agonising. I can feel pain physically ripping through
my chest, through my heart. My ally hurries me along, time is
short, I cannot remain between worlds much longer, I need to*

choose. A huge, overwhelming part of me wants to remain in this world of integrity, of pure light and energy, but visions of my loved ones begin flooding those remaining human parts of me. I crack and crumble, tears breaking open a chasm inside of me. I can feel my ally retreating on the other side. I throw my arms across but my heart does not follow, I am human, my choice is made.

I cannot stop the tears, I am in one hundred million pieces, pieces of ecstatic joy, of wonder, of sadness, of grief. I can feel every feeling, every emotion surging through me all at the same time. It has been the saddest and most amazing experience of my life. I know what an incredible honour it has been to experience the Other in this very real way. It takes days to begin to piece myself together. I will never be the same again.

I have realised that nature is not just kin, but self; there is no separation. That, blind to my waking human eyes, I am connected to the source, to the information super-highway, that pulsating dynamic stream of energy and golden light that connects, that is, all things.

In a strange way this book is, in part, the story of my life. The steps I have taken on my winding path, my mission to make sense of it all, to make sense of this life; *what is the point? why am I here?*

You will perhaps find that it is also your story. The story of a return to nature and how that in itself is an adventure, an unfolding. A journey to the place where you can see, feel, and touch the beauty that is the nature all around you, that is you, and how that is food for the soul like no other. This journey has led me to discover the wildness inside of me. The wildness which also runs through all of nature and how it provides medicine for our undernourished bodies, emotions and spirits. I have realised that the secret, the most important thing, is our invisible connection to and communication with all things.

PART I
The Wild Path

The word "wild" is related to the word "will"; the wild creature is self-willed, autonomous, not domesticated, living by nature's ways not the laws of human beings.
Ralph Metzner

Essentially your mission is not to set the world right, but to simply set yourself right. Then, and only then, will the world begin to be set right.
David Wolfe

Recognising the mind/body/nature connection will be one of the most important actions that a revitalized environmental movement can take.
Richard Louv

You never change things by fighting the existing reality. To change something, build a new model that makes the existing model obsolete.
Buckminster Fuller.

1. WHAT IS REWILDING?

Rewilding is a word that I have seen used increasingly over the last few years. If you search for the word online you get variations on the theme of: to restore an area of land or habitat to its natural, uncultivated, state. Lower down the page there are one or two entries relating to the rewilding of humans. They talk of overcoming our domesticated state, of learning about the natural environment, animals and plants, and reintegrating with those other species.

I believe the first step in reclaiming areas of land and habitat, to saving, refurbishing, *rewilding* them, is to find the wild place inside, to rewild yourself. To feed and nurture that wildness, encourage it to grow and in doing so, overcome a little of your very own domestication. Over generations, as civilised society progressed, we did our best to neutralise wild danger, to make our lives predictable and safe. However, in doing so we unintentionally neutralised an essential part of ourselves, put limits on our own capacity for wildness, and yet still we crave it. I do. I crave for the feeling of freedom that wind in my hair, rain on my skin, dewy grass underfoot gives me. By taming our environment we tamed an essential wild part of ourselves.

So, returning to the online search, my use of the term rewilding is a version of the latter. I am talking about rewilding the self; developing one's senses and natural instincts, rediscovering the natural world so that we can live well with *all* our relations.

When rewilding land, species that once inhabited that place are reintroduced. With time, what occurs is known as trophic cascade. Fundamentally, what this means is that the presence of one species alters the behaviour of another. Animals that had no predator for generations do once more and so their grazing habits and roaming patterns change to allow them greater protection. This in turn allows plants that had previously been heavily grazed to grow to maturity, and new species of plants and trees to re-establish. Along with the flourishing of the flora, more birds and animals return as their particular niche reappears. The whole ecosystem responds and strengthens.

When a person undergoes the rewilding process, allows wildness to re-inhabit their being, the benefits also grow and spread in the manner of a trophic cascade. There is an alteration, a change in the mental health of the person, a change in their physical health, an associated change in the way they interact with the world, their behaviour. This

in turn allows other people around them to feel something different, to perhaps also choose to take a step away from the synthetic existence of modern life. And onwards, and outwards. The whole ecosystem responds and strengthens.

Rewilding is about growing, extending and feeling. It is about being in community with all life and replacing the crumbling, lonely, façade that currently passes for life with vibrancy and colour. To rewild yourself involves more than simply spending time in nature, than wild swimming or foraging for wild fruits; although, of course, they are a great start. To rewild fully you need to immerse yourself in nature, literally *become* nature. It should be remembered that we arrive in this world as small, naked, bloodied animals for whom everything is based on instinct, direct perception and feeling, until we start using our senses. It is not until months, years, into our lives that thoughts start to rule our actions.

We are broken as a people, as a society. Our health, both physical and mental, suffers daily from the choices we have made and habits we have formed, both individually and as an evolving culture. Rewilding is about breaking out of our civilised mould and saying *no more*. It is about laying face down on the Earth, arms and legs spread in a full body hug, full contact with Earth, to reclaim it as part of *yourself*. It is about falling in love ever more deeply with every part of yourself, from the microbes in the soil, to the great oaks, to the stardust we are made from.

> *Forget not the earth delights to feel your bare feet and the winds long to play with your hair.*
>
> Kahlil Gibran

Rewilding is about connecting with the child within that wants to get dirty and play in the mud, splash in puddles and chase butterflies. It is about re-opening your eyes to the wonder in the world. The wonder and beauty in the ordinary, the everyday nature that surrounds you. Even in urban landscapes there are ants and trees, weeds and foxes. Wildness is a missing part of each one of us and without it we suffer.

1.1 The Need For Communication

Communication is key to rewilding. When communication breaks down, even just between two people, it can be very damaging, upsetting and isolating. Over the last millennia or so communication has

broken down between our species, humankind, and the rest of life. Rewilding involves bridging that gap so that we can bond with the wild, with nature, and remember that we are actually a part of it.

We need to reconnect and an essential part of that process involves dropping out of our overzealous logical, analytical, left brains and listening; paying attention to the feelings and thoughts that come to us seemingly from nowhere. It is clear that we all have the capacity because it is one thing we all had built into us in the womb, ready for our emergence into the big bright world outside. It involves perceiving directly without the complication of too many thoughts getting involved, in essence winding back to the skill sets that were everything to us as newborns.

As we grow into little humans most often our faculty to perceive directly, to understand what is there before us, and what meaning that holds, deteriorates. Less attention is given to that ability as we begin to explore with our newly emerging senses and realise the wealth of information we can gather by touching, smelling, tasting, listening; and how we can express our findings, or our needs, with sound. As we develop these last two senses we begin to rely upon language, upon the spoken word to convey meaning and feelings, and thus any life form that does not communicate in this way quickly becomes sidelined.

As digital technology continues to rapidly develop and pervade more and more moments of our lives, our skill sets and brain function align themselves to evolve alongside that technology. An unintended consequence of this is that our capacity to engage with the world around us appears to diminish further. Being skilful with a computer has become more important to us as individuals, and in a sense to our survival in the modern world, than the need to have the skills to find food, or water, or to be aware that we are being watched or stalked. Our abilities, so strong at birth, to *feel* things and understand their meaning as they are occurring around us, dwindle further as our attention focusses on movies, computer games, texting, social media. It has become so that we no longer even register when someone enters or leaves the room we are in.

To *become nature* involves redeveloping your capacity for direct perception and retraining your senses. It involves exploring the wildness that still dwells within you, no matter how diminished, and nurturing it, giving it a space to grow. With refined intuition and acute senses you can gather information about the world around you at all times from just the tiniest

20

perturbation in your environment, a whiff on the air, or change in mood of someone (or thing) near you. Once you are able to gather and interpret information you can respond to it. Opening the lines of communication is opening the lines of possibility.

1.2 Introducing Gaia

Gaia is a term that I will use interchangeably with nature throughout this book, it is a term that envelopes the whole of nature and is in effect an entity unto itself. Gaia, was the Greek goddess of Earth, the great mother of all. In 1979 James Lovelock introduced the Gaia hypothesis; where Gaia, composed of living organisms and inorganic material, operates as a self regulatory organism, shaping and maintaining the Earth's biosphere, ensuring it remains habitable.

All life on Earth, including the planet itself, the minute particles, the magma, the mountains, the lakes and all the plants and creatures that live on the surface or deep within it together form Gaia. Those elements in conjunction create and maintain the conditions necessary for life. Humankind is one of those elements.

One tiny part of the collective known as Gaia, humankind, are considered to have something beyond just a physical presence, something more, something spiritual. It is illogical to me that we alone have this extra something considering that we are simply a single part working together with all of the other components of Gaia to create the specific conditions within which as a whole we can thrive. Does it not follow that if *we* are sentient that by association so are the other elements of this entity Gaia, if not indeed the entity in its entirety? In my world view our sentience implies that Gaia itself should be regarded beyond just a self-regulatory organism but as a sentient being, a spiritual, as well as a physical entity of which we are an inseparable part.

Acknowledging and reconnecting with the rest of life that creates and inhabits this world, is the essential root of rewilding. We are not separate; our aliveness, sentience and spirit is not a phenomena unique to humans, but acting as if it is, in turn creates a breakdown in communication between the parts. To ensure the entity, Gaia, continues to provide the conditions necessary for life there is a danger that the great changes it will need to initiate to achieve that, will wipe us humans clean out of existence.

Rewilding is not, however, about saving the human race, or Gaia; she will do what is necessary to look after herself. It is about remember-

ing what we are here for, and what it takes to sustain our lives. We have drifted so far from even the most basic necessities of life such as the production of our food and source of our drinking water.

Rewilding is about being part of a global community, not just of our own kind, but of all life. It is about recognising the livingness of the world, acknowledging and respecting all forms of life and how that shapes and enhances our own experience as citizens of this planet, and as harmoniously functioning elements of Gaia.

Rewilding yourself, becoming nature, is not grandiose, not hard to achieve and the benefits, once you start to feel them seep into every corner of your life, speak for themselves. It is a call to reincorporate nature and respect for nature into our lives, to reforge links that have been lost. To live a little closer, in heart at least, to how our ancestors did, our ancestors who talked to the animals and plants, who read the wind and the sky.

Being closed to the sentience of our wild relations means we lose layers of meaning. Life becomes one dimensional, meaningless almost, as we miss so much, so many of life's nuances. We miss interactions between species and with apparently inert materials such as soil, wood and stone. Rewilding, recognising our species as part of Gaia, part of an interdependent community of life forms, colours it all back in again. The disconnect, the pointlessness of existence, the grey monotonous drudge, all gone and filled with immeasurable depth of feeling, richness and purpose of being.

1.3 Recognising the Intelligence in Nature

I have already commented that if we as part of Gaia have spirit and sentience then surely it is implied for the rest of Gaia; the same goes for intelligence. Surely the self regulatory aspect of Gaia alone assumes a certain level of awareness, of intelligence. Despite this, intelligence in nature is widely discredited.

There is a belief that one day contact will come with intelligent beings from another planet. That one day we will find some humanesque bipeds with whom we can share a cup of tea, over which we can catch up on the history of their species. That may well happen, however in the mean time it is worth reigning in such expectations. There are plenty of living beings on *this* planet who display self organisation, the ability to make choices (decisions) and to learn. If you can choose between, if you have the capacity to make a decision and to learn from

that, then intelligence is implied. Despite this, intelligent life beyond humanity on this planet is, for the large part, overlooked and ignored.

On nature documentaries the commentary is usually incredibly patronising, and surprised, if there is a display of organisation and intelligence in the animals being filmed. The general denial of intelligence in nature is the overriding paradigm that we live within and yet many of us have had meaningful interactions with the family pet and can accept communication with animals.

If you have experienced communication with an animal, being able to understand what it needs, what it is feeling, then what about the rest of Gaia? I work with plants and have met many gardeners in my private and professional life, a large proportion of whom communicate with their plants. Those communications may not be entirely conscious, and for some are not something they would admit to, but many a gardener will know that a plant wants to be moved, fed or watered way before it displays any visible signs indicating that need. If you can decipher meaningful messages, can exchange freely back and forth with information, then you are communicating and intelligence on some level is implicated.

I know it is a big ask for people to recognise the intelligence in plants, rocks, rivers, mountains, the very Earth beneath our feet. Yet for some the concept will resonate with something deep inside; something so far back in our collective memory it's hardly there, and yet there's a comfortableness and a familiarity to it, a knowing. Rewilding connects us directly with the intelligence in nature. Communicating with other species is something anyone can do, if they would like to try, the skills go right back to the direct perception mode of newborns.

1.4 About This Book

Unfortunately, we have all grown under the illusion that there is a separation between humanity and nature. Over the next chapters I will aim to establish how this is not so, that we are in fact an intrinsic part of nature, there is and can be no separation.

We have adapted our senses and abilities to suit our urban, technology filled lives, so in a sense to rewild is to fine tune ourselves back to the rest of nature. Retune so that we may not just survive in our roaring urban and virtual worlds, but also remember the rest of Gaia, as that is what supports us, and is what we are made of.

It is my aim in this book to disillusion you, where disillusionment is the greatest gift. I will take you to a place where you can see and feel

once again what is truly before you. Where you can be a true part of the global community beyond humanity; incorporating the trees, bugs and dirt too, they are *all* relatives of ours.

We will start with our ability to feel, our intuition. Then work with using our senses and physical body. And finally we will explore the deep mysteries of spirit. This is a soul journey, one that ultimately will feed you with a profound sense of belonging, and an improvement in both your physical and mental well-being.

Rewilding yourself is an ecological reclamation of the self, of your heart. This book is about finding your way to wholeness through nature. It is a call to acknowledge the spirit in all things, the livingness of nature and the recognition of yourself as a deeply interwoven part of it.

🌲

Whether you live in a remote mountain cabin or inner city high rise, opportunities to rewild present themselves all the time. Birds, plants, clouds, they don't halt at the urban edge, they infuse our everyday experience of the world wherever we are. By reaching out and recognising a long lost part of ourselves in them we take the first step away from our domestication, a condition that has formed, shaped, and limited us since our birth. This step away from domestication forms our first step towards rewilding, toward reclaiming and nurturing the wildness that lies in the heart of each and every one of us. Recognition of parts of ourselves in our everyday nature encounters, with the clouds and the birds, is restorative, energising, at last a way home; the beginnings of a new, wilder, path integrated with the rest of Gaia.

I have written for anyone who ever wondered why?; who ever felt they were missing something; or who has ever felt alone and lost. Rewilding is about lifting the veil of illusion and re-entering the livingness of the world. About understanding ones place within this beautiful matrix of intertwined energies and living with a respect and knowing of the beauty that lies both within and without.

As you rewild, as you become nature, you will gain a deeper knowledge and understanding of the whole of nature including yourself. You may find yourself changing; your outlook, desires, behaviour. People will notice and wonder what's your secret as you gain a kind of luminosity, an ethereal glow. And as you begin to care for the earthworms with as much respect as you care for your mother there will be a knowing inside that you finally have come home.

2. CIVILISATION'S CURSE -
Orphans, aliens and other lonely beings

I have given a brief overview of rewilding as a concept, but perhaps the question that now arises is why? Why take time out of your already busy schedule to consider whether grass is intelligent, to start talking to animals, or generally scrabble around outside in the dirt? The answer is not something I can give you within one catchy sentence or a concise paragraph. However, without a strong connection to nature humanity is somehow bereft and we suffer physically, emotionally and mentally. Once on the trail you will notice articles in the media on an almost weekly basis, confirming this. So bear with me as I start in the place I consider to be the beginning; how we fell out of our close relationship with nature and what the consequences of that drift have been. Together they provide enough of a why for me...

2.1 Our Physical Separation From Nature

The root of the word civilisation, is the Latin word *civis,* which means someone who lives in a town, an urban dweller. The move over the centuries towards being civilised people, a civilised society, may have had a more detrimental effect on us both as individuals and as a society than anyone could have imagined.

A very simplistic and general summing up of human history would have it that many thousands of years ago humanity lived very simply, side by side with the animals and the elements, sheltering in caves perhaps, or under the canopy of large trees. With time and developments in our dexterity and mental capacity humans began to build simple makeshift structures with the materials nature provided in that particular locality, no different in essence from a bird making a nest. As we progressed in our ability to carry out complex tasks the shelters we built in turn became more complex and depending on the location and the lifestyle of the maker, more permanent. Still these were simple abodes made from earth, stone, wood, grass and skin.

There are many, many, people on this planet still living in earth, or stick, or stone abodes. In my second book, *20 Amazing Plants & their Practical Uses,* I talk a lot about natural building materials and the

fact that approximately 1 billion people worldwide live in houses made from bamboo[1], that is of course roughly 1 in 7 of the world population! However, especially in more urban and industrialised cultures, there has been a movement away from natural and locally sourced building materials over the last 150 years or more. Large housing estates have been constructed with concrete, plasterboard and breeze blocks to satisfy the surge in demand for homes in locations distant from abundant quantities of natural building materials[2].

As our civilisation developed, industry expanded alongside larger, and larger, clusters of population to service that industrial growth. Concurrently, and as a direct consequence of more urban living, involvement in animal husbandry and the production of food crops lessened for the general populace. As generation upon generation were born and grew without direct involvement in the production of food, connection with and access to nature became of less importance and began to gradually decline. With time people found more urban pursuits to fill the free time they would likely never had were they still tied to tending the land.

Although the migration to urban centres has been ongoing for hundreds of years the current pace of acceleration is astounding. In 1950 30% of the world population lived in cities, 64 years later, in 2014, 54% of the world population lived in cities[3]. The proportion of people worldwide living in urban centres continues to expand and thus the size of these cities also grows. With larger cities it often becomes the case that people have further to travel to their place of work, and so people walk less and less, and are transported by machine more and more. Less working outside and less walking to work or to the shops, has further reduced time spent feeling the elements, the sun, the wind and the rain, on our skin.

Over the centuries our housing has become more urban, homes less natural, and time spent indoors has increased. Meanwhile, so gradual as to be almost unnoticeable, our connection to nature has slipped, stalled and dwindled to almost nothing. It has become so that we are shocked and devastated when nature makes an appearance in our homes; be it flood water damaging our expensive furnishings, or an ants nest requiring chemical extermination lest those darn critters eat some of our sugary treats! *Our physical disconnect from nature almost complete.*

26

An historical element in the breakdown of our physical connection with the rest of Gaia was the burning of the witches across Europe and in the USA. Witch trials occurred from around 1450 in Europe until the late 1800s in the USA. They mainly targeted women with a strong connection to nature. Estimates of the number persecuted and executed during that period for their practices and beliefs vary widely, but it is believed to have been somewhere between 40,000 and 500,000. Female scholars, priestesses, gypsies, mystics, nature lovers, herb foragers, healers and any other woman with so much as a twig in her hair were all potentially counted as witches and killed; even midwives became targets. This, unsurprisingly, drove knowledge of medicinal herbs, relationships with the land, and the practice of Earth ceremonies, underground. Those brave and driven enough to still seek the knowledge and practice it became secretive for their own preservation. This led to the loss of much knowledge and many traditions, especially in the areas of Europe where the persecution and eradication of these ways had been most vehement and thus near complete. We became orphans, our natural connections with all our relations, the rivers, the trees, the mountains, the animals, severed.

Ancestral knowledge of the *green way* continued to be persecuted in indigenous communities by the *civilised* world long after the witch trails of Europe and North America ended. Over the last few hundred years, as we came upon tribes living relatively harmonious lives amongst nature, we tended to deride their wisdom and deep knowledge of plants, Earth and spirit. We viewed them as "primitive" and in our ignorance encouraged them to adopt more acceptable ways and beliefs. Even now, despite a greater level of respect for indigenous cultures, an element remains where we try to "help improve their lives" by imposing inappropriate economic models; subtly inserting a wedge between the people and their environment[4].

Witch hunts and persecutions are ongoing within some African communities although they do not necessarily relate directly to the accused having herbal knowledge. Even within modern *Western* society the historical persecution of the witches still affects our interactions with plants. If you live the *green way* people are often suspicious. If you drink herbal tea made from plants you have gathered and hung in bunches, rather than plastic wrapped from shops, it is not long before

the word "witch" or "witchy" sneaks into people's thoughts and descriptions of you. But a *way with nature* is, and was, the *original way* and for us modern humans that means the path of reconnecting, *rewilding*.

A further disconnect with our local environment may stem from being taught in school of far away places (and problems) but not what is on our own doorstep. Being constantly bombarded with environmental problems far from home in Bangladesh, the Pacific Islands, Alaska, one becomes cut off from local issues and perhaps overwhelmed with the magnitude of it all. *A sense of hopelessness descends*. Our energy goes into raising funds and awareness for distant locations with little knowledge or connection with what is occurring locally. In response we become further dislocated, alienated, from the land upon which we stand.

The cut off from nature has not just been a subtle slide, in many instances it is imposed by circumstances beyond our individual control, the witch killings being an extreme example. However around the world authorities, consciously or not, are continuing to impose restrictions on our access to nature. A few years ago I spent several months living in Bernalillo, a north eastern satellite of Albuquerque, New Mexico. My home overlooked the Sandia mountain range with the Rio Grande in the foreground. Together they formed a wonderful view from my balcony where I often stood watching the moon rise behind the mountain in one direction with the shimmering lights of the city in the other. I had access to the wilderness through a gap in a wall which boarded off an arroyo from my street. I would walk every day, sometimes twice a day, along the dry stream bed to the stand of cottonwoods that shaded the river edge. One morning I began my usual walk only to discover the gap in the wall had been filled with metal bars. Staring through at my wilderness I felt like I had been incarcerated. The only other access to this wonderful nature oasis on my doorstep was through a gate with a pin code at the far end of a neighbouring gated community. I did not have the gate code. However, I was determined and eventually discovered a weak spot in the fortifications that kept human and nature separate. A small section of wire fence existed which, with a little bit of shimmy and limbo, was passable. It was a tragedy that despite living

less than one hundred meters from a wild area leading to the banks of the Rio Grande there was no public access, the nearest point of permitted public entry was a 15 minute drive away, almost in Albuquerque. By foot access had become all but impossible – still tantalisingly visible and yet blocked.

2.2 Our Mental Separation From Nature

Expanding urbanisation has clearly caused a physical separation from nature, but our alienation from the natural environment has deeper roots. René Descartes, a French philosopher born in 1596, had an incredible impact on Western thinking. His philosophy, based in part upon his most famous quote "I think; therefore I am", has led to what is now widely known as Cartesian Dualism, the separation between mind and matter.

The implications of this philosophy, of Cartesian Dualism, the separation between mind and matter, between the conscious and that which is perceived to be unconscious, are immense. This split is even applied to our human form where our conscious minds become something different and separate from our supposedly unconscious bodies.

Our society is still infected with this doctrine as it has remained our impression that we are separate from nature, detached from it and independent from the world, mere onlookers. This sense of separation is what allows the attitude that we can treat the world as an object to be exploited whilst the consequences remain separate from our lives.

This attitude was further strengthened by Descartes' theory that the body is like a mechanical device which will respond to external stimuli with certain predetermined responses or reflex actions. This led to the understanding that the world is filled with lifeless, inert matter, that behaves predictably, without feeling, all just a series of little machines. This belief took the spirit out of living things and enabled the justification for vivisection as reactions were just a motor response and not feeling led; matter being incapable of the sensations of pleasure or pain.

The separation inherent in the belief *I think; therefore I am* has also allowed another very arrogant anthropocentric thought pattern to emerge and dominate Western thinking and behaviour; that of hierarchy. The concept that we, thinking humans, are placed at the top of some kind of invisible triangle of importance where stones and pebbles are particularly low down, with carrots and apples perhaps slightly

higher up, yet still below earthworms, with primates just below us in this table of worth. Such subliminal belief systems have further allowed us to damage, destroy and exploit without a second thought for the animals, plants and minerals taken from their natural environment to support our lifestyles. Just consider for a moment all the products, foods, clothes and other material items that you have used unconsciously today, without a thought. Perhaps in their raw, unprocessed state, they were once living and have been sacrificed for your comfort and lifestyle choices.

In effect, Descartes separated us from the rest of nature, which was reduced to nothing more than an unfeeling bundle of mechanised systems. This released us from empathy, restructuring our relationship with our world to one where the exploitation of finite, living, feeling, entities, or so called resources, and the resulting desecration of natural places, could occur.

The work of Charles Darwin followed 200 years later. He theorised that we evolved from apes, that all life, no matter how distant, are somehow cousins. You would think this would bring feeling, empathy and life back into the world but alas, no. Despite his influence, science and Western culture have clung to our separation. In fact, his work served to reinforce the notion of a hierarchy where we, somehow superior, sit at the top of an evolutionary pyramid with algae and bacteria at the bottom.

For the thinking man, a hierarchy based on degree of evolution would not necessarily have the more complex organisms topping it. Complexity does not automatically infer more highly evolved; as evolution, according to Ralph Metzner's discussion in *Green Psychology,* can be defined as changing adaptations to meet changing environments. Complex, specialised, organisms by their nature have a tendency to be more delicate, there is more that can go wrong - think of a car versus a push bike, for example. This complexity translates as a greater vulnerability to perturbations in the environment; as we know, complexity simply didn't work out for the dinosaurs. In contrast to those extinct fragments of history, a group of single-celled bacterial organisms known as prokaryotes, which originated 3½ billion years ago, are still flourishing. Prokaryotes are the organisms that have been around for the longest period of time suggesting they are the most adaptable and thus the most evolved[5]. So if there needs to be an evolutionary pyramid perhaps those bacteria should top it, and yet our topsy turvy view of the world prevails.

When I teach, I advocate learning from plants as wild and wise older relations, but I do not infer that they are better or higher up the hierarchy than us. We have to realise that we are all *equal* - even the prokaryotes – we *all* have something to share. In fact we are all one – equal parts of one great life force joined by that invisible pulse that connects us all. Hierarchy is so outdated and to progress at all it has to go. I digress...

Another major player in our mental separation from nature was Issac Newton born in the 1640's. An influential mathematician and physicist, through whose findings, his laws of motion and universal gravitation, the idea that the universe is nothing more than a predictable series of mechanised systems was reinforced.

I loved physics at school, so Newton was somewhat of an early hero. However by age 16, when I moved to the senior department and began studying my A Levels, I was told that most of what I had previously learned as laws had limitations. They were not strict laws that applied in every situation; I realised I had been lied to. The truth was bent to fit laws that neatly and cleanly explained our world, except they didn't quite fit, not in every situation. The world is not a mechanical, predictable, thing that can be understood by making it quantifiable. The world was pushed into a square hole to fit a mathematical model.

The work of Descartes and Newton combined changed the world from being a living entity to one that could be broken down into little pieces with corresponding rules about how each of those pieces work. As if by understanding the parts you could understand the whole, like a wristwatch. In their explanations of our world they left no room for free will or chance, for the mysteries of love or spirit.

With a few deft moves, Newton and Descartes had plucked God and life from the world of matter, and us and our consciousness from the centre of our world. They ripped the heart and soul out of the universe, leaving in its wake a lifeless collection of interlocking parts.

Lynne McTaggart

We are each more than the flesh, and blood, and bone that makes our physical structure, more than "matter". If you took a human, or an animal, or a landscape apart and separated it into little bits then built your own from scratch, you would miss the most important part. The something that

runs through us yet cannot be found in any of the parts, the something that makes each of us uniquely who we are, yet paradoxically connects us with all life. That something, that part, is what enlivens us, it is what makes all life more than just mechanised bundles of responses, and without it, without acknowledgement of it, we find ourselves alone. *We have become little aliens on our own planet.*

2.3 Separation From Natural Landscapes And Loss Of Identity

Our loss of connection with the land and with its inhabitants both physically and mentally has also caused, or as a minimum adds weight to, a loss in our sense of identity. Landscape shapes and holds people not just physically by capturing rain, growing plants and sheltering animals, but also in dreaming and the story of the origin of individual cultures[6]. Landforms within the traditional range of a certain tribe help tell their story, with different features of the landscape holding different significance. As the identity of a tribe is woven from their collective stories and memories, the land is an integral part of the stories and thus the collective identity. The high mountain, the fast flowing river, the fork in the trail are all interwoven with the people and the lessons they have learned, the lessons they pass on. The land and the landscape has informed them, has taught them, and is a part of them. The songs and stories handed down through generations tell of the landscape; how to pass safely through the terrain; where to find water, shelter, food; how to hunt both animal and plant; how to act and how not to act.

The role landscape plays is also relevant in modern *civilisations* in urban environments, especially in tight communities where generations of the same family have lived. Stories passed down through those generations, although the history is much shorter, tell the story of their tribe. The corner where this happened, the place in town where it's best to do that, the quickest and safest route to... It is our nature, our surroundings become part of us, our own personal and familial stories. But the modern world has even dislocated us from this feeling of belonging to an urban tribe, as work, studies, and better transportation, have led families and groups to become increasingly scattered across the globe, breaking down further that feeling of tribe and belonging.

People tend to seek an identity, there is an inherent need to belong. When that identity or belonging is to a city where you are anonymous ~ulation is transient, although it fulfils that need in part to

find an identity, it is in a sense quite shallow. You still get that feeling of belonging but the surroundings in urban places are man made and somehow more two dimensional than natural surroundings. We may feel at home in the company of a collection of familiar buildings and they in their own right have a story, a history, to tell but, being man made, there is a missing element. They cannot speak beyond those that built it. They cannot evolve with us, cradle us and teach us, not in the same way a natural living landscape can. If we just associate and identify with humans, and human generated landscapes and society, we remain separate and isolated from the rest of life, our lives too become more two dimensional in response.

If your identity and sense of belonging is affiliated to a group of online friends there are somehow even more dimensions missing. There may be a familiarity and plenty of constantly updating connections, but you never need to really expose yourself; you control which aspects of yourself the rest of the community get to see. If you are not meeting people in the flesh you can hide things from them, you may never look deep into their eyes and hold hands, embrace, share a physical connection, even if it is a hand shake. There is something very artificial within purely cyber relationships, and although you may, in part, be fulfilling your need to belong, if the other members of that community never really see you, never get to touch you, then you remain alone.

🌳

Your local landscape holds the history of your people and helps you develop a sense of place and an ongoing relationship with your ancestors, and the other lives that share that landscape. It helps you carve a sense of self. I feel a sense of belonging when I enter the valley in which I live, where the green on the trees seems richer and darker than elsewhere. It is not the place in which I was born, or close to any of my human family, but the nature is rich and my connection to the land itself is strong. When you love land it is grounding and makes you somehow more sturdy on your feet, stronger with a greater sense of identity. Life without a common identity, a tribe, a sense of belonging, or a connection to a natural landscape, can be lonely.

2.4 The Cycle Of Life

We have been decomposing since the day we were born. From our arrival, milky and sweet, to our musty decay it's a cycle; it's inevitable. It's

the only truth that is the same for all of us from our very first breath. It crosses all cultures, races and religions. It is a species truth, and beyond that a truth for all that lives on, or in, the flesh of our Sweet Earth. It is however another point of alienation from the rest of Gaia because as our lives have become more *civilised* humanity has become increasingly removed from this simple and beautiful fact.

Our elders are shipped off to homes, hospitals, far away stale, sterile places to live their last days. Often, rather than being respected as elders with wisdom and stories to share, the elderly are treated with contempt or disdain by staff in these institutions. How sad for all of us. The loss is many-fold. For the old or sick to suffer their passing in such sterile environments without the smells, sounds and companionship of family life; food being prepared, people chattering, playing, laughing, living. Instead of a place where people feel safe and cared for, where they can play back memories of the life they've lived, many find themselves alone, waiting to die, surrounded by hushed nervous whispers, death, fear and pain. What a shame, not just for the dying but also the relatives, the grandchildren, to not see the person fade and pass in a place where they feel comfortable; to not have the opportunity to sneak into the room and give one last kiss to the flesh as it grows cold and the spirit leaves.

It seems we hide the inconvenient truth of death and dying away from our busy lives. There are complex illnesses and diseases that come with old age that the average family home cannot deal with, but there is also the point that our society is so *advanced* that we must work all our days and cannot take time to care for the needs of the very old or even the very young. As the elderly are shipped off to specialised homes, babies too miss out on family and home while they spend day after day in child care so the parents can work. What is it we are working for? If you cannot take the time to bring up your own child, or care for your ailing parents, what is there? We have broken these links to the cycle of life and instead involve ourselves in other realities, credit and debt, which have almost become more real to us than life and death.

Death will come to each of us and the more we remove it from our daily reality the more it becomes a mystery to us, something we do not understand and thus come to fear. People hang on terrified of what comes next, but it is a natural and inevitable process. Following death, when a natural funeral is opted for, the body is deposited back in the Earth allowing the cycle to complete, the body to decompose and

be reabsorbed by the Earth and make compost, food, so that others, insects, birds, plants, may live.

*The tiny delicate intricacies of each individual snow flake.
The beauty and the impermanence. For something so intricate
and perfect to be formed and then melt away, there for a
fleeting moment. How beautiful to be the best you can be and
then so gently and easily let it go as the sun warms and your
time passes.*

For many of us we do not have to wait until death for the disconnect from life's natural cycles to be apparent and for us to become alienated and isolated from the rest of life as a result. Often mothers, desperate to do the right thing by their newborns, follow expert advice as opposed to their own instinct. Depending on the mood of the moment, that expert advice may recommend the introduction of routine very early on, instead of feeding on demand.

Rather than allowing the baby to follow it's natural cycle of when it needs nourishment, sleep, nurture, and actually connect with it's own body's needs, the infant is required to fit into someone else's schedule. Baby is fed and put to sleep by the hands of the clock, a sure interpretation of animals (human animals) as machines, with no room for our individual differences, no acceptance of the fact that some of us will grow to be huge while others will always be petite with related differences in appetite. This is most peoples first experience of a disconnect from Gaia.

If fed by routine, not demand, when you ask for your most basic need to be met – food – there is no response. What a lonely path to commence this life journey upon. It is a very young age to be introduced to the myth that we are detached from the world, and our actions (asking for food) have no direct relation to what happens in our world (being fed). Unfortunately the preconception that our actions remain separate from what happens in the world around us, for many of us, was one of the first things we learned.

We are taught such lonely lessons so early on. We also find that things we do not need in the moment (sleep and food) are presented to us anyway, with no connection to the timing of our needs. We quickly learn to take it while we can; because if we don't, and then

ask for it later, we will just go hungry, sleepless and ignored, possibly even chided. The impact of these early lessons on our belief systems is far reaching. As we go through life so many of us just take everything in excess when it is presented regardless of potential consequences, whether it is cake, coffee or cocaine - until at some point something breaks. We don't hear our bodies say no, perhaps we don't even know how to hear them, how to listen, as their pleas and cries have been ignored for so long.

Maybe it is time to stop and think, to listen to what our instincts are telling us. How hard it must be to listen to that baby cry, and cry (*only another half hour before I can feed him...*). It certainly would not be the first, or last, time that conventional advice is off the mark or even damaging to individuals (or the entirety of Gaia). I wonder how many health professionals have even considered that dissociating infants from their body's needs so early on may impact their later well-being. With such high levels of obesity and depression worldwide, it has certainly crossed my mind as being a potential contributory factor to our culture's current malaise.

Of course there are always exceptional circumstances, where due perhaps to a medical condition, or an inability to breast feed, routine is the only option available. My mother was instructed to limit my food intake at six months old as I was happy to eat all day long, a trait that remains with me. Sometimes you see dogs kicking over eager hungry pups off their teets; but I'm sure it's not because they have a stopwatch in an invisible pocket and it's not yet time for a feed. Every situation is unique and sometimes there is no choice, however when there is always go with instinct.

Our disconnect with the cycle of life is not just at the beginning and end of our time on Earth. Each day we have certain requirements for life; oxygen, water, food and warmth. Most people in a civilised society get their water from a tap, food from a supermarket and warmth by turning up the thermostat. Few people who have the convenience of modern life give conscious thought to where each of these items come from. Our daily tasks are very often unrelated to our basic needs. We drive to work, sit at a desk, drive home, pop to the supermarket, stick a factory processed meal in the oven, go to bed under a quilt made from synthetic fibres, start again. There is very little meaning in any of those tasks so we drift; our existence develops a sense of meaninglessness

which we try to ignore. Without spring water to collect, food to grow and gather, shelter and clothes to create from locally available materials, there is very little to do that has a relation to fulfilling our basic needs on a daily basis. Even children, with no tasks and chores relating to our basic requirements for life, become disengaged.

Our modern lives, are filled with products that are purposefully made without variation. You can buy a dress or a smart phone from Shanghai to London and the item will look the same even if the size or installed software differs. You can walk along a busy shopping street in Bangkok and see the same shop fronts that you see in New York. The world is undergoing a gradual same-ing process. You never need explore or take a risk as you can eat the same brand burger and drink the same brand coffee the world over. Straight lines, boxes, right angles; shapes that fill our modern lives and yet are rarely, if ever, found in nature. Urban landscapes have become bland-scapes and our lives have become impoverished as a consequence.

We are all a variation on a theme – the human animal. Even identical twins have distinguishing marks, maybe just a mole, but it is a variation nonetheless. Like Mandelbrot and his repeating sequence which is never exactly the same, our slight variation is a common feature of all life. Variation is what we need in our landscapes and immediate environments to keep us alive, keep us readjusting, keep us flexible and able to adapt to the changes that Gaia can still throw at us through storms, seismic activity and the like. It is important to have variation in our lives and be able to respond to it otherwise we are lost and overwhelmed when unpredictable events happen. *Our wildness recedes.*

I have municipal water piped to and from my home yet I live in an area of abundant springs. I choose to collect my drinking water from the nearest spring; I love doing so. I thank the water as I collect it and drink several deep fresh gulps as it gushes from the Earth. I have a supermarket at the bottom of my hill, and there is a Saturday market in town where I can buy all the food I need. I choose to grow as much as I can for myself from my small back garden and the plot of land I rent from the local council, my allotment. I gain an incredible sense of achievement from growing my own food. From the moment I poke a hole in the soil with my finger and plant my seed, to eating the ripe produce, I feel alive. My house has gas central heating, I can control the temperature inside my home with the flick of a switch and yet I choose to use the wood burner in my living room. I make kindling from the

twigs I prune from trees and find underfoot, I have no woodland so I buy in cut logs, but still I stand in the winter sun splitting those logs with my axe. It warms me, feels good, energetic and hearty, and that is all before I even light a fire.

There are many more things I do to connect with the cycle of life, such as foraging for medicinal plants. It is all a choice - how you spend your time, how you live your life. Living without a connection to fulfilling your basic needs, even in just a token way by growing a tomato plant on your window ledge for example, leaves one alienated, disconnected, and without a sense of meaning in ones daily activities.

2.5 Our Separation From Other Humans

Geographical location has led to a rainbow of skin tones and body shapes, beliefs and practices, amongst our human family. Yet when you extrapolate back, most of the major beliefs and religions have a common creation mythology and hold many similar truths. It is just that over time, with the retelling of the story in different times and places subtle differences have grown, and these we have viewed as threatening, or just plain wrong. The stories are the same, just told with different lips.

We are all a unique and individual manifestation of the same thing. Our uniqueness, our own special abilities that set us apart from each other as *individuals*, occur so that with such diversity manifest we should thrive; our differences allowing a flexibility, mutability, so that the beauty of life on this planet survives no matter what. And yet we have turned it upon ourselves. The most basic and essential truth of the universe has been lost along the way. And so we experience our individuality, our uniqueness, as a separation from each other, and the rest of nature. Instead of our greatest strength it has become our greatest weakness. In response we have mined the Earth for weapons of war, exploited, exploded, destroyed the Earth that we are, and those of our brothers and sisters that are most different to us. We are a lonely people scared of each other, of any difference, and rather than celebrating the abundance of diversity we fight wars because of it.

🌳

Technology and its unremitting advances into every corner and moment of our lives has also impacted our connection to other humans and the rest of Gaia. All our devices, smart phones, laptops, tablets, provide a distraction from what is actually going on in our immediate environ-

ment whilst giving us the impression that we are more connected to our human contacts than ever before. Just waiting on a summers evening in a beer garden for a friend to arrive was once a time for watching the clouds and sky change colour, or perhaps the circling dance of a pair of butterflies. Now that time unwinding, subconsciously reminding ourselves of where we live and our non-human kin, is spent texting, calling, fiddling with apps; those few stolen moments amongst nature have been lost. Screens, machines, moving images, the more time we spend entrenched in the world of technology the less time we spend remembering what life really is and actually living it.

Machine built products designed to perform a specific function, just like man made cityscapes, make our world predictable, easy to navigate and thus somewhat dull and monotonous. Even a trip to the supermarket no longer contains any human interaction, no moment of chatter with the checkout assistant, instead you simply scan your own bar codes, pack your own bag, and without a single human encounter get back in your car and drive home. In fact much of the time shopping no longer even involves leaving the house, as it is so often done online. Like banking it is all automated, not a human in sight. As I find my life being filled with technology, human interactions replaced with more screen time, I can feel stress bubbling up inside me; online shopping and banking; adjustments to my website; the constant stream of emails that always seems to be building up. There's no laughter, no human contact, no smiling faces.

We may feel more connected to our human friends than ever, after all there are numerous formats in which to communicate. However, as I've alluded to before, when contact with other humans is maintained and held within an electronic format you miss the subtle nuances; smell; body language; flickers of colour or shadow across the face (even when live video streaming). You miss touch.

As we spend our precious moments on this Earth updating our status for the titillation of numerous vague acquaintances, we miss real time with real people. Research shows that human infants will die if they are deprived of touch, if they are not caressed, massaged or held by another human being. In fact lack of touch in early life can have a detrimental effect in the development of both neuroendocrinological and neurobiological systems. In effect, touch is so important to our development that without it various psychopathologies are indicated including: major depression, post traumatic stress disorder, schizophrenia and anxiety[7].

*Children who are touch-deprived in infancy show tendencies
towards aggressiveness and violent behaviour.*

Ben Benjamin, PhD

Unsurprisingly there are reciprocal benefits for an adult touching or holding an infant, notably lower anxiety levels, less symptoms of depression and improved self esteem[8]. It is not just nurturing touch between adults and infants, there are also general physiological benefits of touch between humans of all ages, including the lowering of blood pressure and heart rate, reduction in stress hormones and an improvement in immune system response[9]. Through human touch we become more relaxed, more able to fight disease and infection, and more alert. In effect, human touch improves our level of health and well-being.

Adoption of technology has lessened our contact with actual humans. Even when in the physical company of friends we often pause the conversation to check incoming communications or update our status. As communication with human connections is ongoing, and often to a much wider group than before joining social networking sites, most of us have not noticed the slip, the slow decline in *real* time spent with people. Our separation from humankind, just like our separation from nature, has been gradual and subtle. But without real life contact, skin on skin touch, pheromones detected and feelings generated, we are affected physically, psychologically and even behaviourally.

2.6 The Price We Pay

*The depressed, anxious, and otherwise mentally-ill are rarely
seen within the greater context of their society, but rather,
as those suffering from a chemical imbalance requiring the
administration of another chemical treatment.*

Alexis Mari Pietak

Convinced of our separation we have dug the Earth for oil, for minerals, for her very lungs (the trees) and blood (the water); and yet nothing brings us the happiness we seek, not sustained happiness. According to a WHO (world health organisation) report, released in October 2012, 350 million people worldwide suffer from depression (*did this happen when we gave up spending sunny afternoons seeing shapes in clouds and watching ants?*). In fact the subsequent WHO "Health for the World's Adolescents" report

in early 2014 concluded that the largest single cause of illness amongst teenagers worldwide is depression, whilst the third largest cause of death among teenagers is suicide. There is no identifiable common cause for all this depression, but one thing is for sure, we are in trouble.

Our alienation from each other and from the natural world most certainly contributes to the current quantity of physical, mental and behavioural problems that beset humanity. Prescriptions for psychotropic medications have risen exponentially since the turn of the millennium. Prescriptions for antidepressants rose to an all time high in England in 2012, up 7.5% on the previous year alone; in some areas as many as 1 in 6 adults are regularly taking them[10]. The use of antidepressants in the USA soared from 11.2 million users in 1998 to an incredible 23.3 million users in 2010[11]. I am not saying that the break in our connection with nature alone has caused this, not at all, but these are huge numbers of very unhappy people and their numbers are increasing.

Amongst children diagnoses of conditions such as ADHD (attention deficit hyperactivity disorder) are also on the rise. There are some really disturbing statistics relating to this and the increase in prescriptions made to treat the condition (remember these are now children we are talking about). An NHS report revealed that in the UK between 1999 and 2010 the number of prescriptions for Ritalin (used to treat ADHD) quadrupled, it continues to rise. This mirrors the USA where they experienced an 83% increase in the sales of Ritalin between 2006-10[12]. All this medicating of our young people while studies have shown that children with ADHD respond well to outdoor activities in a natural environment and to a natural diet with an abundance of fresh vegetables and herbs. Plenty of exercise, even in urban settings, manifests as great improvements whereas screen time, TV and computer games specifically, seems to cause a worsening of the condition[13].

Studies have found that urbanisation has a negative impact on mental health. Urban living raises the risk of suffering anxiety disorders by 21%, and mood disorders by 39%, whilst roughly doubling the risk of schizophrenia, which already is hailed as one of the leading causes of disability worldwide[14]. Depression is also more likely for residents of a built environment[15].

It is not just our health and mental health that is suffering, but our behaviour. Like all animals, there undoubtedly has always been an element of competition between dominant males of breeding age and groups maintaining their territory. However, the quantity and degree of

violence we are currently subjecting each other to, and experiencing as a culture (such as rape, murder, aggravated assault), goes beyond that. People with less access to nature display inhibited cognitive function, poor management of major life issues and poor impulse control; this leads to decreased civility, more aggression, more property crime, more graffiti and more litter[16]. That is not even where it ends as violence against ourselves (cutting/self harm, suicide attempts, over eating, drug/alcohol abuse) spirals out of control. Even the modern trend for plastic surgery is in a way violence towards oneself, going under the knife to change the way you look, it's a rejection of our own bodies, our own piece of nature.

...studies show a relationship between the absence, or inaccessibility, of parks and open space with high crime rates, depression, and other urban maladies.

Richard Louv

We are currently faced with a sorry situation, physical and mental health are in decline, while behavioural issues are seemingly on the increase. Drug prescriptions have increased to combat these problems, but there is a failing; not enough attention or research is going into discovering the reasons behind the current issues. We have been so busy looking for a cure that we forgot to pay enough attention to the cause.

We are led to believe it's normal to go through depression, in a sense it is. The feelings arise to help us understand something is not right, that there is something in our lives we need to change. But as with any dis-ease to treat the symptom with medication (take the depression "away" by prescribing Prozac or similar) is just to push it aside, hide it, hope it goes away. Depression comes along, medication takes away the energy and urgency to make those changes, and allows us to continue regardless of the ill-fit of our lives. Depression is, in part, a symptom of modern society (which in itself is then the disease). The way we live is what is a little out of sorts, out of kilter, and deep down we know it. It's not a mystery. It's in the statistics that as people become more "urban" mental health issues increase. We need fresh air, plants, sunshine, but in our urban environments these necessities can be sparse. Of course

depression, like anything else, has any number of causes but urban living must be regarded as a real and relevant contributory factor.

I have felt the warm sweet pleasure of a hard, sharp, edge of broken glass tracing the lines of my veins. I have watched the blood bubble up from the icy white flesh in dark red pools of warm release. Oh god it felt good... I *know* what it is like to live in a dark, dark place. When entrenched as I was for much of my youth and dizzying urgent moments of my early adulthood in the stagnant mire of my mind, it seemed there was no escape, no respite. Sometimes I would revel in it, allowing myself to be drawn deeper and deeper, the putrid stench infusing into every cell of me. Calmly I would submit, my tears of angst and perplexity with the world washing me ever further, ever deeper. Cutting my skin distracted me from my mental anguish as the physical pain drew me into the present moment of blood and flesh, it made me feel alive.

Rewilding involves discovering and embracing the dark corners of yourself, those wild parts that scare you, that you don't understand, the parts of yourself that don't "fit in". If left unacknowledged and ignored those wild parts will wrench you from the heart of the world, blocking your passionate connection with it. Medication, of course, is essential for certain afflictions and acute cases. However, when medication is relied upon or used for extended periods when not absolutely necessary, it will secure your separation from real life and feelings; and importantly from finding the motivation to explore the darkness and find your own way out.

I have explored my darkness and discovered what those wild scary parts needed, not to tame or banish them, but for them to become a healthy and balanced part of my whole being. It is an ongoing process, a life's work, but I have found better ways than cutting to feel vital life force flow through me. Building Gaia awareness, rewilding, has helped make that stinking pit of despair just a memory. My love for life has grown, and responded, loved me back...

Is it, can it be, as simple as being cut off from source, from nature, from meaning?

Perhaps, even more than the surfeit of touch that so many
human beings experience, it is the lack of Earth and plant
song that causes so much alienation and emptiness.
                                        Stephen Harrod Buhner

In 2005 Richard Louv coined the phrase Nature Deficit Disorder (NDD), he used this phrase to describe the condition of children who were not receiving enough exposure to nature. Levels of stress and anxiety, attention deficit and depression are all liable to be higher in people who do not have enough exposure to nature. In addition, lack of time spent in nature causes the senses to atrophy and alertness to diminish. The concept of NDD more or less sums up what I have been trying to say throughout this chapter - that without nature in our pocket we become deficient, we become *less than*, we cease to thrive.

We learn from touching, feeling, sensing. As Louv pointed out in his work, direct experience of the world is being replaced with learning indirectly through the use of machines. As the virtual world has become our classroom our range of skills and experience of direct interactions with the living world is shrinking. In our machine dominated world there are no rough textures for our fingers to explore. Our world has become limited and predictable. Without direct contact with nature our individual development is arrested. To be able to adapt deftly to changing conditions we need a diversity of resources that machines simply cannot teach us. We need our senses, our intuition, our ability to read the situation for what it really is. All of these skills we can learn and hone in natural environments.

Even in semi-rural locations people are in a state of disconnect. Very few people I meet are in touch with Gaia and their natural selves. Those that are connected are a rare find and most often they work with flower essences, or perhaps they live in a yurt or a cabin in the woods, sometimes they are surfers or rock climbers. People for whom the day revolves around being in nature, they alone are free from this modern condition. Even gardeners and farmers may be in a state of disconnect, separated and insulated from a real connection with nature if they regularly use chemicals and machines.

It is clear that over the last few hundred years humankind have increasingly found themselves cut off from the rest of nature. Not just because expanding urbanisation has caused a physical separation, but also resulting from changes in attitude stemming from Cartesian dualism and the philosophy of science and nature that spawned from those times.

Without a healthy nature connection, without awareness of the meanings embedded all around us, there is a disconnect, a feeling of alienation, of loneliness. Our conscious minds feel this strongly. For many this has manifested as mental health and behavioural issues.

Fresh from the womb we are dropped into a mechanical world that runs on time, like clockwork. It becomes our experience of life, but it is possible to unlearn, to teach ourselves something new; that Gaia is sensitive and responsive. Discovering this, the sensitivity of Gaia, promotes the healing of some of our earliest wounds, and perhaps the feelings of aloneness, of being an orphan on this alien planet. Knowing Earth as more than a set of interlocking mathematical mechanical systems is possible. Living outside of Cartesian Dualism means a major paradigm shift. It means we cannot continue to live as we do, to treat the rest of nature the way we do. It means acknowledging Gaias sentience; it's existence as living, feeling, as alive.

3. RENDING THE VEIL OF ILLUSION

apocalypse (ə'pɪokəlɪps) n. *1. a prophetic disclosure or revelation.*[1]

The Western world exists behind a veil of illusion, the most dangerous and most damaging illusion of our time; the illusion that we are separate from Nature.

This illusion, our separation from nature, makes us distant, takes us away from recognising our bodies and the rest of Gaia as sacred. Our relationship with all of Earth's inhabitants, with each other, with ourselves, even with the moon and the stars, are all damaged as a consequence. Depression, feelings of isolation, behavioural issues, violence to ourselves (self harm, drug abuse, etc.), each other (rape, torture, murder, street violence, etc.), the planet (ecocide, pollution, fracking, etc.), are all symptoms of a society living within the context of the illusion. Every step we take that is not one of compassion, humility and respect, is in fact one of self harm but without recognising our interconnection with the rest of nature we are blind and deaf to this.

We have lost our context, we are drifting, feeling alone. But the veil is thin, we are born from nature, on death we return to dust, to nature. So how is it that in between times we consider ourselves somehow *apart from,* rather than *a part of* nature? Rending the veil, disillusionment, is the greatest gift we can give ourselves.

We have been too long asleep, deaf and ignorant.
Our dreams have grown fitful as a brief glimmer of awareness
rises – there is something more.

It is time for the apocalypse; time to recognise the sanctity of the world, of minerals, rocks, rivers and plants. They are all sacred, equally valid parts of Gaia, and yet we tend to view them as inanimate objects and utilise them without a second thought. Respect for other life and matter has been missing from the last 500 years or more of humanity's evolution. Naturally occurring materials have become nothing more than resources that we are free to plunder and while we remain separate from nature we remain unaffected by the consequences of this.

Nature, however, runs through us. There are thousands of invisible natural systems all having their influence upon us at any one time. Solar flares, inter-planetary influences and sunspot activity all affect us.

The Earth's magnetic field changes slightly according to the relative positions of the sun and the moon, these fields affect water and thus our own bodies (which consist of approximately 75% water). Whether we think so and acknowledge it or not, it is scientific fact. We are clearly part of an interdependent system way beyond the inter-human sphere.

> *...on the skin of our planet, we can be truly successful only when we become aware of its pulse and learn to pace our lives to the rhythm of its deep, untroubled breathing.*
>
> Lyall Watson

Bacteria and mycelium in soil have an affect on tree roots and consequently tree health. The presence of a healthy group of trees affects local cloud production through respiration and thus rainfall patterns, which in turn affect local climate. Local climate affects which bacteria and mycelium will proliferate in the soil and thus create favourable conditions for certain plants to thrive. This is an extremely simplified example of how different elements in nature all affect each other, that they are not only interconnected but that it cycles back round, the end product providing circumstances favourable, or not, for the cycle to repeat itself ad infinitum.

Interconnection is apparent everywhere if we just look hard enough. One unintended side effect of taking prescription drugs, for example, is the presence of pharmaceutical chemical residue in our ground water. Any drug we have taken is at some point excreted from the body, which in turn ends up in waste water. The current system is not equipped to remove these pharmaceutical chemicals and so many of the said chemicals get cycled back into ground and drinking water in trace amounts. These chemicals then act as pollutants in the environment being absorbed by many different forms of life, including ourselves. So while we treat our illnesses (often spawned by our urban lifestyles) with chemical medications we further undermine the integrity of the natural areas that we are missing, and our own health. It is a negative feedback loop. Without awareness of the fact that we are nature and are interconnected with all of nature's systems on the deepest level, our actions will continue to undermine the integrity of Gaia and we will inadvertently make things worse for ourselves.

We live in a time when we can no longer say "there are plenty more fish in the sea". It is a situation humanity has created and the

great illusion has allowed us to do so. If everyone understood that our individual health is intrinsically connected to that of the planet we would no longer be able to over exploit it, we could not hunt species after species to extinction if we *knew* this to be true. Or is it that we are so out of touch, so desensitised by our lifestyles, diets, homes, TV's, computer games and addictions that we know but just lack the motivation to get up and do anything about it? Has humanity become so numb and apathetic that to even make a small change such as how many fish we eat, or where we buy them from, is beyond the majority of people?

Understanding and accepting that we are part of nature, that all our actions have an effect somewhere along the line, and that in turn we are affected by everything we are surrounded by, helps us appreciate that our immediate environment and our interactions with it are important on every level.

3.1 The Health Benefits of Nature

As soon as the separation between humankind and nature begins to be addressed there are immediate and significant beneficial responses. That is, when time is spent in direct contact with the rest of nature there are improvements in physical and mental health, alongside amelioration of behavioural issues. Nature is a healer.

Whilst we remain bereft, separated, from nature problems continue to arise, and yet the solution is palpable, contact with nature keeps us well. I would go as far to say that regular contact with nature is *essential* for good health. When we live under the illusion that we are separate, that we do not need nature and remove it from our lives, when we live dislocated from nature, issues whether in body, mind, or spirit, arise. Without nature as a daily part of our lives we are incomplete. That is why you are reading this, because you miss and yearn for a deeper connection with the rest of nature – why else would you have picked up a book entitled *Rewild Yourself?*

> *...a reconnection to the natural world is fundamental to human well-being.*
>
> Richard Louv

The idea that time spent in nature has a beneficial effect on health is not a new one. Over 2000 years ago the ancient Chinese Taoists recognised the benefits to nerves, health and general disposition, of time spent in

nature. Spending time in gardens and parks, in nature, has been, and is, lauded as a way to preserve your health; that is not in question. Even so considering the lack of its inclusion in treatment plans, and the quantity of pharmaceuticals prescribed instead especially for mental health problems, you would perhaps be forgiven for thinking it was.

Modern lifestyles and living conditions contribute, in many instances, to individual ill health. So, is a chemical laden prescription written in a concrete office by a pale, overworked, doctor in a city centre hospital really going to help? Can it help when it is the concrete, chemicals and urban situation that oft times make people sick in the first place?

It can be so much more simple. Rewilding is taking back our individual connection with nature, immersing oneself and reaping the benefits. It has taken a long time for me to connect the dots, to discover the reason I feel so whole when I'm immersed in nature. It's that I am a part of it, I am an indivisible part of nature. Which is why I feel strange, lonely, and isolated when my connection to nature is broken. Don't just take my word for it, there are hundreds of recent studies which have found the connection between good health and contact with nature.

Studies have shown that bacteria found in natural environments help to develop and maintain the immune system, and that their absence in more urban locations may be a contributor to higher levels of asthma and allergies[2]. Pregnant women who have greater exposure to, and spend more time in, green spaces experience an associated improvement in foetal development (birth weight)[3]. People who exercise in nature feel more restored, less anxious, angry or depressed than those who work out for the same quantity of time in a gym, while those who have less access to green spaces suffer higher levels of stress[4]. There is a University of Essex study comparing a walk in a shopping mall versus a walk in the woods, and no surprises, those walking in nature displayed enhanced mood and self-esteem alongside a reduction in feelings of anger, confusion, depression, tension and even blood pressure. In fact 71% of participants displayed a reduction in feelings of depression after a walk in the country[5].

Rather than list endless studies to prove my point just close your eyes for a moment and breathe. Imagine yourself walking around the shore of an upland lake, the sky is scattered with wisps of cloud, you can hear the trickle of a nearby spring and the trail is surrounded by reeds, tufts of grass, and moss covered rocks (did you just take a really deep breath and feel your shoulders drop?). Now, place yourself

in a shopping mall on a Saturday morning, the sounds of hundreds of voices are echoing off the cavernous roof, you are getting barged by passing pushchairs and shopping bags, it is artificially warm, there is no air (no deep breath here, just a tightening of the chest?). There, we have just proved it in the most simple terms. Even just visualising being amongst nature feels not only fabulous, but also relaxing and expansive in comparison to being in a shopping centre.

It is not just physical health and emotional well-being that benefit from exposure to nature. It can also improve our capacity to pay attention, which would perhaps go some way to explain why sufferers of ADHD display an improvement in their symptoms when allowed free time in nature[6]. It has also been found that in neighbourhoods that have more green spaces there are a lower number of violent and property crimes[7]. Even a simple pot plant or two on the office desk has been shown to aid concentration, and improve general office morale and productivity levels[8].

Our intrinsic need for connection with nature and its link with physical health, mental health and behaviour is so strong that even looking through a window onto a scene of nature is beneficial in comparison to looking over a brick wall. Again no great surprise when you imagine yourself in the two contrasting conditions. My office is in the converted loft space of my house, it has two windows; one looks directly at the wall of the neighbouring house, the other is a skylight looking towards the clouds and the sky. Guess which one I prefer to gaze at when drifting for a moment, taking a pause and looking for inspiration?

Windows with a nature view have been found to leave housing estate residents less fatigued and aggressive; patients requiring less pain medication and shorter hospital stays; improved academic performance and less discipline issues for students; higher morale for teachers; and more productive employees who suffer less stress and enjoy greater job satisfaction[9]. Watching images of nature can reduce muscle tension alongside pulse and skin-conductance readings in just moments[10]. In prisons, even simple changes like having a nature scene painted on the wall has been shown to improve the health, stress levels, and behaviour of prisoners, which as you can imagine has a knock on effect on the morale and well-being of prison staff[11]. I promised myself that I would not let this section become just a list of facts and references, but I can't help myself, the sheer quantity of research highlighting the benefits of

50

contact with nature to our health, even just looking at a painting of it, are overwhelming.

3.2 Nature Therapy

So what can we do with it, all these facts, figures and statistics? Diving into nature, rewilding, clearly will benefit your health and well-being - there is no question. But what if you are already on medication, undergoing therapy, or just feeling so desperate that you need some support, a guiding and friendly arm to hold as you dip your toes back into natures wild waters? There are several well established nature therapies any one of which may help you.

Plain and simple gardening can help improve depression. I will talk more about the wonders of plant growing and having your fingers in the soil in later chapters, however the easement of depression through gardening may be more than what meets the eye. A Bristol University study has linked soil bacteria *mycobacterium vaccae* to serotonin production[12]; so the beneficial effects of gardening could be as simple as dirt getting into your body rather than the therapeutic effects of having your hands in the earth, more likely it is a combination of the two.

Garden therapy has been around for a while and several mental health charities champion its cause using it not only with sufferers of depression, but also dementia and recovering drug addicts. In recent times gardening therapy has been used to give children psychosocial support on arrival in Za'atari, a refugee camp in Jordan for those escaping the violence in Syria. Most of the children arrive unsurprisingly in a rather introverted state, display violence towards each other and consequently struggle to make friends. Through learning gardening the children open up, learn to work as part of a team and most importantly start to build friendships[13].

Having your hands in the earth soothes away worries and brings your focus down to the intricate yet simple fundamentals of life. Gardening is a worthy therapy that you can try alone, or as part of a group such as Green Gym; a Conservation Volunteers program that has even received government support, and is remarkably prescribed for NHS patients by some GPs now in the UK.

Woodland therapy, is well developed in Japan where it is known as *shinrin-yoku*, literally *forest bathing*. It was established by the Japanese government's forest agency in 1982. Walking in a natural environment is particularly restorative and within a forest you receive the

additional immune boosting effects of inhaling the volatile essential oils released by trees[14]. Forest bathing can help increase levels of vigour and improve mood whilst reducing blood pressure, depressive symptoms, hostility and stress levels[15]. In the UK it has been shown to have a beneficial effect on youth with behavioural problems, especially when combined with learning skills such as coppicing and clearing dead undergrowth[16]. Forest bathing is one therapy that you can undertake yourself, all you need is a pair of walking shoes, access to a woodland environment and a little time. Just walk around, notice the smells, the sounds, the colours. Breathe deep. Relax. Take your time.

Finally I would like to mention animal therapy. Many of us have enjoyed the benefits of a four legged companion, how just seeing your dog or cat enter the room can fill your heart right up with love and make you feel loved right back in return. In maintaining kinship with other species people feel less alone. In all age groups from young children through the teenage years into old age, people get so much enjoyment out of having pets through pure and simple companionship. Animals give you contact and are non-judgemental, they give you a wider context for your own life, a sense of being loved and needed, a sense perhaps even of purpose. Owning a pet is linked to having a lower blood pressure, better survival rates after heart attack and less anxiety[17]. Horse therapy has been shown to be beneficial for autism, and swimming with dolphins for just about everything especially Down's Syndrome. Pet therapy, or animal assisted therapy has even been shown to improve the quality of life for schizophrenia suffers[18].

As a teenager I had both a dog and a cat, they were fabulous friends and I loved them dearly. No matter how bad I felt, having the dog come and plonk himself at my feet, or the cat jump on my lap, never failed to warm my heart and make me feel so much better.

One point that we are yet to consider is that some of our mental health and behavioural problems may not be the screams of our own individual minds, but Earth consciousness, our one mind. This becomes more feasible once the connection with all nature is proven beyond all doubt. Once proven it would be viable that we are each subconsciously picking up on the pain of the planet, the species that are daily becoming extinct, their death cries resonating within us and in effect making us ill. So perhaps to heal the current situation within our society we

need to look toward healing our relationship with the planet; rebalancing some of the ecological disasters we have perpetrated. And yet the only way we have a chance of healing the wide scale environmental concerns is by starting with ourselves, another cycle, loop, connection.

3.3 The Ever Pulsating Universe

So through the evidence in the previous section it seems that nature and time spent within it is beneficial for our health, but to overthrow the illusion of separation once and for all, to prove our nature connection beyond all doubt, I will look to the world of quantum physics.

The world as we know it is made up of elementary particles. Quarks and leptons, both elementary particles, form atoms. Some particles including electrons and electron neutrinos (both leptons) can exist separately, but together with atoms form all matter. Atoms form molecules, which form cells, which form organisms.

Elementary particles are in fact composite structures, but they are not made from tangible material. Instead, they are patterns of energy which are continually changing into one another. It becomes very difficult to break the universe down into component parts and put it back together, as the reductionists, Descartes and Newton, did. Instead a basic interconnection of matter (sound familiar?) is revealed.

> ...the properties of a particle can only be understood in terms of its activity – of its interaction with the surrounding environment -...the particle, therefore, cannot be seen as an isolated entity, but has to be understood as an integrated part of the whole.

> Fritjof Capra

Matter is not as solid as it seems. Working simplistically at the level of atoms, each consists of a large amount of "space" with a very small dense quark packed nucleus, surrounded by a cloud of electrons. The extent of this "space" within each individual atom is so vast that if it was removed from the atoms within the human body, the entire human race could be compacted down to the size of a sugar cube. So, what we perceive as a solid object, is mainly space. The space itself is not actually empty but full of fields; we will come to that later.

All particles, electrons included, can act not only as particles, but also as waves (known as wave-particle duality), and thus they oscillate. Solid matter,

then, is a large quantity of vibrating space. This also means that everything in the universe is constantly oscillating, vibrating, pulsating. Vibrations are in themselves energy, and this energy tells us something about the originator of the vibrations. Each vibration holds and transfers information (about the originator of the vibrations, for example), which equates to a communication. This pulsating energy is intrinsic to all life and connects all life. Thus, from the subatomic to the gargantuan, the universe is in perpetual conversation.

Each part of Gaia exits in a state of constant flux, continually adjusting to maintain a condition of relative homoeostasis in the face of all of the micro-perturbations occurring in the environment. To make the micro adjustments necessary to remain resonant with the rest of the universe, attention to incoming vibrations, or communications, is necessary. Being ignorant of the incoming communications, being cut off from nature, means we lose that resonance, we are not in harmony with the rest of Gaia, and we feel lonely and confused as a result.

To add more gravitas to this, to the information held and transmitted by our pulsating atoms, it is worth bearing in mind that every atom that makes your body was in existence before organic life emerged 4000 million, or so, years ago. The atoms that exist within our cells came from rocks and star dust, the same origins as everything else. Our physical fabric, and that of everything on this planet, has common beginnings in the primordial soup from whence sprang life. On the atomic level, certainly, we are *all* relations.

At one point I trained in healing, working with the energy body. I borrowed all my friends and family to practice feeling the differences in their energy flow. Then one person said he had no energy body, he didn't believe in it! Here's the thing, it's not a matter of believing, all matter is energy, that is *all* we are. I feel like I have always known that. In fact each time I read about a concept explained through quantum physics it's as if another piece fits together, that it's familiar and comfortable, and easier to see the whole. It's putting words and reasons to what in the deepest seat of my being are my most basic and earliest knowings.

3.4 Connected By Light

Jeremy Narby, in his book *The Cosmic Serpent*, found extensive references in native mythology, from all inhabited continents, to some kind of spiral ladder which allowed for communication between sky and earth. Using this ladder, the gods could descend to Earth, and humans ascend to the sky. He realised that this imagery of a spiral staircase, ladder or twisted rope, in fact represented the double helix of DNA.

Ancestors worldwide somehow knew of DNA and its relevance and importance in communications with the world outside of oneself.

DNA (deoxyribonucleic acid) is a chemical held in the nucleus of cells. DNA exists in everything that is, or once was, living. It exists in all organic matter, from bacteria to fossils and every living (or dead) thing in between[19]. This means that a body of water such as a muddy puddle or a mountain stream contains DNA in the bacterial, vegetal and animal matter that it carries. Even pebbles, rocks and mountains contain DNA, in the bacteria and fossils that are held within them.

DNA emits biophotons, that is photons of a biological origin. Photons themselves are elementary particles, quanta of light or other electromagnetic radiation, which, like all particles, exhibit the properties of both waves and particles. Despite being weak in strength, biophotons have a high degree of order and an extremely stable intensity. This equates to a high degree of coherence, which means they are distinct signals able to transmit information very clearly[20]. Spontaneous emission of biophotons is occurring constantly in all biological systems independent of any form of external stimulation. So, in effect, there is a constant and independent emission of information from individual DNA molecules[21].

DNA not only emits, but also receives biophotons. This means an incoming and outgoing of individual information bursts on the quantum level. This is a transfer of distinct signals from one to another, it's a communication[22]. So, between the nuclei of our cells we are exchanging biophotons, communicating energy, light. The light being constantly emitted and received by DNA within an organism may connect all the cells, tissues and organs. This biophoton exchange may serve as an organism's main communication network *and* has been found to be self regulatory; in other words functioning in part to maintain homoeostasis within the organism[23] (this is what Gaia, as a whole, does on the macro scale remember?). In essence this means that our DNA is constantly exchanging information whilst maintaining it's state of balance. This phenomena does not just occur within an organism but, as discovered by Fritz-Albert Popp, between the DNA of separate organisms[24]. In other words information exchange, communication, is occurring between individual organisms on the quantum level.

Wherever you are, your DNA is emitting and receiving biophotons constantly. So, I conclude, that whatever you are surrounded by, that is what you are exchanging information, light and elementary particles with. An alpine

wild flower meadow, a conventionally farmed wheat field, a polluted and damaged industrial waste land. Wherever you are, you are receiving and exchanging information and energy from, and with, that which surrounds you.

Biophoton exchange and the implications thereof, are still to be fully accepted by the scientific community; research is ongoing. There is no question, however, that DNA contains a genetic code, the instructions in a gene that tell a cell how to make a specific protein. This code, held within DNA, has been described as a language. The elements that make up this code, or language, (known as A,G,C, and T) have no meaning individually, in the same way that a random selection of letters has no particular significance. It is the way they are combined that determines information content, just like when letters of the alphabet are arranged to make words which then have meaning and significance. Until the discovery of the genetic code, the ability to use language to combine individual units into a stream of meaning was considered a capacity exclusive to humankind, we now know that this is not the case. Anything that contains DNA is generating coded signals imbued with meaning and language.

In some ways the text (coding) contained in DNA acts like a products bar code, in that it can be used to identify the item. DNA can identify blood relatives, even a trace of organic material such as skin caught under a finger nail or dried saliva on a cigarette butt, can identify the human it once was part of. Well decomposed remains can also identify the person or animal that they once were. The language is detailed and precise, otherwise it could not be used for such accurate identification work.

The presence of detailed coding, or language, contained within DNA infers at least a basic level of intelligence. DNA is involved, on the deepest level, in communication. Its presence in all cells allows for information exchange between the cells of different life forms. Not just between the cells of humans, but also between animals, plants, bacteria and fungi. We are invisibly connected to, and communicating with, *all* life.

At this point in time, the purpose of approximately 97% of DNA has yet to be discovered, this huge quantity of information whose meaning remains unknown to us, is referred to as *junk* DNA. Perhaps the purpose of this so called junk is to carry messages with meaning for

56

parts of our being other than the physical and how to make proteins. Either way the presence of DNA in organic matter and constant communication between DNA of different organisms proves at least on one level that we are communicating with other life forms and thus we are intrinsically, and invisibly connected; there is no separation[25].

So to conclude, each of us are comprised mainly of space. Within that space, creating what we perceive as matter, are a whole load of particles that also act as waves. These units of space and particles, known collectively as atoms, group together to form molecules, molecules form cells. Within the nucleus of each cell is a crystalline chemical called DNA. DNA is constantly emitting and receiving light, little quanta of energy, that are embedded with information. This biophoton exchange allows communication between the cells within an organism, but also with cells outside of it. Information exchange occurs on every level from the vibrations of elementary particles upwards. It is an intrinsic activity of all life. Any exchange is on some level a communication. This ever pulsating universe is in perpetual dialogue and we are a part of that whether we consciously acknowledge it or not. Through communication and common beginnings we are connected with everything else.

Part of the rewilding process involves awareness and acknowledgement of this information exchange. It involves opening up to the incoming communications from nature and directing our individual responses. As we unravel the meanings of the world and engage in conscious dialogue, one finds meaning and purpose and a deeper understanding of oneself. We cannot be separate from the rest of nature as we are connected and communicating through the vibrations of elementary particles and our DNA.

Life in all its multi-layered complexity is greater than the sum of its parts, it most certainly can not be reduced to a set of interlocking mechanised systems. There is something that runs through Gaia and all the parts that add up to make her (the golden streaming information super-highway). It is in everything, and yet it is none of those things. The signals being emitted and received by DNA contribute to it but there is also a magic in it for me, an element of the ineffable, the unknowable. This magical element connects all life and carries within it all the information from all time.

When one spends time only in domestic situations, surrounded only by man made products, one misses out on the pure information exchange between DNA that would happen were one to be surrounded

by nature. Something is missing in the conversation when our DNA has no live organic DNA from other life sources to exchange with and is instead met with concrete and plastics.

> *...there is a continuous communication not only between living things and their environment, but among all things living in that environment. An intricate web of interaction connects all life into one vast, self-maintaining system. Each part is related to every other part and we are all part of the whole, part of Supernature.*

Lyall Watson

3.5 Expanding Outwards

At the beginning of our universe was what's known as a singularity, the Big Bang. Everything that we know, the universe, came from a tiny seed much smaller in volume than a single atom[26]. In that first moment everything was entangled and interwoven, touching; from that moment on there has been a continuous expansion. Space between things has given the illusion of separate objects, but energetically everything is still touching. Humans, animals, plants, trees, are all energetic vibrations, connected through those vibrations and our common beginnings. This connection can be envisaged as a net of energy that encompasses and exists within all space, time and form.

> *At our most elemental, we are not a chemical reaction but an energetic charge. Human beings and all living things are a coalescence of energy in a field of energy connected to every other thing in the world. This pulsating energy field is the central engine of our being and our consciousness, the alpha and omega of our existence.*

Lynne McTaggart

We perceive ourselves as separate but in fact we are all part of a unified net of energy, or field[27]. This is demonstrated by the concept of non-locality which refers to the ability of objects, such as individual electrons, to instantaneously know the state of and influence another, despite any degree of physical separation, all without the exchange of force or energy. This can only occur if everything is invisibly con-

nected. It means there is a connection between quantum particles even when apparently separated, which implies the actions of one can always affect the other despite any perceived physical separation. All life, everything that makes up the universe, has quantum properties which means non-locality exists between living things. And yes that means all of our actions create waves affecting the whole.

Even our thoughts are putting messages out into the field, the invisible web that connects all life. Suddenly imaginal hygiene becomes important, the thoughts and dreams we give energy to are being transmitted into the field, so as the mantra goes *be careful what you wish for*.

Taken down to our most fundamental level we, humans, are energy in a constant state of exchange with the all encompassing net of energy or field; what to me is the golden information super-highway. There is no doubt that we are invisibly connected with everything else. The time has come to be aware of our connection with all things and be conscious about what we are both thinking and doing.

What the mystic has always told us about the unity of all life, and what science is telling us about quantum coherency and the non-locality of space and time, is sounding remarkably similar.

Susan Raven

When you begin to recognise the intelligence in nature and our invisible connection to it, you realise that you are never alone. Life and spirit flows through all things, but first you must lift the veil of illusion that has kept you from seeing, feeling and knowing for so long. Switching back on, tuning back in, takes a little time, a little patience, because for most of us it has been so long and yet we can *all* do it. It's what we came to this planet doing – it's simply a matter of remembering how. Remembering what it is like to feel your way around the world with your heart *not* think your way around with your head. For me this is the essence of, and essential pre-requisite to, rewilding

Our reality is made up of layers of meaning, we live in a world of meanings, when we separate ourselves from the rest of nature it makes no sense and

we end up confused, depressed, angry, disorientated, ill. When our connection to nature is recognised and we once again enter into the stream of communications, the world becomes a text that can be translated into something that holds meaning, that touches the deepest recesses of our souls.

The meanings held within Gaia, once translated, direct and shape you. The communications are multidimensional, touching you on millions of different points of contact from elementary particles right up through your physical body, and from the subconscious to the conscious mind. When you travel into the meanings of the world you travel deeper into your own being. *There is no separation.*

Never forget we were born connected and subconsciously we are *still* connected. The apparent disconnect occurs because the conscious mind is not working with the subconscious leading to internal confusion. Being conscious of our connection with, and the livingness of, the rest of nature allows us to make sense of it all. Never forget you *are* nature, you *are* Gaia. Just by sitting comfortably and connecting, communicating with your own body, with your self, you begin the process of rewilding, of reconnection with nature.

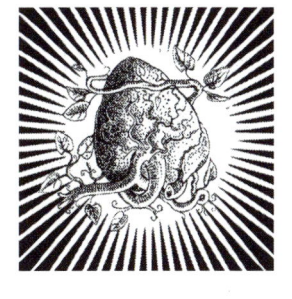

By starting from the ground and tapping into the absolute, unbeatable truth of nature we can make ourselves better. When dealing with plants and animals and the land you cannot be dishonest or fickle. You have to deal with it as it is. That is a good starting point for putting together the pieces of a life. This is not something that can be done second hand. You have to get your own hands dirty.

Monty Don

"...dividing the universe into living and nonliving things also has no meaning. Animate and inanimate matter are inseparably interwoven, and life, too, is enfolded throughout the totality of the universe. Even a rock is in some way alive, says Bohm, for life and intelligence are present not only in all of matter, but in "energy", "space", "time", "the fabric of the entire universe," and everything else we ... mistakenly view as separate things.

Michael Talbot

PART II
Wild Heart

This breathing landscape is no longer just a passive backdrop against which human history unfolds, but a potentized field of intelligence in which our actions participate. As the regime of self-reference begins to break down, as we awaken to the air, and to the multiplicitous Others that are implicated, with us, in its generative depths, the shapes around us seem to awaken, to come alive...
David Abram

Perhaps our deepest fear is not that we would be uncivilized and out of control but that we would be free to rediscover the sacredness of being alive. The enchantment of Gaia and the split between wild Earth and our wild natures would be healed.
Julie McIntyre

4. WHEN EVERYTHING'S ALIVE
Acknowledging the livingness of the world

So far this book has been heavy thinking, left brain stuff, from here on in it will be lifting up and out.

First of all take a deep breath in. All the way in from the soles of your feet to the top of your head. And hold it. Hold it just for one moment. And now exhale and as you do so release all the tension in your body... your shoulders... your jaw... your hands... Now. Imagine a world where everything is alive. Where everything has a consciousness, an intelligence. Imagine what a different world that would be, how much more respectfully we would behave; could you kick a stone if you knew it was living? It would be like kicking a dog, or your friend.

By learning about communication through the vibration of elementary particles, between DNA and the existence of the unified field, we now know that there *is* a living essence and intelligence, that runs through and connects all things. Just like the vision I had when I became my plant ally. Biophotons, energy, light, vibrations, are running between us all, being exchanged by all living things. Everything's alive!

Although I live in the reality where everything *is* alive, where I talk to plants, trees, and earthworms, where I recognise the life in the clouds and streams and rocks, sometimes it is as if everything clicks into a different dimension. Suddenly I can feel millions of eyes looking back at me, I know I am being seen. My senses shift up a notch and I can see in astonishing detail, every glinting mineral in the dust on the roadside, every vein in every leaf. I can hear ten distinguishable birds and leaves of many different textures tickling against each other in the breeze. I can smell blossom and dampness, grass and oak. It is as if the world opens up and invites me in, and like Cinderella, everything around me has a personality and wants to be noticed. This happens so much more, it becomes pretty much normal, once I have been in and around nature for some hours or days, but it also happens occasionally when I am walking the streets on the way home from town. Sometimes I may even be in an entirely man made environment, such as the queue in the supermarket, and I get a massive surge through my feet and I know it is nature calling to me, connecting with me.

If you attempt to rewild yourself without recognising and treating everything as alive it kind of misses the point for me. Anyone can

64

stand naked in the rain, and yes of course they will feel amazing, but without the world upon which you stand being alive and sentient it is just a variation on taking a shower in a regular shower unit, just with less control over the water flow and a better view. We all know that it is not the same, there is something more; that thing, that invisible special feeling, is livingness. It is the fact that everything from the raindrops and the clouds they came from, to the grass underfoot, and the mountains in the distance, are all living beings. Livingness, a term that I first heard used by Stephen Harrod Buhner, means aliveness, it means containing an essence, a spirit, a character; life. Once you recognise and acknowledge the livingness in everything around you, your own aliveness is somehow revived. There is suddenly more meaning in the world, greater possibilities. The separation between yourself and other life is thoroughly dissolved and you begin to be integrated and wild once more. You *become nature*. Without that you are just an eccentric naturist enjoying the weather.

Despite all the research and depressing reading about the detrimental effect that urban living has on our health, we cannot all relocate our lives to rich, verdant wilderness locations – it just isn't practical or realistic. The trick is seeing the wild, the natural, the life that still exists all around us wherever we are. Seeing it when sitting on a sunny step watching ants and bees and the strong green leaves forcing themselves up through the concrete. To be present in that moment, focusing on the natural elements in the scene straight away is medicine for your soul. When I do so, immediately the knots in my stomach loosen, my shoulders roll back, a smile softens my face. Every time. Every time I step outside and consciously greet the nature around me. Every time I breathe deep and choose to notice the scene, choose to sink into the feeling of it, become a part of it rather than just a visitor moving through it untouched. Every time I take a moment to find the beauty in the urban waste, the nibbled corners where nature slowly, silently, is making her return.

By breaking your regular routine, by adding something new and different, such as taking 10 minutes from your morning to greet all your house plants, new possibilities, new thought pathways are created. You are opening the door to a whole new realm of possibility. It is important not to just do it once and think "oh that was nice, I feel better" but

to constantly remind yourself of your connection with all life, to respect and recognise those other lives.

When everything's alive in your world, experiencing it as such is no longer an optional leisure activity or a one off novelty, it becomes a way of being. You begin to notice certain plants, animals or stones more than others, as if they are calling to you. It becomes an essential part of you. Your body reacts, everything lightens, something in your heart lifts as you exhale more deeply than usual. And in that moment you have captured something. It may be small and short lasting, but just for a moment your soul tastes the bliss of being. This is a beautiful thing, that in our busy "doing" lives most of us have forgotten. The changes in the deep self inspired by the acknowledgement of the livingness of all things, are the doorway into the magical realms. From this point on everything opens up and the world is coloured in and fully inhabited.

4.1 The Life in our Immediate Environment

I used to live in a wooden house, elevated on stilts at the front as the hillside dropped away below. Each spring a fox would come and raise its cute but noisy family under the house. The house itself, like all wooden houses I have entered, had an absolute character of its own. Although the wood had been chopped and planked over 70 years before I moved in, it felt alive. The house was a living entity. Because it was entirely natural you could feel it breathe. Not stuffy, no stale air, as air was always circulating through cracks. It was a natural, breathing, biodegradable part of the environment. Being enclosed within chipboard, plasterboard, concrete or MDF feels much less alive, less vibrant. It almost feels like a buffer cutting nature out. I feel stifled and suffocated in modern houses. My current house is brick and over 130 years old, and although not as rich in personality as wood it is still alive, with air circulating through the cracks, with its own sweet decay.

Once you open up to the possibility that all natural things have a livingness it leads one to think about what we fill our immediate environment with. It does matter. It is not just the fabric of our walls and ceilings that have caused a split from the rest of nature, what about all the material products we use in our daily lives, from clothes and bedding to furniture and utensils? Being surrounded by beautiful hand-crafted items made from natural materials leads to a much

more harmonious *feeling* living space than one filled with factory made, straight-lined, chemical infused concoctions.

Even the building or the making of the thing, be it a house or a piece of furniture, layers an energy into it. I have built walls with cob, basically mud and straw. It was a community activity. It was fun and involved much laughter. That shared laughter and warmth was built into the structure itself. Craftsmen who take a pride in their green wood working, thatch or stone masonry, give such a different feeling to the end product than just chucking down another brick on a house the same as all the others. True craftsmen leave a signature, a feeling in the product they make, they leave part of themselves there. But, just as we cannot all go and live in the country, neither can we all build our homes from willow whips and birch bark, it is not practical or feasibly possible for most of us. You can invite the living in, however.

Next time you need to buy something new for your home, remodel or repair a room in your house, just think about what materials would feel better and give more opportunity for a conscious connection to nature. A home can still be modern and sleek yet contain natural elements, from plaster and paints, to fittings and furnishing. Never forget we are constantly exchanging light and energy with what we surround ourselves with. Organic fabrics, responsibly harvested wood, naturally occurring pigments, all make subtle changes to the feeling of our immediate environment and incrementally improve our well-being.

Next time you are in a store handle a smooth beautiful grained wooden chopping board or spoon, smell it, let your fingers explore the textures. Then pick up a moulded plastic chopping board or spoon, the difference is palpable. Expand that feeling to fill each room of your house and you will begin to understand how using natural finishes and products in your home feels warmer and softer, and yet also wilder.

As much as possible attempt to bring wildness into your living space, that way your world is alive not just when you open the front door, but also when it is closed. You can go further than natural furnishings and fittings. Invite wildness in with potted plants, paintings and photos of wild places you love; fill your refrigerator and cupboards with natural, organic foods and medicines. Slowly the wild will re-enter your home and once inside it will quietly stalk you until you find that wildness is gradually reclaiming you.

4.2 Urban Environments

It goes beyond our individual homes. You will find life (beyond humanity) everywhere, all around us, even in cities. Never forget the hidden world beneath your feet, the universe that is the soil, tree roots, rocks, minerals, insect nests and magma. Soil, when not subjected to the batterings of conventional, chemical heavy, agriculture (which in essence renders the substance of soil inert), contains approximately 10 billion bacteria and 1 million fungi in a small handful. Where each bacterium contains 10 million units of genetic information and each microscopic fungus a billion units[1]. Now if that ain't alive you tell me what is!

Despite all that life beneath our feet it can be hard to recognise livingness in urban landscapes, to even come into contact with soil or anything underfoot other than concrete or tarmac. However, nature and life exists even in the most unexpected places. The densely populated areas in our inner cities play host to an urban wildness; dandelions growing between paving slabs; buddleia alongside the rail tracks; foxes and rats (or bears depending where you live!) living off our food waste. Life goes on and can be encouraged, recognised and restored where we live out our lives; where we work, where we play. Interestingly, bees are doing better in urban areas dotted with flower stuffed back gardens than in the monocrop dominated countrysides on the urban fringe these days; which says a lot for our urban green spaces and their value to wildlife, including your own wild life.

4.3 Beyond The Urban Fringe

One of the easiest places to feel the livingness of the world is unsurprisingly in relatively uncolonised deep nature. Take yourself somewhere wild, even just for a day or a weekend. Coastlines are fabulous for this and are usually relatively accessible certainly for those of us who live on an island. Even if the back of the beach is built up with human development you can normally find a quiet fold in amongst the cliffs or a rock pool. Just by standing in the shallows, sand or pebbles underfoot, and salty water splashing rhythmically against your shins, you can feel the life in your surroundings and wildness begin to seep into you.

Most people have the chance for an occasional escape to somewhere wilder than their daily habitat. The wilder, less touched by human development that an environment is, the easier it is to experience it as alive; to appreciate and acknowledge the life that resides there in its many forms.

In my early travelling years I visited the Ecuadorian rainforest, the banks of the Rio Napo, a tributary of the Amazon. I had gone there in search of plant medicine. I came back perhaps with more than I had bargained for, an undeniable knowing of the livingness of the world. I had always spoken with my cat and my dog, loved nature, and supported charities that strove to protect it, but all at once my feeling and understanding achieved another level. It was as if Gaia's green fingers had fully penetrated my heart and I began to experience myself as a living, breathing, exchanging part of nature; nature was no longer "out there" and separate from me.

The layers of sound at any one moment in the rainforest are as an orchestra. Layer upon layer of distinct harmonies, rising and falling. Each layer in turn increasing their tempo to fever pitch, a huge tsunami-like crescendo and then a perceived break. But on listening that break is immediately filled with a multitude of other accompanying layers, each one rising in loudness and energy in turn, or simply as sustained background percussion. The insects, the monkeys, the dripping leaves, the birds. It is a constant pulsating thrumming. It is beyond regular sound as it seems to contain extra dimensions, the vibrations so strong that you can feel it as a life force ebbing and flowing and causing each and every cell in your body to simultaneously vibrate along with the general rhythm. This is the feeling of life, this place is abundantly alive.

And the tall cliffs of green that rise from the river bank. Not just lined with shrubs and trees but a huge deep dark green, seemingly impenetrable, wall that towers 30-40-50 metres into the sky. So imposing, so rich.

And the dampness. How to describe it? When you lie in bed tonight place your hand in front of your face and feel the warmth and wetness of your breath flowing rhythmically in and out. Or, if you share your bed with a partner, face each other and feel the warm dampness of your breath

intermingling around your faces and filling the space. Now imagine being in a very small space with 100 people, all face to face breathing in and out, in and out. Expand that out to cover hundreds and thousands of square miles. But it's plants, animals, birds, all of them, crawling up and along each others limbs to reach the light and air, all intermingling, interdependent, all breathing, transpiring, in and out, in and out, in and out. Then you start to get the picture, the damp, warm, thick air that coats your skin with a certain clammy warmth. Within hours all your clothes, all your luggage is damp. It will never dry while you are here, it will never have that freshly laundered, bone dry, clean feeling that you get at home, but this is life at its most abundant. Everything is alive.

I appreciate that not everyone has the time and resources to embark on such an adventure in search of wilderness. But there is not far to look to find a piece of living nature, because of course, you are it. So failing all else start with yourself. Every single part of you from your little finger, your skin, to your internal organs, are all alive, all living. In the following chapters I will explore many ways of getting back in touch with your bodies so if this seems a little far fetched or tricky to get your head around for now, then simply start outside of yourself with that ant trail on the balcony.

4.4 Developing Our Ability To Communicate

All you have to do is pay attention; lessons always arrive when you are ready, and if you can read the signs, you will learn everything you need to know in order to take the next step.
                                                          Paulo Coelho

Throughout this book I have made a big deal of communication, of communicating with nature. I have attempted to explain why communication is not only possible but constantly occurring whether we are aware of it or not. The point in part is to convince you of the livingness of this world, the fact that everything's alive and that to truly rewild we need to take that on board and each, in our own way, reach out to different points in nature to build relationships of mutual respect and understanding. There are of course different possibilities and levels

of communication. The most basic level is to try to become aware of incoming messages. The more time we spend amongst wild nature the more important it is to be aware of messages generated from outside of ourselves, messages upon which our survival in that moment may depend. But also, as will be explored in Part III, the messages our body is sending us, as this is essential for our physical and mental health, but also our successful re-immersion into the living world, our rewilding.

You can go deeper and deeper with communication and literally talk to, and importantly notice the response from, the plants, the animals, the rocks and the rivers. This is what our ancestors once did, and some indigenous groups still do. It is how they discovered many things such as medicinal plants - not through trial and error as many assume[2]. You do not need to take it to that level initially, or perhaps ever (although with time you will hear whisperings on the wind, you will become captivated as you see, hear, and feel, more and more, you *will* be drawn in). Right now just try to become aware of incoming messages that originated outside of yourself, then those that were generated within, and learn to differentiate between them. Without this awareness you will simply remain an observer passing through foreign terrain, no matter how many cold rivers you swim in.

You may be a sceptic with regard to my notions of livingness and communication, but if you lived in the wild you would live by these truths. If you are ever in the desert sat around a fire at night don't forget to tune into your senses every time you walk away from the flickering light to pee in the bush, as lack of attention to your surroundings – the spiders, snakes, scorpions (etc. etc.) - can get you killed. Growing up in the west, in Western Europe, there is a kind of buffering from the wilds, there are very few wild beasties that can kill us and so we become complacent, often forgetting to be careful and respect nature. So I talk about reconnecting and communicating as a prerequisite to rewilding as for most of us it *is* what we need to do first. If you live in the desert, in the bush, you are most likely already connected, either that or very lucky; as to survive there without awareness, without acknowledging the livingness of nature or being able to read its signs, is next to impossible...

By restoring livingness to the world, acknowledging everything as alive, we inadvertently restore some livingness back to ourselves. It brings added depth to your daily life, enriches it beyond comparison. Suddenly you are no longer alone. This is the first step toward reintegration with the natural world and shaking off some of those ailments, afflictions and behaviours that a life dislocated from nature can contribute to.

Once every living thing around you has life, a spirit, you have to treat those things with the same respect and gentleness as you would a newborn human, a teacup piggy, your lover. The more you do this the more the knowledge that everything is connected is reinforced, it becomes impossible to ignore. The chemicals you are spraying on the weeds (to save time? effort? energy?) are leaching into the soil, the water table, your food, your water, your children's food, your children's water. You are poisoning your living world, your children. It changes everything.

The obvious result is that people who feel this living connection, who approach each part of Gaia as a sacred and enspirited part of the whole, lead a different, more respect filled, more eco-aware and sustainable lifestyle. You cannot damage, pollute, hunt to extinction or wantonly destroy that which is brimming with livingness, instead you hold it as sacred. Awareness and acknowledgement are the building blocks, out of these comes the confidence and ability to start listening to what the world around you is saying, and when you reach that point you really are letting the wild back in. *The rewilding has begun.*

5. FEELING BEFORE THINKING

To engage our wilder side we have to dispense with our very human habit of thinking. That is not to say stop thinking altogether, of course not, but to try and engage your instincts, to *feel* first. When I was apprenticing with Stephen Buhner he always used to say "Feel first think later, if there's time". I have fully adopted that and you will also need to if you are to *become nature.*

Animals do not spend much time thinking, worrying, calculating or assuming, they survive by using their senses and with what they perceive directly. We are so used to analysing, which of course has its place but if you let your logic be in control all of the time you will talk yourself out of a lot of the incoming information. We have all done it, had a feeling about a thing, that it was perhaps a bad idea, or that we should have behaved contrary to habit or what logic told us, and time and again our feeling or instinct was proved right even though we acted against it.

Feeling comes from the heart, thinking comes from the brain. This wild planet is not a machine or a place that can be reduced to tiny predictable sections by logic, I have already discussed the fallacy of viewing the world this way. In part that paradigm is what has got us into this mess in the first place, so it will not get us out of it. To feel your way around the world is to be wild, and to do that you must engage your heart.

Just in case you were wondering the heart *is* an intelligent organ, it has at least 40,000 neurons (nerve cells), as many as are found in various sub-cortical centres of the brain, and they are all simultaneously communicating with each other[1]. Reaching out into the world with ones heart and *feeling* provides us with an intuitive awareness which goes beyond the linear, logical boundaries that limit the brain.

Communications with nature can be felt by using the heart as the organ of perception. Imagine yourself for a moment as a tiny baby in an adults arms, if that adult intends you harm you will know it, you will scream and cry, your body will go stiff. That is an example of a knowing, a feeling generated by direct perception, by using your heart to feel its way through a situation. Now a baby would not have the mental faculty to think its way through that scenario, to talk itself out of feeling that Uncle Mike has a sinister agenda. But as adults, we do and when someone invites you for a drink, or into their car, unless the feeling is very strong and clear it can easily be overridden with thoughts of "don't be silly, he's a nice guy". Direct perception is about trusting that initial

instinct or feeling, looking for it and actually listening to it. Of course we can be wrong, and sinister Uncle Mike could always change his mind, but the more you practice awareness of your feelings, the greater your capacity to trust those feelings. This is feeling before thinking in action. No time to worry about offending that guy from the office or looking like a fool having to walk home in the rain, this is about trusting yourself and what you are picking up from your surroundings, what is being communicated to you.

Going beyond interactions with humans, of which we are of course most familiar, feeling before thinking means picking up when you suddenly get goose pimples, when you feel like something is stalking you. It is about looking outside and seeing bright sunshine but getting the feeling to take an umbrella. It is learning a hard lesson, that is to trust yourself, to trust those feelings, despite being regularly told "don't be so silly" ever since you could first speak. It is not about ignoring everyone else and their advice and experience, but it *is* about being responsible for yourself and making decisions based on what you feel. It is about trusting the world, trusting the messages you are receiving from everything around you and your ability to interpret them and convert that into usable information.

Feeling before thinking helps us remain safe when we are distant from man made recreation areas, when we are in a place with no barriers or fences, no drinking water on tap, no shelter and no corner store. It is essential if we are to thrive amongst the rest of nature, if we are to confidently stride out into the bush and survive. It will take time to build your ability to read the messages coming in from the world, we have spent most of our lives ignoring them; be cautious, be safe, but above all *feel*. The more you feel the better, and the more adept you will become at teasing out the meaning.

> *The human body is a great barometer, and in the early stages of this work, when you begin to receive a feeling response, try not to pounce on it, label it...just mentally stand back and let the feeling truly unroll itself...before applying a mental interpretation. The intellect always wants to keep control...but we have to learn to bridle it when we do this work.*
>
> Susan Raven

There is a reciprocal nature to direct perception, to feeling with the heart, as to touch is to be touched, to see the forest is to feel that the forest sees you. This experience, of being watched, of course alters ones behaviour, in some instances radically. Try walking around outside and as you look at each plant feel *its* eyes upon you, imagine (or believe) that it is watching you back. Feels different doesn't it? Not so much creepy but as if your grandma was watching you play from the kitchen window, there are some things you wouldn't do, right? I feel those eyes upon me as comforting but, as in the home of a relative, my behaviour has become more mindful, more respectful.

6. REAWAKENING YOUR WILD HEART

During my childhood I spent a large amount of time playing outside, often totally mesmerised and enchanted by the moment. The sight of a beautiful flower, the smell of that leaf, the touch of a pine cone, the sound of the buzzing insect, the taste of the dirt. And time, time was endless, and it was always sunny. That's how I remember my early childhood, great chunks of it at least, and how precious? How precious are such memories that still glow warm inside and raise a smile to my lips. Because now, deep into the long and more serious years of adulthood leisure time is somehow lessening as commitments, financial and otherwise, grow. Somehow that connection, those undisturbed moments of deep nature connection, have become rare. To live again such precious moments, to make new sunny nature memories, we have to put time in. It's a commitment.

My generation was lucky, I did have play time outside and I could wander alone beyond my street to the park with the swings. The range of my parents was much greater, possibly even several miles. That of children today is much less than mine was - many do not even leave their back garden unaccompanied. Modern gardens, even those attached to 4 or 5 bedroom homes, are often tiny. There is no room for escape to alternate imaginary realms, just enough for a family BBQ in summer and no more. In fact in the UK alone there are more than 2 million households with no garden at all[1]. The wildness around us is shrinking and in turn our need for it grows and grows.

It has become so rare to swim in wild waters that instead of simply calling such an activity "swimming" as our parents and grandparents did, we now call anything that does not occur in the sanitised conditions of a concrete bound chemically cleaned pool "wild swimming". There are books telling you where you can go and do it, but why not discover for yourself? *Don't be crazy, some places have currents, are deep, are dangerous* – welcome to the wild! There is danger in the wild, that is what makes it wild (*and we hunger for it*). The fact that humankind managed to get this far, to be so prolific on this (*wild and dangerous*) planet was because we used our sense and our senses.

Learn to gauge for yourself, use your heart to intuit whether a place is safe or not. With wild water if you get in, can you get back out? Read the water, learn how to. Play pooh sticks or watch for differences in the surface texture of the water, if the flow is fast that probably means there

is a fast current. Swim with friends, play safe. Be tentative and careful. But don't sit in ignorance, only going where the website, book, or tourist notices tell you. Explore. Discover. Learn to read nature's signs. All of which takes time. I guess that is why we rely so much on other sources, because time is what we all lack in our modern world where computers were supposed to make our working lives more efficient, but somehow swallow up more and more hours each day with each new innovation. You can have an experience in nature and enjoy it as a result of someone else's research, of course you can, and there is nothing wrong with that. But if you do have the time, can make the time, there is nothing better, no experience more profound than discovering, uncovering and realising by yourself.

🐘

We all enjoy and are inspired by different things, just as we all have different levels of access to nature, to the wild. Many people, alienated as we are from the natural world, feel uncomfortable or bored when spending time in it, especially as we are so used to being overstimulated by billboards, traffic, smart phones and the internet. So this chapter is about reawakening your wild heart, those first practical steps. Ways to dip into nature and embrace the wild. Ways to help overcome that alienation, boredom and fear. It is about finding the things that excite you and make you feel connected, make you feel that you are plugged directly into the source. Activities that make you want to spend time outside, keen to do it again, wanting for more. This is about rewilding, about putting an electrical charge through our tired and lonely urban hearts so that they beat strongly once more.

6.1 Embracing The Wild

An experience on the other hand, can be denied and even forgotten, but it cannot be unexperienced. Experience changes you forever.

Eliot Cowan

This is about getting in touch with your wild self and working out what YOU really want. Not swayed by multi-million pound advertising campaigns, but being in touch with what really makes you happy. Nature is not austere or boring. Wildness, Gaia, is about abundance, celebrations,

cycles, fecundity. Make your connections, acknowledge the livingness, open your heart to incoming communications, then dive in deep. This is the key to a richness beyond your wildest imaginings. Do not wait for the weekend or your annual leave to do the things that you love, that you enjoy; find ways to incorporate them into your daily life. Don't overlook the little things, celebrate the ordinary; the dandelion leaf and the trail of ants, standing barefoot on your lawn. The following suggestions are part of the solution, what you can do for yourself to reclaim your rightful place within nature.

Breathing Gaia: My husband came up with this while enjoying the shade of a huge pine at the back of a beach one sunny day. In his moment of reverie he realised what was occurring, that he was sharing something with the tree, and that thing was breath. We humans share the same breath, the same air as the plants and all the animals. Our breath is common. My in breath, your out breath, it is mixed, it is shared. Sit next to a plant, any plant, one in a pot on your window ledge, or a beautiful flower in the park, a weed or a tree, any plant will do. Now become aware of your breath. As you breathe in envisage all the oxygen particles in the air, coming direct from the plant and travelling down into your lungs. On the out breath be aware of all the CO_2 you are breathing out and that in turn being absorbed by the plant. Now close your eyes and repeat this for a few cycles. Maintain an attitude of gratitude at all times. You will find a deep connection with the plant and experience the exchange that is always invisibly occurring between you. This can put you into quite a dreamy state, enjoy it - this is the doorway to the plant realms.

Standing Barefoot On The Earth: To attain maximum impact this is best done first thing in the morning, when disturbance from other humans is likely to be minimal. Just step outside with no shoes, no socks. Let your feet spread, wiggle your toes so they too spread to hold the ground beneath them. Close your eyes and stand for a few moments just feeling your feet and the Earth beneath. Cool early morning dew is a favourite of mine. Most people only ever get to experience barefoot contact with the Earth a couple of times a year, at the beach, or perhaps a summer festival.

Try to make time not just for standing barefoot but also walking barefoot. It is very beneficial for your posture and will affect the shape of your legs. When walking barefoot on natural surfaces there is a transfer of free electrons from the ground into your feet. These free

electrons are some of the most powerful antioxidants known, they scavenge and neutralise free radicals in the body. Walking barefoot will help ease inflammation as well as cell and tissue damage, it even promotes more restful sleep[2]. What's not to love? It is like free reflexology, free wobble-board shoe sole technology, the muscles all the way up your legs, buttocks, core and back all have to work harder. Explore different textures, let your feet mould around different surfaces. Life barefoot is a whole new world.

Hug The Earth: Ever just collapsed to the floor after a long run, a fight with a lover, a traumatic incident, or simply a busy week? As your legs crumple beneath you you become a heap of flesh and bones on the ground, maybe sobbing, maybe breathing hard, maybe washed out, exhausted, or just resting; either way after a short while you feel much better, more energised, revived. So why wait? Try this when it is not a drama or the end of a half marathon. Just lie face down on a lush patch of grass, star shaped, and feel the Earth beneath you. It is almost like you can feel a heart beat, you can certainly feel a pulsing of life. Eye level with the grass, take in the sights, the insects, the dandelions, the daisies. Whatever you see take it all in, along with the sounds and the smells.

Let the lumps and bumps, the contours of Earth, cradle and mould your form, hold you. Most of us only lie in direct contact with the Earth a few times a year, if that. When we do, perhaps just on a surprise sunny day in the park or summer holiday on the beach. It's rarely, if ever, face down in a hug position. But you can do it, hug the Earth, any time, be it secretly in your back garden or as the freak everyone is staring at in the park. Give it a whirl, it is fabulous.

Hug A Tree: Oh yes the old hippy classic, but why not? Have you ever tried? Personally I prefer to sit at the base of a big, strong, inviting tree with my back to the trunk, but I'm not adverse to the occasional hug, it's really grounding. Trees are magnificent beings and if you find one that feels right to you in that moment it can become quite a wise and wonderful friend.

Hands On The Earth: This is something most of us probably do even less than actually standing barefoot. Just take your naked hands (no gloves) and lie them palm down on the ground, spread your palms. Spread your fingers. Close your eyes. Just feel. There is such a strong surge of energy into your palms, this is so simple to do and yet so effective. You may be moved to say a prayer of gratitude for all the Earth means to you, I usually am.

Express Gratitude: For the sun, rain, moon, stars, bees, spiders, flies, plants, for the shade of the trees. Say it out loud. There is always something, always something, to be grateful for. Sometimes that is all there is to keep us sane – that we had enough to eat that day, found enough wood to burn to keep us warm, saw a beautiful sunset, heard birdsong, that we have someone to love, or who loves us, or simply that we are alive. This may not seem that wild, but without acknowledgement of all the elements that make life, one simply takes it for granted and fails to recognise what an entirely complex interwoven web of life, energy and activity each supposedly single, separate life actually is.

Do Something That Scares You: I was told years ago that this was the secret to eternal youth, perhaps it is, but more than that it is also a valuable component in the rewilding process. The reason that it is beneficial with regard to rewilding is that fear causes your senses to tune in and heighten, it makes you alert. I am not encouraging you to do something dangerous, just every now and then try something different, something that you could avoid by sitting in your armchair with the lights on. What scares each of us obviously differs from person to person. Maybe you are scared of trying new foods, or the dark, or heights. Try facing your fears. Try that thing and feel the freedom soar within you as endorphins release afterwards in the realisation that you could do it, it did not kill you. You never know, you may even enjoy it.

Wild animals although not attaching emotion to situations in the way that we do still feel the physical effects we attribute to fear; a release of adrenalin, increased blood pressure enabling blood to be diverted to muscles and essential organs. They are the responses that give wild animals what they need to react with fight or flight. They are also what become heightened in a perpetually stressed person. But, giving yourself a real reason for those hormones and feelings to be there and then importantly to dissipate after the event, gives you a more balanced relationship with those physical effects. Facing your fears, doing what scares you brings all of those chemical reactions into your body, helping you align, just that bit more, with your wild self.

Take A Shower In The Rain: This works best in the tropics or equatorial latitudes where you get tropical downpours on an almost daily basis at certain points of the year. If you live in the temperate zone every so often in summer the heat builds up leading to warm and dramatic thunderstorms, they are the ones to catch. Standing at the edge of a tin roof (not to be recommended if there is lightening!) is particularly

pleasing as the water congregates in little channels, directed by the corrugations. The water literally pours onto your head. I am not sure I have ever experienced anything quite so ecstatic or enlivening as standing naked, surrounded by cloud forest, with fresh cool rain thundering down on my head from the plant nursery roof, cleansing my hot and sticky body.

Sleeping Under The Stars: Camping and outdoor living are of course fabulous for re-engaging your wild self. I have never lived in a tipi or a yurt but know many who have or do, and seeing their lifestyles I notice that every moment is directly connected to the weather and number of daylight hours. Camping is perhaps the lightweights version but I love it nonetheless. I have spent quite a few extended periods camping when I have been on the road, sometimes up to three months or more. Your day is dictated by the elements and you are outdoors from the moment you rise until the moment you go to bed. It is an amazing way, it is invigorating. You lie on the contours of the ground, just a thin mat insulating you. Sun or rain you feel it. Plants, smells, animals and insects, you share each day with them all.

If this is still not enough then I recommend sleeping out (weather permitting of course), no tent, no tarp, just yourself, a blanket and the stars. There is something very cosmic about doing this, watching as the stars seem to progress overhead on a track, yet it is you on the spinning Earth that is doing the moving. Watching stars appear to set on the distant horizon, wow. It makes you feel small, like your problems don't matter so much, and like there is something out there bigger than you which feels comforting. The moon and the phase it is in will have a great influence on what happens if you choose to sleep out. Full moon is the perfect opportunity for a bit of moonbathing (although of course much less ideal for star gazing). How often do you get to lie out and absorb the lunar brightness? It is possibly the pièce de résistance when it comes to sleeping out. I will say no more. Wait for a full moon in summer when it is warm and comfortable enough to sleep out and give it a go.

Wild Swimming: Swimming in rivers and lakes is so refreshing, especially when the water is clear, deep and cool. There is nothing like the smooth silky feel of cool river water on your skin. It's like the most luxuriant fabric touching every fold of your skin, every nook, every hair, wrapping you in its divine embrace. Wild swimming is preferable when done naked, trust me, in fact that *is* wild swimming. Sea swim-

ming for me is the same, I love it. Swimming at night in the sea can be especially rewarding; splash around, there may be marine phosphorescence. If so it makes the whole experience feel like you are in another realm, trailing glow-in-the-dark particles wherever you go; best enjoyed with friends.

A friend of mine goes night swimming, naked, in the sea every full moon of the year with her girlfriends. No matter how cold they still go because it makes them feel wild, alive and magical. Of course, please be cautious and sensible. Never jump into unknown water and most certainly not at night. Learn your water, communicate, listen, look, be responsible but don't let fear put you off, this is an incredible experience that will reignite your wildness.

Wild Crafting: There is an art to what could also be called foraging. You need to know where to look, other species that grow in the same conditions, indicator species that let you know the one that you hunt will follow soon. As you tune in over the years you get to know your quarry better and better, you build a relationship. Nothing tastes quite like a wild leaf nibbled straight from the plant. I truly believe the more wild you eat, the more wild you become.

There are a few fundamental rules that need to be adhered to when wild crafting or foraging - this is becoming more pertinent as this activity gains popularity. Of course you must consider correct identification; and cautions and contraindications if you are collecting medicines, that goes without saying. But it is exceptionally important to only collect that which you need, never take all that you find, be sure to spread seed and don't take the grandfather (the most mature and strongest) plant. I have noticed more and more companies selling foraged foods at markets, to restaurants, even processed as chutneys and jams. I am ethically opposed to anyone making money from foraged foods, it should just be for you. Otherwise, as has happened in parts of India where people have been wild crafting herbs commercially for many years now, some of the species that once were widespread have become endangered.

I even include collecting spring water and gathering firewood in the wild crafting category. Fresh spring water is wild water, drink directly from the spring if at all possible, lips pursed in the flowing water. With firewood again comes a caution. It feels wonderful to collect twigs for kindling from the woods, and even fallen branches, but be aware and respectful as every woodland needs some wood left to rot on the

woodland floor to feed back into the soil and to provide a habitat for insects and fungi.

Traditional Outdoor Pursuits: There are several outdoor pursuits that I have experience of that really help develop one's connection with nature. Pursuits that are slow and sustained enough for you to take a deep breath and feel yourself as part of the surroundings, not just a visitor moving through. My first deep connection with nature, first feeling of being really alive, was whilst trekking in the mountains of North Wales. It was just a sublime feeling that the world was so much more than me and my story and it felt comforting and real.

I also love canoeing/ kayaking because the waterways are so peaceful, and unlike tracks and pathways on land seem to be much less disturbed and populated. I guess the water is always changing and moving so the signs of human disturbance are literally being washed away constantly. You can glide, jump out and swim. You can just be, an amazing experience. I think my favourite moments on the water are when I pause the activity and let the flow of the river take me, I close my eyes and listen to the bird and the animal life, feel the sun and the breeze on my skin.

I have purposefully chosen not to include cycling or mountain biking purely because, in my experience, the attention is on the cycling more than nature. Cycling for me happens too fast for a meaningful connection with nature to be fostered at the same time, but we are all different, so whatever works for you, there is no right and wrong here just ideas I have gleaned from my own experiences. I can imagine surfing, pony trekking and cross country skiing are other outdoor pursuits where a deep connection with nature can be woven and enjoyed, there are possibly many activities I have overlooked through lack of personal experience but you get the general idea.

Standing Outside: I recommend taking 5 minutes outside every day. Begin by taking a deep breath and noticing the air. It changes daily. If you follow this practice throughout the year you will be able to appreciate very subtle changes in moisture content, temperature and odour; every tiny variation that occurs between the extremes. From the gasp of sharp frosty winter air where your out-breath rises like smoke from a dragon, to the sultry days of high summer where it is almost impossible to get a satisfying breath - you will become familiar with them all. Then, observe. Look around, notice the quality of light, th clouds, the sun, the plants. Notice the smell, dampness and decay, h

som, fresh green growth. Listen, even if there is a lack of nature in your area sounds change through the season, as does quality of sound. As the year passes the daily nuances will become apparent to you.

Don't make a big deal out of it. Take your breakfast cuppa outside, stand on the door step, just weave it in, attach it seamlessly into your daily routine. If 5 minutes a day is too much try doing it just every other day, or once a week. Failing all else aim to at least stand outside on the equinoxes, solstices, and the cross quarter festivals. Just so that you not only notice but become keenly aware of, and a feeling part of, the cycles of life.

We are hard wired to be part of the daily (circadian), monthly (lunar), seasonal and yearly (circannual) changes in our world. Different physical reactions within our bodies occur in line with these rhythms and cycles. For example, northern hemisphere babies born in May, are on average two hundred grams heavier than babies born in any other month. The difference is caused by changes in the quantity of hormones produced during pregnancy throughout the year. An archaic echo of a human breeding season, in line with giving birth during the kindest months[3].

The more you stand outside and absorb what is going on around you the stronger the remembering inside of you and in turn the greater the change within you, aligning you to the daily, monthly and seasonal changes.

You can incorporate *breathing Gaia* and *standing barefoot on the Earth*, or any other of these suggestions, with *standing outside* for a deeper penetration of wildness into the corners of your daily life. If you have the time available go for a walk once a week, or more regularly, and notice all of these things, take your time, become part of the landscape.

Sky Gazing: This one is very inclusive because, as long as you have a nearby window, it can even be done by those with limited mobility, from bed. Looking at the sky, noticing the changes in light, clouds, rain, rainbows, lightening. The phases of the moon, the stars, shooting stars, comets. Sun rises and sets. If you are lucky enough you may even get to see eclipses of the sun and moon, total, partial, annular or hybrid. Watching the sky connects us with something larger than ourselves. It is humbling as we can do nothing to control what is happening "up there". It helps us to remember our place within it all. It also connects

~tors who saw the same stars, and friends and family

lanet. Whenever I am missing someone who is far

at the moon and know that they are also standing

nd under the sky, all species.

Wild Watching: Everything from birds to urban foxes can be observed either from hides out amongst nature, from your windows or perhaps even from a greater distance with motion triggered cameras. There is a value to wild watching as you will get to know the wildlife that frequents your local area, who you share your locale with. It can be a good starting point for people who have a genuine fear of wild nature, who are too young to be left to explore the other options, or who have mobility issues that limit their opportunities for getting out there amongst it. But the danger with just watching from a safe distance is that you remain separate, an observer, just a human. Use it as a way in, as an introduction to your local wildlife, a way to build your awareness of your neighbours. And do, if at all possible, step outside. Sit on your back step and watch the ants carve pathways in the dirt from up close. Let one walk over your foot (beware if you are ticklish), let the ant (the wildness) explore and observe you too.

All of the suggestions in this section are basics that can be undertaken with little or no experience, just a respect for nature and common sense (nature sense). This is in no way a definitive list of all the ways in which you can begin to rewild but it is a collection of ideas garnered from my own experiences. More in depth rewilding suggestions will follow in later chapters.

Each activity in this section, when you give yourself in full, can initiate a degree of self-transcendence, of going beyond yourself and your usual conscious mind. This state of being usually comes in to play in moments of extreme danger or maximum exertion, the so called runners high. It is a moment of calm, of being in the zone. It is euphoric. It is what I was experiencing as a child following bees around my garden. Everything becomes more luminous, each blade of grass is as if seen through a microscope. This is your wildness. A moving away from the usual distracted analytical state into one of calm and focus, for want of a less clichéd phrase *being in the moment*. A lion stalking its prey, a squirrel burying a nut, a bird riding the thermals.

These moments provide the reconnection I have been speaking of. The connection with all things, with all life. Connection with something beyond and greater than yourself, but also a deeper layer of yourself.

A layer which is normally buried and restricted by the conscious mind and the limitations we unwittingly place upon ourselves and our abilities. These activities can place us firmly within the cycle of life and can give meaning to being alive.

> *People say that what we are all seeking is the meaning for life. I don't think that's what we're really seeking. I think what we're seeking is an experience of being alive.*
>
> Joseph Campbell

Reintegrating with the wild requires a degree of adventure, an element of unpredictability, something that is not tightly controlled. Computer game addicts share in common with extreme pursuit participants (such as slack liners and base jumpers) a reaction to the boring and mundane of the modern world. People everywhere are searching for that divine connection, that pin-point focus that will draw you out of your thinking mind. I cannot tell you how to find this essential element. For an activity to become *your* authentic adventure you will need to pursue and find it yourself. You can try the exercises I suggest, the ones that appeal, and allow them to evolve so they become your own. Each person in their own way is seeking the wildness in themselves, seeking the thrill of the wild and dangerous. We are hungry for an unsanitised, unpredictable life and the clarity and single-mindedness it delivers. Let nature, your nature, lead you.

PART III
Wild Body

The body of a human being is a highly sensitive instrument; it always knows what is going on around it, but we have forgotten how to listen to and interpret its subtle language.
Susan Raven

Atrophy of the senses was occurring long before we came to be bombarded with the latest generation of computers, high-definition TV, and wireless phones... But the new technology accelerates the phenomenon.
Richard Louv

When people rejected natural food and took up refined food instead, society set out on a path towards its own destruction. ... Food is life, and life must not be a step away from nature.
Masanobu Fukuoka

The sharing of food moves from a quick refuelling to a slow and artful unfolding, and then into a ritual as each serving is consecrated, every bite undertaken as communion. Communion with the life-forms that feed us, with the sun and rain and soil that made the salad possible, with the spiritual and evolutionary power moving through both consumer and consumed.
Jesse Wolf Hardin

7. THIS SENSUAL WORLD
Awakening your senses

We are sensual beings, this is a sensual world. The survival of wild animals depends in part upon the use of their finely tuned senses. Our senses have become latent, they have atrophied through under use as we have drifted from nature. Yet there is not a lack of sensory stimulation in our lives; the converse is true.

In the modern world our senses are constantly being bombarded. As a self protection measure, for individual sanity, we have subconsciously closed each one down, so that they currently function at a fraction of their true potential. A walk along a typical high street can easily overload the senses. You cannot give attention to all the smells, sounds, and colours that you encounter. The fact is we don't need to rely on information from our senses for our survival so it becomes easier and preferable for the most part to simply shut it out. However, in so doing the physical connection with our bodies and the world around us deteriorates. With less attention focused on sensory input there is an associated loss of sensory acuity and a further disconnect with the natural world, enhancing any feelings of dissociation or alienation we may already feel.

For most of us our daily world has become quite sanitised. A suburban environment within a culture of health and safety regulations, risk assessments and fear of litigation has made our offices, homes and housing estates increasingly risk free. This may feel like a safer and better place to live and bring up families but it is robbing us of reliance on our senses and of the need to be tuned into our surroundings.

Danger, the unknown, naturally causes the senses to heighten. It enables you to hear a distant twig snap underfoot, or smell a new presence, someone or something behind you. Danger exists in both urban and wild landscapes. Most people know to avoid dark alleyways late at night or to avoid surfing at a beach where a fatal entanglement between surfer and hungry shark occurred the previous day. Even so, a little bit of edge is good for us – it keeps us alert and tuned in to our surroundings; forces us to stay in touch with our senses and make judgements based on their findings. A little slice of danger causes physiological reactions in the body and reminds us that we are alive.

The fact is that even ventures into the unknown have become a

prosaic following of satellite navigation systems, no need to pay attention to where we are or what landmarks we are passing. We have lost the ability, for the most part, to read nature. We rarely even recognise nature's warning signs of approaching storms, changes in the weather, instead relying on TV, radio and internet forecasts. Even reversing trucks make high pitched sounds to alert one to the potential danger, no need to look up from our feet, or smart phone, and take note of what is going on around us.

Our forefathers could smell an animal approaching, hear a distant rustling of leaves, see changes in vegetation indicative of an underground spring, and sense danger. We rely on technology, we shop in supermarkets; have water on tap; listen to loud music to drown out the boring "silence" when walking in nature; rely on burglar alarms to alert us to an intruder, and CCTV to catch any said perpetrators. We have become lazy and it is easy to understand how so, yet through it we have lost another element of our wildness.

In losing touch with our senses we are losing our ability to experience the world directly, to experience its richness, its texture. As our lives revolve more and more around screen-time our experience of the world becomes increasingly one-dimensional. Our quality of life diminishes. We may have access to what everyone is thinking, their relationship status, news, gossip, minute by minute from around the world, but somewhere in all of that life is passing us by. Overloaded with information our lives have become impoverished as they have become increasingly devoid of true sensory experience.

Rewilding involves a return to a multi-dimensional sensory world. To rewild we must re-engage our senses, literally re-sensitise. Optimally functioning senses tell us so much about our immediate environment and help us to make well considered judgements and decisions. Heightened sensual awareness gives us a much deeper understanding of every passing moment, adds meaning to the world. Our senses ground us in the physical reality of now and allow us to extrapolate meaning from that information. Well functioning senses draw us into the wild and allow us a deeper connection with our own wild nature.

♣

Getting to know and understand the fine tunings of your senses allows them to add depth and meaning to your interactions with the wildness of the world. With time and proficiency you will be able to tune in and

back out with ease, as the situation demands. To become proficient at using your senses you must first learn to trust yourself. Trust in ourselves is essential if we are to believe that the information coming in from our senses is accurate. I have already mentioned how, without trust, we can rationalise away most feelings, we also sometimes do it with direct information received on the tangible, physical plane.

From early childhood we have been taught that we are not trustworthy. Our kindly parents in their attempts to nurture and protect us, made decisions for us. When to eat, what to eat, how much to eat. As we got older we were steered away from various friends and activities and towards others; as a result we never fully developed the ability to trust our own intuition. The current culture of health and safety concerns is only exacerbating this situation. The more rules and regulations in place the less we find ourselves in situations where we need to use our own discretion, to trust ourselves.

The best way to develop trust of your senses is to practice using them in situations where you can verify if you are right or wrong. This will build confidence. It is also important to become trustworthy, and to know that you are. If you promise yourself a day off at the end of the month, or that you will go to a yoga session this week, or even that you will treat yourself to a slice of cake on the way home from work then you *must* do it. If you know that you will not uphold your own promise to yourself, you will not be able to trust yourself. So if you smell a rose and yet can't see one you will never believe your nose. If you taste honey but the ingredients did not list it you will not trust your taste buds. Keen senses are what all our wild relatives enjoy, and are something we must nurture, trust and believe, if we are to join those relations and become a little more wild ourselves.

7.1 Hearing

Sound is a wave vibration with a low frequency of between 20 and 20,000 hertz, this is the range an average human ear can hear, although there is clearly considerable variation between individuals. In urban environments that are heavily populated by humans, there is so much to hear, so much sound. Sound can become a pollution of its own kind, noise pollution.

We are busy in our urban worlds cutting sounds out so that we don't go crazy. Even away from the traffic and sirens of the inner city our suburban homes are full of low level noises. The hum of the freezer

and refrigerator, the laptop fan, the boiler. If you take those things away, one by one unplugging them, you will begin to hear it. The silence. It gathers momentum fast, sweeping through the room until you can hear nothing else but the big cotton wool sound of silence. Try it. I recommend between 3-4am when you are least likely to have any noise from passing traffic, neighbours TVs, late night drinkers stumbling home, early morning risers walking their dogs, or bird song.

It is most likely that you will not be in a situation where you can unplug everything and escape entirely from the incidental environmental noises of distant roads or the elements. Still, try peeling back, layer by layer, each noise-emitting component that makes up your home environment and you will realise exactly how many layers of sound currently fill your world.

I am lucky in that although my house is on a through road on the edge of town it is very quiet, especially at night. As I write this on a sunny April day there is constant birdsong, over the hum of my laptop and the occasional passing car, that is capturing my attention. The laptop I do my best to blank out, the traffic I can not. All the while the background noise whirs on.

The most quiet place I have ever been was on the lava fields of Mt Hekla, Iceland. I spent a day with a friend on the lower slopes of the black ash mountain. We climbed for several hours leaving the few roadside sheep behind until there was nothing, no blade of grass, no bird. We could see the rough road from our vantage point. No vehicle passed all day. The black ash underfoot seemed to absorb what sound there was. We discovered that *no sound* is just as big as *sound*, but although it fills you, you feel empty. In those hours I missed the tweeting of birds and rustling of foliage.

With rewilding the point is to retrain yourself to hear. Of course there will still be much you choose and need to block out, more so the more urban your daily routine takes you. But when you have the chance, be it gardening on a sunny afternoon, a stroll on the beach or just taking a conscious moment outside with your eyes closed, take the time to listen. Listen to all the layers. The insect buzzes, the squeak of fresh snow, the scampering squirrel. The more time you spend just listening, the more layers you will be able to distinguish, to separate and recognise. Practice listening. When you hear something new, turn in its

direction to discover what made that noise. You will become accurate at pinpointing the exact location the noise originated from very quickly and with time more able to discern its likely originator.

It is great once you have worked with sound, with listening. Once your hearing becomes more acute you will not only know when someone is approaching you from behind, but also who it is. Not just whether it is a human or a bird, but who; Bob; Sally; a robin; or a cat. A whole new world opens up. It is like seeing with your ears.

In fact some blind people have developed their sense of hearing to such a degree that they can find their way around with sonar. They are as close as it gets to seeing with their ears. People practising this art use clicking or tapping sounds and interpret the reflection of these sounds from nearby objects to give details of their size, location and density. Some people are so refined at this practice that they can ride a bicycle with no sight. Bearing this in mind the potential for developing our hearing is incredible. No doubt it is easier to train one sense to such an incredible degree of competency when other senses are permanently absent, damaged or impaired but the potential is there. This skill is called human echolocation.

Once you pay attention to sound in your environment your relationship to the landscape becomes stronger. When I first began gardening for a living I spent three days a week working mainly alone at a herb nursery. I had the radio playing all day for company. I knew all the DJ's, all the current affairs, top news topics and hot new tracks. For three summers I gardened like that, with my solar powered radio, a prize possession, never far from my side. At one point I began gardening for a new client, she had acres of land and somehow it felt that playing my radio there was wrong, as if I was imposing too much on the nature that resided there. From my first day on her land I stopped taking my radio to work. Now, when I am outside, my ears are filled with natures symphony. I never feel bored or lonely, no matter how long I kneel with my hands in the earth. There is never a silence, and it is never the same.

Something happens when you hear the sounds of nature. In my experience I feel younger, and more alive. It is a kind of primeval awakening, awareness of your surroundings magnifies intensely. There is a feeling of being here, now, and very much a part of what is going on around you.

As far back as 1950, Dr T.C. Singh of Annamalai University, proved that harmonic sound waves (music) affect the growth, flowering, fruiting and seed yields of plants[1]. It was later realised that bird song, a (natural) form of harmonic sound waves, was the optimum frequency and amplitude to achieve the best results with regard to plant growth[2]. Without exposure to birdsong plants don't grow as well as when they are exposed to it. Could it be that we too suffer when we miss the sounds of nature in our daily lives? Don't forget we were born as wild animals, albeit into a somewhat alien domesticated environment. Could it be that without the sounds of nature in our lives we fail to thrive? Certainly birdsong and other nature sounds have been shown to be beneficial to cancer patients, helping them feel that they are part of something bigger than themselves alone, giving a boost to their state of mind[3].

Sound used for healing is now becoming mainstream in that sound waves are used in modern medicine. A machine called a lithotripter breaks up kidney and gallstones that can then pass safely from the body without the need for surgery. Ultrasound is used as a non invasive therapy for tissue, ligament and tendon repair whilst also providing pain relief. High-intensity focused ultrasound (HIFU) is now used in some clinics to treat prostate cancer. This treatment can closely target tumours causing much less unnecessary damage to surrounding tissue than traditional treatments including surgery and radiotherapy. The purr of a cat which ranges from 20-140 Hertz has been proven to help lower stress and blood pressure and also to promote the healing of muscle, tendon and ligament injuries. This sound vibration can also help clear up infection, reduce swelling, promote bone strength and decrease the symptoms of dyspnoea[4]. There are also many kinds of music therapies for different emotional conditions. Sound is so important to us, the vibrations intermingling with all our vibrating particles bringing harmony (or not) on a physical and emotional level.

When you have the opportunity to listen to the sounds of nature be it surf crashing on the shore, a tinkling stream or buzzing insects, absorb it deep into you; relish it. For me, it is like spring sunshine on my face, food for the soul. Take time to notice how the quality of sound changes with the seasons and with the surface it is being carried across. Sound always travels much further and more clearly over the flat surface of a lake than across a forest floor, for example.

I have noticed different layers and textures of sound in different

places around the globe. In locations where life is less technological, the background sounds are more melodic than the western hum of car engines, sirens, heels on tarmac and heavy doors slamming closed. Instead, you hear the early morning chanting of monks or perhaps the call to prayer, animal hooves on dusty tracks, children laughing and playing, the fluttering of prayer flags in the wind. All of these sounds are melodic, closer to the birdsong and gushing river water that you find in nature.

Pay attention to the sounds in your life. Listen to all the multiple layers, textures and qualities. Practice the art of listening and noticing. Let sound tell you about the world, about your immediate environment, and your place within it. Let sound resonate through your body and notice how it feels, how different sounds make you feel. And, whenever possible, immerse yourself in the sounds of nature.

7.2 Sight

Our sight, like our hearing, is generally overwhelmed in modern urban based society. The more urban you go, the more visual stimulation there is. I would imagine it is the sense we use most, not just when out and about in our towns and cities, but also at work and home. Wherever we are our sight is often not just used to consider real world three-dimensions, but increasingly the flat screened one-dimensional world of TV, computers and smart phones.

The 1-D experience is not healthy for our eyes or our vision, so much so that there is even a name for eye problems caused by excessive screen use; computer vision syndrome (CVS). Over 50% of people who spend their working days at a computer screen suffer some kind of eye trouble[5]. Of course children who regularly use a screen both at school and for leisure activities at home are also at risk, a risk which is being further exacerbated by increasingly concentrating our eyes on smaller more portable screens. One of the ways to help avoid developing CVS is to look away from your screen every twenty minutes and gaze around the room or look out of the window; basically give your eyes a different perspective and thus a rest.

Visual experience of the world with limited dimensions also occurs when watching through the window of a moving vehicle. This is clearly not damaging in the same way using a screen is, our eyes do not

have to contend with glare, screen contrast or flicker, but we do remain separate from that which we are looking at.

Despite the separation there is much to gain from viewing a scene from a passing car and the space to daydream that affords. Throughout my life so many hours have been spent in the passenger seat of cars, coaches and trains, watching the world through a window. I have seen so much, and understood so much about the land through which I am travelling from the landforms, flora, signs of human habitation and agriculture that I have passed. There is a lot to see, a lot to learn by watching the landscape unfold through the window of a moving vehicle. So beware - every time a journey is passed with your head in a book, a smart phone or a tablet, an opportunity to relate to the land, to form some kind of connection to it, is lost.

Don't let a drive by in the car become a substitute for actual time spent in nature. I remember driving to Why, Arizona, to visit the Organ Pipe Cactus National Monument to see the cacti in flower. Awed by the amazing roadside displays of flowering cactus en-route from Tucson I had driven slowly, taking in as much as I could from behind the wheel. Unfortunately having spent so long driving whilst admiring the view, by the time I arrived the flowers had closed up for the day. I missed out on the opportunity to walk among the flowering cacti. I had wanted to see the maximum possible in the time I had available, but this left me compromised and lacking any real time for connection with anything other than the drivers seat and steering wheel.

Despite its value, what you see driving by in a car and what you see up close and personal are two entirely different experiences. What you see when driving lacks depth, and although it has more to it than viewing flat screened technology, being merely an observer in a passing vehicle you lose a great chunk of sensory experience. Once you step out of the car, the experience becomes three-dimensional. Much, much more detail is available visually. You can see shadow and light, close up and wide angle, a full 360° but also the other senses are engaged. There is the waft of musky animal on the breeze, the scuttling sound of a spooked lizard, the scratch of a prickly pear thorn on your calf. You become part of the experience, not just the viewer of a scene.

To retrain your eyes, to improve and expand your visual capacity, first try looking closely, rather than quickly scanning for visual sound bites.

I encourage you to get some colouring pencils and draw what you see. The reason I am suggesting drawing is to help you slow down and notice the minutiae. The visual details that are easy to overlook, tiny details that make the thing unique, that characterise it, and which may give away its identity again at some point in the future. Our eyes are used to giving just a quick scan for interest. Retrain yourself to notice the tiny flecks of colour that would otherwise be lost details on the underside of a leaf, the hairline fractures in a huge boulder. Notice the detail, the tiny, the seemingly insignificant.

Pay full attention to colour - to the many shades reflected by that flower or your friend's hair. At first, when walking in the woods perhaps all you will see is brown and green. With time you will need a new vocabulary for all the myriad nuances you can differentiate in every shade of brown and every shade of green. Our current selection of words to describe colour will suddenly seem clumsy, inadequate and almost meaningless as you strive to describe what you can see.

Once you have mastered noticing minute details, push your vision out a bit, don't just break it down. Look at the whole, the shapes, the shading, the shadow. Look up, look behind you, behind it. Notice the quality of light at different times of day, and year, and how this changes not only the colours, but where your attention is drawn. Look at the spaces between things, the shapes made in the darkness between leaves, the canyons between rock faces. This is a different way of looking, seeing the details *and* the shaped spaces between.

The more you see your surroundings, actually look at and notice what is there, the more you become aware of your place in the world and its cycles; it gives you context. Taking the time to really look helps you notice the subtle differences and changes in your world, it gives you a chance to respond; whether it is fresh prints of a large man-eating mammal, or the dusty evidence of wood worms chowing down on your favourite antique furniture. Being visually aware helps you generate a response to the ever changing environment, brings you in touch with the wild and able to read the messages embedded within it.

To visually connect is a wonderful opening of the universe. I recommend getting hold of a hand lens. It need not be expensive or fancy, mine is integral to my penknife. When you look that close, when you see into that almost microscopic world, wow! Each grain of pollen,

each shining glint of silica in a stone, each intricate pattern in a snow flake (looking at snow flakes especially, is a favourite pastime of mine in winter, mind blowing).

I love looking at flowers through my lens, it shows me so many intricate details that my naked eyes alone would miss. Some years ago I was learning from a Maasai medicine man in the Mukogodo Forest, in the shadow of snow peaked Mt Kenya. Through our interpreter we had been sharing wisdom for several days. My Maasai friend, Pilon, had been introducing many of his medicine plants to me. At one point he showed me a plant with such tiny inflorescences that I immediately took out my lens to get a closer look. Pilon had never seen such a thing and looked intrigued, so I offered him the lens showing him first how to use it. It was such an amazing moment - his eyes grew so wide, his expression was pure wonderment and joy, such that you never see in anyone but the most innocent child. In return he invited me to join him in a sniff of his sacred snuff that hung around his neck. I exploded in one sneeze after another. Tears and snot combined to make a dribbly mess off my face as I rolled on the floor in spasms, my nose doing its best job to expel the snuff as expeditiously as possible. Pilon was also rolling on the floor but in fits of laughter at my reaction. In the modern world we have all seen close up photographs and images from a microscope so I can't promise that your reaction would be as strong; but I can promise that you will be amazed when you see what is always there before us but usually goes unnoticed.

We tend to see what we understand and believe. I am sure everyone has heard the story of the South Americans unable to see the Spanish ships approaching their shores. Ships were outside of their realm of experience and so they did not recognise them and thus did not see them. What we see is actually our brain's interpretation of incoming electromagnetic waves; it is recognition that allows us to make that interpretation. I used to just see green hedgerows and not actually think much about it, perhaps noticing if there were patches of other colours. Now I see hundreds of individual plants in every square metre. I see so much detail: individual leaves, the different shades of each plant and each leaf of that plant. Each of those things tells me something - which is the oldest leaf, which is the youngest, details about the microclimate, whether animals are grazing there. Every step I take in the countryside

is like opening a fabulous detailed book, full of riches that would take months to read to fully appreciate all that is going on in that tiny space. Noticing with your eyes, seeing and recognising, opens the world up like a treasure chest.

No matter how much you work with your sight and paying attention you will still no doubt have to use screens on an almost daily basis. Remember to give your eyes a break every now and then, look away, look at something real. We all also need to venture from time to time into the neon overload of busy shopping streets and city centres. In those places you can keep your blinkers on, or you can choose to notice. Notice what is going on in the back ground, notice the things you have overlooked for all this time, passages, doorways, a new paint job, the grime, peoples shielded expressions. As you work with your sight you begin to notice more and more. The intricacies and beauty of your surroundings, things you may have taken for granted, things you have passed one thousand times but never stopped to look at, never actually seen. You discover a whole new level to the complexity of every thing that surrounds you.

Work with your sight most of all in natural surroundings. Discover and develop a new level of appreciation for the natural world as you see more of it. By seeing more you sink more deeply into it, and become more of an interacting, wild, part of it.

7.3 Touch

When we think about the sense of touch, most often our attention directs to our hands. All day, every day we are touching, testing, probing with our fingers and hands. The information is often relayed directly to the subconscious plane – messages about pleasure, pain, temperature, texture. Little snippets of information that keep us from burning or cutting ourselves and that direct us towards comfortable temperatures and textures. Think beyond your hands and fingers, try using other parts of your body to gather this information.

Our skin spends much of its time wrapped in clothing, insulated from the touch of the world. Find a private place on a warm day and stand naked, feel the warm breath of the breeze caress all 360° of your body. Lay naked on the ground, close your eyes and concentrate on the messages your skin is sending you. Feel the tickle of an insects feet, the soft damp grass, the dry warm dust. Allow yourself time for this,

enough time so that you find yourself melting into the Earth beneath you, becoming one with it. This exercise will leave you with a profound feeling of connection with the rest of Gaia, you will feel wilder. As the boundaries between yourself and other life blur slightly you will remember from where you came and you will recognise the other life-forms around you as extensions of yourself, as your relations.

Walking barefoot has a similar effect. You will get to know the rough and the smooth, and you will most certainly become much more conscious of where you lay your feet, where you tread. It is a very quick and effective way to build your relations with the Earth and with the places you walk. Try different textures: the grass in the park and the cold smooth stones of a river bed. Let your feet learn the different textures, pleasures and dangers, and tell you about them. Many of the suggestions in section 6.1 will have a more potent effect upon you, if your sense of touch is deeply engaged. Training your sense of touch to become more acute is simply a matter of consciously using that sense, of recognising the messages coming in from your skin and interpreting what they mean.

When you walk barefoot with confidence on a surface that is smooth, or that you trust is safe and not slippery or spiky, you become more aware of your whole body, your alignment, how you walk, how you stand. In my experience it has created better posture. In that moment I become aware from my toes to my crown and suddenly walking itself is a very different and more coherent experience. Shoes have allowed us to walk with confidence over any surface, in any weather, but what we have lost is the delicate balancing throughout every muscle and sinew in response to the Earth upon which we walk. Without shoes, my spine uncurls, my shoulders roll back, my head lifts and I am more steady on the ground. It makes me feel alive, well, vibrant, more animal, fitter. It tweaks all my senses that bit more. By connecting through your feet with the Earth you somehow become more whole and more coherent, more aware of your environment and your place within it, *wilder.*

Although our hands and fingers are already heavily used don't forget them in this re-sensitising practice. Use them to become intimate with your environment. Run them over soft round, sea smoothed pebbles and rough, scratchy granite. Feel your way around an arboretum; note the rough and smooth of a cherry trunk, the peeling softness of birch, the flaking discs of plane, the deep crevasses of oak. Experience as many different textures as you can find; explore them all. Really use

those hands, fine tune them. Returning to the skills of the blind once more remember that many blind people read by running their fingertips over tiny raised bumps, Braille. Again great attention to the remaining functioning senses allows detailed information to be gathered.

We are extraordinary sensual creatures, play with it, enjoy it. Take the back of your hand, or a finger, or your forearm and place it in front of your eyes. Now open and close your eyes, slowly, many times. Take time to notice and feel the exquisite tickling of your eyelashes on your skin. We touch our faces with our hands often, but have you ever taken the time to gently caress and explore every contour of your face? Take a single finger. Start at your hairline and gently move it down, around, across, your forehead, your eyebrow, your cheek bone. Trace the lines and shapes made by your nose, your lips. Take your time. There is so much to discover. So many subtle nuances that you have never noticed. Let yourself fall in love.

There is another dimension to touch. It occurs when touching another, whether it is a tree trunk hugged, a leaf through the fingers, a cat stroked or a horse patted. All of these actions involve touch and we give out messages about our intent and state of mind through that touch. We need to receive touch too as I have previously mentioned. Like their human relations primates suffer without touch; infant primates die, whilst adult primates with a deficit of touch become aggressive, we are not alone. We all know how good it feels to be touched. There is nothing like a huge full body hug with someone we love, even just a hand on the forearm or shoulder from a colleague can offer so much support, say so much, on a difficult day.

When *everything's alive* that support and companionship can be felt through our bare feet on the lawn, or back against a tree trunk. Even if you lack regular human touch there is something special that passes between you and other elements of this living Earth if you are conscious of them, their *livingness*, and the exchange.

Using all parts of our bodies to touch, as an interface with the world, helps us feel embedded within it. It gives us a deeper understanding of our

environment and encourages a strong connection to it. The extra dimension that emerges once you consciously touch another being helps you understand so much about the other's life; it is a doorway into their soul.

Explore your sense of touch. Practice touching many different textures and surfaces, not just with your fingers and hands. Be conscious of what you are touching, how it feels physically but also the feelings touching that thing engenders. Using touch in this way allows us a deeper look into the world, a glimpse into not just tactile sensations, but the *feeling* of a place, of a thing. *The pace of your rewilding accelerates.*

7.4 Smell

No perfume is lost to the unguarded nose, and that which bravely acknowledges the smells of the gutter surely feasts on a walk through the garden, truly delights in the olfactory playground of a lover's heated neck.

Jesse Wolf Hardin

Olfaction is the sense of smell. It is stimulated when odorous particles, normally volatile chemicals, attach to olfactory reception sites in the nasal cavity. The information received at the receptor sites is then transmitted to the olfactory bulb in the forebrain for analysis. Our sense of smell, or olfaction, is the detection and perception of chemicals in the air.

Taking in every smell we encounter in our daily lives would be a potentially unpleasant exercise; the stinking corner where drunks habitually urinate; the pungent stench of dog excretion; the rotting odour of decaying food on rubbish collection day. We each use our individual discretion to protect ourselves from these offensive signs of our *civilisation*. We choose when not to breathe in deeply through our noses or analyse the pervasive whiffs too closely.

To help ease our olfactory discomfort we have developed products to mask unpleasant odours such as air fresheners (although these can be highly unpleasant in themselves and irritating to the delicate nasal membranes). But smells are important. They can be indicators of many things, they can affect our well being and help us to understand our environment better. Smells can even help us choose a suitable mate as we detect and analyse the pheromones of the people around us - that is if they are not masked by perfumes, aftershaves or other artificial scents.

Start practising the art of smelling wherever you are, *use* your

sense of smell. Certain smells will be highly unpleasant but take them in anyway. Smell everything. With practice you will strengthen and fine tune your olfactory bulb. Use it for information gathering. Once finely honed at the art, remember that you can remove your attention from it at will, in effect switching to *standby* whenever you choose. I find myself tuning in to my sense of smell with greater intensity and frequency when in nature, or when presented with food; not so much when I'm faced with the open sewers of a third world city, or at the gym. You will begin to notice the subtle differences in the smell of the seasons, the incredible variety of wild flower fragrances and the different layers of smoky and sweet that combine to form the aroma of dry forest scrub.

Over the last 10 years, through teaching workshops and individual work with clients, I have encouraged many people to tune back into their sense of smell. As we place attention on our olfaction it is amazing how much information about the world around us we can unlock, and how quickly; how much intelligence our bodies inherently have if we just pay attention to the signals they are sending us.

Try taking some fresh leaves, use a plant that you know is regularly used for making herbal tea, perhaps stinging nettle. Brew a cup and while its vapours fragrantly rise to meet your nostrils take them in deeply. Close your eyes. First get a feeling for the smell. Is it subtle or strong, sweet or like a swamp? There are so many intricacies of smell and it will take time and practice to tune into them all. Most people I have undertaken this exercise with find it very difficult at first to even detect a smell. Stay with it and don't give up. If you smell nothing the first time try with other teas, different strengths, until you begin to notice the rising vapours as soon as the hot water hits the plant matter.

Once you have practised and mastered actually being able to smell acutely and notice different layers of smell, different qualities, then consider the messages your body is giving you in response to those smells. As you gently inhale your steaming cup of tea follow as the scent travels through your body. Where do you feel it? Where does it go? To your lungs, your chest, your stomach, your head? Breathe in deeply, and again. How are you feeling now? Are you feeling more peaceful or invigorated, perhaps a little happy or a little sad. Maybe as you relax and sink into the messages your olfactory bulb and your body are telling you you may see a colour or a vision. A bright yellow flower or a maiden in a meadow.

Then, read up about the properties of the herb you have been inhal-

ing. You will be stunned as many of the words, thoughts and feelings that sprung to mind as you were inhaling are listed as the plants healing properties. The volatile oils from the plant rose to meet those receptor sites in your nose, which stimulated a part of your brain, the result being that *you* knew the healing properties of that plant, or at least some of them, just by smelling it. This is even more fun when a friend collects the plant and makes the tea for you, so you don't even know what it is, I call this process a blind tasting[6], although perhaps at this stage it is more of a blind smelling. When your friend chooses the plant to be infused there is *no* chance of your head taking over and giving you information of where and what you *should* be feeling. Fine honing these skills means your nose can help tell you about the world, what is good to eat, what is not, what is medicinal, what makes you feel good.

With a little time and practice you will be able to tune in to smell with prowess, with an ability to detect multiple layers along with the origin of the smell and its meaning. You may already notice how perfumes and aftershaves leave a trail behind the wearer, with aptitude you may be able to go much further, to distinguish the brand of soap someone has used from a distance of several metres. Even very subtle aromas emanating from far away will reach you and tell you something about where you are, who you are with. There is a saying "I can smell a rat", once you know what a certain smell is, what it means, then you will literally be able to smell a rat. Once your brain can make the connection between a certain odour and a certain thing your experience of the world will expand as you begin to know what you are smelling. *Your experience of the world, of being an embedded part of it, deepens.*

Olfactory aptitude, just like the other senses, varies between individuals. It has been a long time since our species relied on it for survival, so genes with less than optimal smelling powers have been passed through the generations. As we have had to rely on smell less and less, evolution has failed to weed out the weaker smellers among us. I also believe that our ability to detect different odours varies perhaps throughout our life, like our ability to see. You may have once had perfect vision but now wear spectacles, could once hear perfectly but now need an aid. One thing I do know is that with attention and practice, whatever your start point, you will improve and what you can glean about your surroundings in turn will also improve.

*When exposed to any herb from a wide range of aromatics,
people experience physiological changes very similar to those
experienced by runners, meditators, and music lovers. This
means that regardless of the immediate effects on the mind of
any essential oil, the mere fact that we are interfacing with
a strongly scented plant puts us in the flow of events and
increases our capacity to adapt to stress and change.*

Guido Masé

Our sense of smell has a part to play in our overall health, not just our wildness and connection to nature. The medicinal use of strongly scented plants is documented in many ancient cultures including those of Egypt, China and India. Historically, aromatics have been used in many areas of physical health - from holding back infection such as the plague, to clearing lung and intestinal conditions[7]. More recently aromatics have been proven effective in killing pathogens, helping reduce both maternal and foetal stress, and assisting in the improvement of breathing, circulation and digestion.

Aromatic plants are high in volatile oils, oils that vaporise easily even at room temperature but more so when directly warmed by the sun on hot sunny days. Aromatic plants also release their smell as you brush past them. Deciduous forests are different. There you are not smelling volatile oils so much as the mulchy whiff of the cycling of life. Smells, aromatics especially, have a long track record for balancing mood and mental health.

Aromatherapy is a healing system which engages the sense of smell. It is based on inhaling aromatic plants or their essential oils (although they may occasionally be used topically or internally). Rene Maurice Gattefoss, a French chemist developed aromatherapy in 1928. His work inspired fellow Frenchman Jean Valnet who discovered that essential oils and fragrances were effective in the treatment of psychiatric disorders. Aromatherapy has been proven effective in the treatment of dementia, epilepsy, insomnia, anxiety, depression, headaches and nausea[8]. Some aromatics are stimulating others are sedating. Many are both; the fact is that scent affects mood. Whether you find it in lavender infused bath products to help you relax, or peppermint infused shower gel to help wake you up, aromatherapy is embedded in our lives and how we manage our moods.

I first began to understand aromatherapy whilst living in the Alpujarras in Andalucia, Southern Spain. As I walked and worked high

on the mountain slopes, I realised that with every step, like a flurry of butterflies or fairy dust, a gorgeous aromatic smell rose up to meet my nostrils. It was sublime and captivating and put me in a dream like state. I leant close to the Earth and realised the natural scrub I had been walking through was oregano, lavender and rosemary. I was astounded, never having seen these plants grow so happily, naturally and in such glorious abundance. How poor had I been until this moment, how neglected? It had taken until my late twenties for me to realise the joy of smell. Spending years with the stench of urban decay pervading every street corner, I had closed my sense of smell down, let it atrophy willingly, to save me from the smells we have chosen to fragrance our lives with.

I now understand how at one time walking on this Earth must have been a sensory delight, as so it still remains in the high Alpujarras. I have never forgotten this awakening. Later, in the arid mountainous regions of New Mexico again I felt it so, so strongly. I clearly remember attaining an ecstatic high, an altered state, purely through the smell of the woods at Cedar Crest. A warm, smoky, piney, junipery, delish. It engulfed me as I walked through certain patches. You can feel it being absorbed by your body, entering your blood stream with every deep lungful you take. That time I realised *I knew* how smell was indeed medicine. I realised that volatile oils are more than just a pleasant fancy to the passing nose. Through inhalation (and most often a deep one when it smells that good, no?) they infuse into the blood and travel around as minute particles delivering the blessings of the properties each one holds to places in your body that receive them. *That* is (wild) aromatherapy.

When an area is richly furnished with native plants, the smells become part of the medicine of that place. I wonder whether the smells from a particular area may help treat complaints typical of that bioregion; it would not surprise me. In natural settings we are constantly surrounded by plants and absorb their volatile oils. Just through breathing the plants of a locale become part of us. Just as now, all the artificial fragrances and unnatural chemical smells in the air of our modern homes are becoming part of us.

In Japan where shinrin-yoku, or forest bathing, is an accepted therapy (see section 3.2) research into the beneficial effects of inhaling air containing phytoncides (antimicrobial essential wood oils given off by plants) is ongoing. There are a host of benefits from inhaling deeply

at length in the forest, one of which is greater heart rate variability (HRV)[9]. This is necessary for a strong and healthy heart. People with greater HRV are more able to adapt to changing situations and deal with stress.

On the whole we are accustomed to familiar smells, they barely register unless we are really tuning into the smells in our environment, really using our sense of smell. It is new smells that inform us of a change, a new animal or flower (or bag of trash) in our immediate environment. You see animals reacting, stopping what they are doing, lifting their heads and inhaling deeply, looking for the source of the new smell. A new smell can immediately wake us from a wandering daydream or calm us out of panic. Smells can help us deal with the present moment, activating our wild selves and preparing our bodies for fight or flight. Smells, especially those of a vegetal origin can help us calm, centre and focus. Try crushing a sprig of fresh rosemary, inhaling deeply, and then continuing with a piece of left brain work (great for exams and revising students).

Through breathing in we absorb information about our environment. We inhale its medicine, and through that we connect with it, become part of it, and it a part of us. When natural landscapes are replaced with urban ones this connection is broken as we absorb artificial smells, traffic exhaust, plastics and upholstery. Make time for breathing in natural surroundings and be conscious of how it makes you feel, take that feeling with you and return to it when you need to.

We suffer so many symptoms when cut off from nature. They typically include anxiety, frustration, aggression, depression, insomnia, compulsiveness, attention deficit (see section 2.6). Yet our mental health can be balanced just by going into the woods or meadows and simply breathing in, especially on a day when the sun is shining, gently warming and thus accelerating the release of volatile oils. The smells we absorb through our nose, just like the food we absorb through our digestive tracts can be medicine, mood altering, toxic or benign. Aromatherapy has emerged as a therapeutic practice to help ease the ups and downs of a life dislocated from nature, but we would not need this medicine if we spent hours each day outside in the presence of plants inhaling and absorbing their natural medicine in situ.

...withdrawing the sense of smell leads to depression, fear, and apathy, then perhaps the gradual withdrawal of plant-based aromatics from our culture is also contributing to general malaise, poor attention span, and dark moods. Perhaps aromatics spark the spirit...

Guido Masé

Smell to be well so the saying goes. Let wildness into your deepest recesses by inhaling, by learning the origin of different smells and becoming aware of how different smells make you feel. Let your nose tell you about your world and let yourself become more deeply embedded within it.

7.5 Taste

Our taste buds are regularly over stimulated with artificial flavourings, with sugar, with salt. Depending on what you choose to eat and drink it may be that your taste sense is so used to being overloaded that it finds it hard to register the subtle, the unseasoned. To fine tune your sense of taste it is important to remove, or at least reduce, the quantity of seasoning, sugar and artificial flavourings you consume. At first this may seem drastic and your food may appear bland or even tasteless. Gradually you will build the ability to taste very subtle and delicate flavours, different notes, different layers. With time you will likely lose the desire for heavy seasoning or sugary foods, potentially finding that they leave a burning sensation on your tongue.

Go back to that cup of herbal tea you were using to fine tune your sense of smell. Once you have taken time to smell and experience each message your body received from smell alone, once you have exhausted that approach, then, when you are ready, take a sip. Just a small one. Savour the liquid in your mouth. Swill it around. Slowly, gently. Let it touch your taste buds and then flow around your mouth before swallowing. Allow yourself a moment to really taste it in all it's complexity. Is it spicy or bitter, perhaps sweet or salty? And again, take another sip. As you swallow follow the passage of the warm liquid through your body. Stop! Where do you feel it now? Where is it going in your body and how are you feeling? Does it coat your mouth and throat? Does it feel nourishing like soup? Sip by sip let it diffuse through your body and follow its movements. What is it telling you about itself? Does it feel good to you? Is it something that you need, that feeds you?

Now try this process with foods, not forgetting to fully explore where the smell takes you first. Start with single foods. Try fresh pineapple, it will tell you when you have eaten enough; your mouth will start to tingle. Suck every drop of juice from every mouthful, taste it, luxuriate in the moment, and enjoy the magical gift of fruit. Gnaw away slowly on an apple, take time to enjoy the flavour. Notice all the subtleties a single fruit can bring to your taste buds. As a child I would have been reprimanded for eating this way, it would have been considered playing with my food. But now, with the freedoms of adulthood, I can take my time, stretch my taste buds and allow them to tell me about what I am eating.

You can work through everything in your diet this way. Try a raw carrot, a stick of celery or a handful of nuts eaten one at a time. Chew well, take your time, feel the flavours dispersing on your tongue.

You can repeat this process with everything you drink and eat (both smelling first and then tasting). It is an amazing way to honour yourself and your incredible body, to be so conscious of every mouthful. When you break it down this far, to such a simplistic level there is a true knowing and a communion with what you are consuming. Eating and drinking become sacred acts, become moments of stillness and gratitude.

When you are familiar with the signature of individual ingredients begin to combine them. This works for herbal tea blends and food preparations alike. Become sensitive to what you are fuelling yourself with and how it makes you feel, both physically and emotionally. Try different flavours, both bitter and sweet, foods you have never tried before. If the combination does not feel so good to your newly sensitised body then go back a stage, what did you just add? Remove it and try it alone. Perhaps it is not good for you, does not agree with your individual constitution or body type.

It is also necessary to remain tuned in. Something that tasted good for the first few mouthfuls may start burning or tasting unpleasant. Too much of anything can become a poison. I find this especially true when eating plants, don't forget that many plants are medicinal and too much of any medicine becomes a poison.

When you taste something bitter your body will know not to eat too much. Bitter foods activate the detoxification mechanisms. They are essential for good health but too much can cause us to purge. Enjoy all the different flavours and a good variety of sweet, sour, bitter and

salty; but remain aware of how your body is feeling and know when to stop - when you have had enough.

Use this method when you delve into the world of wild foods. Of course be very careful with identification first, you don't want to eat something inedible. Once confident that you have the correct plant try tasting it slowly, just a nibble, and pause for a moment to absorb the taste. You will rapidly be aware if it feels good to you, if it is a food to add to your seasonal diet.

Through adopting and practising this greater degree of attention to taste when taking in food, you will begin to feel what you eat as both nutrients and medicine. You will notice the effects on your body and mind. You will *know* that food is medicine too. It's not just herbal teas and tinctures that provide your body with healing nutrients, with medicine, but *everything* that you put in it. Food either helps sustain, build, and feed your body or slowly degrade, leach, and damage it.

A developed sense of taste can help you make an informed choice about foods. What you would prefer to eat regularly and in abundance. When to gorge on a certain food and when you've had enough. It helps you to connect with what you are eating. It becomes a re-wilding process. Eventually you may naturally find yourself eating with the seasons, eating what's ripe and fresh, hanging out for a piece of fruit or a large green leafy salad and passing up a candy bar or a plate of fries for its preference. Both the foods we eat and our bodies begin communicating with us as soon as our taste buds are activated. Take the time to listen.

7.6 Fully Inhabiting This Sensual World

In our modern, urban, lives there is so much grabbing our attention we often choose to blank it out. Our senses are bombarded, but at the same time our sensory input is narrow in experience and origin as so many of the stimuli are created by humankind. This and the resulting underutilisation of our senses has led to a general atrophy of our sensory abilities. Natural surroundings are more gentle on us and give us a chance to use our senses without being overwhelmed, using our senses within natural settings is restorative. When our senses are immersed in natural stimuli it is healing for us, as aromatherapy has shown. Using our senses more fully when in nature brings us back

into balance with the world as we become more a part of it, rather than apart from it.

One way to fine tune the senses, to deepen your sensory experience, is to cut out as many inputs as possible so that it is possible to focus in on even the tiniest most subtle stimuli. This is what I was recommending in the hearing section; to strip it right back so that you can experience the individual layers of sensory stimulation, what they are, where they come from. Take it as far back as you can so that, as much as possible, you experience sensory deprivation. It sounds counterintuitive but removing as many sensual inputs as possible, allows clear focus on what is left.

My most intense experience was more by accident than design. I was exploring a cave in Laos with my husband, it went several miles into the deep darkness of the Earth. After walking for sometime we found a ledge to perch upon and sat there. We switched off our torches. There was no light penetrating this far from outside of the cave. None; it was completely dark. I could see nothing, really no difference between eyes open or closed. At first all there was was a dripping sound. Almost immediately I could distinguish several different drips, each coming from a different location, each with a different sound and a different tempo. Still the drips were few and far between. What I then began to notice was a warm damp movement of air on my bare legs and arms, it was enveloping me, absorbing me. A rhythmic flow of warm damp air pushing outwards from the innards of the cave. I could feel the Earth's out breath, all around me, and through me. My senses were tweaked and I was left with a feeling of humility, that I was surrounded by something greater than myself. I felt that I had been absorbed by it, become a part of it. I had not noticed or experienced that feeling previously while I was exploring the cave on foot and with my eyes. I needed to stop and experience the cave in its natural state, without my chatter, movement or artificial light, before I could tune into which senses it was actually touching, and what that meant to me.

Once you become proficient at using your senses, you naturally add the snippets of information you are receiving together. Even a fresh gust of wind arriving suddenly from the west can be full of information. Where I live such a breeze, felt by its cool tickle on my skin, alerts me to turn my head and look for the signals on the horizon. Most often they will

be there, thick grey clouds amassing over the Severn valley, I raise my nose and inhale, yes I can smell it, rain will follow soon. That little cool windy tickle was an early warning that rain is coming. There is an overlap and blending, or intertwining, of the senses. The incoming triggers for one sense activating the others as the body is faced with interpreting the information it is receiving.

Adding pieces of information derived from the individual senses together gives time to respond to the environment, to prepare, to take action. In this scenario it will be something simple; such as taking my drying laundry into the house before it receives a soaking; putting my tools away and planning a few hours of indoor activity; or hurrying to get the job in hand finished before rain stops play. That may not sound too wild but if I was walking in the mountains, where conditions change rapidly, having acute senses and reacting to them could be the difference between life and death.

The truth is once you are well polished at using your senses and can distinguish very subtle nuances, tiny pieces of information that to the unpractised are imperceptible, you have the potential to become dangerous. Mastery of the senses can work like a key, helping to unlock your sixth sense, your *feeling* sense. This sense I also call the animal sense because it is by-passing the logical left-brain thinking, it is felt by the heart, it is *feeling before thinking* (see chapter 5). It is feeling, instinct, intuition. It is an integral part of rewilding, necessary before you can fully inhabit your wild self.

With proficient use of the senses, including the feeling sense, like any wild animal you will be able to discern the weak from the strong, be aware of undercurrents and things that aren't as they seem. This, once again, is where it is important to trust yourself because your mind will talk you out of believing what your senses are telling you if it doesn't fit with what you thought you knew, or what no one else seems to have noticed. It is dangerous because, perhaps for the first time since infant-hood, it is easy to perceive the truth. This can upset the status quo certainly within your social life as your senses and feelings reveal a slightly different story than what you are being led to believe. This is the price you pay for having keen senses, for rewilding. You see beyond the charade to what is really before you. Like a new born baby, or a trusty old Labrador, people will no longer be able to hide

113

the truth from you. You will sense it, feel it. You can of course choose to ignore what you discover, but having access to the truth will change you nonetheless.

You will need to remember how to tune out of your senses so that you can survive in man made environments, so that you don't get overwhelmed and disorientated. But don't forget you were tuned out for years - you know how to do it. The gift is that with a little practice you also know how to tune in and there is nothing like having a multi-sensory connection to your environment for really easing your re-immersion into the wild.

Using your senses to their optimum makes you body smart, helps develop your body wisdom. Your feelings towards yourself change a little as you realise the beauty of your body and all its functions. You begin to see the sacred in yourself and *that* is a turning point. Because if you can learn to love, and respect, and consider yourself sacred, it follows that you will want to treat yourself to the very best. And if you continue to focus on your natural attributes as opposed to your designer handbag selection, then you will automatically know and feel what you need. Sky, wind, grass, raindrops, frosty mornings, mossy caverns ~ you will know what feeds you and will allow yourself to be drawn there. You will begin to understand that you are worthy of the greatest love, of being treated like a new born babe, an old growth forest, an intimate lover.

Perhaps the best advice I can give anyone wanting to re-sensitise, to experience the world with their senses, is to be as a child once more. To drop everything that you think you know, and then feel, sense your way around the world as if for the first time. Try not to miss a single detail, no matter how unpleasant or how minuscule. Take your time. Once you have given attention to everything you have noticed, you will most likely notice more. Stay with it, follow the trail. Then, only when you have felt the touch of each single piece, each dimension, of whatever it is that caught your attention, upon you. Only then, consider what this information is telling you about the world, about yourself.

114

The longer you spend and the deeper you go, the stronger the connection you will feel and the more you will learn. The more you use your senses, the more fine tuned they become. During this process, as your senses become increasingly acute, you will feel more alive, more whole, more wild.

8. EATING YOUR BODY WILD

Having embedded yourself firmly within this sensual world and become conscious of the sensory input you are exposed to, it becomes apparent that what you absorb through the senses contributes to your level of physical and mental health. Beyond the senses, everything you physically put into your body, everything you eat, drink or breathe, also contributes to your physical and mental well-being. These elements, the food, the water, the fresh air, are the raw materials which become new cells, your very body itself. We are literally made of the Earth. Our flesh, bone and sinew created from the fruits of our relatives, from the flesh of Gaia.

There are very few conditions we actually *need* for life but three minutes without oxygen and the brain starts to die. We have little direct control over the quality of the air we breathe, although our choices and lifestyles are what put atmospheric pollution into our lungs. Whenever you are in a location where the air is fresh feed yourself with deep lungfuls. Clean cool mountain air, salty fresh sea air; there are places where you can almost taste how clean it is. Take time to enjoy it when you have a chance to breathe some of the good stuff.

8.1 Water

You can go weeks without food, but only a matter of days without water. Our bodies are made from, on average, 75% water, providing fluid in every cell, lubricating and facilitating every function; even our bones contain 30% water. Water is a solvent which means that other substances can be dissolved in and transported by it. Water is the medium through which nutrients are transported from food into the blood which then delivers them to cells for metabolism. In other words it receives and transmits chemical information, but more than that, its molecular structure also allows it to function as a transmitter and receiver of vibrational information[1]. Information travels in, or through water, as do particulates, which indicates to me the importance of the source and quality of water that I put inside my body.

The health of our body cells relies upon a constant renewal process; to fuel that renewal we eat and drink. Water intake is required to replenish vital fluids and carry away wastes and toxins. If the water we drink is polluted, or of inferior quality, it will impact on our cell health ultimately causing us ill-health and premature ageing.

Wild water that has just gurgled its way through a spring on a

mountainside has a greatly different taste to tap water. It is not just the taste that is different, but the whole chemical make up and energetics (the vibrational information). Chemicals, such as chlorine and fluoride, are used to clean and treat municipal drinking water. These are treated as pollutants by our bodies, which then have to work hard to try and cleanse after consuming them. We celebrate being able to swim in wild water; anyone who has done so knows the difference between that and swimming in a concrete bound, chlorine filled, pool. With drinking water the differences are similar. The effects on your vitality and vibrancy reflect the wildness of the water that you enter, and that enters you.

Water has a natural spiralling action. Watch any natural water course and you will witness this as little eddies visible on the water surface. This spiralling action is a sign of live, wild, water. Healthy, fresh, wild, water also has a highly organised crystalline structure. I direct you to the work of Japanese scientist Masaru Emoto for some amazing photos in which he captures this[2]. Water has a memory and carries vibrational information in its structure, in intricate and beautiful shapes and formations. Emoto, when photographing water which had gone through a chemical treatment process and been fed through straight pipes, found it had lost that highly organised crystalline structure. Tap water and polluted water instead display a disorganised, formless pattern. Water lacking organised structure (tap water) cannot efficiently carry vibrational information and so will not replenish us in the same way that beautifully structured fresh wild water crystals do.

Spirals are to be found everywhere in nature (even DNA is composed of twin spirals). If water cannot naturally spiral it loses energy and other important qualities. This is in part because as it spins it breaks and reforms molecular bonds, creating and recreating, over and over, new combinations of the elements it is carrying. This allows for an ongoing interchange and exchange of electrons raising the electromagnetic energy of the water[3]. Without the spiralling action there is less electron exchange, and so the energy embodied in the moving water becomes less.

It is clear, to me, that wild, energised, water with a highly organised crystalline structure is preferable to chemically treated water with an amorphous structure and low energy. Wild water allows your body to renew and rebuild a more wild and cohesive version of itself. So

whenever possible collect wild water, that is spring water, although, unless you are collecting from a high mountain source, ensure that your spring is regularly tested for contamination by pollution and chemical run-off. It is preferable to store your wild water in an egg shaped earthenware jar. This shape encourages the natural circulation of water, thus avoiding the stagnation issues that beset wild water once it is taken from its source and stored.

If wild water is unavailable to you use a whole house filter, or jug filter, on your tap water to remove the chemicals, and then a device to re-energise the water. There are a number of different products available for re-energising water as a quick internet search will reveal. The most simple being a funnel with a metal spiral in the spout which encourages water flowing through it to form a vortex bringing a healthy flow pattern back into the water as you pour it before drinking. Failing all else stir figure of eight spirals into tap water before drinking to re-energize it.

Most importantly of all remain hydrated. No matter what the quality of your drinking water, if you do not drink enough both your physical and mental health will suffer, as dehydration can exacerbate arthritis, asthma and digestive problems alongside many forms of pain in the body, stress and depression[4]. Dehydration can also affect ability to concentrate and energy levels. All too often when the body cries out for water it is misinterpreted as hunger, and so we eat instead. Unless the snack chosen to sate that perceived hunger is fresh fruit or raw and watery vegetables, it will only make our thirst more intense, potentially leading to overeating and weight issues in the long term. You will never be at peak fitness, wild, sharp and agile if your body lacks fresh water.

Finally, when you get an opportunity, try drinking directly from the source of flowing water, sucking the moving water into your mouth without the use of hands or a drinking vessel. It tastes and feels clearer, fresher. It is not likely that you will be in a position or location to do this very often, so when you do get the chance give it a whirl and drink like a monkey.

8.2 Our Relationship To Food

The ways we gather, prepare and consume food have increasingly changed over the last few hundred years as life for humans drifted from nature and became more urban. As we lost direct engagement with growing and harvesting, we lost contact with what goes into the

food on our plates and how it got there. It is a physical separation, and through it we have lost touch with what it is our bodies are made from, and in turn with our bodies themselves; their wild, animal, nature.

To reconnect with our bodies we must reconnect with our food; one cannot come without the other. The first step towards understanding your food and what you are fuelling and building your body with is to make the food that you eat yourself. Choose fresh ingredients and, as much as possible, make every meal from scratch. Even if that means cooking in bulk at weekends and freezing into daily portions.

If you eat ready meals, convenience food, it will have been prepared in a factory, on a production line, a bit like your car. It will perhaps have been made by machines, stirring ingredients in huge vats and squirting a measured quantity into its plastic tray. It can be contaminated by foreign bodies, not only mice and cockroaches but, as the UK horse meat scandal of 2013 demonstrated, other unintended and dubious ingredients. By eating this kind of food you give control of the ingredients that combine to make *your* flesh and blood over to a company whose entire raison d'être is profit. Even ethical companies that promise a healthier choice are driven by their business plan. Their priority, at the base level, is to thrive and to do so they must make money for the owner or share holders. On its own the drive for profit does not necessarily translate to low quality food and ingredients, but economies of scale do generally mean that it will be made in huge batches by machines. Food that is hand made in small batches would be preferable – the hand that makes it ideally being yours, or one belonging to someone who loves you.

Why is preparation by hand important? Return for a moment to the final section of chapter 3 where I briefly discussed quantum exchange, the vibration of everything, and its connection in one great unitive field, or web, of particles all exchanging energy. Well, that exchange as I mentioned at the time, includes information, it is a communication. Therefore when you are making food, as you prepare it, your intention is being communicated and absorbed by it on a quantum level. When you and your family eat, your bodies not only absorb the minerals and nutrients contained in the physical food but also the messages and intentions imparted on an energetic level. If a big factory production line is making your food then no matter how many seasonings are added to create a tasty dish, it will always somehow be missing something, and that something is the message on the quantum level, the *intent*. If

you eat fresh and ripe, straight from the tree, the communication will be direct from nature, directly from the tree, and the soil, and the sun, and the rain. When you have manipulated the ingredients by chopping, mixing and cooking, but have the intentions of good health and the well being of the recipients in your heart, then that is the message they will receive when they eat it. Don't pass this off as hippy hogwash, this is how the universe works[5].

It is not just how the food is prepared that is of importance when on the wild path. To rebuild a direct relationship with the food you eat you need to be aware of its provenance, its origin and traceability. For each ingredient used it's knowing where on the planet it grew, whether it is fair trade, whether it was grown organically or raised free range. Without a basic grasp of those facts, food is still just something that you buy from the shops, something lifeless that has no more meaning or significance than a plastic cup, or a car part. The easiest way to get to the root of a product's provenance is to buy from local producers.

8.3 Local And Seasonal Foods

Becoming aware of what is in season and what grows locally, or at least within your bioregion, forges a connection with the land and with the plants and animals that grow and graze on it. A great resource is the resurgence of farmers markets. In the UK, most small towns, and even many inner city areas, now have regular markets where local producers can sell their goods directly to the public. Their reappearance is good news. Ever since people began migrating from the land to the towns, local growers always sold their produce at the local market, throughout most of the world this has never changed. Yet over the last few decades, with the industrialisation of food production and appearance of massive supermarkets, this form of commerce was on the decline and in some areas actually disappeared for a while. Now it is possible once again to buy local foods from local producers; to have the opportunity to build your trust and relationship with the person growing your food; to reconnect with the produce that can grow and thrive in your local area. Other options for buying directly from the producers include farm shops, veggie box schemes and deliveries from local farms and fishermen to your door.

Sourcing your food locally will make you more aware of seasonality, which foods are available when. Because of its axial tilt, this oblate spheroid experiences changes in climate in different places at different

120

times of the year; we have seasons. I love the changes that come with the different seasons. Look outside, what you see in July is very different from that which you see in January. No matter where you live very few places do not change with the seasons. Even the tropics and equatorial regions have rainy and dry seasons and variations in temperature and humidity despite the relatively static number of daylight hours. In the winter, where I live, most things have the appearance of being dead or dormant, spring is an explosion of leaf and blossom, summer a ripening of fruit, autumn the last of the harvest and the start of the annual die back. This is the cycle. Technology and transport have overridden it. We can now eat strawberries and asparagus year round, outside of their natural season.

However, despite heating and air conditioning, we cannot climate control the outside environment, so in summer we wear less, winter more. In hotter months we tend to eat lighter foods, salads and fruits. In the colder months we tend towards soups and hearty stews. This ties in perfectly with what is naturally available in those different seasons. The cold months are all about root vegetables, cabbages and food that has been carefully stored and preserved. Hot months are full of fruit and leaves. It is easy to eat with the season, your body wants you to.

Seasonal eating becomes even easier if you choose to grow your own or become involved in a local CSA (community supported agriculture) scheme[6]. As a grower you will have periods of excess where you will get to gorge on a particular fruit or vegetable. By the end of that particular harvest you will be quite happy to not eat it again for eight or ten months. Although, on its return, that first taste will be a celebration and a delight. As a side note, no matter where you live you can grow something. My first foray into growing edibles was a few tomato plants on the fire escape of my building in the East End of London.

It is not always possible or practical to buy from local producers but remain aware of your food's provenance. Start looking at labels and refuse to buy products from the other side of the planet that could be produced locally. Apples grow well in both the UK and New Zealand, most of what appears for sale in UK supermarkets is imported from New Zealand 11,000 miles away. The implications and knock-on effects of this are massive. What a ridiculous waste of transportation and storage! In the mean time orchards and local apple varieties in the UK are

being lost. Reserve your food miles for dried produce such as rice that does not spoil en route and that cannot be grown in your climatic zone. Local varieties are adapted to local conditions such as soil and climate. The balance of vitamins and minerals vary with such things and come through to the consumer as differences in flavour and texture. There is the additional consideration of ripeness. A fruit grown in hot sun and harvested at the peak of ripeness will be so much sweeter than a fruit harvested early then transported and stored for weeks in refrigeration units. It makes sense to eat locally grown as you will get a higher quality end product; fruits and vegetables that are actually fresh and ripe. If you have spent a long time purchasing and consuming imported fruits and vegetables from the supermarket try fresh, ripe, and local and you will experience a flavour sensation that will have you hooked.

Eating local foods means eating the fruits of the land upon which you stand. You are eating the local soil and weather conditions, and they are becoming a part of you, of your physicality. The weather conditions become important to you as you wait for your favourite crops to ripen, red berries and crisp apples. You become less dislocated from your environment as your cells start to be built and replaced with locally occurring elements. The minerals of the local soil become the minerals of your body and Gaia gets to reclaim a little bit more of you.

8.4 The Evolution Of Food Production

Humankind have adopted selective breeding since the dawn of agriculture. Seeds of the strongest, tastiest, most productive and disease resistant plants were saved to be sown the following season. This method is an obvious way to ensure successful crops with desirable qualities suited to a specific area. In agrarian societies seeds have been saved and passed down through the generations, thus through careful selection and natural variation, hundreds of different varieties of each type of plant have evolved. I consider this quite a natural process, the variation between suitability for different soils and micro-climates becoming inbuilt within the naturally occurring seed.

Along came industrialised farming and seed producers, where maximising the potential yield became a science in a sterile laboratory with minimal consideration of the varying environmental factors in different locations. Clever marketing strategies have ensued the world over convincing even the smallest subsistence farmers in rural communities to adopt modern genetically engineered varieties with the promise of

less work and greater returns. What has been lost along the way is the wonderful variation between the seed of neighbouring farms, one plant better suited to the steep bright valley sides, another to the shady damp valley bottom. Suddenly, worldwide, everyone is growing the same variety of seed, and to achieve their promised potential, increasing quantities of pesticide, herbicide and fertiliser are needed. This is the concern of the post GM (genetic modification) world and an issue when attempting to eat yourself wild.

Diversity is key to a wild diet. Like our ancestors once did, modern day hunter gatherers consume an estimated range of between 100-300 different varieties of plant each year[7]. In contrast, currently just three plants, wheat, rice and maize provide more than half of the global plant derived energy[8]. That means that the average person, worldwide, is eating a much more limited range of foods than our ancestors, and than modern hunter gatherer societies. Clearly there are health implications, the answer to which, as conceived by modern agri-business, is to fortify the limited range of foods we do still eat with the missing vitamins and minerals that would be present in a diverse and healthy wild diet. What this translates to is further genetic manipulation of our food plants.

There is a whole generation of modern plants that have been engineered so far from their natural origins that they either do not produce seed at all, or the seed they do produce is not viable. If this pattern occurred in nature it would end there, with that generation, as there would be no viable seed to produce the next generation. Could there be a link between eating such infertile foods and problems with human fertility? The issue is clearly not that simplistic, but somewhere on the quantum level when eating such foods we are absorbing messages about the lack of need for viable seed, worthy of a moment's consideration at least... I digress. Either way such foods are hybrids, they are not as nature intended. After all, the whole of nature is just one long mating frenzy (come on, it's everywhere around us). Evolution, survival of the fittest, life, it's all about having strong viable seed to produce updated, upgraded, stronger, fitter versions of the previous generation and ultimately spreading that precious seed. Think before you buy next time you see seedless grapes or watermelons for sale. These hybrid plants have the seed bred out of them so that we don't have to pick them from between our teeth. They are bred to be sweeter, larger, smoother, more appealing to our ever evolving taste, but they are not wild, and will stunt the growth of our individual wildness when eaten in excess.

Excessively bred plants are very often particularly sweet, even beetroot and carrots have been engineered to a point that is far from their wild, bitter, relatives. Our bodies have to work hard to digest the unnaturally concentrated sweetness and we develop a taste for it. Some plants have been so highly manipulated by breeding that they have become simply indigestible to large sections of the population. Modern wheat provides one such example. Many people have difficulty digesting wheat gluten. Even if you have never registered it as an issue you may bloat a little after eating bread or pasta, perhaps you get lethargic or sleepy as your body struggles to process the unnatural glue you are feeding it with. However spelt, which is an ancient ancestor of modern wheat, although also containing gluten, is much more digestible for most people. Spelt gluten is more soluble, and the whole grain closer to its wild, natural, form.

The strength of modern engineered seed, like modern farmed animal breeds, is weak in comparison to its wild relatives. When left to go feral some cultivated plants, and likewise some livestock breeds, fare better than others. Wild plants do not need watering or weeding, they are tough, they find their niche and they grow. As soon as possible they produce seed or spread vegetatively to ensure the continuation of the species to the next generation. The same is true of wild animals. In my neighbourhood there is common land where deer, rabbits, foxes and badgers survive and thrive year round, but the cattle, which graze there in summer, are collected in winter and cared for under shelter. The wild badgers are coming under fire, quite literally, as they are carriers of tuberculosis (TB) which crosses into the cow population causing all kinds of issues for the farmers. But, the badgers thrive despite the presence of TB within their population. The deer, fox and rabbits too live in great quantity without the need for winter pampering, extra food, hormone or antibiotic injections. Their populations are wild, and they remain able to adapt to the seasons and survive outbreaks of disease. It seems in the non-natural populations, animal or vegetal, there is a kind of dilution of life force and general ability to survive in the wild. By eating these cultivated and bred foodstuffs we are building our bodies with inferior, weak, genes that need pampering and extra help to survive the harshness of the wild. Wild foods are more resilient by nature; they have to be, and by eating them we feed and renew our bodies with a little more resilience, a little more wild spirit.

One step closer to wild food, but still within the realm of cultiva-

tion, is commercially grown organic food. Some organic producers use heirloom seed, seed that has a history of local use and is suited to the local conditions - it may even have been saved by generations of the same family that is currently cultivating with it. The same can be true of livestock bred organically; old, local breeds. If you grow food, it is possible to acquire such seed and then commence the process of saving it for yourself. If you keep livestock (chicken keeping especially seems to be rising in popularity) you can also search out old, local breeds to raise.

Any chemicals applied during the production of crops will be passed on to the consumer, if not directly as residue, then by the poisoning of the land. Every time the land is compromised with pollution, with chemical fertilisers, herbicides, pesticides, run off from manure piles, we are inadvertently being poisoned. Think about it. Remember our connection with everything, with all life. Any chemical put into our environment is also being put into our bodies through the air we breathe, water we drink, soil we walk bare foot upon. Any antibiotics, artificial hormones, and other chemicals injected into conventionally farmed animals remain as toxins in the flesh, even if just in homoeopathic amounts, when those animals are slaughtered and subsequently consumed.

Organic production avoids using chemicals. It is not a perfect system but it is infinitely better for the environment, and the quality of the foodstuffs it produces than more conventional, chemical heavy, production methods. As much as possible buy organic. It, as everything in life, is a choice, but this one is not just for you now but for the future of your children and the integrity of Gaia as a whole. It is an investment in the wildness of the planet, your wildness, and all our futures.

8.5 Wild Foods

Nature was of course the original organic producer. Everything adapted to its local micro-climate and physical conditions. All the plants and animals in a fluid dance, balance but not static, constant micro-adjustments in response to any minor variation in the environment and in the evolution and status of each other. One life form gets knocked back by disease, or becomes too tasty and is over grazed, another will soon arrive to take its place. In the little pockets of nature that still surround us this process is ongoing. Human behaviours and habits generally have a greatly destabilising influence over the natural balance, but that influence fades the further from human habitation and frequency of human interference and disturbance you go.

Wild, uncultivated foods feed you with resilience, with strength. I have grown food for many years watering, weeding, feeding, nurturing. I have never watered a dandelion or an elder bush, never fed a nettle or a bramble patch but year on year despite being cut back, neglected, even sprayed with chemicals by some, they faithfully return bringing diversity to the local ecology and food for your plate - if you want it. If you eat meat, consider that neither rabbits nor deer need antibiotics or winter feed, they know how to survive, how to thrive, in the wild. By eating such foods you are introducing a little more of their wild spirit to yours each time, taking on their characteristics bit by bit. You will get closer to nature, enliven more of your wildness, by eating directly from nature.

As I have already mentioned, there is a slight issue emerging from the recent surge in foraging and interest in wild foods. It is great that people are waking up to the foods nature is providing all around us, even those bursting forth from urban pavement cracks. However, there are a lot of us and so we must be responsible and only take a little, just what we need and nothing more. Could you imagine how impoverished our world would be if enthusiastic foragers pushed the simple delight of dandelion to extinction? Responsibility is essential.

Spread the wild seed, help your favourite foraged foods become more abundant in your neighbourhood. There is always room for a bit of gue-rilla gardening, planting wild edible foods on grassed verges and among municipal planting schemes, so that there will be more than enough wild foods for all our relations. Think carefully about buying anything labelled as wildcrafted, is it collected sustainably? Ask the questions of your sup-plier and if they don't know, it means they have not stopped to ask the question themselves. Concentrate on the wild foods that are local to you, that *you* can collect responsibly. Some wild plants are being stripped, their abundance reduced so much that their ability to continue to the next gen-eration is being threatened. Do not contribute to this.

If you have a garden let the wild edges in. Most of my foraging takes place in my garden and on my allotment. Brambles grow behind the wooden steps up to the deck, the lawn is an orgy of edible (and medicinal) plants. I grow horseradish in a tub and encourage a small patch of nettle to thrive between the St John's wort and evening prim-rose. Elderberry and rosehip overhang my boundaries. Bullace, haws and damson edge my allotment. The wild, very much, has come to me; but still I must go to the wild for deeply bitter sloe.

Wherever you collect from, remember to acknowledge the living-ness of the thing. To ask and thank. To notice where it thrives, whom it lives amongst, its character. Build a relationship with that plant, with that food. If you eat meat and are hunting, the same goes, of course. Whatever you are responsibly harvesting from the wild remember that the more wild you eat, the more wild you become.

You have to eat a little wildness for it to flow through your veins, otherwise everything you eat will have been manipulated by human-kind in some way or other, domesticated, and what sort of animal would that make you? The more wild you eat the more in tune with the land you become; the more you taste it with every sense; the more it becomes you and you become it. On a practical, and somewhat less poetic level, the more wild and local you eat the less landfill you pro-duce (packaging), instead just a little compost.

Slowly we become more like the hare and the hedgehog.

Eat the wild foods you can, when you can. Even if it is just a few leaves of lime, beech or hawthorn (wild indigenous foods, prolific in my neighbourhood) when on a spring walk. You will actually be amazed how little you need. One or two beech leaves makes my whole body sing, yet I can eat a huge plate of store bought spinach, fresh and raw, and not achieve the same feeling, the same satisfaction, the same high. Now we can't all eat wild foods all the time; if you live in a city location it will generally be an occasional treat. Even country dwellers, certainly in the temperate zone, will be limited by seasonality. Spring builds and builds with variety and quantity of wild foods, to a veritable feast, whereas during the dark days of mid-winter the wild pickings are sparse. So wherever you are, you will have to supplement your diet with cultivated foods. Consume them as fresh as possible in their raw, unadulterated, form, and although they will not be able to deliver the messages of wildness that your wild self yearns for, at least they will not be delivering the imprint of factory production lines.

As humankind became more and more domesticated over the last few hundred years, as we migrated to cities and away from the land, the variety and quantity of wild plants the average person consumed de-clined in response. Modern farming has taken over from our herb eat-

ing agrarian ancestors as an efficient way of feeding the urban masses. Most fields are largely devoted to growing carbohydrates whereas bitter tasting foods (the overriding taste of many wild foods) have generally dropped off the menu.

Wild sweet foods, such as fruit and honey, contain fibre that slows their absorption by the body. Unfortunately the modern human sates much of their urge for sweetness with refined white sugar. Such processed sweetness travels very swiftly through the body, through the gut and into our bloodstream. This is problematic as our bodies have not had the chance to evolve quickly enough to remain in step with our changing eating habits. The novel items that we currently consider foods are greatly distanced from their wild, unprocessed counterparts and are proving to be more and more difficult for our bodies to function well upon.

Our bodies need bitter foods. Bitters slow the entry of sugar into the bloodstream, while the taste curbs our appetites as our inbuilt body wisdom reminds us that too much will make us purge, and so we eat less. At the same time, bitters make us more sensitive to insulin[9], so straight away there is an emergence of understanding as to how bitter foods can help us remain well, and perhaps combat obesity and Type II diabetes (symptoms of domestication).

Even just a generation or two ago, bitters were taken as an aperitif, in some cultures it is still very common to consume a plate of leaves before the main course. In such circumstances the body will react to the introduction of bitters, by not only limiting calorific intake and helping to regulate blood sugar, but also by stimulating the release of digestive juices and aiding in liver detoxification. I recommend everyone include them at mealtimes, especially if you suffer with bloating, gas, or any other symptoms that relate to sluggish, congested or inefficient digestion. But bitters do more. Their ingestion also encourages resilience and strength by helping the immune system function effectively whilst reducing inflammatory responses within the body (which when out of balance contribute to many modern conditions).

Many wild foods of the vegetal realm whether bitter or not often have an alkalising effect on the body. As food is digested it needs to reach the slightly alkaline pH of 7.4 before it can can be absorbed efficiently by the blood and utilised within the body[10]. This pH is required for full immune potential and enzyme activity. If it veers off from this average balance point the blood will do what it can to regain its preferable pH. Meat, dairy, cooked, and convenience foods all contribute to

an acidic condition. Once the blood is out of balance, acid forming minerals are precipitated out of the blood and accumulate in muscle, tissue, bone and joints, these accumulations can lead to arthritis[11]. The blood will also leach alkaline minerals from the bones in an attempt to regain its alkalinity, which with time can damage the integrity of the bones and potentially lead to osteoporosis[12]. On the other hand, eating a good quantity of wild, bitter, raw, leaves is soothing and calming to the body, alleviating stress and relieving pain[13].

Your domestic canine companion may end up with arthritis from eating the dog version of convenience food (canned dog meat), but you rarely see wild animals struggling with painful inflamed joints. Maybe it is that as soon as they lose good health they become prey and never get the chance to develop crippling conditions, or it could just be that with a natural life and natural diet they are absolutely unlikely to develop such a condition in the first place.

Wild animals can be witnessed seeking out and consuming the various minerals that their bodies need to function efficiently, that is visiting salt licks. Even yesterday driving back from the DIY store I noticed sparrows nibbling at the road grit (salt) bins at the corner of a steep hill. A wild animal will listen to its body and act to meet it's needs. Not many humans can claim to be that fine tuned when it comes to eating; even if they consider themselves to eat a well balanced, healthy diet (but it *is* possible).

🌰

Cultivated vegetables are the tame relatives of wild plants, as we are the tame relatives of our wild ancestors. Wild plants are so much richer, more resourceful and vibrant than their vegetable cousins. Despite our domesticated condition we still fit together with wild plants like a hand in glove; we were meant to co-exist. They interact with our being on all levels; it is not just our physical bodies that miss their presence when they are absent in our diet, but our state of mind as we miss our interaction with the individual personalities of these, our wild green relatives. I encourage you to collect and eat wild food to expedite the transition from domestic to wild; to grow your wildness. Gathering wild fruits, leaves and roots, connects you with other life, with the land you live upon, and the food you build your body with. Consuming these foods will act not just in your heart and mind, but in your cells, in your flesh. And as currently, many of us suffer from the results of hybrid,

129

processed, unnatural diets to differing degrees, the wild foods in fact are providing medicine, *the medicine of the wild.*

8.6 Wild Medicine

Since the dawn of time plants have been blended into healing brews and potions for all kinds of ailments. Even in this time of modern pharmacology many medicines derive from plant origins, even if the active ingredients are most often isolated, synthesized and ultimately chemically modified. Animals self medicate with herbs and plant foods. In her fabulous book, *Wild Health,* Cindy Engel gives many examples of animals turning to plants they do not habitually eat as a part of their regular diet when they are unwell; when they have an infestation of intestinal parasites, for example. Our ancestors also used plant medicines. They were all we had until quite recently and the advent of modern pharmacology (with it's synthesized and modified versions of plant medicines). Human populations around the world still rely on plant medicines where access to modern health care is limited or absent.

I like to encourage people to forage for medicines in their locale, the same as foraging for food. Make a connection with the wild plants, take the time to get to know what grows where, and how it can be used to help treat minor ailments; colds, flu, digestive issues and the like. Again it will connect you with the land, with the seasons, with other life forms, with your wildness.

Knowing which plant to rub on a sting to reduce the inflammation, and which plant to use as a poultice to staunch bleeding, is a very useful thing[14]. Some herbs, or plant foods however, are more than physical medicines but are also medicines that can help with balancing our emotions, our mental health. Two examples that spring to mind are St John's Wort (*Hypericum perforatum*) and primrose (*Primula vulgaris*). Both examples assist with the treatment of mild cases of depression (amongst other things). St Johns Wort can be ingested as a tea, primrose can be eaten, fresh leaves and flowers mixed in with a spring salad.

Plant medicine goes further, beyond symptomatic treatments. The fact is that food is medicine. When you eat the right foods, in the right balance, your food keeps you well. As I have said before, whatever you feed yourself with will either help build and nourish your body, or help deplete, damage and destroy it; very few things are neutral. Wild raw foods provide essential minerals delivered at the correct pH. Wild raw foods can help your body regain its natural balance, reducing stress, pain, inflammation

and the chances of developing long term and degenerative conditions. I cannot stress enough the importance of diet in our overall physical and mental health; and our fundamental connection to the rest of nature.

Raw plant foods (from herbs to fruits and everything in between) are the single most effective antidote to anxiety, depression, disease, fear, immobility, insomnia, pain, stress and worry!

David Wolfe

The European Nutrition for Health Alliance (ENHA) has estimated that up to 40% of people admitted to hospital in the UK are malnourished on admission[15]. That says two things; that a lot of regular people walking amongst us are actually malnourished (despite the obesity epidemic); and that malnourishment is prevalent in an awful lot of people who are sick and seeking treatment. If your body does not receive all the ingredients it needs to function well then at some point it will cease to function well. Just as a car needs the correct fuel, oil, water, anti-freeze, coolant, and without the correct balance at some point it will end up either at the mechanics for a serious overhaul, or at the scrap yard. There is no great mystery; living and eating more naturally is the key to great physical and mental health. Assuming that the food you eat does not in turn affect your overall health is as foolhardy as assuming that drinking vodka will not affect your ability to drive safely.

Go back to the taste section (7.5) in the Sensual World chapter, read it again and practice it. Become aware of how each thing you put in your mouth makes you feel. Once you become adept at this you can use food to fine tune your health, and with refinement it is possible to be able to take it to the point where you notice that you need something, and know what that something is. When you consume with consciousness and intent, it brings a whole new meaning to eating and herbal medicine, to relationships with food, to life itself. Don't underestimate your own body wisdom.

Wild medicine it should be noted, is not just ingested plants, that is herbal remedies, or even diet. It extends beyond that, to the healing power of nature experiences (in part what this book is about). When entering deep nature with intent there is often an accompanying shift in consciousness, a heightening of the feeling sense, a movement towards feeling your way around the wild with your heart. I have

mentioned this feeling sense several times before, but what I have not yet mentioned is its beneficial effect upon your physiology. Entering such a state in a natural setting leads to a quietening of the autonomic nervous system and the release of endorphins. The knock on effect of which is a lowering of blood pressure, a reduction in heart rate, increased feelings of calmness and tranquillity; the medicine that so many of us need.

8.7 Raw Food & Remedial Work

The design of our gut and teeth are ideal for a plant-rich fibrous diet, not the current norm which is high in carbohydrates and animal protein, while low in fibre[16]. The wild medicine diet should, unsurprisingly, be high in raw fruits and vegetables, as provided by nature. You don't often see a tortoise sat next to a deep fat fryer waiting for his dinner. Cooking, frying, baking, the different processes we put our food through, are all a step away from how food is presented to us in the wild.

Low energy levels can often be traced to enzyme depletion in the body, caused and/ or exacerbated by a diet full of cooked and processed foods. It becomes a negative feedback loop as sugar, carbohydrates and caffeinated drinks are then consumed in a search for energy. In addition, vast quantities of energy are required to digest heavy and processed foods, again leaving us energy deficient. Ever dozed off after Sunday lunch? That is your post meal slump as your digestive system is overwhelmed and all your energy is redirected to deal with it.

Raw foods on the other hand take you to a wild state; energised, more sensitive, more aware. This may well be due to the alkalising effects of such a diet on your system, leaving your body and brain in a more natural condition. With a diet high in raw plant matter (fruits, roots, leaves, nuts) your senses become heightened, including your feeling sense, you become more intuitive. You can feel eyes upon you and turn to notice a spider high up on the wall, not turning and searching for what it is and where, your eyes go straight to it.

Adopting a diet high in raw plant foods has been a very powerful element of my personal rewilding. You will know and understand what I am saying if you choose to work towards it yourself. Some people may experience the state you gain from a high raw diet as ungrounded and find it difficult to participate within society as you usually do (sitting behind that desk all day). It is in fact a state of extreme connection where wildness is flowing freely through you, so yes it can be difficult

to continue with your pre-wild ways, as with all the suggestions in this book it comes with that caveat.

🌳

Raw food is original food, it's what has been here since the beginning of time. Our ancestors learned how to use fire to change the texture, taste, and chemistry of that food. We learned to process and combine foods in different ways to generate different sensations and flavours. But our bodies have not evolved fast enough to effectively gain the necessary nutrients from the modern processed foods. Just in my lifetime foods have changed by an incredible degree, in my mothers even more so. No matter what you think, it would be pretty difficult to argue that the massive jump in intestinal evolution necessary within those two generations has occurred.

It is not just the increase in consumption of carbohydrates and animal proteins, but the explosion in use of artificial flavourings and ingredients (hydrogenated fats, for example) alongside the chemical changes that occur as a side effect of processing. It goes even further when you begin to consider the state of the seed conventional agriculture currently uses; modified and coated in neonicotinoids[17] (if they're killing the bees what are they doing to us?). How do we digest all that with an intestine built for a plant-rich fibrous diet?

No wonder people overeat, their bodies desperate for nutrients to actually feed, to fuel, them with food they can digest. No surprises the "developed" nations are in the midst of an obesity epidemic – it is our bodies natural panic reaction to a diet devoid of nutrition – just keep damn eating until you get something useful inside.

🌳

Adopting a diet high in raw plant food is a complex issue especially as many people feel threatened when it is suggested that they change their diet. So, just for the record, this is not a criticism of anyone, or anyone's lifestyle. Like the rest of the book, suggesting experimentation with a raw plant food diet is just that, a suggestion, something to try in the quest to reclaim your wild nature.

When increasing the quantity of raw plant foods in your diet it is important to look at what is growing around you and take cues from nature. In the summer months it is natural to eat raw. Ripe delicious fruits are abundant, it is easy. In every season (certainly here in the UK) there is something local that you can add raw to your plate. It is

possible to exist entirely on raw plant foods in cool temperate locations but, certainly in mid-winter, the diet becomes extremely limited. At such times of year it also becomes challenging to get a good balance, certainly if you are considering provenance and eating mainly local and seasonal foods (no imported avocados, coconuts, dates – you get the picture). Of course the climate and plants available year round, in places such as California, in Mediterranean and tropical climates, are much more conducive to a year round entirely raw plant diet.

Personally, I vary how much raw I eat. The proportion of raw foods in my diet increases dramatically as soon as the ambient temperature reaches 20°C. In winter, when it hovers around 0°C for weeks on end, there are certainly a few more warming soups involved. But, even in the depths of winter, I always add a raw element to every meal, even if it is just a sprinkling of alkalising wild leaves. In fact, I would recommend adding at least one raw element to every meal as a minimum.

No matter where you live, or the season, you can grow trays of greens within your kitchen to add raw. Sprouted seeds, wheatgrass, pea and sunflower greens, there are many different options. If you have a protected outside area and not too long at sub zero temperatures, you may manage to successfully grow a variety of salad greens throughout the winter. I achieve this in pots which line the south side of my house. Alternatively if you have a strip of land where you can grow there are many kales, cabbages, chard and other tough leaves that will overwinter and can be chopped finely and added raw to any meal.

🌳

Adoption of a diet high in raw plant foods delivers superior health, wild health. It is a wilder way with food, eating food the way nature has presented it. Bitter wild leaves, sweet fibrous fruits, oil rich nuts and seeds, each in their own way have a medicinal effect on our bodies. They help our bodies to remain well, and if currently at a point of dis-ease can help bring us back to a place of balance and efficient function. Embarking upon a diet with a high raw plant content is an adventure in reawakening your body and mind whilst reconnecting with the plants that grow around you, with the landscape, with Earth, and with good health.

🌳

People fast every night when they go to sleep, abstaining from food for eight hours or more. If we followed an entirely natural diet, as wild animals

do, this nocturnal reprieve from eating would give our liver and intestines enough time to clear and process the days intake. However with our modern diets this is not sufficient time for all of the work that needs to be done. Most of us will need some remedial work to bring our bodies to a point of efficient function, a kind of personal wildness reclamation. Being brought up on a standard Western diet means there will undoubtedly be a few toxins lurking about and plenty of wear and tear. Think of a landscape that has been used for industrial purposes and is now being cleaned up so that it can become a nature reserve, not an impossible task, but clearly there would be work to do. A diet high in raw plant foods will kick start your personal wildness reclamation, gradually cleansing and clearing, eventually making much lighter work for your system.

The amount of clear up necessary depends on your starting point but undertaking an intentional cleanse can be very beneficial. It is doing the ground work so that you can actually absorb and benefit from all the wonderful raw and wild plant foods that the wild path will bring into your life.

If you are eating local wild food then the foods that present themselves in spring (in the temperate zone) are naturally cleansing. Stinging nettle *(Urtica dioica)*, wild garlic *(Allium ursinum)*, cleavers *(Galium aparine)*, a few of my favourite spring time leaves, are all highly cleansing. Eating wild foods in spring will help stimulate your liver, your lymphatic system and your digestion. It will help clear some of the residue left over from the more difficult to digest and process cooked foods of winter. A few weeks on a diet rich in wild leaves will leave you feeling bright, vibrant, energetic.

One side effect of a lifetime spent eating unnatural foods is the presence of a layer of impacted mucous in the colon. The colon has a natural lining of mucous to help protect and lubricate it. However, a diet high in processed foods will irritate this layer, causing an over abundance of mucous to be produced, and without a high enough quantity of fibrous foods, an inability to rid itself of this excess mucous. Over time this settles and becomes compacted, lining your digestive tract, interfering with its ability to absorb the nutrients required by the body, and potentially causing, or contributing to, sensitivities and allergies. It also means that eating a plate of wild leafy spring greens may leave you feeling hungry as the nutrients are so poorly absorbed. As you begin to rewild your digestive tract you it may find it helpful to undergo an intestinal cleanse with the intention of clearing some of this backed up mucous[18].

Once you have undertaken a few deep cleanses and are eating a high raw, low processed diet, as a norm, you will reach a new plateau

of health and consciousness. Your body will be more able to absorb the nutrients in your food, allowing you to be satisfied on less, and on a lower carbohydrate, plant-rich diet. Cleansing helps clear the urban, tame, civilised lives from our flesh and blood leading you one step closer to feeling the golden surge of the information super-highway pulsing through your wild veins at all times.

The process of cleansing can be challenging - both physically and mentally. You may get cleansing reactions, such as feeling sick and dizzy, foul breath, headaches, pimples. Do not be alarmed, this is something to celebrate! It is the old stored toxins finally leaving your body. As your body releases stored up toxins, layers of impacted mucous and other debris, you may also find yourself releasing old emotions associated with the time in which each toxic layer built up. And so, you get the chance to cleanse out not just physically, but emotionally and spiritually too. It therefore becomes important when cleansing not only to think of the herbs and juices and plant foods that you are putting into your physical body for the duration of the cleanse, but also what you are consuming mentally. Retreat a little from the daily toxic media influx (TV, internet and printed news). In fact avoid TV in general, especially anything depicting guns and violence.

When considering a cleanse it is really important to do your own research, and be thorough; people often pass on something they hear as fact without really knowing what they are talking about. Trust your intuition, your *gut*. Listen to what your body is telling you. This may be difficult at first but is part of the point of this exercise, to be able to clear and re-sensitise your intestines on all levels.

Feel your way around what is working for you. It is important to only go as far as you are comfortable with and always take good care of your health. Don't go against the advice of healthcare profession-als unless you really feel you know what you are doing; even then it would be safer to find a naturopath and discuss the issue. Never just stop medication, it could be very dangerous or even fatal. *However*, had I just followed the standard advice I would never have deep cleansed or fasted (having Type I diabetes). I certainly recommend that everyone try a full cleanse into a juice fast, followed up with a raw food diet for as long as you can manage, at least once in your life (health permitting); just so you know how incredible and amazing and energizing it feels.

After several years of intermittent deep cleansing, juice fasting, and the adoption of a high raw diet I have thoroughly explored my relationship with what I chose to put inside my body, and how that has an effect on the relationship I have with my body as a whole. Taking my input right down to minimum and then rebuilding my diet again slowly made me so much more conscious of every bite, where it came from, what it's doing and where it's going. It absolutely brought me back in touch with this one little piece of Gaia, my physical body, and the incredible intelligence of my digestive tract.

The more natural, cleaner, plant-based and raw my diet has become, the more sensitive I have become to my sixth, feeling, sense; my animal sense. A clean internal landscape has given me a cleaner, fresher perspective from which to see the world I am part of for what it is, and to make clearer choices about how, and with whom, I interact. I feel more of a living, breathing, integrated part of Gaia; I feel wilder.

8.8 Eating With Awareness

It is important during eating to focus on exactly that, eating. When snacking on the go, while driving or walking, it is impossible to give awareness to what you are eating, it becomes easy to miss messages from your body. Instead take your time, really taste every mouthful, chew thoroughly. Make space for this, actually make meal times about eating. Don't read or watch TV, or catch up with social networking at the same time. If you do allow those distractions into your eating space you will also be eating *them*. Think about it. If you are listening to the news and it is full of doom and gloom, rape and robbery, you are subconsciously swallowing and digesting that alongside your meal. If at meal times you pay attention to your food and your body, you will know when you have had enough. You will more quickly learn about which foods affect you in a positive way. Some foods can leave you feeling light and energetic, while others will leave you feeling grumpy and sluggish. Pay attention and you will be more able to navigate to those foods that make you feel good, that make you feel alive.

Becoming sensitive to what you are eating, awareness as the body of the plant assimilates in its first salivary steps to become part of you, sends a rush like a pulse of electricity through *your* body. Your taste buds, dulled by years of over seasoned, over processed, over cooked foods, with little, or no, life force take re-adjustment to tune in; give it time. Become aware of, and appreciate, the sacrifice the humble pea

has made laying down its life to nourish you. To acknowledge this, to be grateful and savour every juicy bite, brings another incredible dimension to meal times and your connection with other life.

One time when visiting with friends in Ibiza our group included not only English but also Sicilian, Persian and Dutch. Our Dutch friend had been living between India and Morocco for several years. He suggested we discard utensils and eat with our hands "it is like making love (with your food)" he insisted. Somehow he was right. As we ate the delicious, lovingly prepared Persian fare something happened. We all became more involved in our individual relationship with the food on our plates, our chatter slowly stilled, eating became a prayer. Eating was conscious. Afterwards our fingers felt soft, well moisturised from the olive oil infused throughout the meal. It was not like eating fries when your fingers become greasy, or like eating a sandwich or a burger with hands. Something magical happened as our fingers mingled with the rice and vegetables, herbs and oil, and the whole experience gained another dimension.

Taking it a stage further I remember one evening years ago in the back garden with my husband. He was drawn to an elderflower and just reached over with his mouth and took a bite. I did the same. Again it was like an electrical charge, something so much more than when food has passed through the intermediary of hands. Try it. Experiment, but definitely experience. I don't often find the opportunity to eat this way, but in the summer I never fail to pull many, many, raspberries from the bush with my lips alone. In the spring I get down low to nibble some wild greens straight from the plant, the same with mushrooms in the autumn.

Whenever I pick fruit or veg, whether it is for eating or for medicine, I always ask first – holding a thought of what I am harvesting *for* in my heart. I also thank. Imagine the deepening relationship you can develop to food if everything you eat is harvested by you in this way. Of course it's not feasibly possible for most people, even a fruitarian with an orchard. However it is possible to stop and take a moment of pause to thank while preparing and before eating – to thank all the lives that became part of your meal, and all those that contributed along the way, whose flesh now becomes yours. Allow it to become a sacred celebration of life and gratitude, another point of reconnect.

When you body has cleansed, even just a little bit, from the standard diet and begun to be built with a more wild, medicinal, diet it becomes natural to listen to your body and feed it what it wants, what it needs. You may just want to eat chocolate; that is OK. Just follow and listen to every message you receive, pay attention and you will know when you've had enough and, the key part, how your body feels after. If you want to feel well, wild, and tune in to your body wisdom, you will soon recognise what are urges relating to food associations and addictions or to emotional needs, and what your body is asking for to enable it to function well and efficiently. There is a difference, and if you are paying attention you will notice it. If you choose to love and respect your body and start to enjoy feeling clear and clean then, with time, the associations you have with certain foods used to balance out emotional states will begin to drop away. You will become more whole in yourself, more congruent, richer, stronger and by knowing yourself more closely you will find other ways to feed your soul and balance your emotions than with food (or drugs, or alcohol, for that matter).

Learning to know and trust your body (your own piece of Gaia's flesh made from all of the dust, water and fruits of the earth), learning to truly love, respect and listen, engenders a deep sense of being and new degree of self respect. Quiet time spent observing and listening to your body, the same attention you would offer a loved one, is what your body deserves and needs. Treating yourself in this way will accelerate change in all areas of your life, and the relationships you hold with other life.

Our physical bodies are our direct connection with Gaia, the piece over which we have the most control and hence therein lies a responsibility. You can run around protesting, campaigning to save the rain forests, but until you are truly taking care of your own piece of Earth there is not much chance of successfully saving the rest of the planet.

Once you are eating with full awareness, attention to your surroundings at mealtimes heightens. There are few things more pleasurable than al fresco dining whether it is a sandwich on the park bench in a summer time lunch break, a birthday BBQ with a group of friends or a romantic dinner for two at a beach side bistro. It feels good. The air you breathe down as you swallow your food, the sunshine and the smiles, all make for a better dining experience. Eating under the big sky, raw and wild, is the way nature presents our food, and the way our wild ancestors ate. It may not be possible or desirable to do so every

day, but when the weather is mild and dry, taking the opportunity to eat outside seems to feed us on yet another invisible level.

8.9 The Flesh Of Earth Becomes Us

The less raw, wild, natural and local we eat the greater the chasm between us and the rest of nature as we lose touch with our environs, with the soil, the climate, the air and the minerals that are locally rich. The connection to land and to the wild becomes weak. Highly processed foods and impacted mucous lining our colons ensure we remain aliens, detached and dislocated. For wildness to run through our veins, to understand our world and to feel at home where we stand, local, wild, raw, natural foods are essential. Unless your diet is balanced with your local environment and climate, it will not be balanced, you will not be balanced. Nature should determine our diet; what grows, what is ripe. But more than diet being prescribed by the nature that is perceived as outside of ourselves, it should also be directed by the nature that is your body, listen to it. When it's hungry, when it's full; what tastes good, what does not.

The prime consideration is for a person to develop the sensitivity to allow the body to choose food by itself.
Masanobu Fukuoka

Eating your body wild will not just benefit your individual health and enrich your own wildness, but also that of the whole of your environment, of Gaia; there is no separation.

9. YOUR OWN SWEET PIECE OF NATURE

The whole of Part IV, Wild Body, has been about working with your physical self to improve atrophied senses, develop body wisdom and to listen to what your taste buds and digestive tract are telling you. It has been about considering what you eat and where your food came from, about connecting with the land you live upon through the food that also grows upon it; about literally eating yourself wild. It's been about knowing your body, and knowing it as nature. But there is still more to our physical form, to our bodies.

Take a look at your hand. Study every millimetre of it. Marvel at what it can do. Remember that rewilding is about finding the livingness, not just in the world around us, but in ourselves, in our own sweet piece of nature, which we wear as skin, and flesh, and bone. Study each part of yourself and as you do so acknowledge it as beautiful, useful, alive.

9.1 Self-Massage

I have studied massage; I know about muscles, bones, tendons, the body's structure. As I learned different massage techniques, I tried them out on myself to practice, and to see how subtle adjustments in delivery feel to the receiver. As I have done so I have felt each muscle, found places that are tender and sore, places that need a good stretch and places that never usually receive touch. Of course I have had plenty of massage treatments, it was my love of receiving massage that drove me to study it in the first place, but being touched by someone else and touching yourself are two different things. So try it. Become familiar with your body. Feel your way around your structure, your skin, your bones, your blood vessels, your muscles, your sinew. Use your sense of touch to explore your own sweet piece of nature, the silky, the soft, the rough, the hairy. Remind yourself of your wildness by exploring every inch of your physique; celebrate it.

Try using your finger tips and with your first two fingers pressing strongly draw circles across your upper chest, the area that for a woman would be known as décolletage. It feels good. You can feel the warmth of your flesh, the bones of your thorax. This structure, the warm skin, the bones beneath, these are common features with other mammals, with wild animals - it's what we are.

Explore some more. Grab your thighs, fingers underneath, thumbs

on top, and work down the centre line of your thighs using a circular action with a firm thumb - do the same on your arms. Try firmly grasping and pulling the large fleshy pad that sits in the V shape between your thumb and fore finger. Explore and discover. Massage your hands and your feet, your fingers and your toes. Don't stop until you have covered your whole body and discovered what feels good. Take your time. In the process you will have been awakening your skin, your blood circulation and your lymph nodes. You have just massaged your body awake. Even just doing this for a few moments has extremely noticeable effects. It wakes me up, not just my level of mental alertness (although that is affected) but my body - I feel ready for action. Ready for movement.

9.2 The Importance Of Movement

We have been languishing in a state of relative inactivity for too long, often sitting with bad posture, curved spines. You are an animal. Learn about, and how to use, every part of your body. Be active. When do you ever see a wild animal sitting in an office for eight hours each day, another in the car or on the train and a couple more in front of the TV? Don't look at your dog, they are domesticated too, far from their wolfy ancestors. Sedentary work is perhaps unavoidable, however there are certain steps you can take to keep your body active and vibrant.

There has been talk recently about the benefits of alternating between sitting and standing during the working day, so try and set your work station up so that this is possible. Even if not make sure you are constantly adjusting your position. Act as though you are on a long haul flight with mini ankle and shoulder exercises. Keep moving and stretching as much as you can get away with whilst still doing your work conscientiously. You could create for yourself, or may already do, an alternative type of work, physical work, where you are using your body all day. Alternatively try and negotiate some from home days where you will be more able to vary your position and intersperse sitting periods with action. I have created my life so that sitting at my desk writing is alternated with various different outdoor activities, such as gardening.

When you read a long email or document, self-massage at the same time. Something small, subtle and simple such as your hands, forearms or knees. Wriggle your toes. There are hundreds of ways to keep moving, to keep your circulation going, without your boss particularly noticing or objecting.

Of course outside of working hours there is the gym, yoga, swimming, cycling to work; all kinds of active and sporty pursuits in the evenings and weekends. Vary. Weave in different things, stretching one night, cardiovascular another. If sport is not for you at least include some form of activity in your daily routine – walking to the station, running up the stairs, sex.

To become nature you must use your body regularly. To reach peak fitness with the amount of time we must sit each day is a challenge beyond most of us, but don't give in to it, engineer things to be different. Even if it is clenching and releasing your buttocks while sitting on the bus, keep reminding your body that it is alive. And make it fun. Dancing, playing Frisbee, a game of pool - they all involve stretching and moving and will aid your body in feeling lighter, younger, more supple, *wilder.*

Free running, parkour, is a great example of physical, full body, rewilding. Running and jumping, calculating as you are moving, using the human body to its optimum. It is peak performance using skills, senses and intellect alongside physical strength, stamina and agility; like a lion chasing its quarry. It is a beautiful art form, the artistry of the human body. Albeit most often practised in urban environments, it is using the body more or less in the way it was meant, as a wild fit animal. It demonstrates our physical potential as wild human animals. It also involves transcending the human experience, being hyper-focused and extremely aware.

9.3 Hosting Other Lifeforms

There is one more thing I have yet to mention; we are not entirely as we seem. Your own sweet piece of Gaia is more like your very own universe, or at least ecosystem. We are host to a vast quantity of biota, that is microscopic life forms, to put it bluntly, bacteria. In fact these micro-organisms outnumber human cells by 10 to 1[1]. They are on our skin, in our ears and noses, lining our gut *and* they are essential to our health.

A healthy population and good balance of these biota help our bodies to be strong with a well functioning immune system. Being brought up in an environment that is too clean and sterile, too anti-biotic, has been mooted as a causative factor in the development of allergies, eczema and asthma[2]. Certainly lack of contact with the diversity of bacteria found in the wild, which abundantly colonised our ancestors and current hunter-gatherer societies, is implicated in the development

of these conditions[3]. Bacteria are so important to our efficient functioning that an imbalance of micro-flora in the gut has been linked with brain health and the development of autism[4]. We really cannot afford to ignore the massive contribution made to our health by these invisible bacterial hitch-hikers.

Life inside the womb was almost sterile, but the day you were born, your relationship with bacteria began in earnest. The bacteria present in the birth canal change before birth as Lactobacillus become more dominant[5]. As the infant is squeezed and pushed into this reality, it is coated from crown to tips of toes with bacteria. This is the first colonisation with bacteria and prepares the infant for life on the outside of the womb. It is one of the first and most important gifts your mother can give you. Unfortunately, as up to 25% of births in the UK are now by caesarean section, many infants are colonised first by bacteria prevalent on skin and hospital surfaces. Although many caesareans are life saving, when not absolutely necessary (as is the case with elective caesareans) they should be avoided. A child that does not travel through the birth canal is being done a great disservice in not receiving that coat of friendly bacteria that will help build a strong, healthy and resilient personal ecosystem.

What happens subsequently, in early childhood, will influence your population of micro-biota and consequently your ability to cope with allergens and infections throughout your life. Breast milk contains up to 700 species of bacteria significantly contributing to a healthy and diverse personal bacterial ecosystem in breast fed babies. It is also true that a mother's saliva contains bacteria that are beneficial for their infant so, for example, it is more beneficial for a child to have a dropped dummy sucked clean by mum and put back in, than have it replaced with a sterile one. Dogs bring biota into houses, so if you grew up with a dog you were exposed to more bacteria early on and are more likely to have developed a strong immune system. If you had chickens, or maybe lived on a small holding, farm, or often visited one, then again you are likely to have a stronger immune system despite having inevitably been exposed to many more bacteria on a regular basis than in an average suburban household.

It can be difficult if your early years were very sterile, because introducing bacteria as an adult can be challenging for a compromised immune system to cope with. If for example you chose to visit a farm and feed a goat, your ability to fight off the bacteria you come into contact with would be impaired. As a result you would be more likely to

pick up a stomach bug than a friend with a well balanced micro-ecology would. You have to work to welcome and build a robust, healthy, active and well balanced colony of micro-biota. I don't know how easy it would be - I began my life playing on the compost heap, so I guess I am all set with a healthy micro-ecology.

I should imagine that if your upbringing was rather sterile perhaps start with repopulating your gut with friendly bacteria. Use the same process that is usually recommended by an holistic health practitioner to someone who has recently completed a course of antibiotics. Begin by cutting all processed sugars from your diet, any food or drink that contains sugar. Then start introducing food and drinks that contain friendly bacteria (probiotics), such as miso, live yoghurt (but watch for sugar), kombucha and kefir. You will also need prebiotics, such as raw garlic and dandelion greens, which provide a food source for the probiotics allowing them to thrive and repopulate your gut. Once the strength of your gut colony has improved the rest can follow.

Phase out antibacterial hand soap and wipes, except where absolutely necessary, such as in a hospital. Normal soap is fine, you need those bacteria. Build up slowly if you have never had much contact with bacteria before, but get out there and get your fingers in the dirt! Of course not all bacteria are friendly. It is a balance and to obtain a healthy one, a less domesticated, more wild and outdoor lifestyle is recommended. Be hygienic, be clean - but don't be sterile.

Organisms from natural environments are almost absent from urban and semi-urban lives, especially when most people spend up to 23 hours a day, especially on week days, inside. Even fruit and vegetables purchased from the supermarket have been cleaned and bagged before being sold to us without the remnants of soil and dust and all the biota that contains. Spending time outside especially in rural locations and breathing the air, touching natural surfaces, sticking your fingers in the soil, will expose you to environmental bacteria which, with contact, will colonise and repopulate you. Even air carries more bacteria in it in the vicinity of animals, so it becomes important in yet another way to get outside and get amongst it. Foraging and eating wild food, fruit straight from the trees, will introduce certain bacteria to your personal universe, bacteria that for many supermarket shoppers have been missing for a long time. When you have exposure to such bacteria you carry

them back into the home with you, benefiting everyone you live with, a bit like a family dog.

Bacteria are a vital component of the human body. They produce vital nutrients, help us to digest food and provide protection against infectious organisms. Without them we are more susceptible to allergens, digestive complaints and illness. By cutting off our relationship with bacteria, we have broken down part of the invisible connection that we need, making ourselves less alive as we carry less other lives in and on our bodies; in the end becoming allergic to dirt, and dust, and animals, to nature. We have to embrace our own wild ecology and allow it to grow and develop healthily - it is an essential part of our wildness and part of our nature.

9.4 Whole Body Intelligence

Our bodies are wise. We can pick up feelings with our hearts and find out about our environment through using our senses. As we know already, both the brain and the heart contain neurons (so called brain cells), but that is not where it ends. The gut also contains neurons, around one hundred million of them[6]. These cells process and transmit information through electrical and chemical signals. Neurons in the gut, just like those in the brain and in the heart, are capable of remembering and learning, and of responding to situations with feelings - gut feelings. Just like the heart, the gut can be a powerful source of intuition, of feeling the truth behind something before the brain gets involved with its logic and begins to try and rationalise the situation. There is an intelligence, like a third brain, in these cells. As they communicate with each other they are telling you things, things about the world as it really is, fuelling your intuition, and if you listen closely, urging you to be more wild. The neurons are spread forming tissue networks which line your digestive tract all the way from the oesophagus, through the stomach, small intestine and colon.

The third brain works together with the first and second, they are interconnected. The whole of the body is involved in communicating information, in influencing our experience of the world. To be in touch with it, with some of the information being sent around your body, to build an awareness of feeling and intuition rather than simply relying on logic or what our domesticated minds interpret from those communications, is to become more animal. More wild.

Intelligence from the neurons located in different centres of the body informs us about the world. Bacteria line your digestive tract alongside some of those neurons. Bacteria are also intelligent in that they communicate, passing messages between themselves and your cells, working together for the benefit or detriment of their host.

Have you ever had parasites? Or amoebas (amoebic dysentery)? Or even an overgrowth of the fungus Candida albicans? Due to my extensive travelling I have suffered all three at different points in time. In my experience, when I become aware of the infestation or overgrowth and begin acting to remove it I feel an alternate intelligence inside me. Like a devil on my shoulder begging with me to eat the sugars that would feed and keep it alive. I get really strange urges, so uncharacteristic I know they are coming from outside of my usual self. It takes a lot of willpower to overcome those alien urges, to starve and eventually kill off the parasites, amoebas or fungi. It is incredible but once you are aware of that parasitic life form inside you can recognise it, and recognise when it as an intelligent being is trying to influence your decisions. Having this degree of awareness of your body, paying attention when things do not feel right, is living more in line with nature - a further step into the wild.

Being able to recognise early on when things become out of balance may well help you to stay healthier for longer, as when illness (in whatever its form) strikes the sooner it is addressed the more likely the chances of treating it successfully. Your body knows when something is wrong, and if you know the wild well enough then you will know what you need to make yourself well. To reach such mastery of your body requires great focus and determination but it is not beyond the human race if it is not beyond the chimpanzee[7]. Learn how to listen to your body and your wildness will grow.

PART IV
Wild Nature

...sometimes it is better to stay just a little more wild, just a little closer to the soil, with less technology between us and nature.
Guido Masé

In the process of knowing the plants, of holding them in our hands, we come to learn in time that they hold us too. And when we understand that, it is very easy to touch our own faces and in so doing, touch Gaia.
Stephen Harrod Buhner

The wild is a voice that never stops whispering... calling you back to places of vast sky and fast-running light, where solitude hunts for you and the edges of the world get ragged. These empty places are mirrors; they reflect back everything of yourself. They are teachers too, of a thousand lessons...
Daniel Crockett

The initiatory "Walkabout" undertaken by Aboriginal Australians is again such an act whereby oral peoples turn toward the more-than-human earth for the teachings that must vitalize and sustain the human community.

David Abram

10. FINGERS IN THE EARTH -
Skin on skin contact

It is a rare thing in this modern world for our bare flesh to spend time in contact with natural surfaces, which is one of the reasons that many of my suggestions in section 6.1 included it. Walking barefoot across desert and lawn; running your fingers over stone, wood and sand; kneeling, lying, in direct contact, skin on skin, with the Earth. When we do make time for it it feels so good, revitalising. There is an invisible exchange very much like the exchange, the invisible communication, that occurs between you and another human during a moment of physical touch.

I believe this kind of very direct physical contact, not just with humans or other natural and wild organic material, but with Earth itself, is essential for our overall well-being. Touching the Earth, handling soil, rocks and stones, has a part to play in helping us feel grounded (just think about it), centred and to know our place. If you have not had much direct physical contact with the Earth you may not understand this yet, but there is something special, something calming, revitalising and balancing within that invisible exchange. It is like plugging back in to the source, perhaps a bit like rebooting. It provides a remembering of your wild animal self, and through that a self confidence and knowing.

10.1 Gardening

...to maintain my sanity I need at least one full day a week in the garden. It works better than any pill, better than any medicine. Earth Heals.

Monty Don

I have built skin on skin contact with Earth into my daily routine, and with familiarity it has become very much a part of me, a kind of essential therapy that I didn't even know I needed. I have incorporated direct physical contact into both my leisure time and working day, mainly through gardening. My ungloved hands handling soil, my knees in contact with Earth; a muddy, grassy, stony connection. That kneeling position has become my personal prayer pose, a kind of Earth meditation where everything else melts away.

So when I say *gardening* perhaps it is more of a spiritual pursuit than

150

actually micro-managing every square centimetre with military precision. Visitors (of the human variety) to my garden often think it is a completely wild, weedy mess. I do direct and manage a little, encouraging that which grows to stick to a certain patch and not spread too far. I do also introduce plants into the mix, but my grass is long and full of wild medicines. Fruit trees, some cultivated, others wild arrivals, punctuate all the boundaries.

All the while, whenever I have my fingers in the soil, I take my time, absorbing and observing, becoming, and being part of. As much as possible I let nature take the lead. I follow behind just primping and preening here and there to make my patch productive enough to provide food without imposing too much upon the natural processes of the piece of land before me.

Don't think that manipulating nature is not a wild act. Ants farm aphids, herding and protecting them in exchange for the sugary honey-dew excreted by the aphids. Beavers dam up rivers creating still ponds for their own protection and food storage. In fact all plants and animals are constantly modifying their environment all the time. Movement and readjustment is a constant in life, a natural process. Humankind, of course, generally takes the manipulation of nature a stage too far. But, there is much to be learnt about Gaia, and many relationships with other kind to be formed and deepened through the actions of gardening. Through growing, harvesting, watering, sowing, you are manipulating but it can be a gentle process. Choosing not to dig and disturb the incredibly rich and diverse soil based ecosystems, whilst being sympathetic to the plants that voluntarily arrive on the wind and want to grow, are two such ways.

Inevitably, you will have to control the bullies, the excitable vigorous growers, otherwise they will swamp everything else. Gardening is a double edged sword in a way, you are interacting and being with nature, learning about it, loving it, but you are also controlling it. So, be aware, keep your interventions in balance and always encourage the wildness, especially your own wildness.

I garden, in part, so that I have a one hundred percent handle on the provenance of much of my food. But clearly it is more than that, it is the *something* that happens to me when the naked flesh of my fingers comes into contact with the moist loose soil; it is that enlivening invisible exchange. A remembering occurs within me, a remembering of my place here on this Earth amongst all the plants, trees, birds and earthworms. A remembering of what food really is, how long it takes to grow, and of gluts

and lean times. A remembering of the intricacies of my local climate and the cycling of seasons. And a remembering that the land upon which I live is home, and the soil under my finger nails and in the creases, cracks and folds of my skin, is also home. *The connection deepens.*

I know nothing as effective as skin on skin contact with Earth to calm me if I am annoyed or angry. If I am in such a mood I may lie face down on the grass, or with my back against the trunk of a strong old tree, or I may go to my allotment for solace. If I go to work the land I may at first forget myself, grabbing at "weeds", a bit nasty, a bit violent, but within ten minutes, twenty tops, I have slowed entirely. I then begin to soften and together with the plants manage to find perhaps even a funny side to my mood, as a compromise, an apology, or forgiveness grows within me. It is also the best remedy for a late night of over indulgence, as the grounding contact with bare soil slowly clears your head and re-energises your tired and poisoned body.

Gardening is therapy no matter what mood I start with. I usually spend the first few moments, sometimes hours, not entirely present. I spend time thinking of this and that, circumstances or people. But as the time passes I enter into a trance-like state, calmed by my plant friends and my contact with the soil. Little gems of wisdom will pop into my head, solutions, ideas, inspiration. Then that phase will also pass until I simply am, until there is just me doing what I am doing, aware of all the life around me. I have dropped everything (all my human head worries, concerns, thoughts) and become a part of it. No distractions, no unrelated thoughts, just me, the plants, the air that I'm breathing, the sun on my back and the soil between my fingers.

There are other methods people employ to reach that state of beingness - gardening provides mine. It is my spiritual pursuit, my deep connection with source, with animal and plant life, with the wind and rain, with my food, with the very ground itself and through all of those elements working together, with my deeper self.

Perhaps you live without access to outside space, so that not only are your gardening options limited, but walking barefoot is only a rare and occasional opportunity. In such circumstances perhaps more than any other it is worth growing house plants. Even without flesh on flesh con-

tact with Earth there is a benefit to growing plants, to making that deep nurturing connection with another life form. You can still handle soil and encourage life. A few potted plants grown inside on the window ledges will soon add an extra dimension to your life if you remember to acknowledge them as living beings. You can even grow a few food plants; sprouts, wheat grass, micro greens, culinary herbs. Their cultivation, even indoors, still engenders that fundamental connection with growing and nurturing life (other than human) even if the soil is not on the ground. If you have a balcony try leaving a pot filled with soil and see what arrives. If a seed is brought in on the breeze or dropped off by a bird, maybe you will be lucky enough to have your own wild food garden on the fifteenth floor.

🌳

Of course skin on skin contact has many forms, gardening is just one, but it is my way. It is the way I have which I don't need to think about. On a cold morning I perhaps would not otherwise go outside and touch the cold bare Earth with my warm pink fingers. It would perhaps be a chore in the colder months to step outside barefoot to reap the benefits of contact with the Earth for any length of time, and so I garden, it is my communion with the Earth. You will find your way. Make that flesh on flesh direct connection with Earth as often as possible. If you can, make it a daily part of your life, because your wild self hungers for that contact and will be fed by it. The more opportunities you make for this contact the the stronger the wild core of you, and your deep Gaia connection, will grow.

🌳

The invisible exchange experienced during direct contact delivers an energy surge. It is calming yet energising with a confident and balancing, knowing. It makes you feel more whole. You will receive more and more of this, in stronger and stronger doses the more contact you have and the more deeply you are able to immerse yourself in nature. For most of us, access and time available to spend in the wilderness is severely limited. Motivation to explore the wild lands (both internally and externally) may be lacking. But through skin on skin contact with the Earth, even just with a single potted plant in your home, your wildness will receive a little of what it needs to grow and thrive, until you get, or make, an opportunity to go deeper into the remaining wild lands of Gaia.

153

11. DEEP NATURE IMMERSION

Having recognised and acknowledged the livingness in the world, walked barefoot upon and hugged the Earth, smelled your way around the garden, eaten fresh wild herbs, massaged and wiggled your flesh alive. Having incorporated daily deep breaths of fresh air while noticing and becoming. Having felt the rush of energy from burying your fingers deep in soil. As each action and feeling has become part of your daily routine, part of your being, your wildness has been awakening, reasserting itself. With your connection alive and deepened, your senses honed and your ability to feel perturbations in your environment tweaked, any time now spent in nature will have a greater significance, a greater meaning. Whether you are sitting in an urban pocket park or hiking in the Himalayas your experience of Gaia will be enhanced. You will have, at least in part, moved from being an observer and appreciator, to a participator, a true and inseparable part of Gaia.

From day to day sitting in the sunshine at the top of my garden, eyes closed, listening to insects, while I drink my mid-morning herbal tea keeps me connected, keeps me alive and sane. When I take a break from my usual routine my greatest pleasure is going to a place of untamed nature. Whether it is canoeing down the Wye valley, camping on the beach in Mexico, hiking the lava fields of Iceland, or soaking in a hot spring high in the Himalayas, time immersed in wild nature is like recharging my batteries.

It is becoming increasingly difficult to find an undisturbed place of wild nature. But even on the urban fringe there are un-manicured and rarely visited (by humans) edges. Make time to find a place where you can go to, where you can feel the wild and be wild. It is important to make a frequent connection, but that is why I laud gardening and even hugging the closely cropped lawn at a public park, because if you are up close and personal you will find a richness and wildness amongst the other creatures and vegetal species. The regular connection will feed you, calm you, and make you feel more whole.

Despite everything the Earth, Gaia, is rich and strong. Go outside and lay on your lawn, feel the dampness of dusk rise to meet your body. Listen to the symphony of bird call. Feel the chill as it sets in deeper. The day is ending and the cycle continues. Quality of light and colour saturation maintain their dynamic flow as the suns touch fades from the sky and

the darkness of night creeps in. Be bold, stay a moment longer, soak it up.

When you can, even if that is just once a year, or once in a lifetime, make the pilgrimage to somewhere truly wild and immerse yourself. To get the most from any nature immersion experience I recommend that you go alone to the wild (always remembering to tell someone where you are going and when you expect to be back). The place must be free of other humans and obvious human influence. It is essential to be mindful when entering this territory, for it is not the domain of the human. Do your utmost to not damage or disturb, to leave as you found. Don't take your phone, or a camera or an ipod. The reason to take nothing when in deep nature is that even a digital camera screen can be distracting. On wild adventures including African safari and solar eclipse viewing I have noticed people who watch the entire event through their camera or tablet, through a screen. It is a loss and a waste to experience the wild like this. Watching through a screen, you will never be more than an observer. Missing so much, the scene may as well be watched at home on TV.

One vital part of deep nature immersion is to get away from light pollution, to find that place where you don't recognise any constellations because there are just so many stars in the sky (and no reception to run sky map apps). Star gazing away from light pollution remains one of the wonders of the world, especially if when you normally look up all you can see is an orangey glow and Orion's belt if you are lucky.

I was living in Tokyo during 1997 when the comet Hale Bopp was bright and visible to the naked eye. I remember speaking to my mum in the light polluted South East of the UK on the phone "It is like a torch (flash light), you must be able to see it" she insisted, but no, nothing. I like to be in touch with the phase of the moon, to look up as it waxes and wanes through its cycle; but I even lost touch with that in Tokyo such was the extent of the light pollution combined with emissions haze in my neighbourhood. In contrast, when you are many miles from the nearest source of artificial light and can see the night sky unhindered, the milky way appears as a kind of twisted celestial umbilical cord against a backdrop of millions and millions of points of light. Wild nature like this can be truly awe-inspiring. It can touch that magic place inside that never gets activated when immersed in the company and creations of humankind.

So go to the wilderness, make an opportunity. On arrival in your chosen area of wild nature you will undoubtedly need to walk a while to appreciate your surroundings, to find your place. Perhaps you may forage as you go, and through eating the fruits of that place connect more deeply with it, but eventually *stop*. Find a place and just be for a while. No more walking, no nibbling on leaves. No more doing. A time for absorbing, for sharing, for becoming, for being. You may find, as I have done, that when alone in nature clothes have no meaning and that by removing them, whether under the sun or the moon, there is a deeper integration with the wildness of the place and your own inner wildness. Time spent in solitude in the wilderness is the ultimate deep nature immersion experience.

11.1 Facing Fear

Wild places; dank, dark, a rustling behind you, spider's web in the face, the feeling of being watched, of not being alone. Every sound intensified, slight movements made by who-knows-what drawing your attention in a snap second. Smells; a multi-layered palate of fragrance. Wild places, truly wild, scare me. It's a healthy fear - to be alive, awake, alert to dangers both underfoot and potentially in the bushes.

I find focusing in on one thing helps. Watching a curious looking insect continue on its way, proceeding with its usual behaviour, reminds me that not everything unfamiliar is threatening. I breathe a little deeper. I choose a spot to be, to sit and observe, and become. After some time, having taken in the sky, the clouds and the passage of the sun and, or, moon, I take a closer look. First perhaps the obvious, the trees that I can see from my perch. Their trunks and leaves and multi-legged visitors. Then, onto the grasses and wild flowers (*elsewhere people call them weeds*). I take in the beauty and the balance between all the species that I have registered that cohabit in this place. And soon, once I am breathing more slowly and deeply than I ever do in my more familiar human terrain, I realise that they are observing, noticing me back.

Winged insects will visit, alighting on my skin. I remove my shoes so that I can feel the Earth upon my skin, so that I can truly *feel* the place. If it has been hot on my journey to the "place" and my feet have sweated, occasionally I am treated to a butterfly, or maybe two, or three, tickling as they stop to taste the salty residue on my toes. Birds too. They come close and cocking their heads to one side, tilting up one eye to check me out, they seem to wonder what I'm doing there.

There may be a scuttle in the undergrowth, a mammal of some description but they rarely come close except perhaps in the peace of dawn or the big out breath of dusk (or maybe just while I'm sleeping).

The fear really doesn't last long. It's not that scary after all. With time I settle in, relax a little. I become used to the sounds and smells, the aloneness from human company and its replacement by something so much more vibrant, more vital, than a room full of my contemporaries. This feeling starts soaking in gradually, layer by layer, cell by cell settling, reminding me. Reminding me that this is home. This is where my ancestors lived.

Don't live a life too comfortable. Step out of the suburban comfort zone every now and then and do something that scares you. Fear will help you remain able to adapt, it will make your heart vary its rate, beating that bit faster even just for a moment. Fear and facing it is all very much a part of the rewilding process. No matter how deep the over 30's fear has seeped into you (thirty seems to be the age where we gradually find more and more excuses to not take a risk, or face our fears) overcome it, at least now and then. The more you do so the easier it becomes to step out of that comfort zone and remember your wildness.

Overcoming irrational or disproportionate fear is essential, but so is considering the real risks, the danger encountered in nature. Take responsibility for yourself, for your own decisions and actions, educate yourself. Danger in the landscape requires heightened awareness, it requires tuning in to your wildness. One becomes more able to asses the dangers present as you learn to trust yourself more. Initially through using your physical senses and what they are telling you about the world around you, but with experience and practice also through feeling (cognition through the gut and heart), through intuition. Pay attention.

11.2 Metamorphosis As Nature Claims You

To spend quantities of time in wild nature for me is a treat, it feels almost like an indulgence. Despite its value to me I have a resistance to deep nature immersion, there always seems to be something I could, or *should,* be doing and somehow on the surface getting things *done* has a higher value attached to it. But when I spend long enough in the wild those thoughts drop from my mind as nature takes me, absorbs me.

The more time I get to spend without distraction alone in a wild place the more it becomes like a re-birthing, a reconnection directly with source, a remembering of what it is to be human and part of the Earth community.

It gives me a sense of self and purpose whilst at the same time it feeds me with the truth. It becomes a soul teaching. I am reminded of the intricacies of this web of interconnected lifeforms, and that I am just one part of a very complex interrelated organism. As I breathe out my CO^2 is absorbed through the stomata on a plants body, as that plant photosynthesises and releases oxygen I breathe in, and life continues...

When you take yourself off to find a spot in the wilderness you may well notice a heightening of both your senses and physical sensations. You may already have noticed this subtle shift occurring in your regular conscious time spent in nature, in your garden or wherever your regular spot is. The more you have taken note and practised using your heart as an organ of perception, trained your senses, and eaten a diet high in raw plants, the more sensitive you will be.

Perhaps you will notice a visual sensation where the edges of things become incredibly clearly defined, each single blade of grass is definite and individual from all of the others. There is also a shimmering, a sparkling that enters the visual field. Those of you that have previously undertaken a fast, or a low dose of an hallucinogenic drug or plant, may recognise this sensation. It is as though you are seeing more clearly than you ever have before.

It is not just visual. Every breeze may be noticed as a physical sensation across your skin, a rippling caress. Every grain of sand may be felt making its imprint on the sole of your bare foot. Every smell tickling as it dances over your olfactory bulb stimulating and triggering sensations throughout your physical manifestation. The splash of a single droplet of water distinguishable from all the others, despite the deluge of mid-summer rains. It all opens up before you. Deeper, more vital, more vibrant, than anything you ever experience in domesticated, *civilised* life. *Nature has claimed you.*

11.3 Vision Quest

The benefit of time in nature can of course be felt on a short walk during lunch break or simply sitting for ten minutes under a beautiful tree. From a few stolen moments, to an hour every now and then, time spent in such a way helps clear the mind and bring things back into perspective. So imagine the value of spending a large quantity of time dedicated to this, several consecutive days with no interruptions and nothing else to do.

You may want to build up slowly with half a day, a full day, over

night. If you have limited experience alone in nature or wish to delve deep into the wild for more than 24 hours I recommend looking into an organised vision quest type experience.

Deep nature pilgrimage is inbuilt into many traditional cultures from Aboriginal walkabout in Australia, to the vision quest of various native American Indian tribes. Vision quests in their various guises through different traditions often form a rite of passage, especially marking the coming of age. The reason being that time spent alone in nature, with no human distraction, becomes a spiritual journey whether you intend it or not.

Across the planet traditions vary, however there is a general theme. There is preparation time to allow familiarisation with the land and an emptying of the usual day to day timetables and concerns (known as severance). Then, the actual experience itself, which requires solitude in nature and preferably fasting, so that even the body is not distracted with its usual affairs, the task of digestion. This deep immersion is then followed with some time to share and process the experience before the inevitable re-integration with usual day-to-day life.

There are many companies and individuals spread across the different continents offering this kind of experience. The reason I recommend finding such a group, certainly for your first such experience, is mainly because it can be such an immense life changing episode. It is beneficial to share with others after the event, and to have a dedicated team observing you from afar to ensure your safety during your quest. It is something that I believe would benefit everyone even if they only completed the experience once in a lifetime.

Vision quest is clearly something a little more than simple solitary wilderness immersion, there is a conscious spiritual element to it. The spiritual element, as I have already mentioned, is present in any interaction with the wild, but in circumstances when you are occupied with *doing* it can be easy to miss. For our long domesticated bones it is worth really soaking up that isolation from the human world and giving everything to nature. Noticing everything. Feeling everything. And in those moments as the lines become blurry, the lines that demarcate where you end and where nature begins, that is when real connection occurs. Not a logical thought and analysis of biology and quantum physics, but a transcendence of the human condition and a taste of the universe. A warm melding of souls, a release of your need to be human and appear normal, and suddenly an awareness of the flow,

of the light, wisdom, and information exchange. Of the information super-highway. Of it flowing though you, and being a part of it, being able to share and exchange with all other parts thereof. A vision quest gives you space, an opportunity to stop trying to "do" life and actually sit tight for a while and *feel* it flowing through you. It gives you time to feel the wild animal inside you breathe, become more awake, for you to actually notice and experience the animal instincts and impulses pulsing through you.

🌳

I have quested in New Mexico[1]. There was a small group of us who spent several days on the land, finding our spot, and cleansing our thoughts and bodies with a simple diet and a sweat lodge. At dawn one morning, in the yellows and blues of first light, we all walked to our chosen wilderness point from which we could see and hear no other person. My spot was on an incredible ridge, I was greeted by a circling turkey vulture, huge and dramatic, filling the sky. I then sat for four days and four nights, with only water to drink, a small tarp for shelter and a sleeping bag. No other objects. Just me and nature.

Luckily the days were warm. Within hours of reaching my sacred circle I begin stripping clothes until I was dressed as I came to this Earth. Somehow in shedding my garments and possessions, the things that make me civilised, the mental process of stripping away daily concerns and worries also began. By late afternoon on that first day, like a child once more I was revelling in my naivety, the pure wonder and simplicity of my naked soul.

> *To watch as the light fades, and know that you are apart from other humans, to watch as the sun climbs the sky once more and know that you are apart from other humans. And again, and again, and again. Time becomes so long, and so detailed, and so full. And as I lay in the shade of a gnarled juniper in the midday sun, and thanked it from the bottom of my heart for its delicious cooling shade. And as I watched the thunder clouds grow and build on the horizon flashing lightening as they circled around the mountains with thunder eventually splitting over head announcing the storm's arrival. And as I lay for hours watching raindrops collect as diamonds and drop one by one from the trees surrounding me. And as I*

*heard the nearby howling of a group of excited coyotes. All the
time a deeper shedding was taking place.*

*I found parts of myself that I was desperately holding on to
despite the pain they were causing in my life. I fought with
angry tears to hold on to them. Eventually as the days and
nights passed, and the lack of calorific input kicked in, the
energy for fighting to hold on to such painful, detrimental,
parts of my self waned, until broken, battered, and exhausted
I gave in finally, finally letting go. This created a huge void,
a great space within myself to fill with purer energies and
wisdom coming to me directly from the Earth. I had gone up
the mountain with decades of life, decades of domestication,
decades of living under the great illusion and what I
experienced was a great releasing, unfolding, remembering.*

*Returning to my life in this civilised world there is still plenty
of work left to do, a lifetime of unlearning and remembering,
but touching my wildness, becoming untamed, just for a short
while has fanned the flames of my wildness, they will never go
out.*

On the fifth morning, just after sunrise, I left the mountainside returning to camp. I was welcomed with smiling faces and big hugs, simple
foods, a sweat lodge and a chance to share my experience with the
other questers. The whole time I was on the mountain a team of three
sat back at camp saying prayers for our safe return and observing that
each morning I tied a brightly coloured bow on a hanging string that
could be seen with binoculars from a distance, as a sign that I was still
alive. It was good to have the support team, and to know that although
physically alone and exposed to the snakes, scorpions, spiders, javali-
nas, mountain lions, coyotes, sun, rain, thunder, lightening and all the
other life the wilderness held, that spiritually I was being supported
through that time.

Vision quest is a time for clarity, that we never get in our jumbled
busy lives. I encountered the sacred, the sacred in all life, the livingness.
I have taken part in such an organised quest only once, but I would do

it again, just because I felt I could go deeper, relax into the experience more, knowing that there was a support crew back at base camp just in case. I often embark on wild nature adventures by myself without a support team but never for more than 24 hours certainly if I am water fasting, that is the limit at which I feel comfortable. Know your limit. Listen to your body, to your heart. We may have wildness in us, we may be working hard to feed and grow that part of ourselves, but it has, for most of us, been underfed and underutilised for a long time.

11.4 Deep Immersion Activities

There are many ways in which you can immerse yourself deeply within nature. Vision quest is perhaps more like rehabilitation for domesticated animals than a pure wilderness immersion. There are so many ways that you may find more beneficial or more accessible than vision quest. However, for any deep immersion experience care needs to be taken that any activity undertaken is not too technical or involving too much equipment, otherwise it becomes all too easy to slip into using our logic and intellect rather than our animal instincts, our intuition, senses and feelings. For the immersion to be complete it needs to be a solitary pursuit, so equipment requiring a companion for safety, such as ropes and belays, are out. However, provided you have someone back at base who knows where you are headed and when to expect you back there are plenty of activities that will take you deep into your wild animal self.

I enjoy hiking, foraging, wild camping and wild swimming. There are other activities you may pursue in the wild alone, perhaps horse riding or free climbing, neither of which would be within my safe limits. We are each of course different with different ways of interacting with, and delving into, the wild, different levels of experience, skills and confidence. Whatever you choose to do it is essential you know your safe limits. It is also important to pause whatever your chosen activity, just once in a while, don't get carried away with *doing*, pause. Stop long enough to see, hear, feel, taste, listen. To *be*.

Activities in the wild strengthen your animal body and senses, they allow you to realise your physical abilities. Activities feel more animal than just sitting. They do indeed activate your wild animal, they all also have a spiritual aspect. Being surrounded by other living things that all have a life and a meaning gives you meaning, and some deep part of you knows it belongs. Take the time to *feel* your surroundings, to notice

what is going on in and around you. Don't spend all your time distracting yourself with making hides, tracking animals, foraging for dinner, bathing in wild water. Pause long enough to absorb the moment, to relish it. Don't just observe, *feel* it. Feel the wildness coursing through you; pay attention. That way you can return to that feeling again, and again, and again in your daily life. That way in six months time when you are stuck in traffic, feeling down, wondering what it is all about, you can return to your wilderness moment. If you really took time to pause, to feel the wildness within your body, then the memory is more than just mental, it is visceral. Your body will remember the feeling your wilderness adventure gave you. It will feed you with energy and a renewed desire to be outside when you get home and watch where that trail of ants is leading today. Your wildness will lead you back to nature and will remind you to incorporate contact with it as much as possible into your daily life. Day by day, that will provide the medicine you soul has been seeking, the feeling of wholeness and belonging.

11.5 Finding It Where You Can

Attitude, how you view and value things is important. Never forget the intricacies, the beauty, the mystery of nature lies like a universe unto itself in your little finger. Do not overlook wild nature in urban and semi-urban environments. If nothing else because that is where the majority of us live. Any urban area is in fact a complex mix of habitats and ecosystems; the longer it has been established, the more diverse and complex the life there is. Urban areas have their own unique wildlife – foxes, bats, bees, owls, wild plants. Wherever you are, whatever your physical restrictions through location or mobility, it matters not. You can sprout seed in your kitchen, grow a plant, touch a stone.

It will be of far greater value for you to find the nature, the wildness, in your neighbourhood and acknowledge, connect with, it on a daily basis than spend all year waiting for your two week vacation to a top nature destination. I cannot stress the importance of this enough. Rewilding requires maintenance. For the wild part of you to grow and become strong you will need to regularly feed it, otherwise your domestic self will remain in control and the wildness, although it will never disappear, will wither.

People on all levels are waking up to the need for green in our lives. Urban green spaces are becoming more greatly valued and thus are growing in number, not just through the work of activists and

guerilla gardeners, but now, increasingly, through mainstream projects funded by public money.

From the High Line in New York, to the Promenade Plantée in Paris, old abandoned railway lines suspended above city streets have been planted up as green strips, urban parks. In Singapore there are over 200km of green corridors, the park connector network (PCN), connecting up parks and providing nature rich walking and cycling trails throughout the city-state. In London there is a growing awareness of using roofs as green spaces not just privately but on buildings such as Canon Street Station, a trend which began as far back as the 1920's on top of Selfridges. New municipal buildings such as the Library of Birmingham are being built with integral roof gardens on more than one floor, albeit maintained and nurtured by a team of dedicated volunteers.

People around the world are reclaiming vacant lots, and planting them up, in some instances managing to eventually gain official status as pocket parks, safe from development. One of my personal hero's is Ron Finley for growing food along the pavements in downtown LA, greening the environment, feeding and inspiring his whole community. Nature can be, and is, in the city, everywhere you look.

Greening the cities is an important step, providing everyone with greater opportunities to surround themselves with and connect to nature. Even if it has to be on a micro scale it still kindles the wildness inside. Take your focus right down to that crack in the pavement, stuffed with grasses and wild flowers (weeds), ants and earthworms. It is all going on at your feet. Just stop and take the time to notice, take the time to be grateful. Doing so will change your day, will boost your spirit. We don't, and can't, all live in a hand made yurt on a remote hillside. Wherever you are each day the choice is there, it is up to you whether you choose to notice and acknowledge the nature around you or not.

A great adventure to a remote wilderness is wonderful, but, don't forget the ordinary, the everyday, because that is where you live and where the change needs to happen if you want there to be one. Your nature connection needs to be allowed space to grow on a daily basis until your life is consciously entwined during every moment. With persistence, with patience, with an open heart, you will notice changes within yourself as your wildness grows.

Once you have sat with your fingers plunged up to the hilt in soft damp soil and felt the pulse of the planet vibrating up into you, curling

164

and coiling like creepers around your arms, through into the marrow of your bones, and beyond, you will know that your wildness has grown strong. That little piece of nature you have been visiting, acknowledging and loving regularly, be it a plant, a tree, or a scruffy mound of grass, all at once you will know it. It will be a part of you, and you a part of it. It is the same process as when you break through with a person and you exchange something invisible and they become forever a part of you. Even if later you forget them they have contributed to the person you are. Had you never met them and shared that moment of coherence, of connection, of exchange, you would not be who you are now. The same is now true of that little piece of nature, you will take it with you everywhere you go.

🌳

I have had the pleasure of travelling widely across the planet. I have sat alone in distant jungle and desert, on high mountain and tropical island. I have experienced some of nature's most beautiful and least damaged and developed environments. *But* I do not have the luxury of living in one. I live in Gloucestershire, UK. Every tiny corner seems to be trampled and tamed. The small pockets of woodland echo with footfall, voices, and excitable dogs receiving their daily walk. I am fortunate enough to own a garden which backs onto a little spinney, and I rent an allotment from the local authority - a 10x20 metre plot of land where I grow food. It is in these places that I take time to connect with nature the most. My garden is sacred. It gets left most of the time to nature, to just being, and you can feel that. It is wilder than even the nature reserve that sits opposite my front door which is so heavily populated with leisure seekers looking for a little tranquillity and outdoor space in which to exercise.

So find your place. A place in which you feel safe, can relax in, trust. A place where you can perhaps lie back, close your eyes, feel the sun warm your face. Then, begin to tune in to the sounds and smells around you. The perfume of a flower, the buzzing of a bee. It doesn't have to be far, or difficult to reach. To go somewhere extra wild, extra special on occasion is of course a treat, but to bring this into a way of being, into daily life, you have to find a place locally where you can drop into your heart and your senses. Drop out of your head and into your body on a regular basis. Just standing out by your back door barefoot with eyes closed every morning before breakfast is like plugging

directly into the source as bursts of fresh divine Earth energy pulse into the soles of your feet and straight up your spine.

Deep nature immersion allows a glimpse of your place in the grand scheme of things. Deep immersion offers answers, very much like when I retreat to my allotment in anger or distress and within moments of handling the soil find the calm point followed by the resolution, answers to questions I didn't know I was asking, then the peace.

Listen to the voices of nature, the direction of the wind, the messages your own flesh and blood are sending you. Solitary time in the wilderness provides a stripping down, back to the basic building blocks of your soul, a place where meaning in life is revealed. It is a place that you can return to at any time. Even if all you have is a dandelion that landed in a pot on your balcony, seek kinship with it and remind yourself of nature, of your nature and you will know that you are never alone and that somewhere beyond all the urban, techno confusion there is life and there is meaning.

PART V

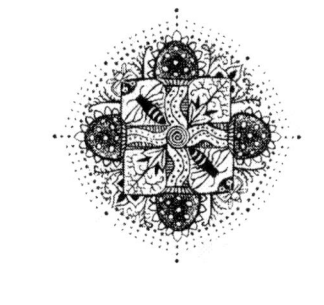

Wild Spirit

There is a basic interrelationship between the health of the Earth and the experience of the sacred. As connection with the sacred grows more tenuous, fewer areas of the Earth will remain alive and wild and sacred.
Stephen Harrod Buhner

The spirit needs the archaic things, the earthly things, the encounter with the nonhuman, with the ancestors... otherwise we remain only half a person, unrealised, like stunted trees.
Charlotte Du Cann

...the ingestion of hallucinogenic plant preparations to obtain knowledge – for healing, for prophecy, for communications with spirits, for anticipation of danger, or for understanding the universe – appears as one of the oldest and most highly treasured traditions.
Ralph Metzner

...in Western Amazonia, which includes the Peruvian, Ecuadorian, and Colombian part of the basin, it is hard to find a culture that does not use an entire panoply of psychoactive plants.
Jeremy Narby

12. ENTHEOGENIC PLANTS AND CONNECTION TO SPIRIT

The deeper into nature we delve the more spiritual the encounter becomes. I have already touched upon this when discussing deep nature immersion and specifically vision quest. Having been raised under the paradigm of nature as machine it can be a challenge to trust and believe in the spiritual element of life. We were raised to ignore feelings, intuition, messages coming in from outside of ourselves. That is the nature of our *civilised* culture. Anyone who claims to feel the spirit in things, to have a spiritual facet to themselves outside of organised religion, is generally regarded with suspicion or thought of as a bit "wacky". But talk to any indigenous group that still lives close to the land and you will discover that, for the *uncivilised,* spirit runs through all things. Embark upon the rewilding process and if you did not feel a spiritual element before, you will begin to as you forge more and deeper connections with nature. Becoming aware of the spirit in all things comes hand in hand with acknowledging livingness and reminds us that everything is sacred, every life.

Denial of the presence of spirit in nature led to the giant misconception, the great illusion I wrote of in Chapters 2 and 3. I believe this separation, this lack of acknowledgement of ourselves and all of nature as alive, enspirited and sacred, is at the core of everything that is wrong with our society. Spending time on a regular basis acknowledging and reintegrating with nature not only brings us back to our wild beginnings but also to a place of spirit.

The more you put into rewilding yourself the more you will find the dimension of spirit opening up. It may feel like life is gradually becoming more and more deeply infused with magic, it may feel like an awakening after a lifetime of slumber. However it feels, grows and appears to you, it is the final essential element to rewilding, to becoming nature. It is not just what you see, but also what you don't see that is important.

🌳

Certain activities can accentuate awareness of spirit; daily nature connections; deep nature immersion; the consumption of entheogenic plants. Many different indigenous peoples across the planet consume

entheogenic plants for healing, for divination, for ritual, for ceremony. They are an intrinsic part of the lives of many, giving wisdom, guidance and healing whilst strengthening and reinforcing nature connections. From ayahuasca combinations for the Amazonian peoples, peyote for the Huichol of Mexico, to Amanita Muscaria for various Siberian peoples. If there is an entheogen that grows in their locale, the native people will know about it and consume it with some reverence as part of their culture.

🌳

The term entheogen was invented by Gordon Wasson and Albert Hoffman to mean a plant that inspires a divine (god or god-like) experience. It's roots are Greek *en-theos-genesthe*, where *en* translates as within or in, *theos* as god, and *genesthe* as to generate. So entheogen is a word for something which generates the god (spirit) within.

All plants have certain qualities that are to greater or lesser degrees mood altering. Breaking the leaf off a growing lettuce, and breathing in as the white sap rises to the point of severance, the smell of freshly plucked lettuce, has the ability to lift you and transport you, just a little bit. When cutting back or brushing past lavenders, the volatile oils released into the air can make you feel relaxed or sleepy. Chopping parsley for adding to food also transports you, just a little, clearing and grounding. Each of the three examples I have used involves smell, the same would also happen if you were to taste either of them. Lack of attention to your senses, surroundings, and how you are feeling, and you could miss all three.

There are certain plants whose mood altering effects are a lot harder to miss. Plants that have special relations with humans that can be traced back for hundreds or thousands of years. Plants that are used by medicine people and shamans as special allies; plants that are generous with their spirit medicine. These are the entheogens, the plants whose effect, or spirit medicine, is so strong that it cannot be overlooked or denied.

12.1 What, Why, Where?

Entheogens come in a variety of forms across the different continents. From fungi to flowers, vines, leaves, roots, seeds and cactii. From the north lands of Siberia almost to the southernmost tip of South America. From desert to jungle. From high altitude to sea level. Entheogenic

plants are spread far and wide, living amongst us, inhabiting almost every landmass, niche and microclimate.

They are wild plants that have been part of human culture for many thousands of years. Peyote dated to 8500 BCE have been found in a cave near Coahuila, Mexico. They did not walk into that cave on their own - our *wild* ancestors were interacting with these particular plants. Other evidence of an ongoing relationship between peyote and humankind include ceramic tiles dated to 100 BCE depicting the cactus. At 2000 years and counting this makes peyote the oldest known entheogen used by humans[1].

Once imbibed, entheogenic plants have the ability to show you yourself, no ifs, no buts; stripped to the core. They shift our awareness so that we can see what needs adjusting and bringing into balance, most especially within ourselves. They assist us in seeing other realities, the hidden dimensions. They help us find connections and perhaps corrections, for the self and this reality. Working with their wisdom allows us to become aligned once more with nature, with Gaia.

The nurturing of our individual wildness requires ingesting wildness and experiencing things we don't know how to explain, or how to control. We tend to fool ourselves that we do know most things, that we are in control, but to take this kind of medicine is a humbling reminder that there are still mysteries out there; big unknowns. Things beyond our understanding and control. Taking this kind of soul medicine is the best way I have found to remind me of that. To put me in my place, if you will.

There is hunger afoot for this kind of medicine. Pensioner mums travel with their middle aged daughters to the Amazon to seek it out, to taste this medicine. It is calling to more and more people but not in the way of drugs, not so that you can "get out of it", distract yourself and forget, but instead so that you can remember a fundamental part of yourself; your truly wild nature and its spiritual dimension.

There is so much information about the various entheogens that has become available in the last few years. I remember only as long ago as 1998 sitting in a café in Guatemala reading *True Hallucinations* by Terence McKenna and feeling a pull, that entheogens were to be my path. Within weeks I was in the Amazon imbibing a mysterious medicine called ayahuasca that I had never heard of previously. Now, for better or worse, we are all aware of many such medicines. There are

websites, books, organised tours, reviews in the national newspapers, mentions and televised consumption on documentaries. Information about entheogens is not only out there it is hard to avoid. I believe there is a significance to this rise in prominence – such as humankind having strayed so far from nature and thus needing to reconnect and receive soul medicine more than ever before.

However, despite the rise in use of entheogens in the *civilised* world it pays to beware for *there be dragons!* This, the poison path, is not for everyone. Follow your heart very closely and never be persuaded by anyone; *you* must be ready. It can be dangerous in those other realms. You can lose your way and find it very difficult to come back. Or you may get fully freaked out triggering a psychotic episode. These are powerful Earth medicines and are not to be played with or consumed without due caution and respect.

For hundreds and thousands of years, a very personal relationship has developed and evolved between these plants and humankind. Stories and ritual have built around these relationships, elevating these plants in human hearts and minds. With the current worldwide interest in these plants they stand bold and exposed. The result in part is that some plants have been legislated against; prohibiting their cultivation, harvest and ingestion. So if you are drawn to work with entheogens it would pay to check their current legal status where you live before proceeding. What bothers me though, is how can a plant, a wild plant, be made illegal? Surely that is like making squirrels illegal, or butterflies?

Admittedly, as I have already mentioned, they are not for everyone and as with all medicines, plant or otherwise, certain people will have a bad physical reaction (some people are allergic to daisies, others to penicillin). They can also have a powerful effect on mental health. Under controlled conditions certain entheogens may have the potential to treat a variety of psychological conditions including post traumatic stress disorder (PTSD) and depression, research is ongoing[2]. However, they are not recommended for self experimentation by those suffering from mental health issues because, as previously mentioned, they could trigger a psychotic episode, or cause the user to become a danger to themselves or others. For these reasons entheogens are deemed as dangerous by the establishment, which is in part why they are legislated against. And yes to a degree they are dangerous, but so too are *Digitalis spp.* (foxglove) and *Laburnum* trees, yet they are grown and celebrated in cottage gardens across the land.

There is something else, another reason. I believe it is because they show you what is really there – what is in front of you. They help you see beyond the illusion to the livingness of this world and thus break down the old paradigm of nature as machine. This contradicts what our current social, political and economic models are based upon and leaves the capitalist paradigm we live under in a frail position. Being party to the truth is liable to subvert us and our obedience. The element of fear driving the legislations against these plants is not just fear of harm to individuals but fear of harm to the current paradigm; how society runs, and how we as individuals are controlled.

🌳

The wisdom, the messages received from entheogens can be life changing, sometimes in a matter of moments. Again, they are *not* for the faint hearted. However, responsible and heartfelt interactions with entheogens are a great way of having direct contact with spirit, with the spirit in nature (and that also means your own wild spirit).

These plants, all plants, are teachers. Plant teachers can lead you beyond the five senses, beyond feeling and intuition to another realm. However, many people refer specifically to entheogens when talking of plant teachers. Learning from them requires inquisitiveness. What you learn depends on what you ask and how you ask. The plants give you something in response; it is up to you to work out what that thing is and what it means. Learning this way means you will never forget, never lose that lesson because it is part of you; you asked it, you discovered it, you felt it first hand, every inch of it until you knew it.

Use of entheogens helps you get back in alignment with nature and your true self, but it requires effort on your behalf. They will show you addictions and habits, relationships that undermine you, your health, your happiness and your connection with nature. It is *you* that will then need to change things, to live and think differently.

The allure of entheogens also attracts joyriders seeking escapism and highs. Yet just a single experience will touch beyond the pleasure receptors and feel like something sacred. Even for the most sceptical it becomes food for the soul. Not many things in life do this, which is why I include it here. I think the further we have strayed from nature, our true nature, and recognising the sacred in all life, the more we all need to be reminded of the sacred; entheogens have stepped forward to help provide that.

174

In popular culture these plants are often referred to as hallucinogens, meaning that they induce hallucinations, which in many instances they do. However, depending on how your brain is wired and which plant you have ingested, you may never hallucinate or see visions. So the term itself can be a little misleading. Some people experience these plants as a visceral feeling that rushes through them permeating every part of their being, others still receive words, direct wisdom, that they need not extract from a flood of visions. Bearing that in mind, it is important not to approach with expectations. If you were expecting to be transported to a psychedelic mindscape inhabited by otherworldly beings, and that does not happen, you may feel disappointed with the results and overlook the nuggets of wisdom you do receive.

Most often I do find myself immersed in visions, sometimes ripped so strongly from myself that all memory of being human, an individual, disappears from my mind, sometimes for hours at a time. Again I caution that for this reason working with hallucinogens is not for everyone and is most certainly not advisable if you are confused or struggling with your mind to begin with.

Entheogens help us bridge the gap between the seen and unseen worlds, between matter and spirit. They are probably the quickest access to the biggest, most life and thought changing experience you can have. They are awe inspiring, humbling. You remember how to be a part of Gaia, who your relations are. You may learn to surf raindrops or allow insects to crawl over you, tickling your skin while you remain unafraid. You may find that you are one with the grass. Like so many of the other rewilding elements, especially deep nature immersion, entheogens can give you a kind of reboot. They can help get you back on track, remind you of the important things, the magic in the universe, but also the things you need to let go of or to work on.

Again and again the entheogens will force you to look at addictions, greed and unhealthy habits. These are all symptoms of domestication. Entheogens push you towards living more naturally; towards the wild side.

For me consumption of entheogens is an essential part of my wildness. Our urban taming is driving more and more people to seek this medicine out. It is becoming mainstream despite criminalisation as people search wider and further in unknown, uncharted, territory for those last sacred, *wild*, parts of themselves.

To work effectively with an entheogen is to swim naked and fearless in an otherworldly sea of meanings and to bring back usable information. Once again this rewilding process brings us to a place of transcending our individual humanity to becoming part of something more than our seemingly separate selves.

🌳

There are so many different entheogens, each with their individual character and medicine. There are of course differences in duration of effects, just as there are a great range of effects. So do your research, don't just jump for the big names straight away. Find the medicine *you* need, one that specifically appeals to you. Try to avoid reading too many "trip reports": all they do is build expectations. Any experience you have as a result of ingesting an entheogen will be unique to you. Try not to obscure that unique interaction with expectations of jaguars and serpents when you live in a flat in Dagenham.

Entheogens do tend to come to you if, and when, it's time. A friend will invite you to a ceremony or perhaps you will buy a magazine and it will fall open on an article about a certain plant. Maybe you will dream about it, or the name of a plant you have never heard of before will enter your consciousness and start ringing in your ears, calling you by repeating its name over and over. Pay attention. Does one plant keep appearing? Perhaps it is more difficult for it to happen this way now that there is so much more information out in the public arena but stay alert, remain sensitive and *feel* your way through the information that becomes available to you.

Perhaps there is an entheogen that lives and grows in your country, in your neighbourhood even. One that you could visit in in its wild environment. One that if legal and safe to do so, you could harvest yourself. There is a saying in folk medicine circles that a plant collected locally is 100 times stronger than one that is not. If it is collected by you its strength is elevated to 1000 times that of a non local plant collected by a stranger. Land provides medicine that the local people need and by learning about it, where it grows, when it grows, how to harvest, how to store and preserve it, how to prepare it for consumption, you begin to build a personal relationship with that plant. Your knowledge and understanding of each other is already growing and building before you ever ingest. When you eventually come to do so (ingest) you are just deepening an already existing relationship. It is the long awaited

176

meeting of long term pen pals, a pregnant woman and her child. The meeting of souls who have already been courting each other with love and patience and dedication.

I cannot list all of the entheogens and where they grow as there are just so many, some of which can be found over a wide range of different countries, even separate continents. Others are more niche.

The entheogens that immediately come to mind include various psilocybin mushrooms; ayahuasca and some of its analogues including either cacao or *Peganum harmala* in combination with psilocybin mushrooms; *Salvia divinorum*; Dimethyltryptamine (DMT) from various sources including *Phalaris spp.* and *Acacia spp.*; Peyote; San Pedro; opium. There are many other entheogenic plants; Iboga, morning glory, Hawaiian woodrose, *Datura spp., Brugmansia spp.*, blue lily, henbane, mandrake, passion flower, nutmeg and fly agaric are all probably a little less well known and less widely used. This is by no means a definitive list; the list, it appears, is all but endless. The reason I have embarked into naming names at all is to inspire you to look beyond the obvious. Different plants, different medicine, will be suitable for different people.

So, as I said, do your research and the same as with food and herbal medicine, think about how local plants will have a greater meaning, bonding you ever closer to the land and the flora of that land. Allowing you access to the spirit medicines and to the shared dreams your ancestors once had on this land. Inspiring you to fall in love again and again with the wild land, wild plants and wild spirits that live where you live.

12.2 Entheogen Etiquette

Entheogen use had a place in many different cultures and although it still does in traditional societies, it has been lost to us. These are new times, a different people and a different culture. We need this medicine for different reasons than those that have grown their whole lives with a connection to nature within a strong community. We live amongst computers in high rises. Our needs are different. The medicines we need are different. I believe the plants are versatile enough to deliver that to us. We need to be able to see things more holistically, to see this Earth as the paradise it still is and still can be, to feel the love, to fathom the unknown, to glimpse the mystery. That is the medicine for modern times. To bring us back to our wild nature.

177

Although we have been drawn toward the rich world of entheogens we are coming from a culture of which they are no longer a part, so we have no formal tradition. Perhaps if you are called by a non-local plant you can opt to be part of an organised group, or travel solo to where the plant that is calling you grows. This way you can imbibe in the plants natural setting with some semblance of a traditional ceremony conducted by local medicine people. If you do not have the pull to travel it is often possible to find a group conducting some form of ceremony away from the land in which the plant grew. These kind of events range from week long country retreats, to evenings in community halls in the inner city, both with the medicine and sometimes a shaman, flown in.

Personally I am not a huge fan of formal organised rituals, although they do serve a purpose. They are of course most relevant when performed within the cultural context that they formed. That is the country in which the plant grows and amongst the people who have been working with that plant over time building a relationship, and through that, developed certain traditions pertaining to its use. In my experience when attending such a ceremony outside of it's original cultural context, importing traditions and perhaps a shaman to oversee the ceremony, it feels diluted. Often highly priced (as making profit becomes a major motivation), over subscribed and distracting. The medicine is rarely strong enough and the ceremony somehow overall lacks substance; heart. Others may have had different experiences, but each time (and there have been a few) that I have been drawn into a formal ritual outside of its place of origin, or performed solely for Western visitors *in* the place of origin, I have found the whole experience rather underwhelming.

That said, such formal group ceremonies for the most part, offer a safe and respectful launch pad for work with entheogens. This is clearly valuable especially for your first few times. As for most young people living today in Western society, my introduction to the sacred plant teachers was not within a ritual, or even a wild setting - instead in a boyfriend's bedsit. Despite the rather unglamorous surroundings, it was nonetheless an eye opening and magical experience that opened a doorway to another realm and another possibility. It showed me that there was a deeper level, there was more than that which we experience in our regular lives.

If you want to explore your relationship with one of these plants outside of a formal group setting there is a lot to consider and I certain-

ly would not recommend working alone for the first few times. My first few experiments and experiences aside I now create my own ritual. Ritual, in whatever form, does help focus the mind and bring you to a place of respect and mindfulness with the plant teacher in question.

Whatever approach you choose to take, and assuming you are choosing a plant that is legal to consume, there are certain guidelines that will help keep you safe, focused and able to get the most from your experience with the plant.

Make sure that the source of your entheogen is sustainable and that it was harvested with consciousness. If you cannot guarantee that should you be investing in it, fuelling the growing industry? Like many herbal remedies that are harvested from the wild some entheogens are becoming endangered in their natural habitat because of unsustainable rates of harvest in recent times. If you are looking to find spirit medicine then the spirit of the plant you intend to ingest when receiving that medicine must be honoured, especially during harvest and preparation. If you want to know the provenance of your food, food for your body, then it should follow that you take an interest in the provenance of this kind of food too; food for the spirit.

It is of utmost importance that any dietary precautions are observed and adhered to, as some entheogens can have serious, potentially fatal, interactions with some of our usual foods. For that reason it is also important that you do not mix ingestion of the entheogen with either drugs or alcohol. To avoid any such issues and in an attempt to clear my body and mind I usually begin with some kind of cleanse. Depending on the plant to be ingested and time available, I usually eat only cleansing raw foods for a minimum of 24 hours prior to ingestion, culminating in a water fast for six hours or more immediately prior to ingestion. Adopting a similar strategy will mean above all else that your body can concentrate on the entheogen and is not still digesting your last meal. If there is no food in your stomach you will get the full impact of the medicine.

During the week leading up to my own personal medicine ceremony I will begin to create a conscious intention, a direction for the journey that will be made with the plant, a question to ask. Without a clear question you will have no momentum and will spend your time distracted by the kaleidoscope colour show, the cogs and cathedrals of patterns and light. You need to ask humbly; ready to feel, experience, and be shown something entirely new. Just wandering in the other

realms enjoying the beauty is fine for the first couple of times, but if you would like to build a relationship with the entheogen, to allow it to work its magic in your day to day life, it helps to be clear about what you would like to know, or need help to change.

Asking a question may not always go as you think it will, as sometimes you will need to face something before you can proceed, and the plant will see to it that you do. No matter how earnest your question, it may feel as if it is not being addressed at all. I often find in these cases with hindsight (which may take literally years to clearly form) that the question or issue closest to my heart was the one the teacher addressed. Sometimes you can be so busy hiding what is on your heart from the world that you even hide it from yourself. The plants will not be hoodwinked in this way. They will take you where you most need to go to help you with your greatest need. It is just a matter of recognising that this is what has happened and in some instances that takes a long time.

Next it is important to choose an environment in which you feel safe and comfortable. Find a place where you are unlikely to be disturbed, where you are physically warm and relaxed. Find a *sitter,* a friend who will sit with and watch over you. Someone you can trust, can throw up in front of, cry in front of, or say ridiculous sounding things without feeling self conscious. Within an organised setting the person leading the ritual will act as your sitter, taking responsibility and making sure everyone is safe and well. If you are working with a group of friends, have one person sit out and observe the proceedings without having imbibed the plant medicine. A sitter is there in case you have a reaction and need medical treatment, or more likely need someone to listen to your ramblings, laugh with, or provide security and hugs.

Immediately prior to ingesting the entheogen I usually smudge myself and the area in which I am to take the medicine, to clear stagnant and unwanted energies and again to help me focus on the sacred nature of the occasion. If my ceremony is to be indoors I may light a candle and have some potted plants or fresh cut flowers, a crystal and a bowl of water in the room. If the ceremony is to be in the open air I may light a fire and choose a spot by running water. This is my way of honouring the elements, noting my place amongst, and dependence upon, them.

I say prayers, thanking the plant for it's sacrifice and asking for it to share its wisdom with me. More recently I have expanded my prayers out to the directions and the spirits of other living beings, prayers of

gratitude and respect. Of course as the medicine is fading within me at the end of the ceremony I say many thanks to the spirit of the teacher, most often tearfully as I don't want to leave their world and return to mine, or perhaps because my whole world has just significantly changed. *Never* forget to thank.

Ceremony can just be a silent acknowledgement before and gratitude after. It can be as simple or as elaborate as suits you. Fasting, cleansing, praying, singing whatever you choose, something that has meaning and significance for you. It is the marking of *your* entry into sacred union with spirit, with the entheogen, that is of primary importance.

Closing your eyes and lying relaxed and relatively still whilst the entheogen is inside you can be very helpful. By lying in darkness you are shutting out the outside world and journeying beyond the five senses, to a place inside. A place where messages and images inspired by the plant are kindling the spirit within, taking you outside of yourself into another dimension but paradoxically also very deeply inside of yourself, a place few of us have ever otherwise thoroughly explored, if at all. It is the universe outside of yourself that also exists deep within yourself, such is the connection between all things.

Wild plants, the wildness in the world, reminds us of our own wildness. These plants are true, they hide nothing from themselves or from the world and they help us to do the same.

Some entheogens such as the cactus San Pedro seem to require movement. It wants you to move so that it can circulate through your body. It wants you to be outside so that you can experience everything breathing in and out, in and out, in and out... Each plant is different, will take you to different places, teach you in different ways. That is why it is important to wait to notice who, if any, are calling to you, who would like to meet you and pass on their wisdom.

Try to maintain a kindergarten state of mind at all times, that is an open mind full of wonder, empty of judgements and expectations. Try to forget what you think you know, what you have read, what you have heard. Those things, those things we think we know, can get in the way of the truth that we are perceiving. A kindergarten state of mind allows us to leave expert opinion behind and meet with your heart; to learn first hand and build your own relationship with plants and nature. Expect the unexpected or drop all expectations entirely, else you may miss what does come.

In the realms where the entheogens may take you, you have no choice but to let go of control. The further you are from your wildness the harder the entheogens, and the doors they open to you, will be to assimilate. The more difficult you find it to relinquish control the more you will struggle. Struggling to maintain the illusion of control is often the basis of a *bad trip*. The more that you have embraced the rewilding process, faced fears of the wild and the unknown, the more prepared you will be to embark on this kind of adventure; a wild adventure of spirit.

12.3 Plant Wisdom

Have fun with your entheogen. Explore the alternate reality that you are taken to. You may meet beings there - they are often playful, especially when you are new. However avoid becoming a what I like to call a "joyrider", consuming entheogens only for kicks, for the fun of it, for the bright lights and pretty patterns. It can be overwhelming in the beginning, and impossible not to be distracted by the incredible intricate beauty and indeed the simple existence of this other realm. But always be respectful, acknowledge the beings as elders, wise older siblings, even during fun and playful moments. Be polite. Ask. Thank. Love. If you are disrespectful sooner or later they will give you a mental slap, something very serious to think about; the teachers are rarely inhibited if you need a telling off.

One thing you will most likely have to face early on, as I've already mentioned, are any addictions or habits that are detrimental to yourself or the planet. Examples I know of include one friend who was told by *Amanita muscaria* that eating sugar was making him small and that he didn't need the comfort of it in his life any more. He told me it was as if the *Amanita* took a knife to sugar and cut it away; he has not eaten it since. One friend who smoked 40 cigarette a day for over 30 years stopped over night after ingesting ayahuasca. Another friend was walking through a beautiful fairy realm landscape only to notice that as far as she could see the ground was littered with her brand of cigarette packets. Another friend was faced with a landscape of doughnuts and sweets with a whole dancing line of chubby beings sticking their tongues out and shaking their butts in her face.

It is not just bad habits that entheogens make us look at, sometimes they help us find resolutions for events that have troubled us. One friend who had taken the difficult decision to terminate a pregnancy met with the spirit of the unborn child and they made peace. I have personally found

myself being taken to an unpleasant scenario that I lived through in this reality. I was made to live through it again through the eyes of one of the other people present. It made me rethink the whole thing, and forgive myself for my part. The wisdom of the plants is medicine on a soul level.

The plants can help us open our eyes to the living, breathing, aware, intelligent universe and overcome our anthropocentric world view. To really experience other life as living and inspirited it can be useful to experience the viewpoint of another life form. For me this has happened multiple times on a variety of different entheogens, for example when I saw through the eyes of another human in the room, as mentioned above. But I have also seen the world the way a mushroom sees and even merged with so called inanimate objects such as a sofa. Entheogen use can give access to these ulterior perspectives and thus can allow real insight into other viewpoints. Once experienced the possibility of developing a biocentric world view, where *all* life is valuable, becomes a real option. Humankind no longer separate and superior, just one life form amongst others.

The more work you do with entheogens the deeper you can go. Jeremy Narby in his 1995 book *The Cosmic Serpent* found that the extensive botanical knowledge of the Ashaninca Amazonian Indians came in visions that they received whilst ingesting Ayahuasca. In fact 74% of the plant based remedies found within the modern pharmacopoeia were originally "discovered" by traditional societies rather than by the logical, analytical explorations of the Western, scientific mind[3]. For most of us it will be difficult to access such detailed knowledge, as opportunities to imbibe can be infrequent. Equally most of us will have plenty of work to do on ourselves, on a personal level, before we start delving into the encyclopedic information available about the universe. However there is plenty of wisdom to glean, and working on yourself, walking away from your domestication and into the open arms of the wild, is what rewilding is all about.

Entheogens can help you notice things that you have failed to notice through either wilful ignorance or just simply because they came so gradually and have been there so long. Perhaps your attention will be taken to a specific part of your body or relationship, maybe it has

not been working right, not for a really long time. Despite the rewilding work your cherished blindnesses have allowed your body and, or, relationships to slowly fall apart without you really paying full attention and discovering what could make things a little better. Entheogens take away the blinkers, help you to see clearly, giving you an opportunity to change things.

Your new way of seeing encourages you to choose to take more care of yourself and the planet. It becomes a positive feedback loop. As your interest in your health and in your food develops, you want to know more about that food, you want to be sure that it is local and organic so you start to grow it yourself. In growing that food you fall more in love with plants and the Earth and you want to know more and learn more. Understanding that only Gaia can teach you of herself, you return to the plant teachers with open ears, open eyes, open heart, open mind, and ask another question.

12.4 Integration

The danger of having so much exposed so quickly, as opposed to gaining such insights through many hundreds of hours of discipline and meditation, is that when you return to everyday reality you bring back precisely nothing. Any knowledge or wisdom gained simply does not stick in this reality where there is no reference point for it, and so the whole encounter reduces to nothing more than psychic candy-floss. In addition it is easy to be bamboozled and confused when after having life-changing visions and insights on return to this reality there is little or no support, and you may even be judged as a drugs freak or just plain bonkers. For that reason it is important for me at this point to emphasise that I consider the entheogens as Earth medicine, most certainly not as *drugs* but as medicine for the spirit direct from the Earth. Just as food and herbal remedies are medicine for the body and emotions direct from the Earth. You can no more describe these plants as drugs than you can a dandelion leaf or a mug of chamomile tea.

So to reiterate, these plants are Earth medicine, spirit medicine - not *drugs*. For that reason as much as any other the whole event should be approached as sacred. Your intent when encountering an entheogen is everything. Without clear intent or a clear question, what you return with is an ineffable selection of bright images, or perhaps a visceral feeling, but it has no context, no meaning, in this reality and thus it eventually just fades away as a vague memory. So, given the

general unfamiliarity with these altered states of consciousness, one of the greatest challenges is translating your visions in to actionable wisdom in this realm.

You may find the whole experience impossible to express to anyone other than those with whom you shared the experience, or whom you know have undergone a similar experience. In locations where the use of teacher plants is commonplace the support system is well set up with multiple generations in each family able to empathise and shed light upon the teachings, to help unravel the true message. As you can imagine it is particularly beneficial to be able to share afterwards, so being part of a community of others whom have experienced similar and will be able to listen without judgement and to empathise can be invaluable. Such a community can help you understand your task and support you in enacting any required changes. If you do not have a group of friends or acquaintances with whom to share in this way there are online communities that may provide such support and a platform from which to share.

Of course any knowledge or wisdom gained from entheogenic encounters is always going to be somewhat difficult to share, even with fellow otherworld adventurers, as it is not of this dimension. What you encountered may well have been fast, very fast, a bombardment of otherworldly symbols and imagery. You may find the spoken word inadequate to describe the alternate dimensions that you travelled in, but there are many ways to process the experience. Writing helps me, not necessarily straight away but a day or two after I fill pages and pages in my journal with all that I can remember. I find it useful to record it in this way because I don't need to explain myself, I know what I mean, but also because it provides a tool for sparking my memory so that I can return to it and seek lessons from it, even years later. For others, art helps to capture the essence of the experience and trigger their memory, for others still it is making music.

It is unsurprising that when a life changing experience happens suddenly, and even more so if it comes from outside of consensus reality, that it can be difficult to integrate. Most often with early entheogenic encounters it is the illusion of separateness that is entirely smashed, which as with all rewilding experiences, makes living within the current civilised world paradigm just that little bit more uncomfortable.

But as more people feel and experience a change in perspective and manifest that as a change in their living relationship with the world, the more it begins to change for us all.

You change after visiting the far realms and whichever method you use to work through your experiences with entheogens one thing is certain: integration of your experience will not happen overnight. It may take many years, or a lifetime, as you evolve, change, digest and assimilate. So be gentle on yourself.

12.5 Developing Life Long Relationships

Not every entheogenic plant you encounter will become your ally. Some plants come and then they go. You may work with them intensely for a while and then they just slide back out of your life, as if their work is done. Others seem to stick around for the long haul, become long term allies (just like human friends). It took me a while to recognise my particular allies as I felt many different teacher plants calling me; I needed to meet them, feel them inside me, hear their wisdom. Now I am more or less settled on a small number that I have returned to again and again over the years for another slice of wisdom.

I am a firm believer that an entheogen will appear to you, become available, at the right time for you. If you find yourself pursuing a certain plant you must always check your motivation. Is it just to tick another experience off your list? To find the ultimate psychedelic high? Be careful of chasing the experience. If the plant is right it will call you to seek it out, or find it's way onto your path.

Long term relationships can't be forced, and you can't choose them; you will choose each other. It is like courting any other relationship in your life, if you both feel the chemistry then you are either set for a dramatic and exciting whirlwind of an affair, or for a lifelong respectful companionship.

When thinking of the long term there is a lot to be said of something that is local, that you can collect from the wild or at least cultivate yourself. I can fully attest to the superior strength of the medicine when harvested, prepared and consumed where it *naturally grows*. I was once berated by ayahuasca for imbibing the brew in a ceremony in France, where the plant had been imported from the far away jungles of South America. I was reminded in no uncertain terms that I should have known better than to take the medicine out of context, especially as I know a relatively local analogue alternative. So think about it, try

186

and explore relationships with entheogens that grow somewhere close, that you can visit in their natural environment.

If you have no contact with the plant before consumption how will you know that it is being cared for as sacrament every step of its journey? That it is not being over harvested? That local populations who have had a relationship with this plant for millennia are not losing out to unscrupulous, over zealous, harvesters (from within or outside of their community) keen to make a quick buck? Beyond the source of the entheogen don't forget there is a context to each plant's medicine.

I grow or wild harvest most of the entheogens I choose to use and so the ritual, the ceremony begins as I plant the seed, take a cutting or gather my harvest. Singing, so often singing, sometimes talking or praying, the plants and fungi seem to like that, to respond to it. Never forget, like all plants, the entheogens are living beings, they like to be acknowledged, spoken to, sung to, loved. If you have the opportunity to grow or wild harvest your own medicines, your bond will already be strong before you imbibe the medicine. The teacher's presence will already be with you; their spirit familiar. There is very unlikely a single native shaman anywhere in the world who is not acquainted with the growing plant before ingesting its medicine, who has not undergone some kind of initiation with the plant, or lived side by side with the said plant all of his or her life.

There comes a point on your journey with the entheogens that you will need to know it more closely than simply through ingestion during ceremony. There will come a time when you will need to know where and how it lives. You will want to know what it needs to be healthy and well. It is the same as with your human friends; you will fall in love.

Always acknowledge the livingness. Maintain an attitude of gratitude. Be open and whole hearted in all your interactions with the entheogens. Over time and with experience you will find one that suits your constitution. There will be a bond - it could be humour, whatever that special connection is with time and familiarity your relationship will flourish and grow. Even so, never force the issue of consuming the plant just because you have grown or sourced it, always check does it feel right for you? Is today the right time? Don't be afraid to ask the plant directly with your heart. It is respectful to work in this way and the entheogen, your ally, will appreciate your conscientious approach.

Another stage in the development of your relationship comes during the preparation to consume. For some of the entheogens this can

be a very lengthy process. During processing you are again interacting, acknowledging the livingness, offering your gratitude and love, and asking your question. Throughout the process you are slowly falling into the dream of the plant which enriches the whole experience. It is a bit like the first time you get to eat fruit or nuts from a tree you have nurtured from a tiny seedling. You appreciate that fruit or nut so much more because you know how long, how many cycles of seasons, days and nights, rain and sun, it took for the tree to mature and produce nuts or fruit. It adds value. The longest preparation time I have ever spent was half a day harvesting, a couple of hours skinning and chopping, followed by a sixteen hour overnight vigil. Stirring, reducing, watching, waiting. I talk of falling in love because that is what happens as you labour all night inhaling vapours, your skin becoming coated, entering the dream. The whole experience is sublime and takes your relationship to a whole new level (and all before you taste a drop!).

We each are at a different stage of life with different needs, capacity to learn and opportunities. So, as with everything in this book, it is up to you to explore albeit safely and legally. Make sure you are always well informed and of sound mind and good health, with a support network and sitter if appropriate.

🌳

My relationship with my primary ally is so deep now, it has reached a new level. When I feel it is time to consume the entheogen, my question comes clearly and quickly. And just as quickly and clearly comes the response. Sometimes just minutes after writing it down, no ingestion. My deep connection, like a phone line direct to the plants intelligence and wisdom, no longer requires ingestion to receive the answer.

12.6 To Imbibe, Or Not To Imbibe?
Remember that all plants are teachers if we are willing to pay attention. Even lying in bed you can learn from plants if you are close to a window. You can watch a tree grow leaves, flowers and fruits, then watch them fall as season follows season and the cycle of life continues. Despite the flamboyance and the loud voices of the entheogens don't overlook what you can learn from a nettle or a fern.

I believe all plants are medicine in some sense, some for the body, some for the mind and emotions, some for the spirit and some for our entirety. But as with all medicines some of us need certain ones and

react well to them - others not. Never forget a peanut is a tasty snack for some, while to others it is potential death. So listen, listen to your body. If you have the chance to sit with and get to know, or to grow the plant in question, do so. Don't read about the plant and base your knowledge on that alone, thinking you already know it; you would not consider that you knew David Beckham just because you have read about him or seen him on TV... It has to be first hand.

If you have been working with your senses, feeling before thinking and fine honing those skills, you will have gone some way to being able to access the wisdom of the plant without ingestion. Just being in the presence of a plant you will pick up on some of its character whether you are conscious of it or not. This is the basis of vibrational medicine. Just try sitting under a variety of different trees and explore how you feel whilst enveloped under the canopy of each one, there will be significant differences.

You may feel uncomfortable with the thought of visiting other realms as a result of ingesting a plant. We have not grown with that as a norm within our culture. If that is the case for you consider growing one of the entheogenic plants at home. One that is perfectly legal to own and grow, and develop your relationship with it. As entheogens shout more loudly than most other plants, especially when they are first brought into your home, you will end up working with them and their truths on a very subtle level on a daily basis as a result. The spirit of that plant will have entered your home and be interacting with your spirit, passing on its wisdom and medicine in subtle ways without ingestion.

I have experimented on working in different ways with entheogens other than ingestion alone. I have found with those plants that have leaves that if I take a leaf that is still intact and attached to the plant into my mouth, close my eyes and be open something beautiful and amazing will always come. Perhaps it is that living with the plant, sometimes for many years beforehand, drip feeds me some of the story, but simply placing a live and growing leaf in my mouth I can tap directly into the spirit medicine of that plant. This is a potential avenue of exploration available to anyone who is nervous or unsure about ingesting. You still get to taste the wildness, and it still gets a chance to infuse into your being.

12.7 A Few Words Of Caution
As entheogens have entered popular culture there is a need to be vigi-

lant; these plants are wild and powerful. Although they hold a deep medicine of great meaning for so many, there is in some circumstances an unhealthy attraction to the power that they wield. I have watched all sorts of inauthentic operations run for the money or the power trip of the organiser or shaman. I have watched people give too much of themselves until they look green or vampire-esque and become more needy than ever. I see zombies lacking vibrancy, giving their power away, destroying distant forests with not one thought for the manner in which the plants were harvested (under sacred ritual, or even with gratitude?). No question over whether it came from a sustainable source, not one question from these peoples hearts and minds, whilst destroying the balance of distant ecosystems. It disturbs me...

If you are drawn to plants that grow in foreign lands it is always best if you can go to the source yourself. Go and take your time, melt into the jungle like snow from the high Andes. If you chose to travel as part of an entheogen package experience it will undoubtedly be intense, ten days to two weeks is standard. Do your homework before you go. You want to be confident that the person running the trip will have your back. The shaman will deliver the medicine, the entheogen will show you the dream then strip it down to the truth. The organiser then has to gather you up and get you back to where you once knew as home. I recommend doing a one day workshop with the organiser or speaking with others whom have previously gone on the trip you are intending. Just because someone is famous within the field or has written a bunch of books does not automatically make them full of integrity or the right person to guide and accompany you.

Some plants are almighty tricksters that will laugh as you spend a crazed three days running the streets naked (this is where the value of a sitter becomes obvious). Proceed with caution. Avoid entheogens that have been tinkered with and made into enhanced strength extracts or isolated as active chemicals. Chemically altered substances can seduce you and lead you to a place of submission and addiction. Be vigilant with yourself, with your motives and with your relationship to the plant; may it remain ever healthy.

We think of feeding our bodies and stimulating our minds, but as memories of greenness fade so does the nourishment of our spirit. There are many ways to nourish the spirit. Not everyone will be called

to come to know one of these powerful and mysterious plants, just as not everyone will be called to stand naked in the pouring rain. But bearing in mind all the cautions, interaction with entheogens has been instrumental to my rewilding process. It allowed me to really think like a mountain for the first time, to really care about each element, hear what the trees and the sad bald eroding hills were saying to me. If you are inclined and if you are ready this could be the extra element that fills you to the brim, that allows you to know in no uncertain terms that we are nature, that we live in paradise but also that our separation is allowing us to destroy it and thus ourselves. Entheogens are the ultimate eye-opener and Gaia connector.

PART VI

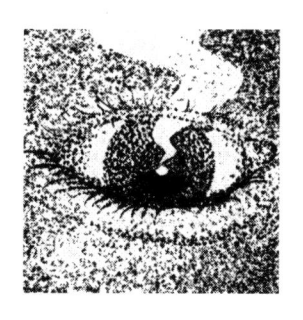

Wild Future

*There is no solution to the "drug problem," or to the problem of
environmental destruction or the problem of nuclear weapons
stockpiles, until and unless our self-image as a species is
reconnected to the earth.*
Terrence McKenna

*We would not be able to regenerate anything outside ourselves
unless we regenerated our own inner landscapes, until our true
wild natures had burst through the broken rubble and tarmac of
our own artificial city-based worlds.*
Charlotte Du Cann

*...at the moment of greatest darkness (or of greatest light), the seed
of the opposite begins to sprout with vigour. At winter solstice,
when nights are cold and deep, the days start to get longer again.
When a cell is threatened or compromised, the seeds of balance
are already sown – but only if that cell is connected to nature, to
its environment, to its xenobiome.*
Guido Masé

Living close to Nature is the greatest wonder you can experience for your spiritual, emotional, mental and physical health. The more natural you are, the healthier and happier you are...
David Wolfe

13. TOWARDS AN HARMONIOUS CONVERGENCE

Each of us is so different having lived in different circumstances with different access to nature and information, different opportunities. So our dislocation from the rest of nature is a personal thing affecting each of us to a different degree and in different ways. Rewilding yourself as presented in this book is an attempt to draw attention to the points of contact with your own wildness, and the wildness of the world, that have most commonly declined or are entirely absent in modern communities and lifestyles.

Throughout the pages of this book and the subjects that have been covered the medicine of the wild, wild nature, wild plants, your wild self has, I hope, become clear. Cultivation of your individual wildness and connection with the wildness of the world provides medicine for the body, the mind, the heart and the soul. We arrived on this Earth as wild bloodied animals; reigniting and maintaining that wildness allows us a better chance of remaining whole, remaining well.

🌳

Acknowledging your bond with the rest of nature, through seeing and feeling yourself as Gaia, you have begun to once again become nature. Of course there never was a separation, but humankind having perceived there to be one for so long opened up a mental chasm between us and nature, created a mental separation. That separation penetrated our hearts breaking them with fear and sadness, loss and loneliness. But underneath it all amongst our DNA and our cells, there has been photon exchange and movement of particles and waves, the communications have been ongoing, endless. On opening to what both quantum physics and your heart can tell you, is the realisation that there is no *becoming*, you already *are* nature, and it is up to you to reclaim that often overlooked connection which exists on the deepest level.

To rewild requires finding those things that feed your own personal wildness, the things that make you feel most vital and vibrant. Work with your senses, your intuition, your feelings, your physicality. Explore and experiment. I have shared what has worked for me. With every tiny change made to feed your individual wildness you are making a change that will feed all wildness. Just like the trophic cascades

activated in areas where top predators are reintroduced, the cascade that rewilding yourself will have is far reaching. Beyond your own physical and mental well-being it will touch your local environment, your human peers and bit by bit, so goes my dream, the whole of Gaia; making it stronger, more coherent, more whole.

13.1 Where Civilisation Is At

Humanity has never been more urban based. In 2008, for the first time in history more people worldwide lived in an urban setting than a rural one[1]. This has coincided with a greater number of people worldwide suffering from depression and higher than ever numbers of prescriptions being written for psychological conditions. Some people may argue that there is no direct correlation, but you have got to be a bit of a fool to not ask the question, right? Worryingly, like most drugs, serotonin reuptake inhibitors (which account for the majority of anti-depressants) don't break down in the environment and instead linger there negatively affecting the health of plants and animals with which they come into contact[2]. This is another negative feedback loop and demonstration of Gaia's interconnectivity. We move away from nature and get sick, we take medication to get better, the residue damages the environment making us all that little bit less wild and more sick.

Humanity is approaching a critical impasse; the whole planet is in crisis. The fact that there are few places of deep nature left, that we have to make an occasional pilgrimage to find a place that is truly wild, is argument enough for rewilding the landscape, the environment. Not just to create a place of balance where wolves and bears are free to roam, keeping grazers and consequently the balance of flora in check, but also for the deep fundamental needs of humanity. The more that has gone, the harder it is for all of us to be well.

However, until we reclaim our own wildness, rewilding isolated pockets of the environment will only ever be a gesture, creating small living museums demonstrating what wild nature could be. It can only ever mean the creation of a few more national parks with a few extra species, perhaps some top predators being reintroduced, but it will never penetrate any further than the periphery unless the rewilding process is also encouraged to take place within ourselves. So that we too can be part of the process, not observers, not scientists monitoring and analysing the results of the process, but a living breathing part of the process. Human actions are integral to the health of the planet; we

cannot just demarcate reserves for rewilding in an altruistic gesture and assume that will be enough - this project needs our hearts.

Without a tangible connection to wild nature our wildness comes out in strange ways. We taunt, torture and terrify each other. We damage, destroy, mine and hunt to extinction. We take drugs and alcohol to escape from this seemingly pointless reality. If we don't take recreational drugs to escape they are often prescribed for everything from boredom with excess energy (where we have become caged animals, a desk our cage from age 4 onwards), to desperate confusion, distress and suicidal tendencies. One of the main reasons for these dark cries of the soul, that are so flippantly medicated by either self or professionals, is that we can't find the sense in it or the contact with other species (even with our own species) that we need to thrive.

Rewilding is not perhaps a panacea for humanities ills, but one by one, as we fall in love with our wild selves, cell by cell, and extend that out metre by metre to take in the grass beneath our feet, the tree shading the spot in which we stand, then slowly, slowly, there will be a change. And for all the people who live in desperate situations, conditions of war, absolute urban poverty, child soldiers, gang culture, we have to make the change, to stand in nature and listen, because they don't have that luxury. If somehow through each of us opening up to Gaia and her wisdom, we can change the piece of Gaia that we are standing in and the piece we are standing on, then maybe, just maybe, it will eventually trickle through and touch everyone no matter how desperate their circumstances.

Like everything in life, rewilding is not simply black and white. There are certain primeval urges that, due to the mess humanity has made of this wild planet, and the fact that most of us will continue to live in a house, drive a car, work in an office, we need to approach with a degree of restraint in order to obtain an outcome of balance, and avoid further destabilising Gaia.

The most basic (and strongest) human instinct, is the one to reproduce. It is absolutely fundamental to the survival of our species and it seems to be the only one people still hear and follow en masse. While the human population on Earth is greater than it has ever been, the last forty years have seen a decline in world wildlife populations of over 50%[3]. Human population and the way we choose to live is directly

pressurising the few remaining areas of wild nature. In turn, our food, water and air have become poisoned. Logically it would be a time to be holding back, and yet we are not. Gaia, however, is trying to balance the human population by reducing our fertility[4]. Interestingly, and not surprisingly, the causes often cited for the reduction in average sperm count are pollutants and toxins in our environment, the perfect cycling. The effects of our behaviours are coming back around to impact our lives. Still, the urge to bear offspring is so strong that we fight against infertility with scientific intervention and fertility treatments. But the truth is in front of our eyes. At some point we will have to slow down, learn to restrain ourselves and live within the limits that the available, natural, and renewable, resources afford us (let nature, no matter how unfair and disappointing it sometimes seems, take its course).

Another human instinct is to hoard. It comes from our wild roots, hoarding the harvest at times of abundance for potential future times of scarcity (winter). But while dislocated from nature this instinct has created yet more unbalance. Our hoarding instinct has transferred from foods to possessions. So that instead of being to our benefit so we can eat when the snow is thick on the ground, our hoarding has served to insulate us from the world, from what is really important, with *stuff.* We have become obsessed with obtaining, maintaining and bettering our collection of stuff at the demise of our real needs. I have experienced times of financial hardship, and also the years I spent on the road, both of which taught me how little we actually *need* and what is most important. It is hard to move away from hoarding. It is hard wired into us, so it is perhaps easier to redirect it. Perhaps towards hoarding nature experiences, knowledge of local plants, survival skills. Instead of hoarding possessions that cost the Earth, hoard the good things that benefit the Earth and that feed us on every level.

There is another current trend, the rise in popularity of which I find interesting and relevant; the study of genealogy. We once lived in clans of kin, surrounded and imbued with relationships, not only to humans but to other life. Not so much any more. So, many people are searching for their roots, where they came from, as if it is a vital piece of the puzzle. It, of course, is, but the most important root and the one that binds us all is that we came from nature. It is not the discovery that we are half Spanish, or that our great uncle came from Ireland that will answer our questions, but the knowledge of our common roots in nature. That is where, I believe, we will learn the most about ourselves, be able to place ourselves, and find a sense of belonging, home.

One area where Gaia seems to be uncoiling her green tendrils and embracing humanity, drawing us back in, over recent years is through the widening influence of entheogens. That is not to say our relationship with such plants is a modern phenomenon, but regular consumption, or even knowledge, of such plants had certainly dropped from mainstream in Western society until recently. One entheogen (or to be more accurate, admixture of two or more plants) that has drawn more attention than any other has to be ayahuasca. It has spread around much of the planet like a craze. Remembering that these plants (like all plants) act intentionally and with direction (are intelligent), I don't think it is too much to say that the recent surge in exposure of these plants is *not* an accident. Perhaps it is because there is such a desperate need for this medicine at this time; a need for our eyes to be opened wide to the interconnectivity of life on this planet. In the case of ayahuasca it could be a rush to get this information to the people of the world before the remaining vestiges of it's home, the wild Amazon, gallop willingly or not to the same culture of consumerism and silicon dominance as everywhere else, who knows. Never underestimate the call of the wild and our ability to heed that call.

At the other end of the realm of experience, we are faced with technology which has certainly played a part in our loss of direct contact with people and the wild. However, we can harness it for the good. Technology is part of all of our lives and will continue to develop and impact our day-to-day experiences. There are all kinds of ways it can be used to help our broken communities connect up and work together again, countless social networking groups that help people find each other, meet up and do their thing. An example from the UK is The Casserole Club which connects people who are able to cook an extra meal with others in the community that need one, engendering human contact.

Technology is an amazing tool for discovering and spreading information. It helps us hook up with movements, workshops, books and trainings. Use it as the fabulous resource that it is, to help you find your way, to learn, to study and to inspire your dreams. However, until you actually action all your knowledge, all your dreams, they are as nothing; so take positive steps to rewild yourself every day. Remember to leave the electronics at home and experience the world for real as much as possible.

13.2 The Wild Utopian Dream

Rewilding allows us to develop adaptive strategies; it makes us more resilient. Think about it. An environment that is wild is more stable, more healthy, more vibrant. Compare the beauty and diversity of a remaining wilderness area to a vast cultivated monoculture. The wilderness area has a large diversity of species, it has multiple microclimates within its borders due to the differing conditions the plant and animal species generate. If there is a fire or a flood, a drought or a storm, although initially the area may look decimated, there will always be a variety of plant and animal life that will benefit, that will be quick to respond and fill the space that the fallen trees have created. Within an agricultural monoculture there tends to be either feast or famine. It either works out as planned, or is a failure requiring government grants and funds to clear up the mess, to compensate and bail the farmers out of troubled times. The agricultural monoculture needs outside help to set themselves straight after something has destabilised it and then tends to continue as before; just as vulnerable. Western, civilised, society has become as the agricultural monoculture - dangerously vulnerable.

Now think about yourself. About your ability to grow and find food, to digest it. To know and feel danger and safety. To know your own limits. To be healthy and strong both physically and mentally.

There may be resistance along the way, along the wild path. There may be a genuine fear of the wild, not just the wild that exists outside of ourselves, but also those wild places that exist within. Perhaps it was through the fear of those places that we allowed the wildness of the Earth to be tamed in the first place. An attempt to control the unknown, the potentially dangerous. You will have to face your fears along this path if you are to go beyond just taking regular walks in the park, rewilding is more than that. Building and deepening nature connections may illuminate the darker, more scary, parts of ourselves but on thorough examination of them, in the light of a deepening understanding of Gaia, you become stronger. By recognising and acknowledging the wildness all around and within you, by rekindling your own connection with the wild, you will develop your personal resilience.

Find your wildness connection in the ordinary, the everyday; the clouds and rain; the changing of the seasons; the earthworms and weeds. Through your own fostered interaction with nature, your understanding of livingness and feelings of connection will deepen, and

in turn your knowing of yourself will deepen until you know what it is you need and where to find it.

As your wildness re-emerges watch as the priorities in your life change, as you and the world around you begins to change. The world will open up to you and although the path may not always be easy, the deepening and enriching of existence will more than compensate. Your world will flood with meaning, you will know what you are here for, what it's all about, and be at last able to answer the desperate cries of the soul ~ *What's the point? Why am I even alive?* By following the wild path, through your personal rewilding endeavours, at some point you end up taking responsibility for everything you contribute (beneficial or not) to Gaia, it is part of the process.

People have spoken of a time, a time of awakening from centuries of slumber, a time of remembering. I join their call and invite you with my words to remember. For the sake of you, me, Earth, all our relations. Remember. Reclaim your wildness. You cannot throw trash or squash insects when you know the world is watching. You cannot go fracking for gas or drive a motorway through an ancient woodland if you understand the livingness of Gaia.

Rewilding is not, can not, be a matter of restoring ourselves, or nature, or the planet to some imaginary golden time of perfect balance. Nature, by its nature, is never static. It is always changing, upgrading, adjusting. It is constantly evolving. However, I believe a state of dynamic equilibrium is possible. A place in space and time where we can move, shimmy and glide together with some semblance of balance in a more fulfilling, wilder, rawer experience of life.

As we each forge our own wild future there is the hope that together we can create a better, more utopian future for all. A place where habitats and species are flourishing, not dwindling. Where rewilding is working not just within each one of us, but within the wider environment. Where top carnivores are being reintroduced to the chosen "wild" areas and the balance within the nature of that place is being redressed, is finding its own happy medium. You don't have to turn your back on modern technology or on urban living. But to rewild yourself you must remember nature, acknowledge you are part of it and that it is part of you. You must feed the wild inside.

13.3 Wildness Pervading
To touch base with your wild self, is to touch base with those further

200

parts of yourself, those parts that put our human lives in context and help us see ourselves more clearly. Yet, this path, rewilding, is not entirely anthropocentric. It's not just about what having contact with what nature will do for you. We need to reconnect because we are dislocated and upsetting the balance, so although it is for our own individual health it is also for the wider health of the planet, there is no separation.

Our entire global social system (except the very furthest reaches) is based upon everything else lacking intelligence and awareness. Current society would fall apart in the face of the truth; that everything is alive and has feelings. It would irrevocably change human behaviour. It would break down the hierarchy, the unintegrated value system that seats humankind above all other life; that allows us to scrape away the surface of the Earth to look for minerals to burn or to decorate ourselves with - we would not do that with the skin of each other.

Growing your wildness is about being back in touch with what it means, what it takes to be alive - food, water, warmth, shelter. Many people are currently so disconnected that they don't even take a vegetable to make dinner with or know what heats their home. It's about getting in touch with primal needs, fulfilling them and interacting in a meaningful way with the water, the vegetable, the fire. It's acknowledging, respecting, recognising a relative, a part of yourself and falling in love with it.

To make space for all these new relationships, relationships with and of the wild, some things will have to go, some of the relationships with things that no longer serve you - perhaps relationships with alien foods and artificial fragrance. Perhaps relationships with plastic furnishings and busy shopping streets. You will choose how much space you need to nurture your wildness, how much you want it in your life and how much of your civilised life you are prepared to shed in order to make that space. Be careful to focus your energy not on fighting the old patterns, on denial, but on exploring and celebrating the new.

As your wildness grows and you have acknowledged your place within the web of life, the realisation dawns that everything you do to yourself, you do to the planet. Likewise everything you do to the planet, you do to yourself. In other words once you remove civilisation's blinkers you will see that however sick, damaged and polluted the world, the same is true for humanity. Through rewilding there is an awakening and a personalisation of the environmental crisis. But instead of being overwhelmed by the magnitude of it all, it somehow becomes manage-

able. Just by concentrating on your own relationship with the wild, your intrinsic connection to nature, your wild and fabulous body, and the fact that you *are* nature. The big issues are broken down and just through perhaps changing and developing your relationship to food you begin to positively feed back into the life support system that is Gaia.

Another valuable lesson the wild teaches is that we are biodegradable. That we grow, flower, produce fruit, then slowly drop our leaves, wither and die, just like everything else. You realise the truth and rediscover your place amongst the great cycle of seasons and life. Our mortality is just one more fact that binds us with all life on the planet; that for each and every one of us, at some point, this life will come to an end. These things, this knowledge, allows you to be strong, to be bold, to be free. The civilised world loses some of its hold and some of the restrictions it has on the way you live. It becomes possible to see through the fine veneer that conceals the deeper, darker truths of our society. You will feel, and see, that which society does not want you to. Being privy to the real truth is somewhat revolutionary, it can make you dangerous, no longer a slave to our culture of consumerism.

Rewilding allows us a sense of humility. An understanding that the world is bigger and more complex than we humans can fully perceive. It allows us to be comfortable in this knowledge and to live with the world's ambiguity, with a tolerance of the unknown. To feel certain about nature and the world is a delusion and takes us back to trying to control it, even just mentally; returning to nature as a machine. Once you have ignited your wild spark you can never live under that paradigm again.

There is a danger when eating large quantities of wild food, just as there is when regularly consuming entheogens, living in the woods, hugging the Earth, or walking barefoot for too long; it becomes ever harder to live in the civilised world and function as we have been trained. You get a bit too close to seeing the golden flood, the information super-highway, running through, exchanging with, and connecting all things, all form; being all there is. To inhabit both worlds you have to pull back a bit otherwise you truly become wild, and a wild thing cannot live comfortably in the civilised world.

13.4 Where I'm At
I have found myself between worlds, wild and domesticated. Able to submerge into one or the other at will, but importantly to pull back

out so that I can continue to function effectively within either. I love the wild, my wild, our wild, and as more people reawaken that part of themselves it becomes easier to draw more of the wild in to my daily life. As the urge to rewild gains momentum, nature and the wild will be drawn back in to all our lives. And like the cracks in the pavement where weeds readily grow, we will grow them too, between our toes, in our hearts, in our minds.

Sometimes I see through the eyes of my domesticated self and I notice the houses, the cars. Other times I see through my wild eyes and I notice that the strip of tarmac is like a temporary accessory that if peeled back like a sticking plaster would reveal the flesh of Earth beneath. It may be scarred but it is flesh nonetheless that in time will heal. I can tell because the plants poke up and out at any sign of weakness, any crack, along the edges, in little accumulated patches of dirt where soil is beginning to form. In cities I notice birds bathing at the roadside in puddles and the fox moving like a shadow in the grey urban dawn. Urban living is not ideal but we all have to work with what we've got. The wild is there waiting to reclaim any crack, any accumulated patch of dirt, within ourselves too, so noticing, appreciating and giving the wild space to grow can only make it stronger.

I know what it feels like to place my feet solidly on the sweet warm flesh of Earth. To spread my toes, scuff the surface and coated in dust feel them meld with the soil and stones. To stand amazed and awed by the vibrant rainbow that hovers above me like a halo of diffracted light. To feel the thick wet raindrops of summer, heavy with life and moisture, splash around me. To close my eyes in that moment of ecstasy and feel the warm kiss of sunlight on my face. *But* I needed to go to the wild extremes, to see and feel untamed beauty before I could recognise the wildness, Gaia, in the ordinary, the everyday; such was the extent of my ennui as my suburban childhood drew to a close. It may be that you need that initial blast of deep nature to jump start your rewilding process too. If you have followed this book and tried a few of my suggestions but are yet to be set on fire by the process, then perhaps go for a deep nature immersion experience. There is nothing like walking barefoot though the milky white ice cold water of a glacial melt stream to awaken you.

My personal love for, and connection with, nature certainly deep-

ened with each of the first few deep nature experiences I had. From hiking in the wild nature of Wales and Scotland as a teen, where my wildness was awoken, to the exponential deepening at my first solar eclipse in Northern India. The eclipse experience was incredibly humbling, to see something so wild and beautiful. As Justice, a South African elder I met on the eve of another total eclipse seven years later, described it, "natural magic". I was barely into adulthood but in that moment under a black sky with just smears of light streaming out into the darkness indicating the position of the sun I truly understood for the first time that we are just human, and that being in control of nature was an illusion.

This was further reinforced a matter of days later when I visited the Himalayas for the first time. As the bus I was travelling in wound its way from the Indian-Nepalese border I began to cry. I cried silent tears all day at the astounding beauty of what was unfolding in front of my eyes. Raging rivers, forests, greenery, huge boulders, the grey dust of eroding mountain. As the sunset glow faded from the sky we turned a last corner and I saw the towering pink tinged snow capped peaks of the Annapurna range for the first time. During the following week I proceeded to trek high into the thin air above the snow line, where each step took all my effort and much groaning breath. When I stopped, looked and felt, my surroundings amazed me. The blue lines of shadow on snow; the rumbles and creaks of moving ice and rock; the delicious but fleeting kiss of the suns warmth on my cold bones and its long long absence behind the mountain wall for the other 21 or so hours each day. I was imbued with the utmost degree of humility.

Full immersion in wild untamed nature is food for the soul like no other. That is what I felt under the eclipse sky and after I pushed my body to its limits on those mountain tracks. On each occasion in a moment of pause, I felt the incredible clear, wild, vibrant, energy that surrounded me and surged through me; a rush like no other.

Rewilding for me has been like taking the back off my wristwatch as an eight year old. It has opened new doors and I have been amazed at what I have seen, felt and experienced. I have realised a new depth of intricacy and invisible connection to the world; that it is a world of meaning and that there are still many more doors to open. Moment by moment, experience by experience, I have been touched by the breath of the living Earth. I have taken it deep into my being, felt it awakening cell by cell, my body, my soul.

My wildness, and keeping it alive, allowing it to flourish and grow, means everything to me - but do not misjudge me. I have not entirely retreated from this modern world to exist in a kind of arcadian idyll, to feed this essential part of myself. I love that I can contact friends on the other side of the world instantly and travel with ease exploring different cultures and cuisines, listen to the song of different tongues, bathe in exotic nature. I believe we should enjoy the gifts that technology has brought us, but I also believe that we should take just enough of each thing. Just enough to fulfil our needs.

In the past I have lived in London, Tokyo, and on several occasions spent months on end in Bangkok. I am no stranger to cities. I do like the buzz of human activity, although to relocate permanently to a city now would be a huge challenge. Still, the absolute secret to rewilding is to find the wild wherever you are and feed it. That way even in this machine dependent era you can remain awake, aware, and conscious, of your connection to Gaia's invisible information super-highway, despite any apparent nature deficit in your immediate physical location. Awareness of both what you are adding to that network (what you are putting out into the world) and what you are receiving from it, becomes a reminder of your wildness and a nudge to keep things on the wild side.

Through rewilding I have fostered respect and kinship for the whole of the natural world. I have rediscovered how it feels to be fuelled by a wild pulse, to eat wild food and drink wild water. To live by the wisdom of my body and my piqued senses. To feel my way around the world and live with sensitivity and compassion. To know my ancestors when I look at the stars and feel my brothers as I walk barefoot across river worn rocks. This is why I write this book, to share my passion for the wild with you and invite you to join me on this wild journey of rediscovery. So that you too may know how good it feels to sit in nature's lap as a part of it, not apart from it. To feel that you are alive and vital, vibrant and passionate; that you are home and complete.

I step from my tent in the dark of the night and stand under myriad stars sparkling like jewels woven into the velvet of this 360° planetarium sky. The warm desert breath caresses my naked skin, soft and gentle as it engulfs me. My feet feel

broad, strong, and sturdy as they connect with every dusty grain, every sharpened pebble, every thorn. As I look across the basin before me, despite the moonless sky and distinct lack of light pollution, I can clearly see the rocky buttes, mammoth and striking before me, black voids thrumming with an otherworldly energy, with the wildness of this place. As I stand and the breeze ruffles my hair, I am strong, and vibrant, and alive. I am part of the landscape, as ancient as the dust I stand upon, and the buttes I stand before. It feels like swimming naked in the ocean for the first time. I belong. I am not scared. My feet are being held by the Earth, and my flesh clothed by the sky. The land, the place, the Earth, has kissed me with its warm breath. I am a child of the Earth, and with the Earth, such a beautiful feeling. I feel whole. I am home.

13.5 The Last Word

During the writing of this book I have noticed that there is a deep, almost urgent, feeling building and growing amongst the people of the modern world. It is the desire for connection to our forgotten part; to nature. Remember this: there is no need for grandiosity, no need to travel and learn from ancient cultures with unbroken lineages, or to study nature conservation, or shamanism (although there is much to learn from each strand). Because, here's the thing: we all come from an unbroken lineage, that of Gaia. Nature surrounds us every day, we, I, you, are Gaia. To reclaim the wild, to rewild, is to notice and acknowledge it. It may take time to feel it fully but we were all born wild, we *all* have it within us. Anyone, everyone, can have that deep, wild, nature connection.

🌳

Don't overcook this, don't over think it. Put down this book and get on with it, never stop, never go back. Walk forward knowing you are Gaia and everything you think and do *does* matter, *does* make a difference. Enjoy the journey, have fun, good luck and know that you never again need be lost and alone in the world.

NOTES

Chapter 2: Civilisation's curse ~ Orphans, aliens & other lonely beings

1   http://blog.greenearthbamboo.com/20090830/bamboo-the-environ-ment/bamboo-is-destroying-our-planet *Bamboo is destroying our planet*. Doug Bancorn. August 30, 2009.

2   Several years ago a friend of mine returned from working in Ghana, Africa. She relayed a conversation she had had with a village elder, he told her that since his house had been upgraded from a thatch of natural materials to concrete with a corrugated metal roof he could no longer make contact with his ancestors during his night time dreams. I have always remembered that story and wondered often about it. Who knows how much our living conditions and lifestyles block our connections, not just with physical nature, but also with elements of world that we can't see, that are invisible?

3   http://www.nytimes.com/2014/07/11/world/more-than-half-the-global-population-growth-is-urban-united-nations-report-finds.html?smid=fb-share&_r=1 *UN finds most people now live in cities*. Mini Sengupta. July 10, 2014.

4   Read some of the books by John Perkins the "economic hit man". His original posting with the Peace corps in the 1960s was to a remote Amazonian tribe. He had been sent to educate the locals about money and finances despite the fact they used no material currency; a seeming wholly inappropriate venture.

5   Metzner Ph.D., Ralph Green *Psychology: Transforming Our Relationship to the Earth*. Rochester, VT: Park Street Press, 1999. pp102-3.

6   Abram, David *The Spell of the Sensuous*. 1996. Paperback edition, New York, NY: Vintage Books, 1997. pp154-179. Contains many detailed stories of different indigenous groups from the Western Apache of Arizona, to the Pintupi of Australia. Stories of how the land has shaped the people and culture, not just in a physical sense through the shape of the landforms, but also the stories that live there.

7   Veenema, Alexa H. *Early life stress, the development of aggression and neuroendocrine and neurobiological correlates: What can we learn from animal models?*Front Neuroendocrinol, 30:497-518. 2009.

8   http://www.benbenjamin.net/pdfs/Issue2.pdf *The Primacy of Human Touch*. Ben Benjamin, PhD and Ruth Werner, LMT.

9   http://www.livestrong.com/article/186495-importance-of-human-touch/ *Importance of Human Touch.* Mary Bauer. Published online January 28, 2014.

10   http://www.bbc.co.uk/news/uk-23553897 *Is England a nation on anti-depressants?*Mark Easton. August 3, 2013.

11   http://www.theguardian.com/news/2013/nov/20/mental-health-antidepressants-global-trends *Antidepressants: global trends.* Mona Chalabi. November 20, 2013.

12   http://www.theguardian.com/society/2012/may/06/ritalin-adhd-shocks-child-psychologists?INTCMP=SRCH *Ritalin use for ADHD children soars fourfold.* Jamie Doward and Emma Craig. The Observer, May 6, 2012.

13   http://www.ncbi.nlm.nih.gov/pmc/articles/PMC1448497 *A Potential Natural Treatment for Attention Deficit/Hyperactivity Disorder: Evidence from a National Study.* Francis Kuo PhD and Andrea Faber Taylor PhD. September, 2004.http://fitness.mercola.com/sites/fitness/archive/2014/10/17/exercise-adhd-medication.aspx *Exercise Can Be An ADHD Medication.* Dr Mercola. October 17, 2014.http://penny-arcos.hubpages.com/hub/TV-Viewing-Video-Games-and-ADHD-Get-Unplugged *TV viewing and video games make ADHD behaviour worse.* Penny Arcos. October 21, 2009.

14   http://www.theguardian.com/cities/2014/feb/25/city-stress-mental-health-rural-kind*Sick Cities: why urban living can be bad for your mental health.* Leo Benedictus. February 25, 2014.

15   http://jech.bmj.com/content/59/10/822.full *Urban built environment and depression: a multilevel analysis.* Sandro Galea, Jennifer Ahern, Sasha Rudenstein, Zachary Wallace, David Vlahov. May 9, 2005.

16   http://willsull.net/resources/Sullivan-papers/KuoSullivan2001crime.pdf *Environment and Crime in the Inner City: Does Vegetation Reduce Crime?* Frances E. Kuo and William C. Sullivan. May 3, 2001.

Chapter 3: Rending the veil of illusion

1   Collins Concise English Dictionary. Glasgow, HaperCollins Publishers, 3rd edition, 1992.

2   http://www.pnas.org/content/109/21/8334.full *Environmental biodiversity, human microbiota, and allergy are interrelated.* Illkka Hanski et al. April 4, 2012.

3   According to a study of 13500 mothers and babies in Bradford, an industrial city in the UK www.borninbradford.nhs.uk and

similar findings in a Californian studyhttp://www.researchgate.net/ publication/258060059_Green_spaces_and_pregnancy_outcomes_in_ Southern_California

4   *Landscape and Urban Planning*, vol. 105, Issue 3 pp221-229, 2012. More green space is linked to less stress in deprived communities: Evidence from salivary cortisol patterns by Catherine Ward Thompson, Jenny Roe, Peter Aspinall, Richard Mitchell, Angela Clow, David Miller.

5   http://www.examiner.com/article/mall-walking-vs-trail-hiking-which-is-better-for-youSeth Smigelski. March 30, 2009.

6   http://www.ncbi.nlm.nih.gov/pmc/articles/PMC1448497 *A potential natural treatment for Attention-Defecit/Hyperactivity Disorder: evidence from a national study.* Frances E. Kuo, Andrea Faber Taylor. September 2004.

7   http://depts.washington.edu/hhwb/Thm_Crime.html *Crime and Safety.* Kathleen Wolf, Ph.D. June 28, 2010.

8   http://www.dailymail.co.uk/sciencetech/article-2519437/Houseplants-make-workers-40-productive-creative.html Sarah Griffiths, December 6, 2013.

9   http://www.theguardian.com/sustainable-business/protect-nature-conserve-health-wellbeing *We must protect nature to conserve peoples' wellbeing.* Tony Juniper. August 30, 2013. The following contains a wealth of articles about the effects of nature upon students and education:http://www.childrenandnature.org/downloads/ EducationsynthesisMarch2010FINAL.pdf

10 http://la570.willsull.net/Built_Environment_%26_Health/Stress_files/ ulrichetal1991.pdf*Stress recovery during exposure to natural and urban environments.* Roger S. Ulrich et al. 1991.

11 http://www.ecobuildingpulse.com/performance-metrics/with-nature-and-justice-for-all.aspx Kim O'Connell, June 7, 2013

12 http://www.bristol.ac.uk/news/2007/5384.html *Getting dirty may lift your mood.* Christopher Lowry, PhD. April 2, 2007.

13 A Save the Children initiative as reported in The Huffington Posthttp:// www.huffingtonpost.co.uk/2014/10/29/secret-gardens-of-syrias-refugee-camps_n_6068550.html *The Secret Gardens Of Syria's Refugee Camps.* Jessica Elgot. October 29, 2014.

14 http://www.theglobeandmail.com/life/health-and-fitness/fitness/ why-is-walking-in-the-woods-so-good-for-you/article4209703/ Alex Hutchinson. Latest update; March 27, 2013.

15 http://www.motherearthnews.com/natural-health/forest-bathing-

ze0z1301zgar.aspx *Your Brain on Nature: Forest Bathing and Reduced Stress.* Eva Selhub and Alan Logan. January 8, 2013.

16   http://www.centreforconfidence.co.uk/flourishing-lives. php?p=cGlkPTE3MiZpZD02NzI

17   http://circ.ahajournals.org/content/early/2013/05/09/ CIR.0b013e31829201e1.full.pdf *Pet ownership and cardiovascular risk: a scientific statement from the American heart association.* Glenn N. Levine et al. May 9, 2013.

18   *Psychotherapy and Psychosomatics,* vol 74, no. 1, pp31-5, 2005. Animal-assisted therapy ameliorates anhedonia in schizophrenia patients. A controlled pilot study. I. Nathans-Barel, P. Feldman, B. Berger, I. Modai, H. Silver. (http://news.bbc.co.uk/1/hi/ health/4171505.stm)

19   Depending variables such as the conditions of preservation, the time of year the animal died and storage post excavation, it can take up to a staggering 6.8 million years before all the DNA bonds in a fossil bone are completely destroyed.http://www.livescience.com/23861-fossil-dna-half-life.html *"Jurassic Park" may be impossible but dino DNA lasts longer than thought.* Megan Gannon. October 10, 2012. Based on a study published Oct. 10 in the journal Proceedings of the Royal Society B.

20   https://www.youtube.com/watch?v=R30YKfEuyo0 *A short discussion of biophotons and coherence* by Dr. Fritz-Albert Popp. April 27, 2014.

21   Narby, Jeremy *The Cosmic Serpent: DNA and the Origins of Knowledge.* 1995. Translated paperback edition, London, UK: Phoenix, 1999. pp125-6.

22   McTaggart, Lynne *The Field.* 2001. Reprint, London: HarperCollins Publishers, 2003. p70

23   http://www.marcobischof.com/en/arbeitsgebiete/biophotonen.html .

24   McTaggart, Lynne *The Field.* 2001. Reprint, London: HarperCollins Publishers, 2003. p70

25   For a really in depth account of DNA and its role in communication a must read is Narby, Jeremy *The Cosmic Serpent: DNA and the Origins of Knowledge.* 1995. But watch out because reading this book may just change the way you understand the world for good.

26   Brian Cox and Andrew Cohen *Wonders of the Universe.* London, UK: HarperCollins Publishers, 2011. p9.

27   For a really accessible read about the field I direct you to Lynne Mctaggart's *The Field.* 2001.

Chapter 4: When everything's alive ~ Acknowledging the livingness of the world

1   Narby, Jeremy *The Cosmic Serpent: DNA and the Origins of Knowledge.* 1995. Translated paperback edition, London: Phoenix, 1999. p110.

2   There are many books that cover indigenous peoples gaining knowledge directly from plants, they include the books I have listed in the bibliography by Jeremy Narby, David Abram and F. Bruce Lamb.

Chapter 5: Feeling before thinking

1   http://subjected2subjectivity.blogspot.co.uk/2007/06/thinking-heart.html *The Thinking Heart.* Azer Mantessa. June 6, 2007.

Chapter 6: Reawakening your wild heart

1   http://www.telegraph.co.uk/news/uknews/5811433/More-than-two-million-British-homes-without-a-garden.html Christopher Hope. July 12, 2009.

2   http://articles.mercola.com/sites/articles/archive/2012/04/29/james-oschman-on-earthing.aspx *Caution: Wearing these can sabotage your health.* Dr Joseph Mercola. April 29, 2012.

3   p46. Watson, Lyall *Supernature.* 1973. Fifth impression, London: Hodder and Stoughton Ltd, 1977.

Chapter 7: This sensual world ~ Awakening your senses

1   Tompkins, Peter and Christopher Bird *The Secret Life of Plants.* 1973. Reprint, New York, NY: Harper Perennial, 2002. The whole of Chapter 10 (pp145-162) discusses the effects of sounds on plant growth. The specific discovery of Dr T.C. Singh mentioned here is found on page 147.

2   Discovered in experiments undertaken by Michael Holtz, detailed on pp136-9. Tompkins, Peter and Christopher Bird *Secrets of the Soil.* Anchorage, AK: Earthpulse Press, 1998.

3   Embody Magazine, Autumn 2013, p13. *From Birdsong to Heavy Metal: How Cancer Patients Benefit from Music* by Fereshteh Ahmadi

4   http://www.collegeofsoundhealing.co.uk/pages/about.html

5   http://www.webmd.com/eye-health/computer-vision-syndrome

6   A name and a process first introduced to me by master intuitive herbalist Nathaniel Hughes.

7   Masé, Guido*The Wild Medicine Solution: Healing with Aromatic, Bitter, and Tonic Plants.* Rochester, VT: Healing Arts Press, 2013. p.65.

8   Masé, Guido *The Wild Medicine Solution: Healing with Aromatic, Bitter, and Tonic Plants*. Rochester, VT: Healing Arts Press, 2013. p67.

9   Masé, Guido*The Wild Medicine Solution: Healing with Aromatic, Bitter, and Tonic Plants*.Rochester, VT: Healing Arts Press, 2013. p60.

Chapter 8: Eating your body wild

1   From a summary discussion of the quantifiable findings of Jacques Benveniste on the memory of water. Ryrie, Charlie *The Healing Energies of Water*. London: Gaia Books Ltd. 1998. p60.

2   http://www.masaru-emoto.net/english/water-crystal.html

3   Ryrie, Charlie *The Healing Energies of Water*. London: Gaia Books Ltd., 1998. pp82-7.

4   Ryrie, Charlie *The Healing Energies of Water*. London: Gaia Books Ltd., 1998. pp104-9.

5   If you would like to know more about the quantum world and intention I highly recommend the work of Lynne McTaggart. For a basic and easy to follow introduction to the world of quantum physics try *The Field*, and for more information on the importance and influence of intention try *The Intention Experiment*.

6   Information about what a CSA is can be found on the Soil Association's website http://www.soilassociation.org/ communitysupportedagriculture

7   Engel, Cindy *Wild Health*. New York, NY: Houghton Mifflin Company, 2002. pp225-6.

8   As stated by Kristof and Stacia Nordin in *The Not So Green Revolution* Permaculture Magazine, No.82 winter 2014, pp37-40. Based on *the state of the world's plant genetic resources for food and agriculture*. A Food and Agriculture of the United Nations report, published in 1997.

9   Masé, Guido*The Wild Medicine Solution: Healing with Aromatic, Bitter, and Tonic Plants*. Rochester, VT: Healing Arts Press, 2013. p155.

10 Anderson, Richard *Cleanse and Purify Thyself: Book Two – Secrets of Radiant Health and Energy*. 1998. Fourth Printing, Mt Shasta, CA: Christobe Publishing, 2001. p45.

11 Reid, Daniel *The Tao Of Detox*. London, UK: Simon and Schuster UK Ltd, 2003. p27.

12 Reid, Daniel *The Tao Of Detox*. London, UK: Simon and Schuster UK Ltd, 2003. p28.

13 Wolfe, David *The Sunfood Diet Success System*. San Diego, Ca: Maul Brothers Publishing, 1999. p170.

14 For much more information about which plants to use as remedies, and how to use them, get a copy of my first book, *The Medicine Garden* (2009).

15 http://www.european-nutrition.org/index.php/malnutrition

16 For a great analysis of our ancestral diets and our frugivorous nature read pp39-51 of Gynn, Graham and Tony Wright *Left In The Dark*. 2007. Second revised edition, Kaleidos Press, 2008.

17 Neonicotinoids are a class of neuro-active, systemic, pesticides used over the last 20 years on a wide variety of crops and are implicated in the recent decline in bee populations. http://bees.pan-uk.org/neonicotinoids

18 There are many do-it-yourself kits available to deliver a deep intestinal cleanse, it is also possible to visit a health spa which offers residential intestinal cleansing programmes. It is essential that you do your own research and background reading to ensure the kit or the programme you choose is a good one and right for you. Personally I have used the Ejuva 4 week body cleanse multiple times (www.ejuva.com) and found it to be absolutely transformational.

Chapter 9: Your own sweet piece of nature

1 http://www.nih.gov/news/health/jun2012/nhgri-13.htm *NIH Human Microbiome Project defines normal bacterial make-up of the body*. June 13, 2012

2 http://news.stanford.edu/news/2003/october15/research.html *Link found between cleanliness, hepatitis A, asthma. Is there a childhood risk in overly clean environments?*Krista Conger. October 15, 2003.

3 http://www.lshtm.ac.uk/newsevents/news/2012/allergy_rises_not_down_to_being_too_clean__just_losing_touch_with__old_friends_. html*Allergy rises not down to being too clean, just losing touch with "old friends"*. October 03, 2012.

4 http://www.autismspeaks.org/science/science-news/spotlight-gut-bacteria-brain-connection-autism *Spotlight on the Gut Bacteria-Brain Connection in Autism*. November 13, 2013.

5 Lactobacillus bacteria live in a healthy persons digestive system, urinary tract and clearly genital systems. They are known as "friendly" bacteria and help boost the immune system, guard against allergens, respiratory infections, eczema and digestive problems. http://www.

webmd.com/vitamins-supplements/ingredientmono-790-lactobacillus.
aspx?activeingredientid=790&activeingredientname=lactobacillus

6   Narby, Jeremy *Intelligence in Nature: an Inquiry into Knowledge*. New York, NY: Penguin Group, 2006. p129.

7   Engel, Cindy *Wild Health*. New York, NY: Houghton Mifflin Company, 2002. pp136-140. This book is a treasure trove of information about how animals remain healthy in the wild. I thoroughly believe that we, like our animal relations, can know our bodies and the plants we need to support them if we just live a little more wildly.

Chapter 11: Deep nature immersion

1   My vision quest was undertaken with a group organised by Trishuwa from the Foundation for Gaian Studies. I thoroughly recommend her programme (when there is one on offer) http://www.gaianstudies.org/Trishuwa_Calendar.html

Chapter 12: Entheogenic plants and connection to spirit

1   Pendell, Dale *Pharmakognosis: Plant Teachers and the Poison Path*. 2005. Revised paperback edition, Berkeley, CA: North Atlantic Books, 2010. pp86-7.

2   http://www.theguardian.com/society/2014/oct/05/healing-trip-psychedelic-drugs-treat-depression

3   Narby, *Jeremy The Cosmic Serpent: DNA and the Origins of Knowledge*. 1995. Translated paperback edition, London: Phoenix, 1999. p38.

Chapter 13: Towards an harmonic convergence

1   http://www.prb.org/Publications/Datasheets/2008/2008wpds.aspx *2008 world population reference sheet*. Population Reference Bureau.

2   Buhner, Stephen Harrod. *Plant Intelligence And The Imaginal Realm*. Rochester, VT: Bear and Company, 2014. pp190-1.

3   Based on a 2014 report by the Zoological Society of London. As quoted inhttps://uk.news.yahoo.com/wildlife-populations-halved-last-40-years-human-consumption-084335464.html#sPqiTOM *Wildlife populations halved in last 40 years by "human consumption and degradation"*. Ludovica Iaccino. September 30, 2014.

4   Sperm count in the average British male has fallen by almost half in the last 50 years. As cited by Dr Rosemary Leonard http://www.dailymail.co.uk/health/article-4243/Infertility-rising-problem.html

BIBLIOGRAPHY

Abram, David *The Spell of the Sensuous*. 1996. Paperback edition, New York, NY: Vintage Books, 1997.

Altman, Nathaniel *The Deva Handbook: How to Work with Nature's Subtle Energies*. Rochester, VT: Destiny Books, 1995.

Anderson, Richard *Cleanse & Purify Thyself: Book Two – Secrets of Radiant Health & Energy*. 1998. Fourth Printing, Mt Shasta, CA: Christobe Publishing, 2001.

Bortoft, Henri *The Wholeness of Nature: Goethe's Way of Science*. Edinburgh: Lindisfarne Press & Floris Books, 1996.

Buhner, Stephen Harrod *The Lost Language of Plants*. White River Junction, VT: Chelsea Green Publishing Company, 2002.

Buhner, Stephen Harrod *The Secret Teachings of Plants: The Intelligence of the Heart in the Direct Perception of Nature*. Rochester, VT: Bear & Company, 2004.

Buhner, Stephen Harrod *Sacred Plant Medicine: Explorations in the Practice of Indigenous Herbalism*. Coeur D'Alene, ID: Raven Press, 2001.

Buxton, Simon *The Shamanic Way of the Bee: Ancient Wisdom & Healing Practices of the Bee Masters*. Rochester, VT: Destiny Books, 2006.

Capra, Fritjof *The Tao of Physics*. 1976. Third edition, London, UK: Flamingo, 1992.

Cowan, Elliot *Plant Spirit Medicine*. 1995. Third reprint, Mill Spring, NC: Swan . Raven & Co., 1998.

Cox, Brian & Andrew Cohen *Wonders of the Universe*. London, UK: HarperCollins Publishers, 2011.

Crombie, R. Ogilvie *The Gentleman and the Faun: Encounters with Pan and the Elemental Kingdom*. Forres, Scotland: Findhorn Press, 2009.

DeKorne, Jim *Psychedelic Shamanism: The Cultivation, Preparation and Shamanic Use of Psychotropic Plants*. Pert Townsend, WA: Loompanics Unlimited, 1994.

Don, Monty & Sarah *The Jewel Garden*. London, UK: Hodder & Stoughton Ltd, 2004.

Don, Monty *Growing Out of Trouble*. London, UK: Hodder & Stoughton Ltd, 2006.

Du Cann, Charlotte *52 Flowers That Shook My World: A Radical*

Return To Earth. Isle of Lewis, Scotland: Two Ravens Press Ltd., 2012.

Engel, Cindy *Wild Health*. New York, NY: Houghton Mifflin Company, 2002.

Findhorn Community *The Findhorn Garden*. 1976. Third edition, Forres, Scotland: Findhorn Press, 2003.

Fukuoka, Masanobu *The One-Straw Revolution*. 1978. This edition, New York, NY: New York Review Of Books, 2009.

Gribbin, John *In Search of Schrödinger's Cat*. 1984. This edition, London, UK: Corgi Books, 1987.

Gynn, Graham & Tony Wright *Left In The Dark*. 2007. Second revised edition, Kaleidos Press, 2008.

Hardin, Jesse Wolf *Gaia Eros: Reconnecting to the Magic & Spirit of Nature*. Franklin Lakes, NJ: The Career Press, 2004.

Harner, Michael *The Way of the Shaman*. 1980. Third edition, New York, NY: Harper & Row, 1990.

Harpignies, J. P. (editor) *Visionary Plant Consciousness: The Shamanic Teachings of the Plant World*. Rochester, VT: Park Street Press, 2007.

Heaven, Ross & Howard G. Charing *Plant Spirit Shamanism: Traditional Techniques for Healing the Soul*. Rochester, VT: Destiny Books, 2006.

Lamb, F. Bruce *Wizard of the Upper Amazon*. 1971. Reprint, Berkeley, CA: North Atlantic Books, 1986.

Louv, Richard *Last Child in the Woods*. New York, NY: Algonquin Books, 2005.

Louv, Richard *The Nature Principle: Human Restoration and the End of Nature-Deficit Disorder*. Chapel Hill, NC: Algonquin Books, 2011.

Lovelock, James *The Revenge of Gaia*. London, UK: Penguin Group, 2006.

Masé, Guido *The Wild Medicine Solution: Healing with Aromatic, Bitter, and Tonic Plants*. Rochester, VT: Healing Arts Press, 2013.

McKenna, Terence *Food of the Gods*. New York, NY: Bantam Books, 1992.

McKenna, Terence & Dennis *The Invisible Landscape*. 1975. This edition, New York, NY: Hapercollins, 1993.

McTaggart, Lynne *The Field*. 2001. Reprint, London, UK: HarperCollins Publishers, 2003.

Metzner Ph.D., Ralph (editor) *Ayahuasca: Hallucinogens, Consciousness and the Spirit of Nature*. New York, NY: Thunder's Mouth Press, 1999.

Metzner Ph.D., Ralph *Green Psychology: Transforming Our Relationship to the Earth*. Rochester, VT: Park Street Press, 1999.

Modzelewski, Michael *Inside Passage*. Boynton Beach, FL: Adventures Unlimited, 1991.

Monbiot, George *Feral: Rewilding the Land, Sea and Human Life*. 2013. This edition, London, UK: Penguin Books Ltd., 2014.

Montgomery, Pam *Partner Earth: A Spiritual Ecology*. Rochester, VT: Destiny Books, 1997.

Narby, Jeremy *Intelligence in Nature: an Inquiry into Knowledge*. New York, NY: Penguin Group, 2006.

Narby, Jeremy *The Cosmic Serpent: DNA and the Origins of Knowledge*. 1995. Translated paperback edition, London, UK: Phoenix, 1999.

Patterson, Barry *The Art of Conversation with the Genius Loci*. Milverton, UK: Capall Bann Publishing, 2003.

Pendell, Dale *Pharmakognosis: Plant Teachers and the Poison Path*. 2005. Revised paperback edition, Berkeley, CA: North Atlantic Books, 2010.

Pietak, Alexis Mari *Life as Energy: Opening the Mind to a New Science of Life*. Edinburgh, Scotland: Floris Books, 2011

Raven, Susan *Nature Spirits The Remembrance: A Guide to the Elemental Kingdom*. East Sussex, UK: Clairview Books, 2012.

Reid, Daniel *The Tao Of Detox*. London, UK: Simon & Schuster UK Ltd, 2003.

Roads, Michael J. *Talking with Nature*. 1985. Reprint, Tiburon, CA: H J Kramer Inc, 1987.

Ryrie, Charlie *The Healing Energies of Water*. London, UK: Gaia Books Ltd., 1998.

Saunders, Nicholas, Anja Saunders & Michelle Pauli *In Search of the Ultimate High: Spiritual Experience Through Psychoactives*. London, UK: Rider, 2000.

Schultes, Richard Evans & Albert Hofmann *Plants of the Gods*. 1979. This edition, Rochester, VT: Healing Arts Press, 1992.

Seed, John, Joanna Macy, Pat Fleming & Arne Naess *Thinking Like A Mountain: Towards A Council Of All Beings*. Santa Cruz, CA: New Society Publishers, 1988.

Shazzie *Detox Your World.* 2003. Third edition, Rawcreation Limited UK, 2007.

Szekely, Edmond Bordeaux *The Essene Gospel of Peace, Book I.* 1928. Reprint, Nelson, BC: IBS Intl, 1981.

Talbot, Michael *The Holographic Universe.* 1991. Reprint, New York, NY: Harper Perennial, 1992.

Tompkins, Peter *The Secret Life of Nature.* London, UK: Thorsons, 1997.

Tompkins, Peter & Christopher Bird *The Secret Life of Plants.* 1973. Reprint, New York, NY: Harper Perennial, 2002.

Tompkins, Peter & Christopher Bird *Secrets of the Soil.* Anchorage, AK: Earthpulse Press, 1998.

Von Essen M.D., Carl *Ecomysticism: The Profound Experience of Nature as a Spiritual Guide.* 2007. Revised and reprinted, Rochester, VT: Bear and Company Books, 2010.

Watson, Lyall *Supernature.* 1973. Fifth impression, London, UK: Hodder & Stoughton Ltd, 1977.

Wolfe, David *The Sunfood Diet Success System.* San Diego, Ca: Maul Brothers Publishing, 1999.

WEBSITES

http://articles.mercola.com/sites/articles/archive/2012/04/29/james-oschman-on-earthing.aspx *Caution: Wearing these can sabotage your health.* Dr Joseph Mercola. April 29, 2012.

http://www.autismspeaks.org/science/science-news/spotlight-gut-bacteria-brain-connection-autism *Spotlight on the Gut Bacteria-Brain Connection in Autism.* November 13, 2013.

http://www.bbc.co.uk/news/uk-23553897 *Is England a nation on anti-depressants?* Mark Easton. August 3, 2013.

http://www.benbenjamin.net/pdfs/Issue2.pdf *The Primacy of Human Touch.* Ben Benjamin, PhD and Ruth Werner, LMT.

http://www.biomedcentral.com/1471-2458/8/17 *Psychiatric disorders and urbanization in Germany.* Jack Dekker, Jaap Peen, Jurrijin Koelen, Filip Smit, Robert Schoevers. Published January 17, 2008.

http://www.bristol.ac.uk/news/2007/5384.html *Getting dirty may lift your mood.* Christopher Lowry, PhD. April 2, 2007.

http://www.centreforconfidence.co.uk/flourishing-lives. php?p=cGlkPTE3MiZpZD02NzI

http://www.collegeofsoundhealing.co.uk/pages/about.html
http://www.dailymail.co.uk/sciencetech/article-2519437/Houseplants-make-workers-40-productive-creative.html Sarah Griffiths, December 6, 2013.
http://digital.vpr.net/post/what-s-your-water-report-points-pharmaceuticals *What's In Your Water? Report Points To Pharmaceuticals.* Mitch Wertlieb and Melody Bodette. February 13, 2014.
http://www.ecobuildingpulse.com/performance-metrics/with-nature-and-justice-for-all.aspx by Kim O'Connell, June 7, 2013
http://www.elsevier.com Frontiers in Neuroendocrinology, *Early life stress, the development of aggression and neuroendocrine and neurobiological correlates: What can we learn from animal models?* Alexa H. Veenema. Available online March 31, 2009.
http://www.examiner.com/article/mall-walking-vs-trail-hiking-which-is-better-for-you Seth Smigelski. March 30, 2009.
http://www.livestrong.com/article/186495-importance-of-human-touch/ *Importance of Human Touch.* Mary Bauer. Published online January 28, 2014.
http://www.marcobischof.com/en/arbeitsgebiete/biophotonen.html
http://www.motherearthnews.com/natural-health/forest-bathing-ze0z1301zgar.aspx *Your Brain on Nature: Forest Bathing and Reduced Stress.* Eva Selhub and Alan Logan. January 8, 2013.
http://www.nih.gov/news/health/jun2012/nhgri-13.htm *NIH Human Microbiome Project defines normal bacterial make-up of the body.* June 13, 2012.
http://www.sciencemag.org/content/early/2013/02/20/science.1230883 *Detection and Learning of Floral Electric Fields by Bumblebees.* Dominic Clarke, Heather Whitney, Gregory Sutton, Daniel Robert. Published online February 21, 2013.
http://news.stanford.edu/news/2003/october15/research.html *Link found between cleanliness, hepatitis A, asthma. Is there a childhood risk in overly clean environments?* Krista Conger. October 15, 2003.
http://subjected2subjectivity.blogspot.co.uk/2007/06/thinking-heart.html *The Thinking Heart.* Azer Mantessa. June 6, 2007.
http://www.telegraph.co.uk/news/uknews/5811433/More-than-two-million-British-homes-without-a-garden.html Christopher Hope. July 12, 2009.

http://www.theglobeandmail.com/life/health-and-fitness/fitness/why-is-walking-in-the-woods-so-good-for-you/article4209703/ Alex Hutchinson. Latest update; March 27, 2013.
http://www.theguardian.com/news/2013/nov/20/mental-health-antidepressants-global-trends *Antidepressants: global trends.* Mona Chalabi. November 20, 2013.
http://www.theguardian.com/society/2012/may/06/ritalin-adhd-shocks-child-psychologists?INTCMP=SRCH *Ritalin use for ADHD children soars fourfold.* Jamie Doward and Emma Craig. The Observer, May 6, 2012.
http://www.theguardian.com/sustainable-business/protect-nature-conserve-health-wellbeing *We mus t nature to conserve peoples' wellbeing.* Tony Juniper. August 30, 2013
http://www.webmd.com/eye-health/computer-vision-syndrome

JOURNALS & OTHER PUBLICATIONS

Anatolian Journal of Psychiatry, Issue 9 pp 238-243, 2008. *Impacts of urbanization process on mental health* by M. Tayfun Turan, Asli Besirli.

British Journal of Psychiatry, Issue 184 pp293-298, 2004. *Urbanisation and incidence of psychosis and depression* by Kristina Sundquist MD PhD, Gölin Frank Msc, and Jan Sundquist MD PhD.

Environment and Behaviour, vol 23, no.1, pp3-26, January 1991. *Restorative Effects of Natural Environmental Experiences* by Terry Hartig, Marlis Mang and Gary W. Evans.

Environment and Behaviour, vol 33, no.3, pp343-67, 2001. *Environment and Crime in the Inner City: Does Vegetation Reduce Crime?* by Frances E. Kuo and William C. Sullivan.

Journal of Vascular and Interventional Neurology 2 (1), pp132-5, January 2009. *Cat ownership and the risk of fatal cardiovascular diseases. Results from the second national health and nutrition examination study mortality follow-up study.* Adnan I. Qureshi MD, Muhammad Zeeshan Memon MD, Gabriela Vazquez PhD, MS, M. Fareed K Suri MD.

Landscape and Urban Planning, vol. 105, Issue 3 pp221-229, 2012. *More green space is linked to less stress in deprived communities: Evidence from salivary cortisol patterns* by Catherine Ward

Thompson, Jenny Roe, Peter Aspinall, Richard Mitchell, Angela Clow, David Miller.

Proceedings of the National Academy of Sciences of the United States of America, vol. 109, no. 21, 2012. *Environmental biodiversity, human microbiota, and allergy are interrelated* contributed by Illkka Hanski.

Proceedings of the Seventeenth Annual Meetings of the Environmental Design Research Association, 1986, pp115-22. *Recovery from stress during exposure to everyday outdoor environments* by Roger S. Ulrich PhD and Robert F. Simons.

Psychotherapy and Psychosomatics, vol 74, no. 1, pp31-5, 2005. *Animal-assisted therapy ameliorates anhedonia in schizophrenia patients. A controlled pilot study.* I. Nathans-Barel, P. Feldman, B. Berger, I. Modai, H. Silver.

Sacred Hoop, Issue 40, Spring 2003, *The Place Beyond Hunger* by Nigel Sheppard.

Scientific American, vol 306, issue 3, The Science of Health, March 1, 2012. *How Hospital Gardens Help Patients Heal.* By Deborah Franklin.

ABOUT THE AUTHOR

Rachel is a plant whisperer, nature dreamer, biophile. She is passionate about growing and foraging for both her food and medicine. Rachel is the author of *The Medicine Garden* and *20 Amazing Plants & Their Practical Uses*. She lives in Stroud, UK, with her husband.

Rachel runs workshops, retreats and 1-2-1 sessions on reclaiming your wildness, plant consciousness and sacred plant medicine. For events and happenings visit her website www.wildgaiansoul.com or follow Rachel on twitter, instagram and Facebook @mugwortdreamer

Printed in Great Britain
by Amazon